GARY S. CHAFETZ

THE
PERFECT
VILLAIN

John McCain and the Demonization
of **Lobbyist Jack Abramoff**

THE PERFECT VILLAIN
John McCain and the Demonization of Lobbyist Jack Abramoff

Copyright Gary S. Chafetz 2008
No part of this book may be reproduced or transmitted on any form or by any means, graphic, electronic, or mechanical, including photocopying, recording, taping, or by any storage retrieval system, without permission in writing by the publisher.

Published by Martin and Lawrence Press,
P.O. Box 286, Groton, MA 01450
ISBN: 978-0-9773898-8-9

Printed in Canada

Cover design: What!Design

July 2008
First Edition

"Congress shall make no law respecting an establishment of religion, or prohibiting the free exercise thereof; or abridging the freedom of speech, or of the press; or the right of the people peaceably to assemble, and *to petition the government for a redress of grievances* [emphasis added]."

—First Amendment, U. S. Constitution.

Other works by the author:

Kathmandu, a novel (Penguin Putnam: New American Library)

Obsession: The Bizarre Relationship of a Prominent Harvard Psychiatrist and Her Suicidal Patient (with Dr. Morris E. Chafetz), nonfiction (Random House: Crown)

The Lost Army, a novel, to be published in the spring of 2008, by Martin & Lawrence Press

To Robin and Alex.

THE PERFECT VILLAIN

CONTENTS

PROLOGUE — VII

PART I EARLY YEARS

- CHAPTER ONE **FATHER OF ABRAMOFF** — 1
- CHAPTER TWO **EPIPHANY** — 8
- CHAPTER THREE **THEN THERE WAS ADAM** — 14
- CHAPTER FOUR **REAGAN TAKES NOTICE** — 16
- CHAPTER FIVE **GETTING ACQUAINTED** — 21
- CHAPTER SIX **PURGE THE BUSHYITES** — 24
- CHAPTER SEVEN **SMALL-WORLD DEPARTMENT** — 32
- CHAPTER EIGHT **A LESSON** — 34
- CHAPTER NINE **JAMBOREE** — 38
- CHAPTER TEN **FUNDING FREEDOM** — 44
- CHAPTER ELEVEN **SCORPION** — 55
- CHAPTER TWELVE **HOME INVASION** — 67

PART II NEWLY MINTED LOBBYIST

- CHAPTER THIRTEEN **TRANSITION** — 72
- CHAPTER FOURTEEN **DISTANT SPECKS** — 81
- CHAPTER FIFTEEN **CAME, SAW, GOLFED** — 89
- CHAPTER SIXTEEN **CROSSING THE LINE?** — 94
- CHAPTER SEVENTEEN **CHOCTAW** — 98
- CHAPTER EIGHTEEN **SNAKE EYES** — 108
- CHAPTER NINETEEN **DISCRETION** — 113
- CHAPTER TWENTY **THE GAME** — 122
- CHAPTER TWENTY-ONE **MOBUTU** — 127
- CHAPTER TWENTY-TWO **INTRIGUE** — 128
- CHAPTER TWENTY-THREE **JEWISH OIL** — 137

PART III SUNCRUZ ARMADA

- CHAPTER TWENTY-FOUR **RECONNECTION** — 141
- CHAPTER TWENTY-FIVE **DEAL OF THE CENTURY** — 145
- CHAPTER TWENTY-SIX **BANKERS** — 150
- CHAPTER TWENTY-SEVEN **WIRED** — 153
- CHAPTER TWENTY-EIGHT **OFFSETS** — 166
- CHAPTER TWENTY-NINE **HONEST HANDS** — 174
- CHAPTER THIRTY **GANGLAND SLAYING** — 178

PART IV ICARUS

- CHAPTER THIRTY-ONE **SMEAR CAMPAIGN** — 189
- CHAPTER THIRTY-TWO **MUSIC, GOLF, LUCK** — 208
- CHAPTER THIRTY-THREE **THE STARS LINE UP** — 220
- CHAPTER THIRTY-FOUR **ADJUSTMENTS** — 229
- CHAPTER THIRTY-FIVE **COUSHATTA COMPACT** — 233

CHAPTER THIRTY-SIX **JENAS**	240
CHAPTER THIRTY-SEVEN **BIN LADEN**	248
CHAPTER THIRTY-EIGHT **SAGCHIPS**	249
CHAPTER THIRTY-NINE **MORE TRIBES**	259
CHAPTER FORTY **QUADRUPLE BOGEY**	264
CHAPTER FORTY-ONE **CALM BEFORE THE FIRESTORM**	272

PART V THE LONG FALL

CHAPTER FORTY-TWO **OPENING SALVO**	288
CHAPTER FORTY-THREE **THE SECOND CASINO**	298
CHAPTER FORTY-FOUR **THE HEARING**	303
CHAPTER FORTY-FIVE **PURGATORY**	309
CHAPTER FORTY-SIX **THE SHU**	312
CHAPTER FORTY-SEVEN **THE MCCAIN REPORT**	318
CHAPTER FORTY-EIGHT **TIGUA REDUX**	329
CHAPTER FORTY-NINE **JUDGE HUCK**	345
CHAPTER FIFTY **TIME MACHINE**	347

EPILOGUE **IT ISN'T WHAT IT IS**	351
ACKNOWLEDGEMENTS	357
FOOTNOTES	357
CHAPTER NOTES	376
INDEX	424

PROLOGUE

A twisted and wicked man, Jack Abramoff was the perfect villain. Blessed with enormous charm and a disarming smile, the former Washington super-lobbyist had no scruples whatsoever. He was a manipulative, racist racketeer who had bribed legions of federal lawmakers and cheated gullible Native Americans out of tens of millions of dollars. Abramoff had confessed and been sentenced to nearly six years in prison. The once arrogant and brash right-wing Republican lobbyist—now broken and broke—was cooperating with authorities, hoping to receive a lighter sentence.

"I never expected that I would have to go to prison," Abramoff says, wearing a dark-green uniform and seated on a purple plastic chair in the prison visitors' lounge, "until it became clear that the media could not allow this play to close without the hanging of the villain."

Over 6,000 articles about the Abramoff congressional corruption scandal had appeared in print. From 2004 to 2006, stories ran on the front page of all major American newspapers. Often the coverage about Abramoff eclipsed that of the President of the United States. Dubbed *"The Man Who Bought Washington,"* Abramoff appeared on the cover of *Time* magazine on January 16, 2006.

Thanks, in part, to the Abramoff scandal, the Democrats recaptured both houses of Congress later that year. Meanwhile, the Public Integrity Division of the Department of Justice plodded along. Nearly one hundred Assistant U. S. Attorneys and FBI agents had been investigating current and former officials tied to Abramoff. Some of the most powerful people in the nation's capital were at risk. They included former House Majority Leader Tom DeLay (R-TX) and House Speaker Dennis Hastert (R-IL), presidential assistant Karl Rove, Sen. Byron L. Dorgan (D-ND), Sen. Ernest "Chuck" Grassley (R-IOWA), former Secretary of the Interior Gale Norton, Rep. Ernest Istook (R-OK), Rep. J. D. Hayworth (R-AZ), Rep. John Doolittle (R-CA), and former GOP National Chairman Ken Mehlman.

The Abramoff probe had already taken down one former congressman. Rep. Robert Ney (R-OH) had pleaded guilty to conspiracy and making false statements. He began serving a 30-month prison sentence on March 1, 2007.[1] Stephen Griles, former deputy secretary of the Interior, pleaded guilty to lying to Congress and had begun a ten-month prison sentence. Because of his close ties to Abramoff, fellow *Time* cover boy, Ralph Reed, the former Christian Coalition leader, had been defeated in what should have been an easy race for the Republican nomination as Georgia's lieutenant governor. Nearly a dozen others had also been convicted.

The Washington Post broke the story on February 22, 2004. The next day, Sen. John McCain used his Senate Indian Affairs Committee to launch a probe into the enormous fees that Abramoff had charged his tribal clients. Seven months later, Abramoff was subpoenaed to testify before McCain's committee, but he declined to answer any questions. Although this strategy was legally prudent, it proved to be a public relations disaster. "Not to defend myself at the hearing," Abramoff says, "was a huge mistake."

In 2006, McCain issued his final report. The 373-page document was trumpeted as carefully researched and "fair, factual, and neutral." McCain had subpoenaed approximately 750,000 Abramoff e-mails and documents and conducted scores of interviews with tribal members and former Abramoff associates. However, the report turned out to be biased and disingenuous. Later, during his 2008 presidential bid, McCain would take credit for bringing down the corrupt lobbyist: "Ask Jack Abramoff if I'm not an agent for change."

Abramoff was accused of exploiting helpless, long-suffering Native Americans, which seemed to tap into a latent sense of national guilt, exhibited by the muted celebrations of the 500th anniversary of the European discovery of the New World. Our guilt now had a living symbol: an outrageous Orthodox Jew named Jack Abramoff.

But there was more. Abramoff had bribed scores of elected federal lawmakers and officials. He was guilty of massive bank fraud in Florida and was somehow connected to the mob murder of one of the state's most prominent businessmen. Further reports of his iniquity kept bubbling forth from a bottomless source. In the 1980s, Abramoff had run an international think tank, secretly funded by the racially segregated South African military intelligence. He had produced a major Hollywood film in apartheid-controlled Namibia, in violation of U.N. sanctions. In 1995, he had tried to secure an American visa for the despicable Congo dictator Mobutu Sese Seko. In the late 1990s, Abramoff had successfully lobbied to allow the Northern Mariana Islands, a U.S. Commonwealth in the far Pacific, to continue paying substandard wages to women, who lived and worked as virtual slaves, and who were forced to submit to unwanted abortions. He had brokered a corrupt deal to influence a critical foreign-aid vote in the U.S. Congress to benefit the Russian mob. And even though he was an Orthodox Jew, Abramoff had represented a consortium of Islamic banks with ties to Osama bin Laden.

And then there was the final straw. After pleading guilty to multiple felonies, he emerged from a federal courthouse dressed like a Mafia don in a black trench coat and a black fedora. Abramoff was just what the doctor had ordered. He was the perfect villain. Later, he shakes his head and smiles: "Fedora? I didn't want to draw attention to my religion by wearing a yarmulke, but I did want to keep my head covered, not to mention the fact that it was raining."

This epic tale of iniquity—almost too good to be true, brimming with so many indisputable facts—was accepted as gospel.

In early January 2006, Abramoff had actually pleaded guilty twice— once in Washington, D.C. to bribery, fraud, and income tax evasion; and the following day in Miami, Florida to wire fraud and conspiracy to commit wire fraud. "The feds probably rushed [the plea deals of my former partners] to make it look like they brought me to my knees, but I was already on my knees, possibly on my belly," says Abramoff.

Aware that prosecutors would later recommend a reduction of sentence based on Abramoff's cooperation, the federal judge in Washington, D. C., Ellen Huvelle, did what was typical and customary. She postponed sentencing him. However, for some inexplicable reason Paul C. Huck, the federal judge in Florida, didn't wait. He announced that he would sentence Abramoff on March 29.

Prior to sentencing, the defendant is given the perfunctory chance to ask for leniency. Abramoff's lawyers prepared a *Memorandum in Aid of Sentencing*, essentially an exercise in futility. They presented the judge with a brief hagiography, citing the former lobbyist's many good deeds, his profound contrition, the improbability of recidivism, and supporting case law.

Judge Huck received an astonishing 277 letters from Abramoff's friends and colleagues. The typical defendant receives only a handful. Urging leniency, the letters painted a portrait of a remarkable man, attesting to Abramoff's high moral code, his incredible—and often anonymous— generosity to friends and strangers, his longstanding selflessness, his strong religious beliefs, and his devotion to his family. The letters sounded heartfelt and moving, not coached. One writer told how Abramoff happened to overhear him talking to a man with cerebral palsy in desperate need of a new hearing aid: "[Abramoff] contacted me later to say that he would cover the $2,500 cost of the hearing aid. His only stipulation was that the recipient not be told of the source of the donation."

Captain Andrew J. Cohen wrote that he had been reassigned as the chaplain to Bolling Air Force Base in Washington D.C. But Cohen and his large family suddenly found themselves without a place to stay, and their temporary military stipend did not cover the cost of a hotel and food: "When Jack and Pam Abramoff heard that a new military family was…in such a predicament, they graciously opened their home to us, and I and my wife and five children took up residence for a month and a half in the Abramoff's home." Another letter described how Abramoff had anonymously donated $400,000 to a school for special-needs children.

"[The letters] were so important to me," says Abramoff. "As a result of this experience, I felt so beaten up that I started believing that I [was]… the most evil man there ever was. These letters reminded me—I had forgotten most of these things, that I had money and I just gave it all away to the people who needed it—it reminded me that I was a good person."

The media essentially ignored them. The letters were simply a ploy. Abramoff had been tried and convicted. He was as guilty. End of story.

Yet, one letter, written by Michael Goland, a long-standing Abramoff friend, alleged with great specificity that Abramoff had had virtually no involvement in the wire fraud to which he had just pleaded guilty. Furthermore, Goland asserted that Abramoff's guilty plea had been coerced. He could not afford the millions of dollars in legal fees and he wanted to spare himself, his wife, and five children the ordeal of multiple trials that might drag on for a decade and still result in a guilty conviction on a technicality, after which he would be sent to a maximum-security prison with violent offenders. Under those circumstances, the only sane, risk-averse course of action was to plead guilty.[2]

Goland's claim troubled me. However, any further exploration of this story seemed futile, because Abramoff's lawyers had thrown up an immovable roadblock. They'd forbidden him from talking to any reporters, writers or filmmakers. Except for several brief interviews, Abramoff—the symbol of greed and excess—had essentially never spoken. There were only two ways to obtain the other side of the story, if there was one. Either interview people close to Abramoff and conduct a thorough review of all relevant documents, or contact Abramoff directly and somehow persuade him to talk, which is what I did.

This book is an exhaustive analysis of the evidence. It also contains many hours of exclusive, extensive, and unconditional interviews that Abramoff granted to me.

The first one took place in the early afternoon of June 17, 2006, at Eli's, a kosher delicatessen, near DuPont Circle, in Washington, D.C. When I walked in, Abramoff was seated alone at the table near the door. He had a black yarmulke on his head and was nursing a diet root beer. The international pariah seemed relaxed and at ease, except for a habit of chewing the inside of his lip. I almost didn't recognize him. He had added over 50 pounds to his 5' 8" stocky frame. He noticed my look of surprise. Grinning, he says, "The good thing about the weight is I can walk around Washington and no one recognizes me."

We shook hands and I sat down across from him. For the next six hours, Abramoff answered my stream of questions on an off-the-record basis. However, whenever the conversation ventured near matters related to the on-going federal investigation, he refused to comment. We split the cost of the food and drink.

Abramoff could not meet again for several weeks, presumably because he was holed up every day with federal prosecutors. Reportedly, these meetings would often last ten hours, after which he would be given "homework"—hundreds of pages of his own cryptic e-mails to decipher for the meeting the following day.

The second interview took place in early August, at a sushi restaurant in downtown Washington D.C. (Most sushi is considered kosher). I made it clear that these interviews could proceed only if this was *not* going to be an "as-told-to" book. I would carefully sift the evidence and draw my own independent conclusions. Abramoff would receive no remuneration from the publication of the book and would have no control over the manuscript.

In the ensuring interviews, which were fit in whenever he wasn't meeting with the prosecutors, it became clear to me that Abramoff had been badly traumatized. He was probably suffering from a version of battered woman's syndrome. The media had beaten him up so badly that he had come to believe everything that had been said about him. We discussed this at length. "You start to get brainwashed. When someone says something often enough—thousands of articles, every day, several times a day, some days ten stories on the front page and inside that are all bad—pretty soon you start believing it," says Abramoff. "And the worse it gets, the more it seems like what they're saying about you must be true, like you've got it coming or else they wouldn't keep doing it." He pauses and adds, "I don't think there is something called a coincidence. Everything is a message from God, and God sent me plenty of messages and I didn't listen, so he set off a nuclear bomb." However, thirteen months earlier, he had told a reporter from *The New York Times*: "I've been shocked at how I've been portrayed in the media. The Jack Abramoff who has been made into a caricature and a punching bag in the national media is not the Jack Abramoff who I think exists. If I read the articles about me, and I didn't know me, I would think I was Satan. [The experience has been] "Kafkaesque."

To me, what also seemed apparent was that he was suffering from the Stockholm Syndrome as well. Not unlike Patty Hearst, he had fallen in love with those in control of his fate—the federal prosecutors.

"I believe that the prosecutors I've been working with are honest and sincere people who want to get at the truth in order to clean up the American political system," says Abramoff, "and [I have] seen no indication…[of their willingness] to bend the facts to fit preconceived theses."

Perhaps he was being cautious so that he could extricate himself more quickly from the federal noose around his neck. When I suggested this, he bristled.

In fact, it soon became clear when I eventually met his family members that Abramoff had indeed never defended himself to his wife and children, or to his elderly parents. Like everybody else, they too had assumed he was guilty. When I presented him with my theory that perhaps he was the victim of a perfect storm—generated by misleading *Washington Post* articles, a vengeful Sen. John McCain, and a Justice Department that preferred to coerce guilty pleas rather than risk going to trial—Abramoff would smile and roll his eyes. No matter how persuasively I presented the evidence, he refused to consider it. In his mind, he had badly erred and God was justly punishing him for his sins.

Abramoff certainly didn't buy my perfect-storm thesis. "I benefit the Choctaws [his Mississippi Indian-tribe client] for ten years and now I owe them millions of dollars?[3] It's totally out of proportion," he says. "Either I subscribe to [the fact that] everything is random and chaotic as it would be for an inkwell to fall on a sheet of paper and produce Shakespeare; or it could be a perfect storm, but still someone is blowing the wind around."

That perfect storm was launched when a Louisiana butterfly began fluttering its wings on September 21, 2003. On that day, an obscure Louisiana newspaper, *The Town Talk*, reported that Abramoff, a prominent Republican lobbyist in Washington D.C., had been paid millions of dollars by the Choctaws to defeat any and all threats to its profitable casino. One of Abramoff's lobbying rivals brought the story to the attention of Susan Schmidt, a veteran reporter at *The Washington Post*.

Schmidt wrote her first story in February 2004. Her article, which seemed fair, told a tale of $45 million that several Indian tribes had paid Abramoff to lobby on their behalf when there were "no new major issues for gaming tribes on the horizon." She eventually won the 2006 Pulitzer Prize for single-handedly launching the Abramoff corruption scandal.

Unfortunately for Abramoff, Senator John McCain happened to be a senior member—and soon the chairman—of the Senate Indian Affairs Committee. McCain could not have detested Abramoff more. The senior senator from Arizona believed that the lobbyist had been involved in the infamous "black baby" smear campaign during the 2000 South Carolina GOP primary, which McCain had lost to George W. Bush, who had then gone on to secure the Republican nomination and the presidency. After the *Post*'s first story, McCain immediately launched a full-blown probe. Seven months later—and three days before Abramoff was slated to testify before McCain's committee—Schmidt wrote a devastating piece that painted Abramoff as the most callous, underhanded swindler who had ever lived. The timing was ruinous. Her story, however, contained a glaring omission that no one noticed.

At the Senate Indian Affairs Committee hearings, McCain released several Abramoff e-mails, in which he seemed to disparage his former Indian clients, calling them "troglodytes," "morons," "monkeys," and "idiots." Most of the Native American clients who had remained loyal to him—many had already turned against him—now deserted him with a vengeance.

There was a public uproar. The Department of Justice felt compelled to make an example of Abramoff. Even though he had been secretly cooperating with federal investigators for over a year in their quest to implicate congressmen and other ranking officials, Abramoff was indicted, arrested, eventually forced to plead guilty, sentenced, and then allowed to remain free for several months in order to cooperate with investigators.

But in late September 2006, Judge Huck—a staunch right-wing Republican—made a questionable and unconventional decision. He decided that enough was enough. Even though Abramoff's cooperation had only just begun, Huck announced that the former lobbyist must begin serving his 70-month sentence on November 15th. It was time to pay the piper, Judge Huck told Ed Nucci, acting head of the Justice Department's Division of Public Integrity, in a telephone conference call. Nucci begged the judge to let the piper be paid later, because one way or the other the piper would eventually get paid. Huck refused. His decision had a devastating effect on the investigation.

"Jack is the greatest anti-corruption weapon they've ever had, because he knows how all this stuff works," says a source close to the investigation. "There are at least 40 members of the Senate and Congress who are in as bad positions as [Rep. Robert] Ney, if not worse, but the feds are working at a glacial pace. It took them nine months to do Ney and there is a five-year statute of limitations on all the others. Now, with Abramoff in prison, things are going to go even slower."

Perhaps coincidentally, the day after Judge Huck's decision, the House Government Reform Committee issued a disquieting report: Abramoff and his staff had had at least 485 contacts with the White House, including 79 with Karl Rove and his personal assistant, Susan Ralston, who happened to be Abramoff's former personal secretary. The report declared: "There is evidence that White House officials at the most senior levels of our government repeatedly took actions that benefited Mr. Abramoff and his clients." Some observers suspected that once the investigation began edging towards President Bush, Judge Huck stepped in and killed it by sending Abramoff off to prison. Abramoff would now be jailed on the relatively minor wire-fraud charge well before he could complete his cooperation. "The stuff in Florida is like a parking ticket versus al Qaeda," says a source close to the federal probe. "Was it worth it to throw away this investigation over a parking ticket?"

Hours before Abramoff was scheduled to report to prison, Schmidt sent his lawyer an e-mail: "Is Abramoff going to [the] Cumberland [federal corrections institution]? What time will he arrive? Will there be a photo op?" It seemed callous, but this was what reporters typically do.

To avoid the press, Abramoff, his wife, and his five children arrived at the admissions building of the federal prison in Cumberland, Maryland at 6:15 am on November 15, 2006. Sobbing, Abramoff and his family hugged and kissed goodbye. He and his lawyer, Pamela Marple, then walked inside where Abramoff assumed his new identity: federal prisoner 27593-112. Waiting for Marple to return, his family could not stop sobbing. Abramoff's oldest son became so distraught that one of the guards walked over to inquire if he was the one surrendering. His mother explained that it was his father who had just reported to prison.

"Jack?" the guard asked.

She nodded.

"Please don't worry. Everything will be fine. We'll take very good care of him." Perhaps the only kind words the Abramoffs ever heard during this entire ordeal were uttered by a prison guard.

Soon thereafter, it became evident that Judge Huck's strategy was working. The five-hour, 260-mile roundtrip drive from Washington D.C. was too much for federal prosecutors to endure on a daily basis. After his first year in prison, The Man Who Bought Washington had met with prosecutors far less frequently than in the past.

Abramoff soon became ensnared in a virtual Catch-22. Because the investigation would now be moving so slowly, soon too much time would have elapsed before Abramoff's cooperation was completed for him to benefit much from a reduction in sentence.

The perfect storm kept blowing.

When Abramoff's mother died after a 16-month battle with liver cancer on June 26, 2007, the Bureau of Prisons refused to grant him a furlough to attend her funeral in Los Angeles, even though such furloughs were routinely granted for other inmates in federal prison camps.

It seemed the perfect villain was getting exactly what he deserved.

PART I
EARLY YEARS

CHAPTER ONE
FATHER OF ABRAMOFF

Fleeing poverty and persecution, Jack Allan Abramoff's grandparents were toddlers in 1901, when they emigrated with their parents from Odessa, Russia, and settled in the greater New York City area. At the turn of the nineteenth century, there were a handful of automobiles. The Wright Brothers had not yet achieved powered flight. Suffrage for women was twenty years away. And President William McKinley had just been assassinated.

Twenty years later, Abramoff's grandparents met, married, and moved to Atlantic City. They bore two sons—Bernard, born in 1924, and Frank (Jack's father) in 1927. Atlantic City was a resort destination for residents of New York City and Philadelphia. Abramoff's grandfather, a wholesale produce broker, struggled to make a living. Most of the time, his family lived in run-down rooming houses. Often, they relocated because they couldn't pay the rent. Abramoff's grandmother prepared meals on a hot plate or a sterno stove. Often, Frank and Bernard went hungry. The Great Depression arrived and Frank contracted rickets. To make matters worse, his father came down with rheumatic fever, forcing his two young sons to drop out of grade school and earn a living. Frank's father never fully recovered.

"I worked for 60 cents a shift at a drug store," says 79-year-old Frank Abramoff. "I was a soda jerk, stock boy, and delivery boy from 6pm to midnight. That's ten cents an hour."[4] Frank glances out the window at the golf course next to his luxurious retirement home in Rancho Mirage,

California, near Palm Springs. A full head of graying hair capped his 5'8" stature, and he still speaks with a slight South Jersey accent. Often, his eyes mist over when he spoke about his son Jack. At night, he can see the glow from the nearby casino operated by the Agua Caliente, one of the six American Indian tribes that his son had pleaded guilty to defrauding.

Screwed to Frank's memory was an image of the Hindenburg—the largest aircraft ever built—slowly drifting over Atlantic City's famous lighthouse on May 6, 1937. "We were listening to the radio an hour later when the disaster happened," he says, "and no one believed that I'd just seen it. And to this day, no one believes me. Everybody thinks the Hindenburg went straight from New York City to Lakehurst New Jersey, but it didn't."

In early 1942, immediately after Pearl Harbor, his brother Bernard enlisted in the Army. He was shipped off to the Philippines, leaving Frank as the family's sole breadwinner. In the spring of 1942, 60,000 recruits invaded Atlantic City for basic training. Frank lied about his age and landed a job in the local PX where he worked 12-hour shifts and was quickly promoted to manager. He began servicing all hotels housing servicemen. In his spare time, he sold newspapers on the boardwalk and worked nights at a supermarket. He barely slept.

"[Within a year] I saved up enough money and bought a luncheonette for $900," says Frank proudly. "It did so well that a couple of years later, I sold it for $3,500. I gave the money to my parents to live on. Then [at age 17] I enlisted in the Navy."

Assigned to the USS Saratoga, Frank saw action near the Northern Mariana Islands and Iwo Jima. Frank says that poverty and war instilled in him a strong work ethic and a deep sense of patriotism—values that he says he passed on to his three children. After the war, Bernard and Frank returned home to Atlantic City, a seedy seaside city with an unkempt beach, a rotting boardwalk, and rows of run-down penny arcades. During the war, however, Frank had done so well playing poker that he took his winnings and opened a restaurant with his brother. One day, Frank and a friend attended a local beauty contest, because his friend's 15-year-old sister, Jane Divac, was a contestant. Frank ended up driving her home but didn't see her again for five years.

The loquacious, self-confident, and entrepreneurial Frank was soon hired by a manufacturer of vending machines. He placed them in hotels and department stores throughout the Atlantic City area. He was so successful that he and a friend purchased the former Charles Hotel. On a whim, Frank designed and built a miniature golf course on the back lot of the hotel. The golf course became so popular people queued for hours to play. He built three more. With investors, he launched Fairway Miniature Golf. It constructed miniature golf courses, driving ranges, and "par threes" up and down the Atlantic seaboard.

In 1951, Frank's father died. The following year, Frank reconnected with the pretty and diminutive Jane Divac, who was barely five feet tall. Three years later, they were married in the former Teplitsky Hotel in Atlantic City. The newlyweds, nominally Jewish and registered Democrats, purchased a middle-class home in Margate, New Jersey.

At the time the conservative and reticent 1950s were a collision course with the vocal and confrontational 1960s. The Abramoffs launched a family. Their first child, Linda was born in 1956. Jack (named after Frank's father) was born on February 28, 1959, and Robert was born in 1961—all in the Atlantic City Hospital. By 1960, Frank had constructed over 300 miniature golf courses, driving ranges, and par threes around the world. He was determined to grow the business.

Frank met and befriended Mark McCormack, who had just founded a sports agency, International Management Group (IMG). It would eventually become one of the leading sports management agencies in the world. (Its clients would later include Jack Nicklaus, Rod Laver, Bjorn Borg, John McEnroe, Chris Evert, Andre Agassi, Pete Sampras, and Tiger Woods.) With a handshake, McCormack had just signed up his very first client, a golfing friend from college, named Arnold Palmer. "I realized I needed a marquee name," says Frank, "so [McCormack and I] brought in Arnold Palmer, and we merged [Palmer's] company with mine." It was the notoriously conservative Palmer who persuaded Frank to become a Republican. And it was Palmer who gave Jack his first golf lessons at age ten.

In the spring of 1962, Frank ran an ad in *The Washington Post*:

> **Here's a once-in-a-lifetime opportunity for you to become affiliated with Arnold Palmer as the only Arnold Palmer Putting Course operator in your protected franchise area. Profit now with the magnetic Palmer**

> name in this completely NEW CONCEPT in Miniature Golf...Mr. Frank Abramoff of the Arnold Palmer Putting Courses Inc. will be at the opening of the new 38-hole Championship Putting Course...to speak to persons interested in securing ...[a] franchise for their area.

"Well, I went on to build 200 more miniature golf courses, driving ranges, and par threes in Australia, Japan, South Africa, Denmark, and England," says Frank. "Then we went on to do clothing, endorsements, licensing, personal appearances, TV shows, and the golf courses that Arnold himself designed. I was the senior vice president and director of operations of Arnold Palmer Enterprises. By the mid 1960s, the company was doing $50 million [a year]."

Frank paused and pointed to a framed black-and-white photograph on the wall. There were ten people seated around a dining room table, smiling at the camera. "There's Jack. He's eight years old, sitting next to Arnold's wife, Winnie, and their daughters, Amy and Becky. And there's me next to Arnold and Mark [McCormack]." (Many years later, Palmer and McCormack would sponsor Jack Abramoff's application to the exclusive Congressional Country Club near Washington, D.C.)

Frank's wall was covered with photographs: Frank and/or Jack with Sugar Ray Robinson, Groucho Marx, Joseph Cotton, Joe Lewis, Phil Gramm, Jack Kemp, Arnold Schwarzenegger, President G. W. Bush, and President Ronald Reagan, as well as a dozen photos of President George W. Bush with Jack and/or his children. In fact, Abramoff later says that his children became so fed up with having their photos taken with the president that they refused to meet him anymore.

On January 26, 2006, Bush told reporters at a White House press conference, "I, frankly, don't even remember having my picture taken with the guy. I don't know him. But I can't say that I didn't ever meet him." And White House spokesman Scott McClellan asserted that "there were only a couple of holiday receptions that [Abramoff] attended, then a few staff-level meetings on top of that." The White House refused to release any photos, claiming that they would be used for "pure political purposes" and "they're not relevant to the investigation. Of course, the relevancy of the photos to a federal investigation was for the Justice Department, not the White House, to decide. Tabloid magazines immediately offered Jack Abramoff $1 million for the rights to these photos.

Although desperate for money to pay his legal bills, he declined to sell them. In June 2008, the House Government Reform Committee would release six of the 12 Bush-Abramoff photos on the wall of Frank's office. Jack Abramoff says that at one of these photo shoots, as he was shaking the President's hand, Bush looked around and asked, "Hey, Jack, where are the kids?" (President Bush did not respond to a written and faxed request for an interview in May 2008.)

In the early 1960s, while Frank's business was booming, his brother, Bernard, had become a licensed real-estate broker. He was eking out a living, selling depressed Atlantic City property. By 1965, Frank, now president of Arnold Palmer Enterprises, was earning an annual salary of $150,000 a year, equivalent to over $1 million in 2006 dollars. "[Palmer] was a kind, nice, decent fellow...a real gentleman, but we never discussed politics," says Jack Abramoff years later.

By the late 1960s, Palmer's career was waning and Frank decided to make a radical career move. On March 16, 1969, a small business article appeared in *The New York Times*, announcing that Frank had taken a job as "president of Diners Franchise Systems, a new subsidiary of Diners' Club." Many years later, the press would repeatedly misstate Frank's employment history, reporting that he had been "President of Diners' Club." Years later, the press would continue to misstate Frank's employment history at Diner's Club. As recently as December 29, 2005, *The Washington Post* reported that "Abramoff['s]... father...had a wealth of connections from his days as president of the Diners' Club credit card company..."

"Alfred Bloomingdale [founder of Diner's Club] asked me to organize a franchise system world-wide. I was president of the new company and I owned 50%. But it was short lived. I didn't like commuting to New York," says Frank. "When I told Al I was leaving, he told me that he didn't blame me and he bought out my interest, but we stayed close friends."

In the summer of 1969, Frank relocated his family to Beverly Hills, California and launched a new company, called Target Marketing: "I represented movie stars, TV personalities, and I formed an alliance with CMA (Creative Management Agency). I did the same type of commercial marketing for lots of famous people."

In 1972, Bernard launched Jerome Realty; four years later the New Jersey legislature legalized gambling in Atlantic City. The new law, however, did not allow any "sawdust casinos" or honky-tonk slot-machine parlors as in Nevada. Atlantic City was honky-tonk enough. Only casinos that operated in tandem with large hotels (with a minimum of 500 rooms) were permitted. Suddenly, real-estate values soared.

Frank saw an opportunity: "Right after the 1976 referendum [to legalize gambling], I told my brother, 'It's going to be the only crap game between Las Vegas and England.' I went back and optioned as much land as possible. The idea was to assemble property and flip it…I put three casino deals together: Marlborough Blenheim Hotel, Sands Hotel, the Playboy Hotel and Casino…I was flying back almost weekly…I got out in [19]84. I saw real estate go from $2 a square foot to $200 in a single year."

Frank and Bernard made millions and aspired to open their own casino, apparently seeding in Abramoff a yearning to fulfill his father's dreams. Frank and Bernard lacked the wherewithal to launch a casino, because it required lots of cash, bribery, a willingness to break legs, and an iron-fisted control over the building trades. Organized crime was enamored of casinos (along with garbage collection), because casinos were a business in which the cash could easily be skimmed. According to a May 1, 1979 front-page story in *The New York Times*, "Developer with Alleged Mob Ties Investing Millions in Atlantic City," Bernard Abramoff "brokered" nearly sixty real-estate transactions, worth millions of dollars, for developer Angelo Pucci, who made the purchases under various names and entities. Bernard and Frank insisted they knew nothing about Pucci's underworld ties. Soon, there were published reports that Pucci's partner was Paul Volpe, a major organized-crime figure in Toronto. Three years later, Volpe was stuffed into the trunk of his wife's car, with two bullets in his head. The murder has never been solved. What ever happened to the sixty parcels Pucci purchased? According to Lee Garell, one of Frank and Bernard's partners, Pucci defaulted several years later and the properties then reverted back to the sellers.

In 1979, Frank and Bernard, along with Lee Garell, made a rather odd purchase. They purchased "Price's Pit," a 22-acre toxic waste dump near Atlantic City. Later, the federal government declared "Price's Pit" the third most hazardous superfund toxic clean-up site in the country. In 1982, a federal appellate court ruling noted, "Upon purchasing the property in 1979, [the Abramoff brothers and Garell] acknowledged in writing that this site had been used as a landfill. Although two of the three partners were licensed real estate brokers, no one inquired whether hazardous wastes had been deposited there. Neither did [the buyers] inspect the property or take steps to determine if the landfill had been properly closed."

This was puzzling. Frank and Bernard were born and raised in Atlantic City. Bernard was a licensed real-estate broker and Frank was a real-estate developer. Presumably, both should have been well versed in the flora and fauna of the neighborhood. According to court documents, Frank and Bernard acknowledged purchasing a land-fill site, and soon thereafter carcinogens from Price's Pit were leeching into private wells, not to mention seeping into Atlantic City's drinking water. When asked about it, Frank chuckles: "My brother, may he rest in peace [Bernard died in 2002], got me into one of the worst deals I ever made. We had no idea what a toxic waste dump was. I couldn't even spell toxic. But if [the Superfund] ever cleans up the property, it'll be worth a bundle." As of the spring of 2008, Frank still owned a 54-acre tidal marsh just north of the Pleasantville toll barrier on the Atlantic City Expressway. He was planning to develop into a $60 million factory-outlet mall with 120 stores and eight hotels, which would be the biggest non-casino project in Atlantic City history.

Frank also owned the parking lots surrounding the Atlantis Casino Hotel, which later went bankrupt and was resurrected as the Claridge Hotel and Casino. When Donald Trump tried to purchase the site at foreclosure auction, Frank and two others held a $6.5 million lien on the property. (In fact, Jack Abramoff later listed himself as co-owner of the very parking lots on his financial statement when he purchased SunCruz Casinos in 2000.)

In the early 1990s, Frank explored opening a casino in the Commonwealth of the Northern Mariana Islands, a U.S. territory that, with Frank's help, would later become one of Jack Abramoff's first major lobbying clients. One can't help but wonder how Sophocles, with *Oedipus Rex* and *Antigone* under his belt, would have mined this story. It seems uncanny that, many years later, Jack Abramoff would unconsciously engineer his self-destruction by teaming up with Adam Kidan—a man who had close ties to organized crime—in the purchase of a fleet of casino boats. Maybe the ancient Greeks were right. One's fate is predetermined by the gods. In modern parlance, Freud would say that adult behavior is influenced by early childhood experience. What is clear is that Jack Abramoff seemed irresistibly drawn to casinos. Not only did he purchase a fleet of gambling boats, he was the lobbyist for six Native American tribes that operated casinos.

CHAPTER TWO
EPIPHANY

One of Jack Abramoff's earliest memories was an eleemosynary one. When he learned that an old-age home in Atlantic City was in financial distress and that its residents might be tossed into the street, he took action. To raise money for the elderly, six-year-old Jack Abramoff decided to sell his stuffed animals on the sidewalk in front of his home. "Jack went out and did a yard sale, selling his toys for the Seashore Garden's Home in Atlantic City. The story was in the paper—*The Atlantic City Press*," recalls his father, Frank, proudly.

Then young Abramoff had another inspiration. Why not hold a street carnival to raise money? Amazingly, the idea caught on. The carnival proved to be a huge success and allegedly saved the day. Jack's mother, Jane, believed that this early venture illustrated her son's good heart and foreshadowed his leadership skills, his sense of initiative, and his inclination to help those in need. This triumph remains, to this very day, "one of Jack's proudest accomplishments."

Four years later, when Jack's father announced that he was relocating the family to southern California, ten-year-old Abramoff's reactions were mixed. He would miss his friends, but he also found himself excited to be moving to a warmer climate. Frank purchased a comfortable dwelling on Tower Grove Drive in Beverly Hills. Several months later, a minor earthquake shook the house, which frightened young Abramoff.

In 1972, the Abramoffs moved to an upscale house on tree-lined Elm Drive, just north of Santa Monica Boulevard. It was an affluent area with Danny Thomas, Robert Young, Gene Hackman, and Kenny Rogers as neighbors. Jack Abramoff was attending the local K-8 elementary school, as well as Sabbath services and Sunday school at Temple Emanuel, a Reform synagogue.

In that the voting age was lowered from 21 to 18, which meant that college students, among others, could vote in local and national elections.

The year 1972 was pivotal for another reason. It was the year when Abramoff experienced an extraordinary spiritual awakening. The cultural and social landscape of America had undergone a mutinous metamorphosis, and the Vietnam War was winding down with Henry Kissinger declaring, "Peace is at hand." While many adolescents were defying authority, experimenting with drugs and free love, and finding provocative ways to express themselves, something else was churning in the psyche of 12-year-old Jack Abramoff. He too decided to go against the grain, by rebelling against rebellion. He journeyed back in time and embraced the traditions of his great-great-grandparents. Abramoff recalled years later that at his Bar Mitzvah, "I quickly came to the conclusion that [the message of secular Judaism] was gibberish."

One weekend, his family went to the Pacific Theatre on Wilshire Blvd and saw *Fiddler on the Roof*. Abramoff was transfixed. It was a stirring musical about persecuted Jews living in squalor in eastern Russia, who somehow found meaning and hope through their faith. The impressionable Abramoff suddenly had a religious epiphany. He hadn't had any exposure to Torah-based Judaism, yet he found himself craving the orthodoxy of his ancestral past. He felt dismayed that his family had lost its religious roots. "I made the decision that I would become religious in order to preserve the faith in our family," said Abramoff. A cynic might wonder if this the act of a narcissist, trying to attract attention? Was this the only way he could stand out in a sea of free spirits? Was this just an example of a distressed psyche taking refuge in religion?

Abramoff's epiphany did appear at the dawn of puberty. His hormones were kicking in. The typical response is an awkward exploration one's sexual urges. Instead, Abramoff may have reacted by suppressing them with a sudden and fierce focus on a strict and puritanical form of Judaism. Whatever the reason, his decision to convert to Orthodox Judaism at the tender age of 12 was atypical. Additionally, he remained steadfast in maintaining a deferential attitude towards women.

It was not an adolescent fad or a whim. The 12-year-old boy embarked on a long and indefatigable voyage of devotion and faith. He began attending the conservative Sinai Temple on his own. He purchased books on Judaism with his own funds and began to teach himself Hebrew. The most important book he read at that time was *To Be A Jew* by Hayim Donin. "I read that book from cover to cover several times over and decided that if I was going to be a Jew, that's the kind of Jew I was going to be," says Abramoff.

On the Sabbath, the teenage Abramoff would walk to the Conservative synagogue five miles away, because he didn't realize there was such a thing as Orthodox synagogues. His parents became puzzled and concerned. Their son's mysticism represented the very world from which Frank's parents had escaped. When asked many years later about his son's decision to become an Orthodox Jew, Frank hesitates, and then says, "I didn't like it. I didn't like it at all."

During one Jewish holiday, Abramoff misconstrued a religious regulation and ended up walking to synagogue in his socks, believing that wearing leather shoes, a sign of comfort, would be a sin on a holy day. (He was right about the leather; wrong about the shoes.) In September of that year, Abramoff was particularly distraught when eleven Jewish athletes were murdered by Palestinian terrorists at the Munich Olympic Games. He began to see himself as fervently devoted to Zionism.

By the eighth grade, Abramoff was attending the prestigious Hawthorne Elementary and Middle School in Beverly Hills. He had already demonstrated his keen intellect, his strong will, his political inclinations, his leadership strengths, and his social skills. He was well liked.

"[Abramoff] was an excellent student and never caused any trouble," recalls Milton Rowen, the school principal at the time, many years later at the age of 87. With one exception. Abramoff decided to run for president of the student council. His opponent was David Factor, scion of Max Factor of cosmetic fame. The vote was held on a Friday. Three days later, on Monday, Abramoff was allegedly disqualified for campaign spending violations.

"We had certain rules about the amount of money that could be spent, and there was [to be] no electioneering outside of school," says Rowen. "He had his mother come up with hot dogs in her car and give them out to the kids." Thirty-two years later, the media would seize this incident as an early sign of Abramoff's predilection for political corruption. Unfortunately, *The Los Angeles Times*, which broke the story—subsequently carried by newspapers and magazines around the country—didn't dig deep enough.

On Thursday, Abramoff was knocked unconscious playing flag football and did not attend school the next day, when the ballots were cast. George Forges, the Civics teacher in charge of school elections immediately counted the votes and declared a tie. According to the school's constitution, a tie required a second vote on the following Monday. But there was a problem. Earlier in the week, Abramoff had invited his entire class, including his opponent, to his backyard for a Sunday-afternoon barbecue, two days after the election. The barbecue, where Mrs. Abramoff "handed out hot dogs,"—but not from her car—did not constitute a campaign violation, because the barbecue was supposed to have taken place after the Friday election.

On Monday morning, as he was handing out ballots for the re-vote, Forges learned of the barbecue, which raised an intriguing legal dilemma. Was the barbecue a campaign violation? Forges called Abramoff and Factor into his office. Rowen, the school principal, did not attend the meeting, and Forges, when contacted, says he simply can't remember, except to say that Abramoff was an excellent student. According to Abramoff, Forges realized that Abramoff had not intended to violate campaign regulations, because he could not have anticipated the tie vote on Friday and the re-vote the day after the barbecue. Nevertheless, the barbecue could be construed as an inadvertent campaign violation that could have influenced the election. Abramoff says he did the honorable thing and withdrew from the race, because technically he should have immediately cancelled the barbecue after learning of the Friday tie vote. Jane, Abramoff's mother, says years later that she distinctly remembered her son saying, "Hey, Mom, it's no big deal. It's more important to David. He wanted to win so badly, so I withdrew."

This barbeque may have been one of the earliest examples of what would later be Abramoff's favorite expression: "Thinking outside the box." He had shrewdly calculated that by issuing invitations to the eighth grade class before the election—to a barbecue scheduled for after the election—it might win him a vote or two, possibly tipping a close election his way.

In 1973, Abramoff entered Beverly Hills High School, probably the only high school in the world that could boast of a working on-campus oil well, which overlooked the gridiron where Abramoff would excel. Bill Stansbury, his football coach, remembered Abramoff many years later for his hard work and leadership skills. Although Abramoff was somewhat short, about 5'8," Stansbury noted, "…for his size, he was extremely strong and very aggressive." Abramoff did manage to distinguish himself as an all-city and all-conference football center. His coach remembered one play against their arch rival, Inglewood High School, in which Abramoff blocked an opposing player and knocked him unconscious.

"The football coach was always afraid that Jack was going to kill somebody if he hit him head-on," Rowen recalled, who enjoyed attending the high-school football games. The square-jawed, broad-shouldered Abramoff was also a regional weightlifting champion. As a senior, he became the school's first member of the 2700 club, because he lifted a combined weight of 2700 pounds for the power squat, dead lift, bench press, and clean and jerk. He also held the school record for the power squat, lifting 540 pounds on his back. President George W. Bush, many years later, reportedly said to Abramoff, "How much can you bench, buff man?"

A former high-school classmate, Dr. Jonathan Aviv, admired Abramoff's interpersonal style, including his conflict-resolution skills. "[He] would mediate between hot heads in the lunch room, on the playing field, or in social gatherings." Dr. Aviv also claimed that Abramoff launched a program to help poor high school students with their educational expenses, and was somehow able to persuade Sylvester Stallone, who had just completed his first Rocky film, to help him raise funds.

In addition, Abramoff organized two fundraising events for the Sugar Ray Robinson Youth Foundation. "[Jack] arranged for the Los Angeles Rams [now the St. Louis Rams] and a group of motion picture stars, that me and my friends introduced him to, to appear at the fundraisers. There was James Caan, Elliot Gould, Ernest Borgnine, Bill Cosby… Sugar Ray was a friend of the family, and yet they call [Jack] a racist," says Frank bitterly.

In his senior year, Abramoff ran for president against David Hirsch. Even this election proved controversial. Regulations forbade a candidate from hiring a professional design firm for campaign banners or posters. One of Abramoff's campaign signs appeared to violate the ban. When confronted, he explained that a co-worker at the Beverly Theater, where Abramoff was the weekend manager, had fashioned the poster. When school officials confirmed this, the matter was dropped. Abramoff lost the race by a close vote. He received some consolation when he subsequently captured the presidency of the high-school letterman's club.

Timothy Noah, a year ahead of Abramoff in high school, remembered him as a glad hander. In an article Noah wrote for Slate.com, titled "The Making of a Sleazeball," he admitted that he used to call Abramoff "Abraham Jackoff" behind his back. In early 2006, George Clooney picked up on Noah's comment when he accepted a Golden Globe award for best actor. He said, "I want to thank Jack Abramoff, you know, just because...I don't know why. Who would name their kid Jack with the last words 'off' at the end of your last name? No wonder that guy is screwed up." Abramoff had other detractors in high school. Another Abramoff classmate, who does not want to be identified, says, "He always had a very vaudevillian, bombastic, exaggerated personality. There was clearly some insecurity deep within him that made him have to prove himself in all kinds of ways. There was a side of him that kind of came from the Borscht Belt."

Another detractor was Jonathan Gold[5], later a food critic for *The LA Weekly,* who was a year behind Abramoff in high school. "I was walking down the hall to history class, and [Abramoff] hip-checked me...I went sailing down the stairs with my cello. He was laughing about it with his friends. I suspect he forgot about it five minutes later," said Gold. "I didn't." Nearly three decades later, Gold, who described himself as a "chubby white guy with long red hair," was delighted to read about Abramoff's misfortunes. "It's more that I could have wished for. Who wouldn't feel satisfied that he was getting his comeuppance."

"I don't remember the guy at all," Abramoff says years later. "And I would have never done anything like that. I think he's conflating something that happened with someone else and pinning it on me to make his story more interesting."

In his senior year, with a 3.4 GPA, Abramoff applied to three colleges: Stanford, UCLA, and Brandeis. Located in a leafy Boston suburb, Brandeis was his first choice.

"I made the waiting list," says Abramoff. "This stretched into the summer. I mentioned it to Sugar Ray [Robinson] and on his own he called the admissions director to help me. I did not ask and was shocked, but grateful, that he did so."

Brandeis accepted him.

During the summer before college, he continued to work as the manager of the Beverly Theater, as well as the Westwood Avco Theater, dreaming of a career in Hollywood.

In the fall of 1977, Abramoff moved to Massachusetts, the most liberal state in America, to begin his studies in Waltham. Was his choice of Brandeis—ostensibly because of its kosher kitchen and abundance of like-minded Jews—motivated by its location? It was as far away from home as he could possibly go. There was still tension with his father over Abramoff's decision to become an Orthodox Jew. However, his decision to attend Brandeis was also motivated by the fact that the college did not have a football team. He did not want to be tempted into participating in a sport whose matches were usually played in college on Saturdays. Abramoff says he was determined to remain an observant Jew, who strictly observed the Sabbath—as dictated by Jewish law—which begins on Friday at sundown and continues until three stars appear in the sky after Saturday's sunset.

CHAPTER THREE
THEN THERE WAS ADAM

Raised in humbler circumstances, five years younger than Abramoff, Adam Roland Kidan was born on July 30, 1964. His parents, Steven Kidan and Judy Freeman, brought him home to a rented apartment in a modest three-story brick tenement in Brooklyn, New York. When Kidan was six, after his sisters, April and Arlyn, were born, his father deserted the family. The father never made contact or provided child support.

Kidan's formative years were "an emotional roller coaster." He vaguely recalls a series of men romantically linked to his mother, who held a series of menial jobs. Kidan was an excellent student and was active in Boy Scouts. When he was ten, his mother met Andy Amato, 25 years her senior. A loving father figure had finally entered Kidan's life. Amato, who weighed in at 235 lbs and was 6' 4", was mobbed up. He controlled the numbers racket[6] in the Brownsville section of Brooklyn. Kidan claimed that Amato—never a "made man," only an "earner"— was a gentle guy, who had to occasionally break a leg or two. He paid a percentage to the Mafia for protection. As a teenager, most of the wise guys in Brooklyn, including Lenny DiMaria and Eddie Sciandra, would drop by Kidan's house.

But Amato's livelihood was doomed. After much hand wringing, state legislators voted to create the New York State lottery. The larger payoffs killed off the numbers racket. Now unemployed, Amato—along with a group of fourteen friends—decided to launch a casino. His partners included a state assemblyman, a district judge, and Eddie Sciandra, Amato's best friend. Sciandra later became the consigliore and then acting boss of the Buffalinos, the family that allegedly murdered Teamster President Jimmy Hoffa. In the early 1970s, they pooled their resources and launched a small casino and hotel operation in St. Maarten in the Caribbean. Sciandra's friends on the island greased wheels and palms. The casino—managed by Amato—was small, but profitable. Kidan tells of how Amato would often fly him down to St. Maarten on school vacations. (A reporter from a national publication would later call Kidan a liar, claiming the St. Maarten's Casino and Beach Club didn't exist.)

In December 2006, Kidan was forced to go into hiding, because he declined to go into the witness protection program. He had secretly leased a three-story brick townhouse, not far from the one in which he grew up. Kidan was now the chief witness in a sensational Mafia murder trial in southern Florida. He gives his visitor a quick tour of the first floor, which serves as a living room and office shows photos of Kidan's shaking hands with presidents Ronald Reagan, George H.W. Bush, and George W. Bush. On the fireplace mantle is a card from the President and First Lady congratulating Kidan on the recent birth of his daughter.

Kidan is stocky, jowly with a shaved head. He looks like Melvin Laird—President Nixon's defense secretary. Kidan has his slightly heavy eyelids and almost transparent eyebrows. He is calm and affable; some might call him glib. Others have called him a pathological liar. He is the same height as Abramoff— about 5' 8." Despite all that Kidan has been through—bankruptcies, disbarment, media denunciations, two felony guilty pleas, and now fear of extermination by the Mafia—he looks young for his age. Kidan is a business broker now, advertising on the Internet, making 10% of every deal he brokers.

Several feet away, a large, wall-mounted, flat-screen TV spews out Fox News. A story about Jack Abramoff flashes on the screen. Kidan's name is mentioned.

"I'm still in disbelief that it came to this and I'm even more so that I'm a part of it. It's upsetting to have a front-row seat." Kidan pauses. "It's sickening."

CHAPTER FOUR
REAGAN TAKES NOTICE

When he arrived on the Brandeis campus in the fall of 1977, Abramoff must have looked like a freak—not the kind with long unkempt hair, filthy sandals, patched blue jeans, a ripped work shirt, beads, bangles, bandanas, and body odor. He was a reverse freak—a right-wing, short-haired Orthodox Jewish weightlifter, who did not drink, smoke, or curse and who wore dark suits, garnished with red ties and wing-tipped shoes. He spoke with a soft voice, had a gentle manner, and a ready smile. A born mimic, with an infectious sense of humor, he could make people—friend or foe—laugh. "The hair was immovable, always done up. I don't think I ever saw him not in a suit," said a conservative activist and an old friend.

In his freshman year, his dormitory roommate was Robert Brown, also an Orthodox Jew. There were few Orthodox Jewish college students at Brandeis. Most attended Yeshiva University. Abramoff found himself even more in the minority, both because he was Orthodox and politically conservative. He was amazed when he learned that his room had once been occupied by Angela Davis, a black feminist Communist, later tried and acquitted of murdering a judge.

As a young man, Abramoff never passed through the oats-sowing period like many of his peers. He hardly dated in college, although he says that he'd fallen in love with a woman he would have married. When it came to the opposite sex, he was essentially shy. He played in a flag football league and kept lifting weights. His major was English Literature, with a minor in Opera, which led to his senior thesis on Shakespearean operas.

Some of his classmates were listening to Jimmy Hendrix's creative rendition of the Star Spangled Banner, which deeply offended Abramoff. Others were still hanging posters on their dormitory walls of Vietnam War era hippies burning the American flag and effigies of Richard Nixon.

In contrast, Abramoff flaunted his conservative religious views and his right-wing politics. He mirrored many of his leftist peers by becoming a typical in-your-face activist. He argued that a conservative political ideology flowed directly from the Old Testament—that opposed abortion and homosexuality, and favored limited taxation.

Not surprisingly, Abramoff was taken aback by the droves of left-wing groups whom he abhorred as Communist sympathizers. He was confounded by the activists came in so many shapes and sizes: radicals still seething over the Vietnam War, Black Panthers who loathed whites (especially Jews), peaceniks who favored unilateral nuclear disarmament, bra-burning feminists, and gay and lesbian militants. "I was outraged that seemingly normal American students could so hate the country I loved," says Abramoff.

He joined a Republican club on campus, organized and led sparsely attended rallies in which his colleagues tried to drown out their leftist brethren by singing protest songs like *God Bless America*. "Most [of the] kids [at Brandeis] were political with liberal proclivities, but not activists," says Abramoff. "Of course, the radical Communists hated us, but we were all the weightlifters and former jocks and so they didn't mess with us."

At the same time, Abramoff pursued his study of the Talmud with a new friend, Orthodox Rabbi Rod Glogower, and increasingly embraced the importance of charity in achieving a truly spiritual life. "We learned [the Talmud] together. There was a [class]," Abramoff recalls. "He bore himself in such a dignified way, an elegant way. Just seeing him inspired me."

Decades later, Glogower would remember Abramoff with equal affection. "My wife and I lived in a tough neighborhood, and when we would walk to and from the campus, I often got anti-Semitic comments from passing cars, windows would roll down," Glogower said. "When Jack heard about it, he was extremely upset and protective of me. I have never forgotten the sense that he was a guy who would be in the trenches with me."

Abramoff's passion and political resolve impressed Morton Blackwell, a former Reagan aide, who later recalled Abramoff's sterling reputation. "I met and trained Jack Abramoff during the [summer of] 1980... [He] was clearly one of the most outstanding of the 300 graduates [of the Reagan Youth Staff Schools]...Jack graciously declined [my offer of employment, saying,] 'I'm going back to Massachusetts and organize enough students there to carry Massachusetts for Reagan.' I laughed and replied, 'Jack, if you carry Massachusetts for Reagan, we'll win in a national landslide.'"[7]

Back on campus, Abramoff's political enemies considered him a demagogue, but many of his admirers were touched by his kindness and thoughtfulness. Though single-minded in his political views, he seemed far less self-absorbed in his private life. Several classmates were impressed by Abramoff's generous nature. In his sophomore year, an acquaintance, Neil Sunkin, was devastated by his father's sudden death. "I had lost most ties to my Jewish faith and had forgotten how to read Hebrew or pray," Sunkin said. "So that I could pray for my father, Jack made a tape recording for me of the Mourner's Kaddish…During that year, Jack often helped me to pray for my father, going to services [with me] at an early hour of the morning for a year."

This foreshadowed an astonishing spirit of generosity—a quality revered in Orthodox Judaism—that seemed to take root and flourish during Abramoff's years at Brandeis. In the ensuing decades after college, Abramoff's acts of kindness and charity became legendary. After the Congressional scandal broke and Abramoff had been publicly vilified and was about to be sentenced for the SunCruz wire fraud, there were literally hundreds of people who sent letters to the judge on Abramoff's behalf, begging for leniency. The judge received 277 letters, from Jews and non-Jews alike, attesting to Abramoff's extraordinary generosity. Some of these dated back to his high-school and college years. In contrast, Adam Kidan, who was sentenced along with Abramoff, received only two letters, one from each of his sisters.

Jerrold Hercenberg, a neighbor of Abramoff's, recalled that a local rabbi, deep in debt and without health insurance, found himself overwhelmed by medical bills from his child's recent auto accident. "A call was made to the Abramoff family. The very next day a check was delivered from Jack Abramoff to the family for $10,000," wrote Hercenberg, who added that there was no request for repayment. Jeffrey Klein, the former treasurer of a Jewish elementary school, confided that he knew of many occasions in which Abramoff made similar anonymous donations. "There were a few unfortunate occasions where a school family was struck with a dire circumstance—a fire that uprooted a large family from their home, a serious illness, or loss of a job. As the treasurer of the school at the time I would receive a call from the Abramoffs that they [would] help cover the tuition bill...The families in question never even knew who specifically had helped them out," wrote Klein.

The list goes on and on. Abramoff helped pay many families' medical bills or provided them with necessary medical equipment. He assisted struggling families in purchasing a home or paying for a Bar Mitzvah. And over the years, he took into his home many children and families who required housing or emotional support. The media viewed these 277 letters with great suspicion, assuming them a ploy orchestrated by Abramoff's lawyers to influence the judge. Yet there was no question that hundreds of people, despite Abramoff's public disgrace and humiliation, continued to feel privileged to be counted among his friends. His generosity during his adult life distinguished him. The fact that this blossomed in college, when mindless self indulgence is not uncommon, was unusual.

In his senior year, a meeting of all the Massachusetts chapters of the College Republicans was held at Brandeis. Only eight people showed up. They went around the room asking who wanted to be the next state chairman. No one did, so Abramoff raised his hand and was instantly elected. "It changed my life," he says.

At that time, he had befriended Harvard graduate Grover Norquist, then a student at the Harvard Business School. They would become and remain lifelong friends and allies. Norquist would go on to establish himself as one of the country's leading conservative anti-tax activists, founding Americans for Tax Reform. Abramoff and Norquist grew the Massachusetts College Republicans from six chapters and about 300 members to more than 45 chapters with over 5000 students across the state.

"In 1980, I actually supported [GOP Congressman from Illinois] Phil Crane. He was by far the most right wing and the most pro-Israel candidate in the race to unseat Jimmy Carter," says Abramoff. "One night, my roommate, David Sidransky, and I were watching the presidential debates as Crane shredded his Republican opponents and declared that the American Embassy in Tel Aviv should be relocated to Jerusalem. But his single digit support nationally meant that Crane was soon out of the running and we had to go back to supporting Reagan."

Eight years before, in 1972, Nixon was elected to a second term as president by every single state in the union, with the exception of

Massachusetts, which voted for his Democratic opponent, Sen. George McGovern. Abramoff and Norquist were quite dismayed, however, when Reagan selected George H. W. Bush, a moderate, for his running mate. When Bush landed briefly at the airport in Boston on his way to Maine[8], Abramoff gently urged Norquist not to greet Bush with a huge sign that read, "Reagan-Kemp for President."

The Iran hostage crisis was still caught in the nation's throat. Carter had just sent commandoes on a botched, tragic, and humiliating raid to rescue American diplomats held hostages in Teheran. The nation was mired in a recession. There was double-digit inflation, and the prime interest rate had reached 21 percent. Pollsters predicted that President Carter would carry Massachusetts by less than 10,000 votes. Abramoff did not want that to happen. He devised a creative strategy to finesse votes for Reagan. He requested the Bostoner Rebbe, one of the nation's most influential Orthodox leaders, to publicly endorse Reagan. Abramoff pointed out that the Orthodox Jews and Christian right-wing Republicans shared much in common. Both were ardent supporters of Israel, and believed in private or home schooling, school vouchers, and local governmental control. Both were opposed to abortion, birth control, sexual promiscuity, and big government. Both were fiscally conservative and strong supporters of the military.

Abramoff tried to arrange a photo shoot of Reagan and the Rebbe, but the candidate was too busy preparing for the presidential debates, so Reagan's daughter, Maureen, was sent in his place.

Abramoff explained to Maureen, who was politically liberal and a feminist, that the Rebbe could not shake hands or be photographed with any woman other than his wife. Maureen was confused. "So what am I doing here?" she asked. Her meeting with the Rebbe went smoothly until a male campaign aide tried shaking hands with the Rebbe's wife, also strictly forbidden. Fortunately, this did not diminish the Rebbe's support for Reagan. Political observers later estimated that the Rebbe's endorsement produced at least 3,000 additional votes for Reagan in Massachusetts, not to mention many votes from the Rebbe's followers in New York.

Later that same day, Abramoff and Norquist—both wearing "Jews for Reagan" buttons—went to Rubin's Delicatessen, a kosher restaurant in Brookline, to celebrate. A National Public Radio reporter happened to interviewing Jews entering the restaurant for lunch. Speaking into the reporter's microphone, Norquist declared, "I've been a Democrat all my life, but enough is enough. This time I'm voting for Ronald Reagan." The next day, *All Things Considered* aired the interview with Norquist, who isn't Jewish.

Abramoff's second strategy was brilliant. He went around the state talking local college students into registering to vote. They were then handed a stamped absentee ballot application, which they were asked to fill out at once. Abramoff then mailed it for them. To his astonishment and delight, Reagan captured the Bay State's 14 electoral votes by a margin of 3,829. He was the first Republican to carry Massachusetts since Dwight Eisenhower in 1956. And the President-elect gave the lion's share of the credit to 21-year-old Jack Abramoff.

As his senior year wound down, Abramoff made the fateful decision to run for office. Thanks to his "Massachusetts miracle," as well as a vigorous campaign funded by his father, Abramoff was unanimously[9] elected National Chairman of the College Republicans, under the aegis of the Republican National Committee. "I held a fundraiser for Jack at home," Frank Abramoff says. "Most of my friends were Democrats and Independents, but we still managed to raise about $6,000" One of the people who attended the fundraiser was attorney Marc Levin, who would later introduce Jack Abramoff's to his very first tribal client, the Mississippi Choctaws.

In June 1981, Abramoff graduated from Brandeis *magna cum laude* and moved to the nation's capital. He had been accepted to law school at Georgetown University, but deferred enrollment so he could focus on his new $12,000-a-year job[10].

CHAPTER FIVE
GETTING ACQUAINTED

In the fall of 1982, Adam Kidan began attending George Washington University in Washington, D.C. Grants, work-study, and student loans paid his tuition. "I was a lowly freshman on scholarship at George Washington University in D.C., and I joined a little campus club for Republicans," Kidan says later. "On a lark, I picked up the phone and called the office of Newt Gingrich [R-GA]." Kidan invited Gingrich—a former history professor, who was being touted as a future GOP leader of Congress—to speak at a student rally for Republican candidates. "Never in a billion years did I think this powerful guy would accept, but he did. As a result, I became the vice president of our club. When Gingrich showed up, I ended up introducing him." It just so happened that Jack Abramoff tagged along.

After the rally, Abramoff walked up and introduced himself. He told Kidan that he liked the way he had handled himself. "I was floored," recalls Kidan. "Jack was the National Chairman of the College Republicans. He had an office at the Republican National Committee headquarters! I thought he was a god."

Abramoff remembers it differently: "This is nonsense. I was not at his rally for Gingrich and did not meet him there. I met [Kidan] when he applied for a job."

Abramoff hired him for a national radio program for college students. That September, Abramoff launched *Fallout*, a weekly radio show with a debate format. Years later, Abramoff remembers Kidan as "an eager beaver and a hard-working young man, who seemed smart and a good guy, and he did a competent job on the show." The weekly panel included Kidan as moderator, Abramoff as chairman of the College Republicans, and a representative from the College Democrats. *Fallout's* more famous guests included Attorney General William French Smith, Jack Kemp, G. Gordon Liddy, Barry Goldwater, Pete DuPont, Tom Brokaw, and Peter Jennings, along with several prime ministers. The shows were taped, copied onto cassettes, and shipped free of charge to campus radio stations around the country.

The reason *Fallout* had access to the powerful was that Abramoff had access to President Ronald Reagan. Kidan smiles as he remembered Reagan's 72nd birthday party. "Thanks to Jack, fifty of us [College Republicans] were invited to present a cake to the President on the South Lawn of the White House as he stepped off the helicopter. Luckily, it was snowing so hard that the presentation was moved inside. I have great photos of President Reagan, Jack, and me eating birthday cake together in the Oval Office," says Kidan. "Heady stuff for a college kid!"

Abramoff shakes his head: "It was never to take place in the South Lawn. How could it? It was February [6th]."

Reagan, the oldest President ever elected, told them how great it was to have college students who supported his politics. It hadn't been that way when he'd been California governor in the late 60s. At that time, UCLA students were hurling stones at his official limousine. Black Panther Eldridge Cleaver, who was running for President as a candidate for the Peace and Freedom Party, was holding rallies on state campuses, inciting thousands of students to chant repeatedly in unison: "Fuck Ronald Reagan."

"The President seemed to be genuinely enjoying himself," says Kidan. "I was standing next to Abramoff when Nancy [Mrs. Reagan], still wearing her plastic smile, pulled Jack aside. 'Cut him off,' she hissed. 'My husband needs to go upstairs and take a nap.' Jack was speechless. I was trembling. Finally, Jack sputtered out, 'But Mrs. Reagan, he's the President of the United States. I can't interrupt him.' She looked Jack in the eye and snarled, 'You're running the show, aren't you? Well then, just do it.' The First Lady strode out of the room. Jack just stood there, smiling, and did absolutely nothing. Reagan had another piece of birthday cake and fifteen minutes later he joined Nancy upstairs."

Abramoff says that Kidan was nowhere nearby when that happened. "It's just his ego-driven need to be a player. [Kidan's] retelling of the Nancy Reagan encounter is just a retelling of what he [later] heard from me."

But something noteworthy did occur that day. Abramoff's future wife was also in attendance at the White House. "I was with him on the day Jack met Pam," Kidan says, proudly. "Ralph [Reed] introduced them. She's from Tennessee or Kentucky. I can't remember....She ended up being his secretary for a while, then his wife. Now they have five kids."

A recent graduate of University of Georgia, Pamela Alexander—an intelligent, good-looking, thin, petite blond—was looking for a job. She had just moved to the Washington D.C. area to live with her grandfather in Alexandria, Virginia. At the suggestion of Ralph Reed—she had never met Reed, only spoken to him once by phone—she called Abramoff, who arranged for her to be interviewed by one of his staff. At the end of the interview, she was invited to Reagan's birthday party. Several days later, Abramoff hired her as his communications director, not his secretary.

Raised in the Protestant faith, she had joined a Jewish sorority in college and became increasingly curious about the religion. On Friday nights, she would join other staff members who would meet at Abramoff's for dinner. Often, she would join in reciting the Kiddush, a prayer said at the beginning of the Sabbath meal. Over the course of several years, without prodding from Abramoff, Pam converted to Orthodox Judaism.

Meanwhile, *Fallout* had become a huge success. Initially envisioned as a ten-minute campus show, it quickly blossomed into a 30-minute format that was eventually picked up by 194 stations around the country. Kidan said that college students would actually come up to him and ask for his autograph. "This is patently absurd," says Abramoff. "How could they recognize him? By his voice?"

In the process, Kidan says he and Abramoff were good friends: "There were hundreds of other college students buzzing around Jack, and to be the one that got close to him gave me confidence, but now looking back, meeting Jack turned out to be the worst thing that's ever happened to me. Sen. [Conrad] Burns [R-Mont.] said that he wished Jack had never been born. I just wish I'd never met him."

Abramoff has a different memory. The implication that Kidan and he were "pals, or that he was closely involved with Grover or Ralph is laughable," says Abramoff. "He was a good employee who seemed like a good guy. That's it. We did not socialize."

CHAPTER SIX
PURGE THE BUSHYITES

When Abramoff assumed control of the College Republicans in 1981, it was little more than a frat house, barely 10,000 strong. His timing was perfect. In the early 1970s, the GOP had suffered two almost fatal humiliations. For the first time in American history, the vice-president and president—both Republicans—had resigned from office in disgrace. And yet, within a decade, right-wing evangelical Republicans were on the verge of a remarkable comeback: The Republicans would capture five of the next seven presidential terms and eventually both Houses of Congress, advancing their ideological agenda, especially in the Supreme Court.

Conservatives exploited Roe v. Wade—the 1973 U.S. Supreme Court's legalization of abortion—to galvanize its demoralized "silent majority." By 1975, Kevin Philips had coined the "New Right." Conservative think tanks were sprouting up like weeds, sown by Richard A. Viguerie, Bill Kristol,

Howard Phillips, Paul Weyrich, and Terry Dolan. The Heritage Foundation, the National Conservative Political Action Committee (NCPAC), and William F. Buckley's Young Americans for Freedom, to name a few, were spewing out God-helps-those-who-help-themselves rhetoric. Funds were pouring in from wealthy conservatives, such as Joseph Coors, Nelson Bunker Hunt, and Richard Mellon Scaife. By 1979, the Moral Majority was beating its breast and attracting national following.

Most importantly, conservatives and neo-conservatives—fed up with long gasoline lines, double-digit inflation, a deep recession, high interest rates, and the Iranian hostage crisis—could finally rally around the best teleprompter reader of all time. His name was Ronald Reagan, the former Democrat, film actor, and labor-union chief. With his election to the presidency, the conservative Camelot had been consecrated. And thanks to Reagan's astonishing electoral victory in Massachusetts, Jack Abramoff, the new chairman of the College Republicans, had the President's ear.

After a whirlwind tour of college campuses in Texas, Delaware, Virginia, Arkansas, California, Illinois, New York, Pennsylvania, New Jersey, and Maryland—Abramoff capped it with a 20-minute discussion in the Oval Office with President Reagan. "[The president] was very excited with what we are doing," Abramoff told a reporter for *The Atlantic City Press*. The chairman of the College Republicans informed the president that his organization was destined to become a force to be reckoned with in the upcoming 1982 mid-term elections. "Meeting the president was scary and extremely intimidating, but he was very kind and soothing," Abramoff says.

Although he could be brash, Abramoff was soon viewed by his legions of admirers as someone with boundless energy and "man of steel" core beliefs. "Jack was a very friendly guy. He was always happy, always smiling. He seemed to enjoy what he was doing," says Jeff Pandin, a College Republican from Capital University in Columbus, Ohio. "What was so appealing about Jack was that he was the opposite of politically correct. He wasn't going to water it down to make it more attractive to the middle-of-the-road folks. He was always full steam ahead, no breaks, no compromises. And that was very appealing."

As national chairman, the first thing Abramoff did was audacious and counterintuitive. To the consternation of some of his superiors at the Republican National Committee (RNC), he drastically reduced membership. He purged the "Bushyites," those allied with Vice-President George Bush's kinder, gentler viewpoint. Dan Cohen remembered the blood letting. "We were more 'in-the-trenches' conservatives. Our heroes were people like Jack Kemp and Newt Gingrich and Ronald Reagan." What remained, according to Abramoff, were the hard-core "young enthusiasts who were imbibing on conservative political tracts, the sexy intellectual material that was forbidden in [the mostly liberal colleges]." Later he added, "We probably made it very dictatorial, but we wanted the College Republicans to remain conservative."

At Grover Norquist's request, Abramoff passed resolutions calling for the elimination of the Federal Reserve and the authorization of the private minting of coins. Abramoff crystallized his vision for the battle ahead in his group's annual report: "It is not our job to seek peaceful coexistence with the Left. Our job is to remove them from power permanently—[from] student newspapers and radio stations, student governments, and academia." Abramoff ordered his organization to distribute to college campuses nearly 1000 copies of a book called *Target America: The Influence of Communist Propaganda on the U.S. Media*, which claimed that the Soviet Union had planted thousands of KGB agents in the United States, posing as American reporters, to conduct a "massive secret propaganda campaign." Abramoff's favorite movie was Patton, and urged his own troops to memorize Patton's famous movie speech, substituting *Democrat* for *Nazi*. "The Democrats are the enemy. Wade into them. Spill their blood. Shoot them in the belly!" Abramoff later says that all they were doing was goofing around: "It's had been turned into a nefarious foretelling of what a monster I became, but it was just a fun joke, for goodness sake."

Some of his Republican elders didn't get the joke and were appalled by the rhetoric. They told Abramoff to tone it down. "Often, you choose your words carelessly," said William I. Greener, then Republican National Committee communications director. "The goal is to win, not to incite." Looking back at that time, Abramoff shrugs and says, "Look, we were the college kids, the troublemakers, the radical conservatives. [The people on the Republican National Committee] didn't want to shake things up. We were the first troops landing on the beach. We weren't the usual group of kids they were used to dealing with. We were: 'Join the revolution.' We were bizarre to these guys."

Later, in 1984, some of his Republican elders become outraged when Abramoff announced his opposition to the reelection of Senator Charles H. Percy (R-Ill.)—whom he describes as "a partisan Democrat in Republican's clothing." As a result, it led to the election of liberal Democrat Paul Simon. "Percy was viciously anti-Israel and so we preferred Simon. An enemy in the huddle is much worse than an enemy across the scrimmage line," says Abramoff.

Adam Kidan describes Abramoff as "an ultra right-wing lunatic," but one who had an important job to do in order to achieve a stronger conservative presence on college campuses: "[Jack] was very instrumental in pushing back a lot of liberalization. And someone like that needed to come along to bring parity back on college campuses where it wasn't that way for a long time. He accomplished a lot. Whether you liked him or not, he was very effective."

Kidan remembers the day Ralph Reed, a 19-year-old student from the University of Georgia, showed up at Abramoff's office in 1982. Abramoff says later that he'd met Reed in an elevator in Chicago the previous year and hired him on the spot: "My impression was that he was a young, skinny go-getter who was willing to work for free, because that was all we could afford to pay." Abramoff quickly became close friends with the baby-faced intern, who crashed on Abramoff's couch for the entire year, "since I could not pay him enough for him to be able to afford his own apartment."

Reed later became the public face of the Christian Coalition, which he would turn into a national political powerhouse. But much later he would be ensnared in the Abramoff scandal, which would sink his 2006 bid for Lieutenant Governor of Georgia.

Perhaps it was Abramoff's dearth of administrative skills, or his youthful exuberance, but one overarching theme in Abramoff's life, a chink in his armor, was his failure to manage money. It was one of his three Achilles' heels. He never saved a dime. He spent obsessively and impulsively. The College Republicans were always begging for money. Payments to vendors were often late. Abramoff's superiors wondered where all the money was going. "Our financial maturity still needed development," Abramoff admits. "We were like kids in a candy store." Over twenty years later, Louis Ruebelmann, Abramoff's accountant, was bewildered that a Washington power broker like Abramoff remained so naïve about money. Years later, despite the tens of millions that Abramoff allegedly defrauded from American Indian tribes, he never got around to paying off his own home mortgage.

Money woes plagued Abramoff at the College Republicans, which triggered the emergence of his second Achilles' heel. This affliction is essentially universal—presidents, federal prosecutors, lawmakers, businessmen, and lawyers all suffer from it: creative ways to reinterpret laws and regulations. Why not bend the rules, Abramoff wondered, and set up a charitable foundation to solicit tax-deductible contributions for conservative causes? However, Mark Braden, in-house counsel for the Republican National Committee (RNC), expressly forbade it. He informed Abramoff that it would be against the tax code for nonprofit foundations to "engage directly or indirectly in political activities." "Jack was a freebooting pirate as far as I was concerned," Braden recalled. "He had a strong belief in his own correctness. It was damn the torpedoes, full speed ahead."

But liberal groups had been flagrantly bending those very tax rules for years. There were an abundance of left-leaning tax-exempt public-interest research groups on college campuses across the country. These groups, many of them inspired by consumer advocate Ralph Nader, were opposed to nuclear power, supported abortion rights, and advocated for environmental and consumer protection and safety in the workplace. What Abramoff found so outrageous was that many of these nonprofits were funded in part by mandatory fees, collected from students during college registration. He told *The New York Times* that these groups promoted liberal politics "instrumental in leading anti-Reagan and anti-free market forces on campus." He added that the mandatory funding was patently unfair to students who did not share the views of those leftist groups. (Technically, students could apply for a refund, but few ever did.)

The College Republicans launched a letter-writing campaign with threats, such as "our lawyers are looking into this situation" and that "no school wants to be involved in court litigation that may drag on for years." Two lawsuits were actually filed. Eliminating these mandatory fees would also diminish the funding "that the organized left [would have] to lobby against President Reagan," added Steve Baldwin, Abramoff's projects director. Abramoff's efforts did have the support of the Republican National Committee. William Greener III, its director of communications said, "To the extent that they are trying to diminish the strength of groups opposed to the President, especially when those groups receive obligatory funds, that's something we generally support."

Operating on the premise that what's good for the goose is good for the gander, Abramoff created a tax-exempt public interest group, called USA Foundation, which quickly solicited $250,000 from right-wing donors. "We didn't steal students' money; we raised it from voluntary contributions," says Abramoff. In 1984, headquartered in the Heritage Foundation, he helped stage "Student Liberation Day" to celebrate the one-year anniversary of America's triumphant conquest of Grenada, a tiny and defenseless island in the Caribbean.

As head of the USA Foundation, Abramoff wrote, but should not have written on College Republican stationery: "While the Student Liberation Day Coalition is nonpartisan and intended only for education purposes, I don't need to tell you how important this project is to our efforts as [College Republicans]. I am confident that an impartial study of the contrasts between the Carter/Mondale failure in Iran and the Reagan victory in Grenada will be most enlightening to voters 12 days before the general election." When a reporter challenged Abramoff's impartiality, his spokesman, Jeff Pandin, responded that Abramoff "wears two hats. When he has his College Republican hat on, he's partisan. When he has his USA [Foundation] hat on, he's nonpartisan."

"Jack was an idea man, not a detail man. I can believe that he did some dumb things, but he's not a crook. He would no more line his pockets than murder puppies. It's just not his personality," Pandin says years later. "He's extraordinarily nice. I want people to know he's not the bastard that's coming across in the press. Jack's a great guy, and I have no reason to believe that he would change. A person's character doesn't change."

Nonetheless, back in the summer of 1981, Abramoff penned a letter to Roy Cohn, asking for a contribution to the College Republicans. Cohn happened to be the legal counsel for the leading Mafia families of New York and Canada. Abramoff's letter to Cohn was dated July 8, 1981:

> ...Alfred Bloomingdale, a close personal friend of my family, told me to contact you immediately...Although we [College Republicans] are an arm of the RNC

[Republican National Committee], we must become financially self-sufficient…

"Cohn was a major Republican donor," Abramoff later says. "Had I known he was mixed up in the mob, I would not have written to him." In the letter, Abramoff went on to say that he had obtained the RNC contributor list and needed seed money from Cohn into order to milk the list. Richard Bond was RNC deputy chairman at the time. He scoffed at Abramoff's claim that he had access to the contributor list as "outside the realm of reality. That list is like the Holy Grail… You can see his early prevarication." Abramoff says someone at the RNC had slipped him the list and that Bond was mistaken.

Ever desperate for cash, Abramoff decided to raise money by staging events that would grab media attention. Perhaps such antics might attract new members and contributions. Abramoff co-opted the New Left by harnessing the tactics of the merry pranksters of street theater. College Republicans started invading and shouting down nuclear-freeze rallies. When Democrats held an upscale fundraiser, Abramoff hosted a soup kitchen for the homeless across the street. "He'd have a long line of homeless people being served dinner by the College Republicans while the fat-cat Democrats were going into the Hilton to eat their foie gras and filet," recalled David Barron, former head of the Young Republicans.

Abramoff's College Republicans solicited a few contributions by hanging "adopt-a-contra" posters around town, imploring:

Only 53 Cents A Day Will Support A Nicaraguan Freedom Fighter.

The most notorious manifestation of youthful Republican exuberance was on Thursday, August 11, 1983. It was staged in Layette Park, across from the White House. At 6 P.M., Abramoff and his cohorts constructed a 24-foot wall of concrete blocks and draped a Soviet flag over it. "We hope this will not be a riotous event!" Abramoff said. Two hours later, with press photographers' cameras flashing, Abramoff's flock poured kerosene on the flag, set it on fire, and used sledgehammers to flatten "the Berlin Wall." All the commotion undoubtedly woke up President Reagan from one of his legendary naps. After the demolition, 500 protesters, shouting slogans, marched with torches and banners to the Soviet Embassy where they burned the leaders of the Soviet Union and East Germany in effigy.

Abramoff declared, "Germany has been divided between freedom and tyranny by the Berlin Wall for too long." Most Americans would have agreed with him.

"We felt we were the sword and shield of the Reagan Revolution," Abramoff recalls. Abramoff's four-year stint was certainly controversial. Originally, his offices were located in the first floor cubicles of the Republican National Committee headquarters at 310 First Street. Later, Abramoff claimed that the College Republicans were moved to a different site, along with all the other outreach groups. Others claim his organization was kicked out for being too boisterous and impertinent. Yet there was no doubt that Abramoff single-mindedly willed the College Republicans—with assistance from executive director Grover Norquist and Ralph Reed—into the largest student political organization in the free world. In recognition of his achievement in transforming a sleepy social club into a potent force of over 1,200 chapters and 150,000 members, Abramoff was invited to address the 1984 Republican National Convention.

"It's funny. I had never appeared before such a large group of people. However, the Teleprompter blocked my view, and I actually could not see anyone. It was probably a blessing. " Although he was supposed to give a canned speech, written by a party elder, Abramoff had memorized his own. He took a deep breath and then launched into an oration patterned after the rhyming style of Jesse Jackson. "My superiors didn't like it, but the delegates loved it," Abramoff says. "They were tired of hearing boring speeches. And Reagan got elected despite it."

Abramoff began: "Fellow Republicans, I come before you today, representing American students, the future of our Republican party, a group, I am proud to say, that leads all others in support of our President, our principles, and our Reagan revolution. Just as it's the job of all revolutions to make permanent their gains, so it is our job to make permanent our popularity among youth, a permanent fixture on the political horizon."

At this point, a smile crept over his face. He knew he was about to depart from what his elders had scripted for him. "Today, our party readies itself to mount the wave of the future. Will we ride that wave to glory, or will it send us crashing ashore? If we're the party of tax cuts, and not the party of 'ifs' and 'buts,' then we're riding our wave. If we're liberating students from Grenada, and not bowing down to a Cuban dictator, we're riding our wave. And if we're the party of composure and not the party that ducks disclosure, then we're riding our wave..." He stopped to clear his throat: "If we equivocate, capitulate, accommodate, and negotiate, we'll crash ashore. If we try to outspend big fat Tip O'Neill, or rush to Geneva to cut a deal, we'll crash ashore...."

Some of those that followed Abramoff to the podium included Sen. Howard Baker, former President Gerald Ford, Sen. Bob Dole, Sen. Barry Goldwater, Vice-President George Bush, and President Ronald Reagan. After all the sermonizing was over, a former heroin addict and token black man by the name of Ray Charles, led the conventioneers in singing Abramoff's favorite song, "America the Beautiful."

CHAPTER SEVEN
SMALL-WORLD DEPARTMENT

In early 1985, as he was handing over the reins of College Republicans to his successor, Abramoff still found himself so overwhelmed with responsibilities that he decided to shed control of the USA Foundation to his friend, Adam Kidan. Soon thereafter, however, the nonprofit ran out of funds and quietly expired. But Kidan had already been plotting his own future. After graduating from Georgetown University, he would move back to New York City and attend the Brooklyn School of Law. Kidan and Abramoff lost touch with one another. For thirteen years, they had no contact.

During semester breaks in college and law school, Kidan continued to fly down to St. Maarten to help out his "stepfather" at his casino as a chauffeur and a gofer. "It was a fast-paced and exciting environment," he says. "And one of the perks was lots of beautiful women." Eventually, he says he became one of the casino's goodwill ambassadors, greeting and glad-handing people. He liked to roam the tables spotting cheaters— those who counted cards, or used listening devices or signals. "It wasn't like the movies. No one would take them into the back room and break their hands," Kidan says. "We'd just ask them to leave."

He passed the New York bar in 1989, and started helping Amato with legal and regulatory issues. In effect, Kidan says he became the casino's legal counsel. One day Eddie Sciandra, the Buffalino consigliore, Kidan invited to one of Manhattan's finest restaurants. Over after-dinner cognac and cigars, Sciandra asked Kidan to become the Buffalino legal advisor. His first assignment would be to iron out a contract dispute with a boxer. Kidan says he politely declined. After that, Kidan decided to stop going to St. Maarten and that he would essentially have no further business dealings with mobsters.

Soon thereafter, Kidan opened a law office in his tiny Manhattan apartment. On the side, he opened a bagel store in the Hamptons with Michael Cavallo. Soon, they opened a second store and called the chain New York's Best Bagels. Kidan and Cavallo then launched a bagel factory to supply their stores and others. Years later, investigative reporters would claim that Cavallo was "an associate of known gangsters," and was "now deceased."

Kidan laughs. "He was a young mortgage broker who was dating my sister. They've got the wrong Michael Cavallo." According to the press, Cavallo introduced Kidan to mobster Anthony Moscatiello, an introduction that would have seismic repercussions years later. On September 26, 2005, Moscatiello, along with two mob associates, would be charged with the murder of Gus Boulis, the man who had sold a flotilla of Florida gambling boats to Abramoff and Kidan. "Cavallo didn't introduce me to Tony [Moscatiello]. I met him through Lenny DiMaria, a Gambino big shot. Lenny was a friend of my stepfather. I'd known him since I was a kid. I did some small-time legal work for Lenny. He was looking at some property down in Florida. He, Moscatiello, and I flew down there together to look at it," says Kidan. "Funny thing is, Boulis ended up buying that same property ten years later. Falls into the small-world department, doesn't it?"

Kidan said that Moscatiello became valuable to his bagel business, because "this is someone I [knew] who [had] experience in feeding large groups of people." These large groups of people included family weddings for John Gotti, the Teflon Don, boss of the Gambino crime family. In 1991, Kidan's bagel business went belly up. At age 27, Kidan was bored with the law and decided to explore other options.

"I wanted something bigger, faster, edgier, sexier," Kidan says.

CHAPTER EIGHT
A LESSON

Abramoff's third and final Achilles' heel was his compulsion to be hectically busy. Even though his voice was calm and gentle, he marched through life as if hooked up to an intravenous amphetamine drip. Always juggling too many balls, Abramoff says, "I can't remember a lot of the details of what I was doing twenty years ago," he says, "because I was always trying to do fifty things at once."

Since he could not possibly keep track of every ball, he dropped a few. Early on, his fervent focus was on stopping the threatening firestorm of Communism, the arch-enemy of mankind. Communism was anathema both to freedom and to religion. To a Communist, freedom was self indulgent and inefficient; religion, the opiate of the masses. Because he was busier than humanly possible, he was often oblivious to nuance and shades of gray, and he became blinded by the sight of his righteous pursuit. Any alliance, no matter how tainted or fouled, was worthy if it served the purpose of keeping the Communist Armageddon at bay. Any country—no matter how despicable but opposed to Communism—became a comrade-in-arms in the great holy war.

It should be noted that such cognitive dissonance—others called it realpolitik—was not uncommon. During WWII, the United States became an ally of a lesser evil, the Soviet Union, to defeat a greater evil, Nazi Germany. And in China, bitter foes Chang Kai-shek and Mao Zedung joined hands to defeat the Japanese invaders. The United States had opposed democratically elected governments—Iran (1952), Chile (1974), and Hamas (2005)—and supported brutal dictatorships—Augusto Pinochet, Saddam Hussein, and Fulgencio Batista—in pursuit of its national interests.

Overwhelmed, Abramoff was forced to delegate. He allowed his many lieutenants to attend to the Lilliputian details. In the process, he couldn't help but lose contact with much of what they were doing. The fact that he was besieged to the point of bewilderment certainly contributed to Abramoff's destruction fifteen years later when he purchased SunCruz Casinos. He says he trusted his main partner, Adam Kidan, to attend to all the myriad details. "[Abramoff] can do 20 things at once—'Call this person in Saipan; change my flights to Hong Kong, make sure my Kosher food is packed and ready to go'—he's doing e-mails while he's talking on his cell phone—'is my driver ready? Okay tell him I'm coming down in two minutes; send my bag down to my car.' There was always a dust cloud around him," recalls Kidan.

While Kidan was negotiating the complicated purchase of SunCruz, Abramoff was bursting at the seams, leading a 20-person team of Washington lobbyists with an ever growing list of clients. He was a relentless fundraiser for the GOP and a docent for congressmen, senators, and their staff on numerous junkets to storied golf courses in distant lands. Abramoff was toying with prospecting for oil in Israel's Negev Desert. He was launching and financing an Orthodox Jewish High School. He was opening a kosher restaurant and a delicatessen, donating mounds of money to many worthy causes and individuals, and devoting himself to his wife and five children, two of whom struggled with learning disabilities. He was practicing Orthodox Judaism, which meant sacrificing one day a week during which he could not touch his Blackberry.

Back in his mid 20s, Abramoff's life was no different. While taking night classes at Georgetown University Law Center and wrapping up his second term as national chairman of the College Republicans, he served as executive director of the political action committee for the Conservative Caucus and was on the board of directors of a local Jewish high school. He took the red-eye back and forth from to the Republic of South Africa, where he had broken bread with Russel Crystal, leader of a right-wing National Student Federation, which was allegedly in bed with the South African military intelligence services[11]. "Regardless of what has come out about Crystal since, he was never openly or privately pro-apartheid," says Abramoff. "He was an anti-Communist, not anti-black. Otherwise, I would have never worked with him."

Then, out of the blue, Abramoff was offered a $150,000-a-year job as director of Citizens For America, conveniently housed—along with the USA Foundation—at the Heritage Foundation.

Back in 1983, President Reagan had asked Jack Hume and Lew Lehrman—members of the president's so-called "kitchen cabinet"—to establish a grassroots organization to lobby on behalf of insurgents fighting Communism. Their organization—Citizens For America—became the seed that would germinate into biggest scandal of Reagan's presidency. Hume was the world's largest processor of dehydrated onions and garlic. Lehrman was the founder of the Rite-Aid drugstore empire. In 1982, he blew a cool $7 million in his failed gubernatorial bid to oust New York's Mario Cuomo, but Lehrman's narrow loss briefly trampolined him into the national spotlight.

Hume and Lehrman persuaded some of the nation's wealthiest right-wing cowboys to pony up for Citizens For America. These included Nelson Bunker Hunt, Ivan Boesky, J. Peter Grace, T. Boone Pickens, and Joseph Coors.

Lehrman hired Mark Holzman as executive director. He was soon replaced by Jeffery Bell, who had lost a New Jersey senate race to Bill Bradley in 1978. Their job was to lobby for the entire Reagan agenda, including finding ways to provide "humanitarian" aid to the Nicaraguan Contras. Congress had just unanimously passed the Boland Amendment[12], which forbade the CIA from providing assistance to the Contras, who were trying to overthrow the Communist Sandinista government in Nicaragua. Two years later, when Bell's term was up, he urged Lehrman to hire Abramoff. Lehrman immediately offered him the job, and Abramoff accepted it.

His brief tenure as executive director would propel him to the edge of controversy and scandal. Abramoff, who was close to the scandal's central figure, should have breathed a sigh of relief, because he had unwittingly dodged a bullet. The "Iran-Contra" scandal was the bullet; Lt. Col. Oliver North its marksman.

In the 1980s, America was still in the ostensible throes of the "domino effect." The theory was that if a country fell to Communism, the contiguous country would fall next, and so forth, until it reached America. China had succumbed to Communism in 1949. Cuba, only 90 miles from Florida, had tumbled in 1959. Ethiopia became Marxist in 1974. And, of course, there was the humiliation of the communist takeover of Vietnam. At least America could point to a few victories. In 1974, the CIA had managed to topple the democratically elected, but Socialist, president of Chile, Salvador Allende; and in 1983, America invaded the tiny Caribbean island of Grenada, nutmeg capital of the world, and ousted its communist government[13].

However, in 1979, Nicaragua, a Central-American nation only a few dominoes away, had fallen under the sway of Communism. When Reagan became president, he declared that the Sandinista-Communist regime in Nicaragua was "on our doorstep" and supported an insurgency led by the

Contras. By late 1984, Congress, increasingly mistrustful of the Reagan Administration, decided to ensure that the president did not deviously circumvent its will. It passed the so-called Boland II Amendment, which prohibited any American governmental agency from aiding the Contras, except for an annual $24 million in humanitarian aid.

Without American military assistance, the Contras were doomed, so Reagan decided to bend the rules. He directed his national security advisor, Robert "Bud" MacFarlane, to seek funding for the Contras by soliciting other governments. When a $1 million contribution came in from Saudi Arabia, MacFarlane ordered his deputy director for political-military affairs, Lt. Col. Oliver North, to funnel the cash to the Contras. A few months later, when Reagan could not convince Congress to overturn the $24 million humanitarian cap, he made it clear MacFarlane who allegedly told Col. North to find a way to keep the Contras alive "body and soul." This request launched the "Iran-Contra Affair," the name given to an illegal enterprise that operated within the halls of the White House. It became a scandal that should have cost Reagan his presidency, or at the very least, led to his impeachment, especially since the Democrats controlled the House of Representatives.

Both of Reagan's national security advisors—first MacFarlane and then Admiral John Poindexter, together with North—apparently hatched and implemented a scheme to illegally and secretly divert millions of dollars to the Nicaraguan Contras made from inflated profits in the illegal and secret sales of military hardware to Iran. Why sell American arms to Iran, a loathsome country that had recently released 52 American embassy staff, held hostage for 444 days from 1979-1981? Reagan hoped that by improving diplomatic relations with Iran, it would assist in freeing a handful of Americans held hostage in Lebanon.

At the time, not only was the United States legally prohibited from selling arms to the Contras, but to Iran as well. In fact, Reagan had been urging his European allies to ban arms sales to Iran. When the secret Iran-Contra operation was finally exposed in the fall of 1986, there was a hue and cry from Congress and the media. Reagan was forced to fire Col. North and demand the resignation of his national security advisor, John Poindexter. Several months later, Congress launched a televised probe into the "Iran-Contra Affair." What eventually save Reagan's presidency was the doctrine of "plausible deniability," jargon for untruthfulness.

His closest advisors apparently committed perjury by insisting that this madcap scheme was conducted under the president's nose without his knowledge or consent.

Had these role models implicitly tutored Abramoff in the art of creative, "think outside of the box" ingenuity? Abramoff later scoffed at this suggestion. What was so damaging to the rule of law was that high crimes and misdemeanors—all for a "worthy" cause—did not necessarily lead to prison or disgrace[14]. The nation's capital—filled with lawmakers and lawyers—seemed obsessed with skirting and fudging the law without breaking it. Depending on one's point of view or party affiliation, when you did so, you were either being ingenious and creative, or shady and devious.

In the greater context of the American capitalistic system and how it conducts its business and government, the fact that Abramoff would later "push the envelope" and "think outside the box" in vigorously lobbying for his clients and acquiring wealth did not necessarily make him a criminal.

Rationalizations notwithstanding, it seemed what was criminal was the system itself.

CHAPTER NINE
JAMBOREE

Abramoff became head of Citizens For America and was quickly put in touch with Col. Oliver North. In a memo dated March 15, 1985, North mentioned that Abramoff had been assigned responsibility for organizing briefings by Contra speakers, phone trees "to targeted congressional offices urging them to vote for aid to the freedom fighters in Nicaragua," and "rallies throughout the country." Soon, Abramoff was being touted as "one of North's closest advisors in the 'private sector.'" According to *The Washington Post*, Abramoff was in touch with North almost daily. Andre Bogolubov, Abramoff's successor at Citizens for America, complained how Abramoff used to bring up North's name constantly: "It was Ollie this and Ollie that."

In the May 1985 issue of *Conservative Digest*, Abramoff signed a petition, appealing to Reagan to stop "trying to sell 20 million Black

Africans into Communist slavery." Abramoff was even opposed to UN-sponsored democratic elections in Namibia, illegally administered by South Africa since 1966, because he feared there would be a Communist takeover. He was chomping at the bit. What more could he do for the anti-Communist freedom fighters around the world? His friend, Jack Wheeler—a right-wing intellectual adventurer, who had fought alongside the anti-Communist Laotian guerrillas and the Afghan mujahideen—had an idea. Inspired by President Reagan's declaration that "support for freedom fighters is self-defense," Wheeler suggested that they stage an international publicity stunt. The Soviet Union held regular summits for all its puppets—the Sandinistas, the African insurgents, the PLO, and Cuba—to plot strategy and offer self-congratulations. Why not the anti-communists? Abramoff loved the idea.

But where? South Africa and Israel were willing to host the summit, but they were politically radioactive. "Preparations were difficult," Abramoff says later. "We had to find a place where everyone wouldn't get killed. The Soviets wanted to kill most of these guys. We thought about Taiwan. Ultimately, it came down to the part of Angola controlled by Savimbi. We had to keep it secret until the last minute so the Soviets and Cubans wouldn't know where we were."

Abramoff turned to his friend, Russel Crystal, head of the libertarian South African National Student Federation, whom Abramoff had met in 1982. They agreed on Jamba, a flyspeck in southeastern war-ravaged Angola. Granted independence by Portugal in 1974, Angola had quickly become the site of one of the many proxy wars staged by the United States and the Soviet Union in their ongoing brawl over world hegemony, known as the Cold War. The fact that millions of innocent civilians lost their lives in the 30-year Angolan civil war was considered a collateral pity. Jamba was the rebel headquarters of UNITA (The National Union for the Total Independence of Angola). UNITA, funded in part by the CIA and by South Africa's apartheid government, was leading an insurgency against Angola's Communist government, which was heavily defended by thousands of Cuban troops and hundreds of Soviet advisors.

Organizing the event in Jamba was a logistical nightmare. Transportation, lodging, medicine, and communications equipment had to be delivered to a remote and camouflaged jungle camp subject to aerial attack from Russian MIGs flown by Cuban pilots. Savimbi would feed everyone. Crystal, who had links to South African military intelligence (which was fighting its own leftist insurgency, led by Oliver Tambo and the jailed Nelson Mandela), told Abramoff not to worry. The South African government was only too pleased to provide assistance and security for such a worthy cause.

Abramoff turned to Col. North for help. North immediately dispatched Reagan speechwriter Dana Rohrabacher (later a GOP congressman from California) to Nicaragua to hand-deliver the invitation to the leader of the Contras. Despite the assistance of the South African government, logistical problems cropped up. The Laotian guerrillas, for example, had trouble catching a flight out of Thailand. The Pakistani government wasn't overjoyed about letting the mujahideen slip out of the country. Yet with stunning speed, the Jungle Jamboree in Jamba took shape. In the first week in June, the delegates and the media began arriving in Johannesburg. They were then ferried on rickety Douglas DC-3—the "vomit comet," which took evasive action to avoid Cuban radar—to a dirt airstrip in southeast Angola, and then driven a two-hour bumpy ride to Jamba.

"The whole concept was so audacious and really a little bizarre," says Jeff Pandin, Abramoff's former College Republicans spokesman. "The fact that it even came off was incredible. Jack thinks big. He thinks outside the box. Back then, there were always people around who could restrain him and keep him focused. But without any restraints, I could see him getting into trouble [if he were] surrounded only by 'yes' men."

Bwana Jack arrived on Friday June 3rd, to avoid traveling on the Sabbath. Later that day, the first leader Abramoff greeted was his host, "Dr." Jonas Savimbi, the bearded head of UNITA. His guerrilla-chic attire included a holstered pistol, green army fatigues, and a green beret. Next, was the tall, white-haired Adolfo Calero, leader of the 15,000-man Nicaraguan Democratic Force, who towered over everyone. He appeared ready to hit the links. His outfit included a white lightweight zip-up jacket, white shirt, and beige slacks. The bespectacled, bearded Ghulam Wardak of the Islamic Unity of Afghanistan mujahideen arrived in traditional garb: a turban with a long tail that dangled down his back like a braid, a knee-length tunic over baggy beige pants, and a green vest. He brought his son as translator. The final guerrilla generalissimo was the diminutive Pa Kao Her of the Ethnics Liberation Organization of Laos. He was a full head shorter than his counterparts. Despite the heat and dust, he was dressed in a dark blue business suit, blue-striped tie, and leather shoes.

Abramoff particularly admired Savimbi, whom he affectionately called the Che Guevara of the right. Savimbi had actually visited America many times, would soon meet with President Reagan, and retain a top Washington lobbying firm to help burnish his image. His many detractors claimed that he had a fondness for burning his enemies at the stake and shooting down humanitarian-aid flights heading to towns controlled by the Angolan communists. Abramoff dismissed these accusations, later well documented, because "[The Soviet Union] has a full-time director at the KGB for disinformation." A few months later, Jeanne Kirkpatrick, Reagan's first ambassador to the U.N., would praise Savimbi as a "linguist, philosopher, poet, politician, warrior...one of the few authentic heroes of our time." Others had grown to appreciate him as well. According to Don Steinburg, an American ambassador to Angola, Savimbi was "the most articulate charismatic homicidal maniac I've ever met."

Next up was a pageantry of nubile, braless UNITA women in short-sleeved orange blouses, blue skirts, and orange hats, who chanted revolutionary slogans as they raised their fists. The participants filed into a small stadium and sat before microphones at a long table. Behind them was a colored banner depicting two clasped hands—one black, the other white—inside a circle that represented the planet earth. Nearby were the stenciled words: "Angola—Jamba 1985." Savimbi opened the proceedings with some platitudinous remarks and spoke too long. Finally, he concluded with the stirring words: "The Russians will never stop, unless we stop them."

Calero told those in attendance that he had just learned that one of the Russian generals he was fighting in Nicaragua had recently been transferred from Angola. "We have fought the same enemy," he declared. "We have known the same enemy. But we did not know each other until this opportunity."

Due to the inept translators, when Ghulam Wardak and Pa Kao Her delivered their speeches, no one had a clue what they were saying.

Finally, the balding Lew Lehrman, basking in the media attention, pointed out that the goal of the "Democratic International" was to energize one another and coordinate efforts to help stamp out the world-wide scourge of Communism. He then read a hearty letter of support from the leader of the Free World, in which he concluded, "Your goals are our goals. Good luck. God Bless you. Sincerely, President Ronald Reagan." He neglected to mention that the letter was actually addressed only to him, not to the rebel leaders. Lehrman distributed a communiqué for all to sign, declaring, "our solidarity with all freedom movements in the world and…our commitment to cooperate to liberate our nations from the Soviet imperialists." He then handed out framed copies of the Declaration of Independence and other patriotic tchachkes.

The Jamba Jamboree was extensively covered by the mainstream press, playing prominently on Tom Brokaw's NBC and Dan Rather's CBS nightly news programs. *Time* magazine surmised that the meeting may have launched "a new lobby to urge Congress to support the Nicaraguan Contras and other anti-Communist guerrillas." Three weeks later, when Congress raised the $24 million cap to $100 million in aid to the Contras, most observers attributed that accomplishment to the Jamba Jamboree. Although Lehrman took the credit, it was Abramoff who really deserved it. Several months later, Reagan granted an additional $15 million in assistance to UNITA.

On Monday, Abramoff and Lehman departed on the Learjet Lehrman had leased. "On the plane ride home, he told me he wanted me to fire Grover [Norquist]," Abramoff later says. "We fought about it all the way back, from Jamba to Jo-burg, Jo-burg to London, and then on the Concorde back to New York. I was furious about this. He was my friend, and he had done nothing wrong. The problem was that Grover was effective." With great reluctance, Abramoff fired Norquist, but managed to get him three months' severance pay. This briefly put a brief strain on their relationship.

Why Abramoff and Crystal organized a costly follow-up meeting a month later in early July in Johannesburg, nobody knows. However, an important message of love and support from former South African Prime Minister P. W. Botha proved to be the event's crowning jewel. While in Johannesburg, Abramoff continued to bond with Crystal, a fellow Jew. They discussed the possibility of establishing an international right-wing think tank. Crystal introduced Abramoff to Craig Williamson, an obese student activist, who was equally enthusiastic about the think tank. "[Williamson] definitely gave the impression of being a shady character," says Pandin, who met him once in Johannesburg and once in

Mozambique. "He does not inspire a huge amount of confidence when he tells you something."

In Johannesburg, Abramoff renewed his friendship with South African Rabbi David Lapin, whom he had met on a previous visit in 1983. "I was struck by his brilliance and his majestic personality, and he began tutoring me in the Talmud," says Abramoff. "Since that time, he has been my family's rabbi." Nine years later, Lapin's brother, Rabbi Daniel Lapin, would introduce Abramoff to Tom DeLay, an ambitious congressman from Texas. "It always annoyed Jack that so many Jews were liberal Democrats. Jewish outreach to conservative Jews was what [Daniel] Lapin was all about. He became Jack's go-to guy," says Pandin.

Within a week of his return to Washington, however, Lehrman fired Abramoff for overspending. Abramoff remembered it differently. "Lehrman's brilliant, a genius, but he has some flaws," Abramoff explains years later. "He always treated me very well until the end, and I'm grateful for the time I was there. Basically, this is what happened. His job was to raise the money, but he hated raising money, so he'd donate his own money instead. We were spending money hand over fist, doing a thousands things that cost money, like lobbying for Reagan's initiatives from the MX missile, to the Clark Amendment, to the Tax Reform Act. So when I met with him, he told me he was taking away financial responsibility of the organization and he was going to bring in his accountant. Frankly, what I should have said was 'Fine.' Instead, I quit. I was too immature at the time to realize that that wouldn't have been a bad idea. I told him I'd be happy to stay for the transition. He told me that he preferred that I clean out my desk by 5 pm that day. And that effectively caused the organization to collapse."

The Washington Post's Sidney Blumenthal reported that Lehrman accused Abramoff of "lavish spending" and financial "mismanagement." A Lehrman spokesman grumbled, "It was one big party...[Abramoff] had gone hog wild."

Abramoff had a sweet tooth when it came to money. He couldn't budget it or hold on to it to save his life. "I was the only person who could exceed an unlimited budget," Abramoff later quips.

Nonetheless, Abramoff had pulled off the impossible, and the Jamba Jubilee had been a great—though quickly forgotten—success.

The following year, there was a brief hullabaloo over groups like Citizens For American. One news report claimed that Col. North had diverted $5 million in arms-sales profits from Iran to groups that supported pro-Contra congressional candidates, and Rep. J. J. Pickle (D-TX), head of the House Ways and Means Committee, threatened to launch a probe into the funding sources of conservative tax-exempt groups linked to the Iran-Contra scandal.

Abramoff told a reporter, "We didn't get any money from the Ayatollah."

CHAPTER TEN
FUNDING FREEDOM

Abramoff's tenure at Citizens of America lasted only six months. Although now unemployed, he kept charging ahead at full speed. There were other offers, but he turned them down. Weary of politics, Abramoff decided it was time to make money. But politics was hard to resist. "Russel [Crystal] came to the States to see me. I was thinking about making movies at that point. He asked me just to be the chairman [of a new think tank]. 'Do us the favor.' So I reluctantly agreed. I'm almost certain it was unpaid or had a nominal salary," Abramoff says years later.

The think tank would be called the "International Freedom Foundation" (IFF). Abramoff would be its founding chairman; Crystal would head up the satellite office in Johannesburg. Abramoff signed the incorporation papers and IRS application for tax-exempt, non-profit "501(c)3" status, which were filed and approved. The purpose of the educational foundation was to "expand free markets and individual rights throughout the world."

But first there was the formidable task of raising funds, the bane of fledgling nonprofits. Where would the vital lubricant come from? Crystal assured Abramoff that he had located a group of wealthy South African businessmen who were only too happy to seed a think tank of such paramount importance. "I can't believe that the group of businessmen I met in South Africa lied to me," Abramoff says many years later. The checks arrived like clockwork. No need to squander energy on fundraising. The IFF's first listed address was Abramoff's apartment in

Silver Spring, Maryland. Later, its offices were located at 200 G Street in northeast Washington, D.C. He hired staff—Colleen Morrow, Duncan Sellars, and Jeff Pandin—and began formulating the specific goals the organization hoped to achieve.

When later questioned about the IFF, Abramoff was perplexed. Why even discuss it, he wonders? "I was not really all that involved. [Crystal] had direct and constant contact with the staff, and I had very little to do personally with any of it."

The IFF's relevance was that years later the media would pounce on it as an example of Abramoff's lack of scruples and his implicit racism, when they exposed that the IFF had actually been secretly funded by the white-ruled South African government.

"Well, I guess I did leave my name out there," Abramoff concedes.

At the time, he says he had actually begun working full-time for his father, Frank, who owned the land in Atlantic City that was leased by the Claridge Hotel and Casino, as well as other nearby parcels of terra firma that Frank hoped to develop. In his spare time, Abramoff completed a 15-page film treatment he would later turn into a Hollywood feature film.

In mid August of 1985, Abramoff read in *The New York Times* that a member of the National Security Council staff, Col. Oliver L. North, "has emerged as an influential and occasionally controversial character in ... nurturing connections among anti-government rebels in Nicaragua, their conservative supporters in this country, and the rest of the administration." Essentially, this was the first mention of the soon-to-be infamous Col. North. The Iran-Contra scandal, however, would not yet erupt upon the news cycle for another fifteen months.

In January 1986, the International Freedom Foundation formally opened its doors. This venture would prove not be a think tank in which soporific monographs were published infrequently and never read. The staff worked feverishly to make the organization a *force majeure*. Although headquartered in Washington, D.C., the IFF soon opened other offices in Johannesburg, London, Hamburg, Brussels, and Rome.

Eventually, the IFF had a paid staff of 20. They aggressively organized forums, seminars, fellowships, and a speakers' bureau. The foundation published the monthly *Angola Peace Monitor*; the monthly *Freedom Bulletin*, with local editions in America, England, and South Africa; and a weekly newsletter that eventually had a circulation of nearly 220,000. But that was just the beginning. It also published *Laissez-Faire*, which explored European and Third-World relations; the Soviet Perspective; *The Sub-Sahara Monitor*; and other journals with scholarly articles on foreign policy issues. Even powerful Republican politicians would eventually participate in the foundation's activities, including Sen. Jesse Helms (R-NC), Reps. Dan Burton (R-Ind), Philip Crane (R-IL), and Robert Dornan (R-CA), former CIA director William Colby and Henry Kissinger.

Checks continued to arrive from Russel Crystal. Was anybody suspicious about where the money came from? "Russel never said where the money was coming from, and I had the sense not to ask…because he didn't put any strings on it. Basically, he said, 'Here's the money to support the cause. Run with it,'" says staffer Pandin years later. "A lot of us just weren't sensitive to the race question. We didn't think of it as really that important. There was stuff much more important than that. Jack wasn't a racist. He didn't care about race one way or the other."

In the late 1980s, the world was a considerably different place. The Soviet Union's nuclear arsenal was still threatening the Free World, and a brutal white supremacist government ruled the Republic of South Africa. The official policy of strict segregation of races, was poetically called "apartheid." The government, however, had come under heavy pressure to end its racist policies. It was universally ostracized, except by right-wing Christian Republicans, a few Orthodox Jews, and Israel, as well as defense hawks and zealous anti-Communists. There was a UN arms embargo against South Africa. The European Community had imposed a limited trade ban on the country. Corporations and individuals were ridding themselves of all South African investments. Finally, on October 2, 1986, Congress overrode President Reagan's veto and passed the Comprehensive Anti-Apartheid Act. It was the only Reagan veto ever overturned.

"I thought [this act was] stupid, because the people who were going to suffer were the poor, not the propagators of apartheid. I thought less contact with the USA was a bad idea, not a good one. It was with contact with the USA that the RSA [Republic of South Africa] would become a true democracy. The truth is that I now think I was wrong and that sanctions had a big impact in ending apartheid and causing what has been for the most part a positive political transformation in [South Africa]," says Abramoff years later.

Most Americans believed that the South African government—terrified that rivers of Caucasian blood would flow if the black majority ever seized power—was desperate to hold back the tide, even though its days were clearly numbered. Besides the usual torture and assassination of its own black African freedom fighters, South African military intelligence had conducted shrewd clandestine operations, whose purpose was to combat sanctions and sway world opinion. At the same time, there were elements in all branches of government that accepted the inevitable but hoped to persuade Mandela and the African National Congress (ANC) not to "kill the golden goose." Despite world-wide sanctions, the golden goose was the country's robust economy.

"We decided that the only level [at which] we were going to be accepted was…to paint the ANC as Communist surrogates," admitted Craig Williamson. "The more we could present ourselves as anti-Communists, the more people looked at [the apartheid regime with at least some] respect. People you could hardly believe cooperated with us politically when it came to the Soviets." There was irrefutable evidence that the Soviet Union, which Reagan had dubbed the "evil empire," was the ANC's chief arms supplier, and that Nelson Mandela had once lavishly praised Communism. Therefore, the fear of a Red South Africa was hardly paranoia or lunacy.

But the inevitable forces of change would finally reach South Africa. In early 1990, four years after Abramoff founded the International Freedom Foundation, F.W. de Klerk, the white president of South Africa, would unexpectedly free Mandela after 27 years in prison. By 1993, the IFF would disband, because its funding suddenly evaporated. In April 1994, South Africa would hold its first democratic elections, and Mandela would become the president of a country that could not be placed into orbit around the Soviet Union, for one simple reason: the Soviet Union no longer existed. To the surprise of the entire world, it had dissolved itself on December 31, 1991.

President Mandela had taken the astonishing step of establishing the controversial Truth and Reconciliation Commission in 1995, because he was determined to prevent his country from being torn asunder by retribution. Former white South African government spies and assassins, as well as "dirty tricksters from other political persuasions," were offered total amnesty—immunity from prosecution—if they publicly confessed their crimes and apologized to the victims or their families. Soon a cathartic, though horrible, torrent of secrets began spilling out. One of the more tepid revelations was that Abramoff's "independent" think tank, the IFF, had been a front for the South African government.

In 1995, New York's *Newsday* conducted a three-month investigation and concluded, "The [IFF's] broad objectives were to try to reverse the apartheid regime's pariah status in Western political circles…[and] to portray the ANC as a tool of Soviet Communism, [in order to undercut] the movement's growing international acceptance as the government-in-waiting of a future multi-racial South Africa." South African Army spokesman Col. John Rolt conceded that the IFF indeed "was a former South African Defense Force project."

Even though the IFF was technically in violation of federal law, the American intelligence community under Reagan looked the other way. "We knew that the IFF was funded by the South African government," said Herman Cohen, who ran the Africa desk for the National Security Council. "It was one of a number of front organizations." The South African government had been supplying at least half of the foundation's annual $3 million budget. Russel Crystal in Johannesburg, not the IFF staff in Washington, had been pulling the purse strings, determining how much money each branch received. Crystal also admitted that some of those funds came from doing "jobs" for South African military intelligence, and payments for those services were often paid directly to the Washington headquarters.

Williamson claimed that "[Abramoff and the IFF] ran their own organization, but we steered them. That was the point." In sworn testimony before the Truth and Reconciliation Commission, Williamson also confessed that he had been a spy who had committed a number of atrocities back in the 1960s and 70s, including the murder of Ruth First, one of the most prominent white-opposition figures, and the murder of the wife and baby daughter of Marius Schoon, another white dissident. These crimes were not dissimilar to those committed by America's Central Intelligence Agency. Just to scratch the surface, these had included the assassination of Congo's Prime Minister Patrice Lumumba in 1961, and the attempted assassinations of Jamaican President Michael Manley and

Cuba's Fidel Castro, as well as its indirect involvement in the death of Salvador Allende.

South African military intelligence felt justified in spending millions on the IFF operation, dubbed "Babushka." A former South African police official, Vic McPherson, testified: "They [the IFF] were all very good, those guys... They were not only just good in intelligence, but in political warfare." At least two unnamed sources reportedly claimed that Abramoff had been well aware of the source of funding. "As chairman [of the IFF], he understood where the money was coming from. He knew exactly who he was playing with," an unidentified source told *Harpers Magazine*. The source's statement contains an intimation of presumption, not certainty. At the time, Abramoff denies the claims emphatically. He says that the foundation had been "funded by hundreds of contributors in the United States, Europe, and Israel," some of whom he had personally met on a visit to Johannesburg in 1986.

Years later, Abramoff would add, "The IFF... was vigorously anti-Communist, but it was also actively anti-apartheid... In 1987, it was one of the first conservative groups to call for the release of Nelson Mandela, a position for which it was roundly criticized by other conservatives at the time. While I headed the IFF, we accepted funding only from private individuals and corporations and would have absolutely rejected any offer of South African military funding, or any other kind of funding from any government—good or evil."

Others claimed not to know where the money was really coming from, including Rick Sincere, a former IFF staffer, who never met Abramoff. "It was a well laundered operation," he told *Harpers*. "We'd get tips to apply for money from certain European foundations and they'd approve our grant applications. What I didn't realize at the time was that it was all pro-forma and we were pre-approved. The staff thought it was the hard work of fundraising."

Duncan Sellars, who succeeded Abramoff as chairman in 1989, told *Newsday*, "This is nothing I ever knew about. It's something that I would have resigned over or closed the foundation over. I would have put a stop to it."

Jeff Pandin expressed amazement when he was told that funds had come from South Africa's secret police. "I worked for the IFF from Day One to Day End," he said. "This is complete news to me."

The most compelling evidence that may exonerate Abramoff came years later from Russel Crystal, who, at that point, had had a falling out with Abramoff, and would presumably have been forthcoming in revealing Abramoff's complicity. When questioned, however, Crystal acknowledged that Abramoff had not known where the money came from. Since it was Crystal who had arranged for South African Military Intelligence to supply the funds, he would have known with absolutely certainty how much Abramoff actually knew.

How much of the apartheid government's dirty work did the IFF do in return for the millions it received from South Africa? Surprisingly, the answer was full of contradictions.

When Oliver Tambo, head of the ANC, met with George Shultz, Reagan's Secretary of State, on January 28, 1987, in Washington, D.C., conservatives of all stripes howled in protest. The IFF helped organize a rally opposing the meeting. About thirty demonstrators shouted, "ANC means KGB." Others lugged tires around their necks to protest the alleged ANC-sponsored "necklace killings," in which suspected government informers were eliminated by placing a tire filled with gasoline around their necks and set ablaze.

David Sanders, a spokesman for the Conservative Caucus, of which Abramoff was a senior member, blasted the administration for "entertaining one of the leading terrorists in Africa." Republicans introduced congressional resolutions, which the Democrats quickly tabled, that denounced the meeting for sending the "wrong kind of message" as America fought terrorism in the Mideast. Even future GOP presidential candidate Sen. Bob Dole declared that Shultz's meeting with Tambo could only be viewed as an endorsement of terrorism.

Also in 1987, when Sen. Edward Kennedy (D-Mass) held hearings on how the apartheid government was oppressing black children, Abramoff counterattacked with a classic tit-for-tat. He sponsored hearings before the House Republican Study Committee, chaired by his good friend, Rep. Dan Burton (R-IN), on the oppression of children by Nelson Mandela's African National Congress. One of the witnesses was Alan Keyes, an African American who opposed sanctions. Keyes was Reagan's Assistant Secretary of State for International Organization Affairs. (In the 1996 and 2000 Republican primaries, Keyes would make two frivolous bids for president.)

On the heels of the Burton hearings, Abramoff's foundation published two articles. The first, "The Role of Youth in Revolutionary Warfare," attacked Mandela's African National Congress. The second, "Suffer the Children," accused Randall Robinson's anti-apartheid group, TransAfrica (based in Washington, D.C.), of being a mouthpiece for Soviet and Cuban terrorism.

Yet paradoxically, Abramoff's foundation also praised the South African government for releasing Govan Mbeki from prison on November 5, 1987. He was an ANC leader and member of the South African Communist party, who had been imprisoned for treason for 24 years[15]. Why was Abramoff's foundation praising the release of a Communist?

The Johannesburg Star extensively quoted Russel Crystal: "If Mbeki... renounce[s] violence and engage[s] in peaceful negotiations with the government, we will have come a long way toward real and lasting reform."

In the same article, comments by Pandin went further. He said, "Since we have made the case for [Nelson] Mandela's release, we have heard favorable noises from many quarters." Indeed, the July/August 1991 issue of Spur magazine (UK) pointed out that "the International Freedom Foundation (IFF)...has consistently opposed the apartheid system in South Africa." Abramoff's Freedom Bulletin repeatedly took the position, as early as 1987, that apartheid should end and that Nelson Mandela should be released from prison. This hardly squared with the position the South African government wanted the foundation to take. Apparently, *Newsday* and other media omitted the fact that IFF openly opposed apartheid and supported Mandela's release from prison, because it would have diminished the story's impact. (*The Washington Post*'s Susan Schmidt would employ the same device—omission—years later in her condemnation of Abramoff.)

Nonetheless, the IFF's London office seemed to be operating on its own wavelength. It published an anti-sanction screed, "Understanding Sanctions," written by David Hoile. Several years earlier, Hoile had attended a right-wing student conference sporting a badge with the beguiling motto: "Hang Nelson Mandela." The London office also attacked OxFam, a world-wide private relief agency, simply because of its opposition to apartheid.

In 1990, when the popular and respected Mandela paid his first visit to the United States shortly after his release from prison, the IFF placed ads in various newspapers vilifying Mandela for his ardent praise of Cuba's Fidel Castro, but by then, Abramoff was no longer affiliated with the foundation. As a result, Mandela failed to receive the honorary "key to the city" from the mayor of Miami, Florida, home of the world's largest concentration of anti-Castro Cuban exiles.

Mandela's admiration for the evil triplets—Castro, Arafat, and Khadafy—was not in dispute. All of them, along with the Soviet Union, had long supported the ANC in its epic struggle against the apartheid government. Just as Abramoff had unabashedly allied himself with anyone who opposed Communism, the fiercely loyal Mandela allied himself with anyone who supported the ANC. That didn't necessarily make Mandela a Communist, just as it didn't necessarily make Abramoff a racist.

Abramoff was hardly flying solo. Most conservatives—some of them African-Americans such as Alan Keyes, Jay Parker, and Colin Powell—were also opposed to sanctions against South Africa. Not only did they see the ANC as a ruthless terrorist organization, but they feared that Mandela would turn South Africa into a communist state. If conservatives lived in constant fear of the Red Menace, then it was perfectly rational for them to try to prevent South Africa—despite its apartheid government—from descending into a Communist hell.

"Conservatives did not want to see blacks degraded," says Abramoff. "They wanted them to have all the rights that whites had. They just didn't want to see South Africa go Soviet, where neither the blacks nor the whites would have had anything but slavery."

An exhaustive examination of the IFF's publications confirmed Abramoff's claim that the foundation's single-minded raison d'etre was to defeat Communism, not to perpetuate apartheid. Was the South African military intelligence satisfied that it was getting a bang for its buck by manipulating Abramoff? Or was it the other way around? It seems that each managed to scratch the other's back.

Had these scandalous allegations surfaced earlier—on the heels of Abramoff's dismissal for alleged financial malfeasance at Citizens of America back in July of 1985—President Reagan would never have named Abramoff to a five-year term on the prestigious U.S. Holocaust Memorial Council, a mark of prestige for an Orthodox Jew in the Washington, D.C. area. Yet on May 3, 1986, Reagan did just that.

In addition to his college and law-school degrees, Abramoff's only listed affiliation in the presidential announcement was "vice president of Boardwalk & Associates." What reason did he have for omitting the College Republicans, The USA Foundation, The Conservative Caucus, and Citizens of America? Boardwalk & Associates was the name of one of his father's real-estate companies[16]. Meanwhile, Pamela Alexander, now employed by New York Life Insurance Company, had converted to Judaism. She became an increasingly important friend and confidante in his hectic life. Although they had never formally dated, they had grown closer over time. Always respectful, and unassertive with women, Abramoff had never proposed to her, but they had reached an understanding. In fact, he never bought her an engagement ring. One day, she simply went and picked out one that she liked. It was somehow understood that they would marry.

On July 13 1986, at the Woodley Park Sheraton Hotel, now a Marriot Hotel, they were wed by Rabbi Melvin Rishe, a prominent attorney, who lived across the street from Abramoff and was also his racketball partner. Over four hundred people attended the service, including family members of the bride and groom, as well as Jack Kemp, Phil Crane, Ralph Reed, Grover Norquist, Paul Erickson, Jeff Pandin, and Michael Goland. Since Abramoff is allergic to alcohol, he consumed grape juice during the ceremony. Adam Kidan, who in St. Maarten with Andy Amato at his casino, was not invited. Oliver North planned to attend, but could not at the last minute.

It was in the fall of that year that the illicit Iran-Contra scandal erupted and Reagan was forced to fire North. Nevertheless, Abramoff wisely distanced himself from North. When interviewed by *The Washington Post* a couple of weeks later in December, Abramoff said, "I [used to] talk to [North] maybe once every three weeks, sometimes more frequently, sometimes less."

In the spring of 1985, *The Washington Post* reported that Abramoff had been speaking to him almost daily. Was this the same kind of distancing that Abramoff would experience twenty years later, when a stampede of congressmen, senators, and a sitting U.S. President would rush not only to disavow their friendship with Abramoff, but to deny any knowledge of him whatsoever?

"I don't ever recall backing away from him," says Abramoff. "In fact, I met Brendon Sullivan in my effort to help him by being willing to testify on his behalf, if there was anything I knew that could help."

By mid-July 1987, under a grant of limited immunity, Col. North was delivering an electrifying performance before a nationally televised joint House-Senate committee investigating Iran-Contra. Often whispering to his lawyer, Brendan "I'm-not-a-potted-plant" Sullivan, North proudly admitted that he had lied under oath to Congress, illegally shredded documents, obstructed justice, and accepted illegal gifts. What seemed to incense Abramoff the most, however, was the committee's brazen refusal to allow North to present his homespun slide show, which North had used to promote the Contras at private fundraisers in the homes of conservative donors.

In order to right this egregious wrong, as well as to hone his skills as a budding film producer, Abramoff urged the IFF staff to release a 30-minute video of North's slide show for $8.95. The foundation actually sent a film crew to Nicaragua to interview contra leader Adolpho Calero, who provided a stirring introduction to the video, which also included battle footage of his guerrillas in action against the Cuban-backed Sandinistas. Executive producer Jack Abramoff arranged for the distribution of the Col. North blockbuster, "Telling It Like It Is," and even ran a 30-second radio commercial to promote it. Only 1,000 cassettes were actually made, however.

The truth was that Abramoff had long ago begun drifting away from politics and had essentially relinquished the IFF reins to Duncan Sellars, Colleen Morrow, and Jeff Pandin. He was fed up with politics. The Blumenthal article had hurt him. He wanted to make money and couldn't do it as a conservative in politics since he would always be subject to the guys with the money. He decided to "go out and get rich and then I can call the shots and won't have to be beholden to crazy rich people."

This interest had actually first emerged just before Abramoff graduated from Georgetown Law School in 1985. Entertainment Law had been one of his favorite courses, but after graduating from law school, he never took the bar exam. "I prepared to take the bar, but the day before the exam, I had to fly to South Africa for *Red Scorpion*. Then I prepared again and the same thing happened when I had to go to Malaysia," he says later.

Like so many people in their twenties driving a taxi, parking cars, and pumping gas in southern California, Abramoff was dreaming about making it big as a Hollywood producer. He didn't know that making a Hollywood movie was like climbing Mt. Everest without oxygen. Indeed, there are many successful screenwriters and producers, earning a decent living in Los Angeles, whose work has never been produced. Abramoff says later, "The concept of I can't do something had never entered my mind. I didn't have the mental maturity to understand what I couldn't do." He was on his way to taking his first film project all the way to the big screen.

CHAPTER ELEVEN
SCORPION

When the Congressional scandal broke in early 2004, Jack Abramoff was the devil incarnate, one of the most sinister creatures that had ever slithered out of the slime. But how had he managed to hoodwink so many smart and sophisticated people for so long? The answer was simple. He could scheme, deceive, manipulate and seduce better than the best. His callous greed, his unscrupulous disregard of the laws, and his racist contemptuousness made him America's Iago—an unadulterated evil genius.

On further investigation, however, there were some inconvenient inconsistencies. Maybe the black-and-white portrait of Abramoff was more a caricature or cartoon. Was it possible that once again the media, in league with his political foes and overzealous prosecutors, had become the ringleaders of mob rule, of a Salem witch hunt? Had a highly accomplished and complex man—who had made some regrettable choices that had left him vulnerable—been unfairly demonized?

Well, hadn't he collaborated with the reviled apartheid South African government? Or was it possible that he was simply a foolhardy militant patriot, willing to enter into any alliance that would help stop the spread of Communism? "How had I collaborated with them? By making a movie in Namibia? I did not make any deal with the South African military," says Abramoff. "I made a deal with a commercial film-equipment company in South Africa!"

Were his derogatory remarks about his American Indian clients, in which he referred to them as "troglodytes," "morons," and "monkeys," further manifestations of his rampant racism? "Scanlon and I were goofing around. And I wasn't referring to all Indians. In one case, I was referring to two Indians waiting outside my office who were giving Chief Martin [of the Choctaws] a hard time," says Abramoff. "In e-mails I've called my own kids monkeys, but notice that McCain didn't release those."

Wasn't he the architect of a vast criminal enterprise, in which he seduced and bribed scores of elected officials and their staff? Or was he simply the most astute and gifted lobbyist who ever lived?

But wasn't the case closed? He had pleaded guilty to numerous felonies. Didn't that certify *a priori* his guilt? But were his guilty pleas proof of culpability? Was it possible that Abramoff had confessed because the prospect of protracted trials would have traumatized him and his family more than they could financially or psychologically endure?[17] Was it possible that Abramoff's guilty plea was nothing more than a risk-averse approach recommended by his legal team? Plead guilty, cooperate, and get your life sentence reduced to two or three years. The strategy was to get it behind you, so you can start your life over and see your wife and kids again.

Finally, wasn't Abramoff nothing more than a snitch for cooperating with federal authorities against his erstwhile powerful friends? Why hadn't he just keep his mouth shut and take his lumps like a man? Former Defense Secretary Caspar Weinberger refused to testify against his co-conspirators in Iran-Contra and as a result was rewarded with a presidential pardon. But no matter what Abramoff did, a presidential pardon from George W. Bush was not in the cards.

Or was it possible that Jack Abramoff's fall from grace was simply a perfect storm, where myriad events coincided at the worst possible moment to produce nightmarish results? Abramoff's destruction took place in the context of the shark-infested waters of Capitol Hill, omnipotent prosecutors who had lost their bearings or were seeking high-profile convictions, and journalists craving that all-mighty Pulitzer Prize.

It is impossible to quantify how much influence a lobbyist wields over the votes that lawmakers cast. But it is not secret that edgy lawmakers are always on the fundraising treadmill, desperate to keep their jobs. If a lobbyist and his client raise funds for a lawmaker, then that lawmaker will hardly want to bite the hand that feeds him. If a lawmaker—in good conscience, of course—happens to cast a vote favorable to a client's interests, then campaign contributions will continue flowing from that client into the lawmaker's campaign coffers. If the lawmaker fails to vote for the client's interests, then the client's contributions will be directed to a lawmaker who will. And finally, if a lobbyist cannot produce favorable results for his client, then the client will fire the lobbyist and hire someone else who can. Some call that Human Nature 101.

As a lobbyist, Jack Abramoff may have been too good for his own good. He may have become too effective, too visible, too powerful, too confident, and too arrogant. He may have become the object of too much jealousy and resentment. Furthermore, he unapologetically exhibited his Orthodox Judaism in a sea of right-white Christian Republicans. Was there a smidgen of anti-Semitism in singling out Abramoff for annihilation? "The so-called right-wing Christians had nothing to do with what happened to me and have for the most part stood by me," insists Abramoff, "and the anti-Semitism theory sounds like bunk." Had he also become the quintessential symbol of an intrinsically corrupt system crying out for reform? Was he singled out in part because of our collective guilt about the unconscionable exploitation of Native Americans dating back to 1492? Or was he simply a sleazy manipulator who had broken too many rules and gotten caught?

Jack Abramoff's admirers report that he was hardly the insincere, smooth-talking, charming snake-oil salesman that one might expect. They said it was difficult not to feel the force of his unassuming charisma. He clearly loved the company of others. It was easy to understand why he had so many friends, some of whom go back to nursery school. As a longstanding Abramoff friend says, "There is a good reason why Jack was on a first-name basis with all 535 members of Congress." Regardless of speculation into the nature of his soul, Abramoff's many qualities were on display as he moved full throttle into his next adventure.

He was an avid film buff—dating back to his road-to-Damascus transformation after watching on the big screen Fiddler on the Roof at age 12. It wasn't surprising that when he left politics he decided to pursue his dream of becoming a Hollywood producer.

Virtually any film student can produce and finance a motion picture using personal credit cards and a Super-8 video camera. In 1994,

Kevin Smith wrote and directed *Clerks*, a black-and-white film. It cost $27,000 to produce and grossed over $3 million in America, launching Smith's career. Abramoff, not about to take the road less traveled, embarked on the more traditional journey. In a single leap, as a rookie film producer, he co-wrote, produced, and released a major Hollywood film. He somehow managed to sign up an emerging action-adventure star and raise an extraordinary $16 million.

His film was not going to be shot in a local convenience store, in a candle-lit dining room, or on the back lot of Universal Studios. His would be shot on location in one of the harshest and most controversial regions of the world. The project would demand the expense and expertise of blowing helicopters out of the sky, and obtaining and obliterating a Soviet tank, along with all the other accoutrements of war, including machine guns, armored personnel vehicles, and mortars, not to mention stunts and special effects. "The claim that we used a Soviet tank is bizarre. I don't recall that we had one," says Abramoff. "It was just a tank the film-equipment company supplied to us."

Abramoff had the social skills, confidence, and fortitude to defeat nearly impossible odds and shepherd his goals to completion—just like all bootstrapping titans of industry who probably, without exception, have shaved a corner or two. Of course, he wanted to turn a profit, but he also wanted his film to serve a higher moral purpose. It would display the evils of Communism and the saintliness of the cold warriors

Published reports repeatedly claimed that without assistance from the South African government, Abramoff's budget would have soared into the stratosphere. Thanks to its support, he had ready access to an African landscape, exotic Bushmen, and scores of black military personnel, as well as military equipment and ordnance. Abramoff disputed these assertions: "What assistance? We paid the going rates to lease the equipment to film the movie. The company we paid was not part of the government. The only role the government had was in granting investors a film credit and other normal things like permitting…I'm missing where I had some advantage that other films did not have there or that other films don't have elsewhere in the world."

Abramoff ended up producing *Red Scorpion*, an action-adventure film, starring Dolph Lundgren, which played in thousands of movie theaters around the world. *The New York Times*' Frank Rich described it as "seriously God-awful." Stephen Holden, another reviewer for the *Times* observed, "The movie's reflective moments belong to Mr. Lundgren's sweaty chest." Abramoff's hometown paper, *The Los Angeles Times*, called it "a numbskull live-action comic book." However, *The San Diego-Union Tribune* was slightly kinder; noting that it "is better than many [action-adventure films] and sometimes even flirts with character development, which is unheard of in such epics."

On April 19, 1989, *Red Scorpion* opened in 1,268 movie theaters across America. Anti-apartheid protesters picketed outside many of those theaters. "There weren't enough picketers," Abramoff later says. "It would have been better if there had been more. Controversy sells."

When the movie opened, Adam Kidan took a date to see it. "It was an action-adventure movie," he recalls nearly 20 years later. "I didn't even know it was his. I was in law school at the time. Then I saw the credits and blurted out loud, 'Holy shit, Jack Abramoff!'"

Red Scorpion was conceived shortly after Abramoff returned from Jamba, Angola. A local filmmaker approached him in Washington, D.C. and asked if he would help fund a documentary about Jonas Savimbi. Abramoff didn't flinch. "Why would you want to make a documentary?" he asked. "Nobody watches documentaries...You should make an action film." Abramoff sat down and scribbled down a plot for his own anti-Communist thriller:

> **When a top Soviet special-forces agent, sent to Angola to assassinate the country's black anti-communist rebel leader, watches as Russian helicopters gas innocent African women and children, he switches sides and joins the rebels' cause.**

In the fall of 1985, Abramoff went to see Sylvester Stallone's *Rocky IV*, and decided that one of its actors, Dolph Lundgren, should star in his film. Abramoff had written a 15-page screen treatment and ran the idea by his younger brother, Robert. A graduate of Boston University, Robert was finishing up his last year at the University of Southern California Law School. His only film experience had been a brief stint in the business affairs department at Warner Brothers Television. After forming a production company, Regency Entertainment, they needed someone to write a script but couldn't afford to pay much. Somehow, the Abramoff brothers stumbled across a would-be screenwriter, a recent graduate of the American Film Institute in Los Angeles.

"I had written a script that never got [produced] but made the rounds. [The Abramoff brothers] liked what I'd written and called me up," says Arne Olsen, from his home in Vancouver, British Columbia. Why hire an unknown screenwriter just out of graduate school? "Because I was cheap. They [eventually] paid me $100,000 and this was before I'd joined the Writers Guild. They were smart enough to know that [since I wasn't in the union] they wouldn't have to pay me residuals," recalled Olsen. "Hey, I was thrilled!"

The Abramoffs showed the screen treatment to Olsen. He says he immediately recognized it as a Rambo rip-off. Others would later call it the African Rambo. For an initial payment of $10,000, Olsen went right to work. Three months later, he showed the Abramoffs a first draft. They made extensive suggestions and then flew him to South Africa. Olsen met with the casting director, Moonyee Lee, and spent a couple of weeks touring South Africa. When he returned to Los Angeles, Olsen learned that the producers had offered the starring role to Dolph Lundgren.

Lundgren, a blond Swedish karate-champion with an engineering degree from Australia, had turned down a Fulbright scholarship to MIT in 1983 to become an actor. He was one of 5,000 people who had auditioned for the role of Ivan Drago, the "steroid-enhanced, genetically engineered" Soviet boxer in *Rocky IV*.

Thanks to his performance in that film, Lundgren had found himself on the cusp of stardom. He seemed the perfect archetypal Soviet villain for the Abramoff script that was slowing evolving. Abramoff's partners, Gary and Greg Foster, called up Lundgren's agent and offered him $400,000, plus a meeting with President Reagan. According to Avi Kleinberger, the film's production manager, "In [Lundgren's] living room somewhere, there is a photo of him [shaking hands] with [President] Ronald Reagan." Abramoff conceded he may have arranged for Lundgren to tour the Oval Office.

The Abramoffs arranged for Lundgren to meet Olsen at a restaurant. Lundgren had been hired as the bodyguard for the tall, flat-topped Grace Jones when she had starred opposite Roger Moore in the James Bond thriller, *A View to Kill*. He and Jones, nine years his senior, were now dating.

For the next six months, Olsen continued to meet with the Abramoff brothers during the endless process of script revisions. "They were total gentlemen to me," Olsen recalled. "Robert, the younger brother, was quite sweet and gentle. Jack, the older brother, was the man in charge. He was the super "A" type personality, which is the personality a lot of producers have. They've got to be pretty tough people or else the movie doesn't end up getting made."

Olsen says that the director, Joseph Zito, rewrote the script "pretty extensively. I was leaning toward the more cerebral and mystical, like the scene in the desert with the bushman…I was a little disappointed in the final cut."

However, Olsen was impressed with the brothers Abramoff, two rookie producers in their late 20s. "This wasn't their profession," said Olsen, "[not] what they'd do for the rest of their lives. It was a lark. They wanted to get a message across, but at the same time they were going for exploitation and of course trying to make money."

Actually, the Abramoffs went on to write and produce a sequel, *Red Scorpion 2*. Abramoff also expended considerable time and energy in trying to produce *The Emperor's Gold* and *Cyberstrike*. Neither was ever completed. As for Robert, he remained in the entertainment business and ultimately had many films to his credit.

While Olsen was redrafting a script and Dolph Lundgren had signed to star, Abramoff was able to negotiate a "negative pick-up deal." He talked Warner Brothers into distributing the film and then took that signed contract to the Bank of Minneapolis, from which he borrowed $6 million. But Abramoff also had to persuade Performance Guarantors, essentially an agent for Lloyd's of London, to insure the $6 million bank loan—a tall order for a 27-year-old Orthodox Jew, who had never produced a motion picture. If the film were ever completed, Warner Bros.—which owned the domestic, foreign and sequel rights—would repay the bank plus interest and distribute the film. In addition, the Warner Bros. contract specifically forbade locations that included the Republic of South Africa or Namibia.

Abramoff had been advised to hedge his bets, however. With a mockup of Dolph Lundgren on a *Red Scorpion* poster, he had already sent his brother Robert to the Milan Film Market, where several distributors expressed keen interest, just in case a back-up distributor was needed.

The first director Abramoff hired rewrote the screenplay with a new scene that would have added $1 million to the film's $6 million budget. Abramoff vetoed the change, and the director stormed out. "The first chance I had to act responsibly with money and the guy quits," Abramoff says years later, laughing. At Warner Bros., Lisa Henson, Jim Henson's daughter, recommended Joseph Zito, who had directed two films starring Chuck Norris—*Missing in Action* (1984) and *Invasion U.S.A.* (1985). Abramoff immediately hired him.

For the film's location, Abramoff considered Kenya. Sidney Pollack—director of (1985) *Out of Africa*, starring Meryl Streep and Robert Redford—told one of Abramoff's partners that the corruption in Kenya made filmmaking difficult. Pollack recommended Mexico, but Abramoff decided to send someone to scout locations in Swaziland. Despite published reports to the contrary, Abramoff says Russel Crystal played no part in raising funds for the film. "I raised [the money] from investment banks, some of whom were Jewish, but none were friends of mine from the [South African] community, nor were they religious."

Abramoff finally settled on Swaziland and flew there to arrange the filming permits. The country had the ideal terrain and dirt-cheap labor. Most importantly, the transportation costs would be minimal. He'd be renting the military hardware from a film-equipment firm in South Africa, but nothing would be shot in South Africa, which would have violated the Comprehensive Anti-Apartheid Act, passed over Reagan's veto, on October 2, 1986. The existence of land-locked Swaziland—a tiny kingdom surrounded on all sides by the Republic of South Africa except on the east by Mozambique--was true serendipity.

Abramoff had not anticipated that the movement of large quantities of military equipment into Swaziland would trigger an attack of regal paranoia. The advisers to the king began whispering in His Highness' ear that Western film crews had a nasty habit of engineering *coup d'etats*. The fact that the apartheid government would have quickly intervened was irrelevant. The Swazi king got cold feet. Impediments and interminable delays began cropping up. Abramoff had already spent nearly half a million dollars in pre-production costs. He mounted an all-out charm offensive, visiting seemingly sympathetic government ministers, who passed him along to others. But it became clear that permission to film in Swaziland had been rescinded.

Next, Abramoff approached Lesotho, another independent black country completely surrounded by the Republic of South Africa. For six weeks, government ministers told him to "come back on Tuesday." One problem was that Abramoff had already converted most of his money, budgeted for the film, into the lilangeni, the currency of Swaziland, which could only be converted into currencies belonging to the South Africa Rand financial zone. Due to the world-wide economic boycott of South Africa, no other countries—except Botswana, Namibia, Lesotho, and South Africa—would accept the lilangeni. He considered Botswana, but rejected it as too dangerous.

Meanwhile, Abramoff had been paying costly "per diems" to all the cast and crew idly waiting in Johannesburg for the production to begin. He had to find a new location and raise more money fast. There was some dispute over where these additional funds came from. Craig Williamson, the notorious South African spy and assassin, later alleged that *Red Scorpion* was funded in large part by the South African military. Abramoff indignantly called this claim "an outrageous lie." He had briefly met Williamson only once and says that Williamson had had no involvement in the film whatsoever.

South African lawyer Peter Leon drafted the contracts for the local investors in Abramoff's film. Because of the anti-apartheid boycott, the South African film industry was moribund. As an exercise in futility, the government had fashioned tax incentives, hoping to lure investors with truly astonishing tax deductions. "Sometimes the deductions totaled twice or three times the investments," Leon said. Moonyee Lee, the casting director, remembered that everyone was so excited because a Hollywood film was being shot in South Africa.

But actor Carmen Argenziano, who played a leading role as a wicked Cuban colonel, said, "We heard that very right-wing South African money was helping fund the movie....We were pretty upset about the source of the money. We thought we were misled. We were shocked that these brothers, who we thought were showbiz liberals—Beverly Hills Jewish kids—were doing this."

Finally, after a costly two-month delay, Abramoff realized he had no choice. It was either film in Namibia or the movie was dead. He put in a call to Rob Friedman at Warner Bros., with whom he had signed the distribution contract, to notify him of the decision. According to Abramoff, Friedman said, "Just keep it quiet."

The "independent" nation of Namibia, once known as the South-West Territory, was a former colony of Germany, located on South Africa's northwest border. After WWI, the League of Nations had handed over administrative control to South Africa. But in 1966, the United Nations had passed a resolution calling for free elections. The apartheid government had happily complied, copying what the United States and the Soviet Union had done innumerable times. South Africa held "elections" and created a puppet government. But virtually no governments sent ambassadors to Windhoek, Namibia's capital. The "country" was not granted a seat at the UN General Assembly. And Namibia was subjected to the same economic and military sanctions as its puppeteer. "I strongly advised him against filming [in Namibia]," said Leon.

But Abramoff had no other viable options. The film was already over budget and shooting in Namibia was going to be a logistical nightmare. There would be costly delays. "You had to travel back to South Africa to get a nail," said Avi Kleinberger. Still, Abramoff decided to go ahead. Maybe no one in Los Angeles would find out about Namibia. Kleinberger agreed that taking the risk would probably work out. "It was a huge country and the chances of getting spotted—that somebody from the west would find [us]—was not great."

Furthermore, the South African government had essentially banned all Western journalists from Namibia, so there would be no snooping reporters seeking a scoop. The logic of this rationalization was flawed. Even if cast and crew weren't spotted on location in Namibia, there were too many people involved in the film to keep it a secret. The post-production work usually took at least a year, a long time for a large cast and crew to remain mum. Abramoff would have to fib about where the film was shot. Word would surely leak out and Warner Bros. would have no choice but to "indignantly" back out.

Nonetheless, Abramoff marched forward. He advertised for extras in Windhoek newspapers for "light-skinned Namibians" who could play Cuban soldiers. He ordered cast and crew to Namibia. If and when problems emerged, he would deal with them. Unfortunately, they emerged sooner than Abramoff would have ever guessed. The problem proved to be Grace Jones, Dolph Lundgren's statuesque black girlfriend. In

November 1987, Jones flew to Namibia "to patch up [her] relationship with Dolph."

Stardom had gone to Lundgren's head. He had been playing the part of a petulant, promiscuous child. Abramoff and the other producers had reportedly been somewhat intimidated by their temperamental leading man, who was eight inches taller than Abramoff, as well as a former karate champion. He reportedly tried placating Lundgren by housing Jones for two months in a $3,000-a-month villa in the coastal town of Swakopmund, close to where *Red Scorpion* was filming. Abramoff later says Jones only stayed a week. He also denies paying for the villa, or that Lundgren had ever been a bully. "Dolph was always a professional on the set," Abramoff says years later. "He never threatened or intimidated anyone." Abramoff also claims that Lundgren's girlfriend at the time was not Grace Jones, but model Paula Barbieri, O.J. Simpson's future girlfriend (who would dump Simpson the day after Nicole Brown and Ron Goldman were murdered by an "unknown" assailant.)

How could the censored Namibian press—which was allowed to indulge in celebrity gossip—fail to take notice of the famous, garish Jamaican movie actress in their midst? The stories that started appearing in the local newspapers were truly sensational because Lundgren and Jones conspicuously flaunted their (technically illegal) interracial relationship in public. Lundgren, opposed to apartheid as were most Swedes, ignored exhortations to be discreet. It didn't matter. Abramoff's secret was safe. Who would ever read *The Republikein*, a conservative Afrikaans-language quotidian, published in Windhoek, which ran a story about the famous interracial couple? Apparently, someone at *The New York Times* did.

On January 9, 1988, the *Times* ran a story, which must have made Abramoff's hair turn white:

> **South Africa provided tanks, trucks, troops, jeeps and mortar for the filming of an American adventure movies cheduled for release next summer, according to South-West African publications.**

Defying a boycott of South Africa by many United States artists, Americans wrote, directed, produced and starred in the film, Red Scorpion....

Local journalists, who had visited the sets in Windhoek and Swakopmund, claimed to have counted as many as 40 South African Army vehicles, including Samil troop transports and Casspir and Buffel armored personnel carriers. Some of the vehicles sported the telltale "R" license plates of the South African Defense Force. More troubling was the insignia of the notorious Operation Crossbar, the South African counterinsurgency commandos, who ruthlessly hunted down and slaughtered Namibian guerrillas. "This license plate claim is a total lie," says Abramoff. "The story on which this is based was a total piece of junk... The outrageous claim was that what was really going on [on location] was that South African troops were killing SWAPO[18] guerilla fighters and that this was being filmed by me, buddy of Ollie North!"

Only a few weeks earlier, South Africa had actually invaded southern Angola to prevent Soviet and Cuban forces from eradicating Jonas Savimbi. The South African government confirmed that assistance had been provided to *Red Scorpion*, because "[t]his is equipment that could not be provided by the private sector. The filmmakers are paying for this assistance," which allegedly included a Soviet-made T-54 tank and mortars captured in Angola. Again, Abramoff disputes this: "The private sector always provides [military] equipment for films."

Condemnation was instantaneous. Arthur Ashe, the black American tennis star, co-chairman of Artists and Athletes Against Apartheid, said, "We would oppose any participation by an American...in a film project of which the South African Government is a part....It's hard to see the film as anything less than an endorsement of South Africa's [apartheid] policies." Others called for the film to be "condemned, boycotted and blacklisted." Randall Robinson, executive director of TransAfrica, whose group had been vilified as a Communist stooge by Abramoff's International Freedom Foundation, got his comeuppance. Robinson declared "[t]hat this propaganda film would come to the American screen as legitimate entertainment is shocking." Rob Friedman of Warner Bros. told the *New Times* that his company had "declined to be involved even before [Abramoff] decided to shoot in Namibia." Years later, Abramoff shakes his head: "Oh really? What about our signed contract?"

Many entrepreneurial tomcats would have tucked their tails and slinked away. Not Abramoff. In fact, the Warner Bros. repudiation saved the day. Abramoff approached his back-up distributors who had earlier expressed interest and selected Shapiro-Glickenhaus, because it was willing to pay $8 million for the foreign rights only. This would not only cover the Bank of Minneapolis loan, but would provide an additional $2 million to help defray the ever-expanding budget. More importantly, Abramoff could now sell the domestic and sequel rights as well.

CHAPTER TWELVE
HOME INVASION

While Abramoff was in South Africa producing a big-budget film, Adam Kidan was building his law practice in New York City. He had teamed up with three other lawyers and formed the law firm of Duncan, Fish, Bergson & Kidan. Most importantly, he had won a new client, Napoleon Barragan, an Ecuadorian immigrant, who had launched in 1976 a bedding retail company called Dial-A-Mattress.

Kidan was living in Manhattan, dating a beautiful woman, and driving a fancy car. Life was good. His mother Judy had finally found "the love of her life," an Israeli businessman named Sami Shemtov. Born in Iraq, Shemtov moved to Israel when he was two years old, later became a decorated Israeli soldier, and earned an engineering degree. In 1967, he moved to New York. Soon, he married, produced three children, and divorced. In 1992, when Kidan was 28, his mother and Shemtov got married. "My mother had finally found all the things she'd been hoping for—a loving partner, a beautiful home, and the financial security to enjoy the finer things in life," says Kidan.

Shemtov was dark and handsome, and exuded confidence and charm. He owned an electrical supply company in Ohio, along with several other legitimate businesses. But Kidan says he never really trusted him. "There was something about him I couldn't put my finger on, but my mother was so happy, so I kept it to myself," he recalls.

Kidan and his two sisters got along well with Shemtov's three grown children. Close in age, all six would drop by the Shemtov's Staten Island mansion on weekends. Kidan and his sisters had the normal, stable, healthy family life they'd always craved. "Briefly, my sisters and I experienced a peace of mind we had never known," recalls Kidan. That peace of mind was shattered on February 18, 1993.

Around 10 pm that evening, four young white thugs, associates of the Bonanno crime family, parked their stolen car near the Shemtov's house. From his ex-wife's new boyfriend, they had learned that Shemtov secretly owned a string of adult video stores and kept hundreds of thousands of dollar in his home safe. A late-model Lincoln Continental, its engine still warm, was parked in the driveway. Bonsai trees lined the slate path leading up to the dark mahogany front door, illuminated by a brass lamp. Inside, Judy Shemtov was fixing herbal tea for her husband. He had just returned from a business trip. Upstairs, Kidan's 23-year-old sister, Arlyn, was blow-drying her long red hair. Al Bello, an old friend of hers, was expected momentarily. They were going to the movies. Anticipating Bello's arrival, Judy had not activated the security system with video surveillance and an alarm linked to the local police.

Judy brought the cup of tea to the living room, where her husband was relaxing in front of the TV. The doorbell rang. Outside, next to the front door, was a mezuzah, a small Jewish talisman meant to ward off evil spirits. Walking into the foyer, Judy said, "I'll get it. It must be Al." She crossed the parquet floor to the front door. "Al?" she called out, unlocking it.

Hearing the lock turn, two burglars forced their way in. One of them shoved a gun into Judy's face. "Give us the fucking money and no one gets hurt!" he demanded. Terrified, she froze. "Tell us where the goddamn fucking safe is, lady!" the second one shouted.

Her lips moved, but she couldn't speak. The burglars weren't sure what to do. "Where's your fucking husband?" one of them screamed. "He's got the combination!" Shemtov came running into the foyer, startling the burglars. The gun accidentally went off. It sent a .45-caliber bullet into base of Judy's brain. She landed on her back in the foyer. As the burglars ran to the waiting car and sped away, Arlyn cradled her mother's head as she bled to death.

Minutes later, the burglars were speeding over the Verrazano Narrows Bridge, connecting Staten Island to Brooklyn. One of them opened the window and hurled the murder weapon into the icy water below.

Kidan had spent the night at his girlfriend's. He woke up in the morning and headed to his office. A few minutes later, his car phone rang. It was his sister Arlyn. At first, he couldn't understand her. "Adam. Mom's dead! She's been murdered! Last night, someone broke into the house and shot her."

Kidan didn't feel a thing at first. He was in the middle of a nightmare. All he had to do was wake himself up. In shock, he pulled over to the side of the road. Then, on the long drive to Staten Island, he started making calls. The Jewish faith required burial within 24 hours. He called his rabbi at Temple Emanuel to plan the service. The rabbi recommended the Frank E. Campbell Funeral Home on Madison Avenue on Manhattan's Upper East Side. Kidan arranged for flowers and a caterer. Later that day, he went to the morgue to identify his mother. That afternoon, he visited his maternal grandmother to inform her that her daughter was dead. Next, he hired a plastic surgeon to cover up the hole in the side of his mother's face. In the early evening, he brought the mortician's fresh clothes for his mother to wear in her casket.

Several days after the funeral, he drove back to his mother's grave and sobbed for hours. Years later recalls with a shudder, "It was the most horrific thing that's ever happened. Your heart and mind go crazy. You start wracking your brain trying to figure out who could have done something like this and why. It haunts you day and night. Was it random? Was it, God forbid, someone I knew? The years go by and you're agonizing, knowing they're out there somewhere, wondering if they'll ever be brought to justice." The way he dealt with his grief, he says was to devote himself to financially supporting his relatives. Shemtov, who had promised to reimburse him for the $50,000 in funeral expenses, never did.

"After my mother's death, money took on a whole different meaning for me," says Kidan. "I became the sole provider for my grandmother. One of my sisters was still in school. I paid her rent and all of her college tuition. I was so busy providing, caring, working, that I never really mourned her."

* * * * * * * * * * * * * *

On March 28, 2006, Kidan and Abramoff were sentenced to five years and ten months and began serving their sentences later that fall. "It's not what I envisioned when I dreamed of becoming governor of New York when I was a starry-eyed kid," Kidan says.

In November 2007, shortly after giving a deposition to Florida state prosecutors in the Boulis murder case, Kidan was attacked by three fellow prisoners with Italian surnames and ties to organized crime. He survived the attack and for his own protection was placed in isolation at the adjacent low-security prison. Three months later, he was quietly transferred by bus to Philadelphia, PA., to Brooklyn, NY, back to Philadelphia, and finally to a low-security—not minimum-security—prison in Elkton, Ohio.

PART II

NEWLY MINTED LOBBYIST

CHAPTER THIRTEEN
TRANSITION

Abramoff soon learned that the most successful Hollywood producers often endure periods of disappointment and failure. Perhaps his success at producing *Red Scorpion* was beginner's luck. The sequel, *Red Scorpion II*, was a dud. "I was involved enough [in *Red Scorpion II*] to get it set up. The movie was made as a Canadian tax deal. If I had gotten a story credit, it would have disqualified the Canadian tax credit, so I got executive producer credit instead," says Abramoff. "It was made for HBO." Except for the title, *Red Scorpion II* was a sequel that had nothing to do with the original.

Abramoff, a film buff, who often quoted lines from famous movies, didn't give up, however. Later, *The Washington Post* exploited this in an unattributed slander in the lead paragraph of a story: "Jack Abramoff likes to slip into dialogue from *The Godfather* as he led his lobbying colleagues in planning their next conquest on Capitol Hill. In a favorite bit, he would mimic Michael Corleone facing down a crooked politician's demand for a cut of Mafia gambling profits: "Senator, you can have my answer now if you like. My offer is this: nothing." Twenty years later, he was still a movie freak. His *Fiddler on the Roof* transformation had assumed epic proportions. Virtually all of his friends and colleagues were acquainted with this legend.

"*The Godfather* is one of my favorite films," says Abramoff, "and I did frequently quote from my favorite movies and television shows, such as *Seinfeld*. But did it define me? Of course not. Clearly Schmidt and others wanted to configure me as a mafia don. Of course, I helped with the hat."

After *Red Scorpion I* and *II*, Abramoff labored on other scripts and story ideas, hoping to score again, this time with better results. "Who doesn't learn from his mistakes," he says. With filmmaking, he wanted to make money and promote his political philosophy, but he wanted artistic success as well. When he watched the final cut of *Red Scorpion*, he cringed. He wouldn't see it again for another 10 years. At Brandeis, his final thesis was on Shakespearean Opera and focused on Falstaff. Abramoff possessed an intellect capable of appreciating sophisticated and subtle drama and yearned to produce a transcendental film of Shakespearean proportions about anti-Semitism and the need for tolerance.

In nearly 10 years in the film business, far from the world of Washington politics, Abramoff traveled for weeks at a time, sometimes to distant lands to meet with writers, actors, investors, and government officials. Yet he continued to reside in Silver Spring, Maryland, with its close-knit Jewish community. After the birth of his first son, Levi, in 1987, another son, Alex, in 1989, then Daniel in 1991, and finally his twin girls, Sarah and Livia, in 1993, he found it increasingly difficult to spend so much time away from his growing family.

The one film project that came closest to fruition was *The Emperor's Gold*. The screen treatment, written by Abramoff, was based on reports that the Japanese had left behind a huge cache of gold in the Philippine jungle during WW II. The story followed four rival teams of treasure hunters—American, Japanese, British, and Malaysian—who work the clues in quest of the prize, and the American hero falls in love with a Malaysian girl. Abramoff had managed to raise $7 million from Malaysian investors. With a polished screenplay rewritten several times, he had hired a director and was ready to start shooting.

Datuk Paddy Bowie, an English woman who has lived in Malaysia for over half a century, had introduced Abramoff to several local investors. She recalls that as the first day of filming approached, the leading financier suddenly pulled out of the project. "This left Jack high and dry…The [film] contract stated that if production did not begin by such and such a date, the other investors could ask for their money back, but only if they did so by a certain time.. When one of them later tried to get his money back, Jack had already left Malaysia and the production company had folded," says Mrs. Bowie, "so [the investor] sued me instead, because I had introduced him to Jack. Jack did a very noble thing; he surrendered his film rights to [the investor], which was worth more than $1 million, to save me from embarrassment."

After Abramoff's film career ended, Mrs. Bowie, now in her 80s, kept in touch with him, and was tangentially involved in two other incidents for which Abramoff was later vilified. The first was the 2000 golf junket to Scotland that Abramoff organized, which included Tom DeLay. In London, Abramoff stayed in Mrs. Bowie's home. "Nelson Mandela has stayed there as well," she says.

The second involved Abramoff's controversial lobbying for Malaysia. Relations between Kuala Lampur and Washington had deteriorated because the country's long-term Prime Minister, Dr. Mahathir Mohamed, seemed undemocratic and bigoted. He had jailed political opponents and human rights activists, and had made several anti-Semitic comments. For example, in 1997, he noted that "The Jews robbed the Palestinians of everything, but in Malaysia they could not do so." In 2003, he gave a speech in which he declared: "[T]oday the Jews rule this world by proxy. They get others to fight and die for them."

In 2001, however, Dr. Mahathir wanted to meet with President Bush during the Asia-Pacific Economic Cooperation summit that October. A month before, September 10, Abramoff e-mailed Ralph Reed:

> **Abramoff: I have a one-month subcontract for you if you can help me. We need to get Rove to see if we can break through the current posture of State on Malaysia and the PM meeting with Bush at the APEC meeting at the beginning of October.... If it works there will be a lot more.**
>
> **Reed: Sure.**

The following day, Islamic terrorists attacked the World Trade Center and the Pentagon, and Malaysia immediately declared its support for the war against terrorism, which pleased the United States. Bush and Dr. Mahathir spoke briefly at the October meeting and then met again in Washington on May 14, 2002[19]. Mrs. Bowie and Dr. Mahathir were also good friends, but she says Abramoff never asked her to arrange an introduction to the prime minister. Abramoff was eventually paid $1.2 million for his assistance, which was quietly funneled through American International Center, a "think tank" run by Michael Scanlon.

"I was always concerned about [Mahathir's] comments about Israel and Jews, but...I felt it was okay to represent the nation...not him," says Abramoff many years later. "I was not paid to get him the meeting. That is false. He got it himself. I was paid to help the nation [with its relations with Congress.]" Abramoff also admits that he and his firm, Greenberg Traurig, violated the Foreign Agents Registration Act, by not reporting that he was acting as a lobbyist for a foreign government.

Abramoff had to finally conceded that supporting his wife and five children on the "very much up and down existence" of filmmaking was something he should not continue.

In the meantime, Abramoff was worried that his children would not be able to receive a proper Jewish education. He believed that there was a growing divide in Orthodox Judaism between the "insulated, xenophobic, almost ridiculous" fundamentalists and the modernists, who were diluting their faith. Abramoff wanted to create a "third way," which would "combine the aspects of a fine prep school with a yeshiva[20]...something unheard of in the Orthodox world," said Abramoff. He decided to set up a charity, called the National Institute of Torah, in which he launched a small program to home school ten students, including two of his children. At first the school operated out of his home and eventually evolved into the Eshkol Academy. After several years, he changed the charity's name to The Capital Athletic Foundation. This nonprofit foundation and the Eshkol Academy would later be singled out by *Washington Post* reporter Susan Schmidt and Sen. John McCain as yet another example of Abramoff's perfidy, because the foundation was used to fund sniper scopes and other military equipment for an Israeli settlement in the occupied West Bank, as well as a 2002 golf junket to Scotland. He concedes that what he did was improper.

In December 1993, *The Washington Times*[21] ran a "DOERS PROFILE"[22] on Abramoff, in which he described himself as a motion picture producer who was "tenacious, balanced, studious." His Walter Mitty fantasy was "Conducting the Metropolitan Opera." The books he listed at his bedside were "The Bible, The Generation, All for the Boss, and Rabbinical Mathematics and Astronomy." His favorite clothing store was "Visa in Kuala Lumpur." But most portentous was his motto: "The world is based on gratitude and indebtedness." By the fall of 1994, Abramoff was looking for a job closer to home.

And then there was an amazing stroke of luck. Suddenly, Washington was rocked by a major political trauma. In the mid-term Congressional elections that November, the Republicans won eight new seats in the Senate and an extraordinary 52 in the House of Representatives, a stinging defeat for President Clinton. For the first time since the 1950s, the Republicans controlled both the Senate and the House. However, these Republicans weren't moderates. They were right-wing ideologues, who brooked no arguments and took no prisoners. They were the kind who vocally disliked the first President George Bush and loathed Sen. John McCain. And these particular Republicans were blunt and unapologetic. Access and influence were dependent on right-wing credentials and money, which seemed to verge on outright bribery. "The Republicans wanted to promote their own and raise money to stay in power," says Abramoff, "which is no different than how the Democrats did it." The new speaker of the House, Newt Gingrich (R-GA), didn't mince words to reporters: "If you want to play in our revolution, you have to live by our rules."

In 1995, Tom DeLay (R-TX), the deputy Majority whip, became majority whip, the third most powerful post in the House. Elected by his fellow Republicans against the wishes of Gingrich, DeLay made it clear that making political contributions was requisite to gaining access to the power brokers. He would tell lobbying firms about "Project Relief" (later called the "K-Street[23] Project"). "You've contributed too much money to Democrats," said DeLay. "You've got to contribute more money to Republicans. We're in power now…We keep a very close eye on the money. There can be no revolution in policy without a revolution in fundraising." Why was K-Street so important to DeLay? It meant campaign contributions, as well as the security of a high-paying lobbying job if one were to lose the next election. "We're just following the old adage of punish your enemies and reward your friends," said DeLay.

Called many things, including "The Prince of Darkness," "The Exterminator" and "The Meanest Man in Congress," DeLay would later describe Gingrich as "the visionary"; Majority Leader Dick Armey as "the policy wonk"; and himself as "the ditch digger who makes it all happen."

DeLay was referring to was his prodigious fund-raising abilities. It was this feverish pursuit of campaign contributions that eventually made him more powerful than the Speaker of the House.

It is impossible to understate the importance of Tom DeLay's pivotal role in Abramoff's ascendancy to the pinnacle of influence and power as a Washington lobbyist. DeLay's reputation for vengeance and his ruthless exercise of power made him so feared that when he expressed support for an issue that was important to Abramoff, his close friend and major fund-raiser, anyone who put up resistance did so at great peril.

Born in 1947, more than a decade before Abramoff, DeLay was expelled from Baylor University for drinking and vandalism. In 1970, however, he graduated the University of Houston with a degree in biology. He avoided military service during the Vietnam War, later explaining that his decision was purely altruistic: he didn't want to rob a minority of the chance to earn a decent wage in the military. Eventually, he launched an exterminator business, called Albo Pest Co.

Businessman DeLay would soon complain bitterly about excessive taxation and government regulation. On three occasions, the IRS slapped him with tax liens for not paying payroll and income taxes. He loathed the Environmental Protection Agency, because it banned a certain pesticide he favored. His critics would accuse him of indifference to poisoning the environment with carcinogens and agents that caused birth defects.

After 11 years in business, he was fed up. In 1978, he attended a Fort Bend County Republican Committee meeting and voiced his disgust with governmental regulations. He argued so persuasively that party officials urged him to run for the state legislature. He agreed and won, and was reelected twice. Although married, DeLay developed a reputation as a playboy and alcoholic, often consuming a dozen martinis at receptions and fundraiser. His enemies dubbed him "Hot Tub Tom." Shortly after his election to the U.S. House in 1984, DeLay suffered a crisis of confidence, became a born-again Christian, quit drinking, and later claimed that he "was no longer committing adultery."

In the meantime, in early November 1994, Abramoff realized that he had become a hot property: "After the [GOP landslide and the] conservatives took over, there was this disconnect between the new Republican majority and the lobbying firms. They were filled with Democrats with no access to the new leadership in Congress. They started to panic. I was approached by a friend who ran a small lobbying shop. I'd just gotten back from a long trip. It was the third time I'd been away for six weeks in a row. The reality of setting up movies was starting to weigh me down, and I realized that I needed to do something closer to home." Abramoff thought lobbyists were "evil." They violated his sense of right and wrong, but he soon found a way to rationalize away his misgivings, and he had mouths to feed.

A highly regarded aviation attorney named Jonathan Blank was the managing partner at Preston Gates Ellis & Rouvelas Meeds[24], a mostly Democratic law firm based in Seattle, with a lobbying branch in Washington, D.C. The father of Microsoft's Bill Gates was one of the firm's named partners. Although Blank kept his conservative political philosophy mostly to himself, he had struck up a friendship with Abramoff at the Woodside Synagogue. They saw eye to eye on many issues. They also happened to live across the street from one another in Silver Spring, MD, a suburb about a half hour from downtown Washington, D.C. After checking out Abramoff's conservative credentials, Blank offered him a job. Abramoff says he was flattered and agreed "to join Jonathan's firm as a lobbyist...I told him I wouldn't do things that were against my ideology." He was hired on December 30, 1994, six days before the Republicans assumed control of both houses of Congress.

"I think a lot of K-Street law firms were a little nervous about conservatives. When I went to work at Preston Gates, I think they looked at me like some exhibit from the zoo," says Abramoff. The firm's official announcement stated that Abramoff "maintains strong ties to Speaker Newt Gingrich, Majority Leader Dick Armey, Majority Whip Tom DeLay, and Republican Policy Committee Chairman Chris Cox and their staffs." Nine years later, Gingrich, along with President George W. Bush, would claim that he didn't know who Abramoff was.

According to Larry LaTourette, a former partner at the firm, when Abramoff arrived he was "a fish out of water...Preston Gates didn't know what to make of him. They were as button-down-proper, don't-rock-the-boat a place as you can imagine. [Abramoff] talked in black-and-white terms—'We've got to declare war on these guys; we've got to march to victory'—powerful words that you don't usually hear in D.C."

As for DeLay, there was minor disagreement over who introduced him to Abramoff. But even this bit of trivia sheds light on another example of what stood out in this narrative. Virtually everyone with any close affiliation to Abramoff became tainted.

That was the case with brothers Rabbi David and Rabbi Daniel Lapin, whose reputations have been besmirched by the Abramoff scandal. Abramoff met David Lapin in Johannesburg while making *Red Scorpion*. (Lapin would eventually become the head of Abramoff's Eshkol Academy.) "I wound up spending Sabbath in [Lapin's] community," says Abramoff. "I was stuck by his brilliance, his majestic personality, and we became friends. He is very charming, a wise rabbi, who I feel is my rabbi and he's my family rabbi since that time." Eventually, David Lapin introduced Abramoff to his far more conservative brother, Daniel, who operates Toward Tradition, a Judeo-Christian charity that strives to strengthen relations between Jews and Christians. Some critics refer to Daniel as the "field commander in the religious right's war to reunite church and state."

Daniel Lapin, an Orthodox Jew, was one of the lone Jewish voices who supported Mel Gibson's The Passion of Christ and defended the efforts of Terri Schiavo's parents to keep their comatose daughter alive. He was an ardent opponent of abortion and homosexuality, considered the Anti-Defamation League "a dangerous organization," and one of his favorite programs was The 700 Club.[25] In 2000, Daniel Lapin hired and paid $50,000 Lisa Rudy, the wife of Tony Rudy, one of Tom DeLay's top staffers. Two of Abramoff's clients made a total of $50,000 in contributions to Daniel's charity. He had been questioned by prosecutors and denied any wrongdoing. Also, in 2000, Abramoff wangled a $1.2 million no-bid contract for the brother, David Lapin, on "ethics-in government" from the Northern Mariana Islands. Later, auditors were unable to determine what exactly Lapin had been done to satisfy the contract.

"The idea that [Lapin] did no work or did not deliver is absurd," says Abramoff. "He has reams of materials he did for them. This is just typical slander by [the press], which only serves to impugn both Lapin and me."

Nonetheless, it was Daniel Lapin who apparently introduced Abramoff to DeLay. "Some [news] articles claimed that I introduced them while others, including one in *The Washington Post*, have the two meeting at a DeLay fundraiser, introduced by Edwin A. Buckham [DeLay's chief of staff]," said Daniel Lapin. "Although I have no clear recollection of having formally introduced them, it is certainly possible. I was at several Republican Party events at which both Tom DeLay and Jack Abramoff were present."

Soon, Abramoff had run-of-the-mill access with the new Majority Whip. "[Abramoff's] someone on our side," said Buckham, "he has access to DeLay." But Abramoff wanted more. He wanted to become DeLay's bosom buddy, which someone with Abramoff's intelligence and charisma had a reasonable shot of engineering. But hundreds of people were vying for DeLay's attention. Abramoff needed a magic bullet. Grover Norquist, Abramoff's friend from College Republican days, supplied it.[26] In 1985, Norquist founded Americans for Tax Reform (ATR), an anti-tax lobbying political nonprofit. He co-authored the 1994 "Contract with America" that defined the new GOP majority in Congress, leading to Newt Gingrich's election as House Speaker and Tom DeLay as Whip. "I don't want to abolish government. I simply want to reduce it to the size where I can drag it into the bathroom and drown it in the bathtub," was Norquist's most famous quip.[27]

As neonate lobbyist, Abramoff was incredibly fortunate that Norquist and Ralph Reed were essentially his best friends. "Grover gave Abramoff priceless credentials as a conservative lobbyist loyal to conservative causes," said J. Michael Waller,[28] who once attended weekly ATR meetings, but became disenchanted with Norquist.

In February 1995, at Abramoff's behest, Norquist wrote to DeLay urging him to meet with the newly minted lobbyist: "Abramoff is moving his clients to help our side, both through PACs and through giving to our coalition groups." In July, Norquist told a reporter, "What the Republicans need is 50 Jack Abramoffs. Then this [Washington, D.C.] becomes a different town." In a 2004 National Public Radio interview, a couple of months before Abramoff pleaded guilty in court, Norquist said, "To this day I can't find anything he did or he's accused of doing that's illegal, immoral, or fattening."

Adam Kidan, Abramoff's future SunCruz Casinos partner, recalls one incident that illustrated how close Abramoff and DeLay would soon become. "One time [Jack and I] were flying to the US Open on a corporate jet and Tom Delay, the House Majority Whip, is paging Jack. It's midnight. Jack puts it on speakerphone, probably to impress me. DeLay says, 'We're on the floor, about to vote on a bill. How should we vote on this bill?' And Jack's telling him how to vote."

Abramoff bristled at this recollection: "This is a contemptible and typical lie by Kidan. There is absolutely no truth to it. I rarely talked to DeLay on the phone and certainly he would never ever ask me how he should vote on a bill in this fashion."

Jonathan Blank must have been pleased by the memo that went out in March 1995, announcing that their newest recruit, Jack Abramoff, someone with no Capitol Hill experience, had managed to persuade Tom DeLay, the new Majority Whip of the House of Representatives, to interrupt his busy schedule to meet informally with the partners of Preston Gates in their fifth-floor conference room. "It was a big deal," said someone who attended the meeting. "[Abramoff] was able to deliver DeLay very fast."Abramoff had brilliantly hitched his star to DeLay's chariot. For a while, the ride was intoxicating. As one of his old College Republican friends, now a prominent television commentator, pointed out, "Jack had ten-year-old connections with Grover [Norquist], Ralph [Reed], and the RNC [Republican National Committee]. He had an intro to Preston Gates. He had an intro to DeLay, and now the GOP was back in power. To have parlayed [all of this] into the career that followed is no less remarkable. He made it happen."

Abramoff's next big hurdle was rainmaking. He needed clients and fast.

CHAPTER FOURTEEN
DISTANT SPECKS

Later, the rap on Abramoff would be that he was willing to exploit naïve, gullible, and defenseless American Indians. If true, it made perfect sense for Abramoff's detractors to say that he had no compunction about helping billionaire Chinese and South Korean textile tycoons exploit defenseless, underpaid, Third-World garment workers, mostly women, who were also forced to be sex slaves and have abortions. At least the diabolical Abramoff was consistent. If there was a disreputable and dishonest cause where bushels of money could be raked in, the deceptively soft-spoken Abramoff would be the first to elbow his way in. Of course, he would then try to persuade you that he was doing it for the greater good and a higher calling. That was the prevailing point of view.

"What was appealing about Jack was that he was the opposite of politically correct," recalls Jeff Pandin, Abramoff's colleague from College Republican and International Freedom Foundation days. "He wasn't going to water it down to make it more appealing to the middle-of-the road folks…and that was very appealing to us young conservative Republicans."

Abramoff's aversion to liberal politically correctness—making a film in Namibia despite UN Sanctions, allegedly working with the apartheid government in South Africa, trying to help Mobutu Sese Seko get a US visa, supplying sniper scopes to Israeli settlers in the West Bank, etc.—would eventually attract plenty of airplay in the liberal press, along with the allegations of defrauding Indians and bribing Congressmen, which only intensified federal prosecutors' zeal in focusing their crosshairs on Abramoff.

How was it possible that a handful of tiny islands over eight thousands miles and an 18-hour plane ride from Washington could get the nation's capital so bent out of shape. Abramoff's allegedly malignant effect on the Northern Mariana Islands, one of his first clients as a lobbyist, remained a major bone of contention more than a decade later. The squabble over the palm-fringed U.S. commonwealth—fourteen specks of volcanic rock east of the Philippines with a native population of about 53,000—was complex and contentious. Liberals and conservatives were miles apart and agreed on little.

In 1944, 5,432 American soldiers, mostly Marines, lost their lives liberating the Northern Mariana Islands from the Japanese. After the war, the islands became a UN mandate administered by the United States. In 1976, the population voted to join the U.S. as a commonwealth (similar to Puerto Rico) and ten years later they became American citizens. But Northern Mariana Islands[29] won two concessions, which social activists later called loopholes. According to its covenant with the United States, the islands could set its own minimum wage and control its own immigration. "They ceded their territory to the U.S., but only if they could maintain a viable economy. Their population was small, so they needed to bring in workers and therefore needed local control over immigration," says Abramoff. "But to compete with the Asian [textile] industry they needed to pay sub-US minimum wages and they still had to pay enormous costs to ship to the 50 states. These were not loopholes."

Eventually, Chinese and South Korean textile manufacturers seized the day. Factories started sprouting up, because clothing manufactured in the Northern Mariana Islands—Ralph Lauren, J. Crew, Tommy Hilfiger, Arrow, Liz Claiborne, Anne Taylor, Brooks Brothers, Abercrombie & Fitch, J.C. Penney, Sears, Wal-Mart, The Gap, Montgomery Ward, Eddie Bauer, and Levis—was exempt from import quotas to the United States (a savings of 50%) and could carry the coveted "Made-in-USA" label, which implied that the garments had been stitched together by American workers. In fact, the seamstresses were third-world laborers imported as "guest workers" from Bangladesh, Thailand, Sri Lanka, the Philippines, and China. Mostly women, they were paid $3.05 an hour, well below American minimum wage at the time of $5.15 an hour, but still about ten times what they would have earned, for example, in Guangdong, China.

Soon, the duty-free economy of the Northern Marianas was booming, making it less dependent on federal handouts, which thrilled the Republicans. Democrats called it "an Americanized Kuwait—where low-paid second-class foreigners do the drudge work," (which described those who toiled at construction sites, drive taxis, landscape lawns, and clean homes throughout the United States.) The Northern Mariana government used the billions in new tax revenues to pay its burgeoning welfare recipients and to develop its tourism industry—luxury hotels and four world-class golf courses. More than six thousand miles from Los Angeles, these Micronesian islands came equipped with beautiful white corral beaches, swaying palm trees, and azure blue water. Most of the tourists were Korean and Japanese on package tours.

Soon the guest workers held 90% of the jobs and far outnumbered the indigenous population, whose unemployment rate soared to over 14%.[30] Only the natives (now American citizens) could legally own the land, which they profitably leased to tycoons who constructed and operated the factories and resorts. Since the local government didn't want to displease the golden geese, some claimed there was limited enforcement of labor and housing regulations for the guest workers. The garment workers were allegedly crammed into "sweat shops" in allegedly unsanitary and dangerous conditions, allegedly working impossibly long hours. Often they were allegedly not paid overtime. If they became pregnant, they were allegedly forced to seek abortions or else lose their jobs. Many underage women were allegedly lured to the islands under false pretenses and forced to work as nude dancers and perform sex acts on stage in local karaoke and topless bars. These alleged abuses soon came to the attention of social activists, TV and print investigative reporters, and finally to liberal congressmen. "These people are working under the protection of the American flag, and they're being exploited as if they were in the worst Third World country," said Rep. George Miller (D-CA), who had sponsored hearings in 1992 to strip the Northern Mariana's wage and immigration exemptions. Abramoff later called Miller—who represented the extremely liberal East Bay area near San Francisco—a toady of the unions, dead wrong, and a liar.

"I would not have defended those islands if I felt that these things were going on, and I am confident they were not going on," says Abramoff. "And yet there was this continuous imputation of my bad motives, naïveté, skullduggery, and greed—all the while that I could look at you with a straight face as if to say that I knew these allegations to be true, but that it was somehow okay with me."

William Branigan of *The Washington Post* also ran stories. The abuses cited by the media—female workers in horrific working conditions being cheated out of over-time wages or sexually abused with impunity—were, however, only anecdotal. The Northern Mariana governor, Froilan Tenorio, said he was determined to eliminate the abuses, which he called isolated. Raising the minimum wage, however, would only cause the textile industry to relocate to Bangladesh or Thailand. Fearing the passage of Rep. Miller's bill, the Northern Mariana government panicked. They were told they needed to hire a Washington lobbyist. In yet another stroke of luck for Abramoff, they turned to his father, Frank, for help.

"I knew Guam and the Marianas well from [having served there during] the war," says Frank. "I had been contacted by some people who wanted to put a casino on the island of Tinian,[31] where the Enola Gay[32] took off from, so I spent a lot of time there. I met a young, well-connected attorney, Randy Fennel, the mayor, the leaders of the community, then the governor. I brought in a friend of mine who is an architect of casinos. I even became friendly with the family that owns a lot of land in the Marianas. Well, just after Jack became a lobbyist, I got a call from Fennel. He said, 'We need representation in Washington.' So I introduced him to Jack." The introduction proved invaluable. The Northern Mariana Islands—the government and textile manufacturers—would eventually end up paying Abramoff nearly $11 million for his services in stopping 29 bills that would have ended the immigration and wage exemptions. In fact, one bill passed the U.S. Senate by unanimous consent; another had 234 sponsors in the House! Yet Abramoff was able to kill them all.

He faced a formidable obstacle, because the evidence—which began accumulating long before he ever arrived on the scene—seemed overwhelming and distressing. First, in 1991, Willie Tan—a textile manufacturer and the islands largest employer, who later would work closely with Abramoff and contribute generously to DeLay's favorite charities—was sued by the US Labor Department for paying 1,350 foreign workers less than the local minimum wage and forcing them to work about 90 hours a week without paying them overtime. The following year the US Occupational Safety and Heath Administration (OSHA) hit Tan with over $240,000 in fines for locking and blocking fire doors, lack of proper ventilation, filthy toilets, and overcrowded conditions.[33]

In 1993, *The New York Times* published an influential story describing conditions for foreign workers in the Northern Marianas as "something close to servitude." Young Filipino women were being lured to the island under false pretenses and forced into prostitution at local bars. The Governor of the Northern Marianas was indignant. "It is an insult to us," he said. "There's no slavery here," but conceded there was room for improvement. The media barrage and governmental pressure continued after Abramoff became the lobbyist for the Northern Marianas.

In May 1996, President Clinton wrote to the Northern Mariana governor criticizing the Islands' labor practices as "inconsistent with our country's values." A devastating piece—Shame on American Soil—appeared in *Readers' Digest* in 1997. It described rampant exploitation and rape of foreign female workers with impunity.

In January 1998, a Department of the Interior report called for the end of the Northern Mariana immigration and wage exemptions, because it had created intolerable conditions that included "forced abortions… the trafficking of minor girls and young females for sexual purposes," and "the non-prosecution of local individuals who [sexually] assault [female] workers." Days later, a senate committee issued a scathing report in which it declared "Only a few countries, and no democratic society, have immigration policies" like those in the Northern Mariana Islands. In February, *Time* magazine ran a story in which Clinton official Allen Stayman[34]—director of the Interior Department's Office of Insular Affairs[35]—was quite blunt about the widespread abuses in the Northern Mariana Islands: "The local immigration and labor departments are essentially organized crime."

In early 1999, a $1 billion class-action lawsuit was filed against 18 American retailers and apparel companies, claiming that the 15,000 garment workers on the Northern Marianas had been deprived for their basic rights. Abramoff asserted, however, that this class-action lawsuit was based on lies and only served to line the pockets of the lawyers, while the claimants receive crumbs. And in May 1999, ABC News investigative show, 20/20, ran a shocking expose of rampant abuse on the Northern Mariana Islands—Tom DeLay made a cameo appearance—in which government officials and textile tycoons were made to appear evasive and buffoonish. For Abramoff's baptism as a novice lobbyist, this was the equivalent of scaling Mt. Everest.

"It's much better than many places in the United States," Abramoff says. "There's no place in America that has more OSHA inspectors per square foot than [the Northern Marianas]. This propaganda comes from UNITE.[36] It didn't want [the Northern Marianas] to have a minimum wage lower than the one in the states." Was he deluding himself that these reports were wild exaggerations of labor unions and social activists? Or was he simply amoral to the core? Did he really believe that the Northern Marianas exemplified the kind of capitalism around which conservatives should rally? Did Abramoff's representation of the interests of Northern Mariana Government and its textile manufacturers demonstrate a callousness of the soul? Wasn't it obvious that the rich and powerful were always going to exploit the weak and destitute? All defendants deserve legal representation, but do all clients deserve lobbyists? What does it say about a lobbyist who chooses these kinds of client? Or were Abramoff's claims correct that these allegations were the lies and exaggerations of pro-union social activists? Furthermore, were they asserting that the more than 100 congressmen and staffers—mostly Republican, but some Democrat—who were later brought to tour the Northern Mariana islands by Abramoff were engaged in a massive cover up?

There is no denying the ruthlessness of globalization. Factories go where costs are lower, because most buyers are driven by price, not conscience. If a competitor produces the same Polo shirt for less, you will quickly go out of business and your workers will unemployed. Of course, working conditions in some third-world countries would make those in the Northern Marianas seem lavish. And what about the fact that the American media—which tend to exploit the anecdotal—were denied access to countries with censorship or were indifferent to the abysmal conditions in third-world countries? In October 2007, there were reports that 10-year old children in India were working 16-hour days, handstitching clothing for The Gap. "Some…said they were not being paid because their employer said they were still trainees." That's where the jobs will go if Miller succeeds." Abramoff says.

"The government of the Marianas came to me," he explains. "They said that Congress was about to trash their economy, take away their minimum wage and immigration controls which they had negotiated when they joined [the United States.] If this happens, we can't compete with Asia."

Abramoff didn't give a damn about what the liberal media considered politically correct, because he believed in what he was doing. It could be argued that because he was surrounded by colleagues and political associates who shared his views, Abramoff never pondered its cumulative effect until it was too late. He was unwittingly filling an ever-deepening pool of ill will that would eventually release a flash flood of pent-up resentment.

How did Abramoff block Congress from reforming the Northern Marianas? How did he counter claims that the faraway islands were nothing more than a reprehensible sweatshop on American soil? First, he declared that his clients were exemplars of the conservative cause, persuasively framing them as models of free-market capitalism and local control. And Tom DeLay would soon agree. Gushing how they were a "perfect Petri dish of capitalism…my Galapagos Island," DeLay would later tell the governor of the Northern Mariana Islands, "You are a shining light for what is happening in the Republican Party, and you represent everything that is good about what we're trying to do in America in leading the world in the free-market system."

But at least one conservative didn't buy it, imputing that the driving force behind these claims was self-interest. "Why [the Northern Marianas] would become a conservative issue was beyond so many of us," said J. Michael Waller[37], a former acquaintance of Grover Norquist. "Now to some of us [the Northern Marianas] is a huge Chinese sweatshop. To those of us getting money from those Chinese sweatshop interests, [it] was a wonderful experiment in free market and low taxes at work."

Abramoff's second lobbying strategy was risky. He called it "utter transparency." Basically, he said, "Please come see for yourself what's going on and make up your own mind." It was a gutsy strategy, because if the abuses were as blatant and as pervasive as the social activists, labor unions, and liberal media claimed, the stream of "tourists" that Abramoff would soon bring to the Northern Marianas—congressmen, staff, and journalists—would probably be hard pressed to deny what was allegedly so apparent. But the very first person Abramoff had to persuade was himself. The second was a named partner in his lobbying firm, the well-respected Lloyd Meeds[38] of Preston Gates Ellis & Rouvelas Meeds. "He and I are 180 degrees apart politically," Meeds told a reporter in 1995, "but he is a very innovative and very productive guy." Together, they traveled there and saw the conditions for themselves and concluded they were greatly exaggerated.

Abramoff immediately informed the Northern Mariana Government that "Meeds has an excellent relationship" with Rep. Doc Hastings (R-WA) and others, who sat on the House Subcommittee that oversaw the Northern Marianas, which was considering Rep. George Miller's proposals to "gut their economy." These 14 islands would soon become Preston Gates' biggest lobbying client, accounting for one-quarter of the firm's lobbying revenues.

But Abramoff insisted it was about more than money. Defending the Northern Marianas was the honorable thing to do. "They don't have a Congressman or a delegate to the United States," Abramoff told a reporter. "It's the farthest territory from the United States. Nobody knew anything about it. And the federal bureaucracy, which for so long had a paternalistic and almost colonialist rule over these guys, said let's make a move on their economy."

Landing this client was a coup for the firm's new hire.

CHAPTER FIFTEEN
CAME, SAW, GOLFED

Why was such a stink made about the Northern Mariana Islands? Why did the liberals and conservatives become so animated over something most people couldn't find on a map? During the Cold War, the United States and Soviet Union could not attack one another militarily, because each had thermonuclear weapons capable of wiping the other out. Therefore, they fought proxy wars, mostly in third-world countries. These included Korea, Vietnam, Cuba, Nicaragua, Angola, and Ethiopia, costing hundreds of thousands of lives. The Northern Marianas became an ideological proxy war between conservatives and liberals. In many ways, the venom reached levels on par with abortion rights and gay marriage, each side viewing the other as inhabitants of an alien reality.

"[Abramoff] spent a lot of time, effort and money to protect a system that was a growth industry for sex shops, prostitution, abuse of women, slavery, illegal immigration, worker exploitation and narcotics, and he did it all in the name of freedom," said a furious Rep. George Miller.

Abramoff dismissed these claims as ridiculous: "Congressman Miller has an agenda, and he wants the facts to fit his thesis. No lobbyist could have convinced Congress to support the system he describes." If asked, most of the workers would have said that, yes, they became wealthy by Asian standards. They're the ones who could return to their villages and build the biggest homes. Miller did not consider for a minute how his actions would destroy the hopes and dreams of these people. "Instead, Miller would find the few workers who complained to publicize his allegations. The truth is that many of the workers that he highlighted had filed labor protests as a means of avoiding being sent back home after their contracts had expired, because the law provided that a worker with an outstanding complaint could not be asked to leave the [Northern Marianas]," says Abramoff. Miller vigorously denied this, saying that many workers secretly approached him at his hotel, claiming the official tours were a sham.

"You know what all this fuss is really about?" Abramoff told a reporter in 1998. "It's that the people of this beautiful island finally have broken out of U.S. dependency. They live on a warm, tropical island with beaches and they've always been dependent, but now they want to make their own economy and not be on welfare. I think what's going on here is the radical left simply is not happy about that." What about the 234 congressmen—both Democrats and Republicans—eventually sponsored a bill barring the Northern Marianas from using the "Made-in-USA" label on clothing manufactured there? Later, Tom DeLay would go even further, denouncing [opponents] as "evil." Abramoff, the newly minted lobbyist, was able to persuade Preston Gates, a traditionally liberal firm, that it should basically convert itself into a tour-guide operation singing the praises of the Northern Mariana Islands as a free-market paradise.

In a review of the law firm's voluminous billing records for this period, it became clear how much time, effort, and money went into arranging the all-expenses-paid "educational" visits for congressmen and staff—mostly Republican, but some Democrats—as well as conservative journalists. It appeared that under the aegis of Abramoff, Preston Gates arranged for over 100 visitors.[39] As expected, these "junkets" would soon be viewed as a "lavishly funded public relations [stunt]." The Preston Gates billing records clearly stated that the all-expenses-paid guests were accompanied by Preston Gates personnel, who arranged briefings with representatives of the Departments of Commerce, Finance, Labor and Immigration, the Office of the Attorney General, members of the local legislature, and federal officials from the Departments of Labor and Interior, as well as visits to various apparel manufacturers.

Sounds like guided tours. Of course, time was also set aside to party. Why let stunning beaches, world-class golf courses, and historic settings go to waste? Saipan, the largest of the Northern Mariana Islands, was littered with beached ships, tanks, and other artifacts from the 1944 American invasion. One sobering attraction was the rocky Suicide Cliff at the island's northern tip, where as many as 18,000 Japanese soldiers and civilians jumped to death rather than surrender.[40] On a runway on the island of Tinian sat two small obelisks, marking the spot where the atomic bombs dropped on Hiroshima and Nagasaki were loaded onto the U.S. B-29 bombers. Among the many junketeers Abramoff brought to the Marianas were conservative columnists and think-tank pundits. Even this would generate a typhoon of controversy years later when it was revealed that many of these scholars had been paid by Abramoff to write articles and editorials extolling the virtues of the Marianas.

In the world of lobbying, this practice was actually more the rule than the exception, something the print and TV media neglected to mention.

At least BusinessWeek Online fessed up: "For years, rumors have swirled of an underground opinion "pay-for-play" industry in Washington in which think-tank employees and pundits trade their ability to shape public perception for cash."

Doug Bandow, a former senior advisor to President Ronald Reagan was the first lamb brought to slaughter. In 1997, Bandow, then a senior fellow at the libertarian Cato Institute and a syndicated columnist for Copley News Service, gushed about the Marianas. They were a "stunning economic success." When confronted in 2005 about his alleged payola, Bandow conceded that Abramoff had indeed paid him about $2000 each for between "12 and 24 articles." He apologized, calling it "a lapse in judgment." The Cato Institute and the Copley News Service promptly fired him. Suzette Standring, the president of the National Society of Newspaper Columnists, was unforgiving. What Bandow did, she said, "isn't a lapse in judgment, it's soul-selling."

Another one of Abramoff's paid writers, Peter Ferrara, a senior policy adviser at the conservative Institute for Policy Innovation, however was unrepentant about advancing the concerns of a lobbyist's client. "I do that all the time," Ferrara says. "I've done that in the past, and I'll do it in the future." His boss, Tom Gianovetti, backed up Ferrara, refusing to fire him: "I have a sense that there are a lot of people at think tanks who have similar arrangements."

Even Grover Norquist had pitched in. According to e-mails from McCain's Senate Indian Affairs Committee, over the course of several years, Abramoff had paid the anti-tax guru to write approximately 50 op-eds favorable to Abramoff's clients in *The Washington Times*.

Abramoff is unapologetic: "The mission of a lobbyist is to get his client's case before the decision makers of Washington. In the Republican Congressional era, one of the most important tactics was to set forth the ideological and philosophical underpinnings of a client's wishes, and how these were consistent with conservative Republican thought and belief. To do this, scholars and writers of the conservative bent were needed." He says that he never asked any conservative writer to take a position that they would not have naturally reached on their own. Most of these writers were otherwise employed by think tanks or were very busy with their own issues. "In order to get important and effective writers to focus on my clients, I—like so many others in town—would arrange for financial compensation," says Abramoff. "It was not a matter of paying someone to take my position. It was paying someone to take the time to focus on an issue which they were not focused on."

Years later, an award-winning filmmaker spent three weeks in the Northern Marianas, shooting footage for a documentary on the islands' labor abuses. He maintains that conditions were actually far worse than previously reported. He says that Abramoff would ferry congressmen and staff from Washington D. C. to these blissful islands where his "fact-finding" tourists would visit several textile factories. The Third-World seamstresses would deferentially nod and smile when the factory foreman gently asked them if they were happy. While Abramoff's "fact-finding tourists" were being herded back to their five-star hotels for golfing, scuba diving, and a pig roast hosted by one of the islands' textile tycoons, the seamstresses would resume their miserable existences. "Abramoff's evil genius was that he realized these abuses could be hidden in plain view," says the filmmaker. "He brought all these people and they didn't see a thing."

Nonetheless of all the junketeers that Abramoff persuaded to visit the Northern Marianas, only one really mattered: Majority Whip Tom DeLay. If he blocked a vote, no matter how overwhelming a bill's support, it would die. But Abramoff had to make a Herculean effort in order to persuade DeLay, the third most powerful man in Congress, to make the 36-hour round-trip plane flight to these distant specks in the far Pacific. The billing records of Abramoff's firm for 1996 and 1997 confirmed that Abramoff had 187 contacts with DeLay's office, including 16 direct contacts with DeLay and 104 conversations with Ed Buckham, DeLay's chief of staff.

In the meantime, the initial Preston Gates contract with the Northern Marianas—from June 1, 1995 to June 30, 1996—had expired. Mysteriously, believing he had the authority to do so, Governor Froilan Tenorio continued to pay Abramoff's firm. Despite the lack of a valid contract, the local government paid his lobbyist $5.21 million until January 11, 1998.

Finally, after all the details had been ironed out, DeLay took the long first-class flight for a "fact-finding trip" to Northern Marianas over New Years 1997/1998. In addition to Abramoff, DeLay's entourage included his wife and daughter, and several aides, as well as several staff from the office of Dick Armey, the Speaker of the House. The ensemble stayed at the Hyatt Regency Saipan, a luxury hotel where suites cost as much as $1,000 a night. The grounds of the hotel occupy 14 acres of lush tropical gardens and lagoons, and include a magnificent beach on the open Pacific. DeLay was kept very busy on this historic visit. He met with the Governor, members of the legislature, and a Roman Catholic Bishop. He also toured several "sweat shops." Afterwards, he described some of the workers' housing as below American standards, but noted that the garment factories were clean and air conditioned. "I didn't see anyone sweating," DeLay reportedly joked. Together, Abramoff and DeLay toured several factories with a Chinese interpreter in tow.

"DeLay was not about to be brainwashed by anybody," Abramoff says. "He asked [the factory workers] tough questions about their situation, and after that he was convinced that the attacks against the island were more ridiculous than ever."

During his visit, DeLay was dogged by an ABC camera crew from the investigative news program 20/20. "The 20/20 crew had been following us around the island. At one point, they were hiding in the bushes," says Abramoff, shaking his head. "DeLay saw them and invited them to come into one of the factories, but they said, 'No, we'd rather not,' because they wanted to make it appear as if they were secretly ambushing DeLay." After the TV show aired on May 24, 1999, Rep. John T. Doolittle (R-CA), who had visited the Northern Marianas in February, circulated a scathing letter to every member of the House. "The real shame was that in its report on the Saipan garment industry, 20/20 decided to jettison the facts, as well as any degree of balance, and piece together a story fraught with bias, mistruth, and sensationalism in order to win a TV ratings war." A favor to Abramoff, the letter would be the first of many Doolittle would perform, for which he would be investigated eight years later.

On each evening of his five-day visit, DeLay was the honored guest at a sumptuous reception. The most notorious was the first. Hosted by William Tan, with whom DeLay had brunched and golfed earlier that day, the pig-roast dinner was served at the exclusive Pacific Islands Club. A naturalized U.S. citizen, Tan was the wealthy textile tycoon who had agreed in 1992 to pay $9 million in overtime back pay to his workers.[41] His other business interests included several hotels, a bank, and the islands' largest newspaper—the *Saipan Tribune*.

After Tan warmly introduced him, DeLay stood and turned to Abramoff, who was seated nearby. What DeLay would say next would haunt him years later after the scandal broke. "When one of my closest and dearest friends, Jack Abramoff, your most able representative in Washington, D.C., invited me to the islands, I wanted to see firsthand the free-market success and the progress and reform you have made." The House Majority Whip went on to say how much he was dismayed by the Clinton administration for trying to "kill prosperity on the islands. You are up against the forces of big labor and the radical left."After dinner, DeLay and Tan went off to see a cockfight, according to one of the participants. "I was at the dinner," says Abramoff. "I never heard about this, and I doubt it's true."

DeLay's taxing schedule required additional relaxation, so he and his family snorkeled in the corral-encrusted lagoon on the exclusive Managaha Island. An avid golfer with a single-digit handicap, DeLay played an additional two rounds on the island's Lao Lao Bay Golf Resort. Abramoff made certain that only top golfers played in DeLay's foursome: "I knew Tom, whose handicap is under 10, did not want to play golf with players of lesser skills, to put it mildly." Upon his return home, DeLay's critics and the press pounced on him for too much golfing in the Marianas. This trip, along with two others that DeLay would take with Abramoff—one to Moscow and the other to Scotland—would prove embarrassing for DeLay and felonious for others.

CHAPTER SIXTEEN
CROSSING THE LINE?

In early 1998, the newly inaugurated governor of the Northern Marianas, Pedro Tenorio, who had just succeeded his nephew, Froilan, announced that he would not renew Abramoff's contract, which would expire in the fall. Why wouldn't the new governor renew the lobbying contract that had clearly saved the island's lucrative status quo? "Teno was a peace time consigliere, not a war time," Abramoff says. "He simply didn't realize how precarious the situation was. Later, he did and signed [a new contract with us]."

When Abramoff's contract ran out, it was immediately picked up by a consortium of local textile manufacturers—called the Western Pacific Economic Council, which, of course, included Willie Tan. In 1999, this consortium paid Abramoff a whopping $1.8 millions in fees. "Well, that's what we billed," says Abramoff, "but we were only paid $400,000." But Tan didn't want to keep paying Abramoff even that sum. He wanted the government to pick up the tab by renewing the lobbyist's contract. Later, federal prosecutors concluded that Abramoff's "thinking outside the box" might have crossed the bright red line into criminality.

In interviews conducted with his former colleagues, they agree that Abramoff was always bubbling forth raw ideas for creative solutions to intransigent obstacles. If someone spoke up, however, and pointed out that his suggestion was illegal or unethical, Abramoff would sheepishly back down. But when surrounded by obsequious underlings intimidated or awed by his intellect and charisma, Abramoff's creative—and possibly illegal—schemes might move forward.

Benigno Fitial, owner of several bars on the Northern Marianas,[42] had worked as a textile executive for Willie Tan and was an avid golfer. Fitial was now running as the underdog candidate for speaker of the 18-member House of Delegates. He was two votes shy of victory. A criminal investigation would later focus on why two local lawmakers changed their minds and voted for Fitial, who then orchestrated the renewal of Abramoff's contract.

The first thing federal investigators would discover was that Fitial held DeLay in the highest esteem. After all, he was Majority whip of the U.S. House of Representatives. Two years earlier, in April 1997, Fitial had played golf in DeLay's foursome at a Houston fundraiser for the DeLay Foundation for Kids,[43] and had won the putting championship. Right after the tournament, he traveled to Washington to lobby lawmakers on behalf of the Northern Marianas, as well as to sing "Happy Birthday" to DeLay in his office. He promptly sent Ed Buckham an e-mail: "[DeLay was] happy after the golf tournament because he beat me by one stroke." Fitial also expressed gratitude to Buckham for "stopping legislation from getting on the floor of the House." The e-mail was signed: "YOUR 'ADOPTED' BROTHER BEN."

Secondly, it was no secret that one of Abramoff's parlor tricks in bending the will of Congress was his recognition that the staffers wielded the real power in Congress. "Earmarks, Christmas-tree bills[44], non-germane earmarks and insertions into the *Congressional Record*, most of the time you can handle it through the staff, because if the staff is opposed, they will find 100 ways to subvert it," says Abramoff. His strategy was not hiring former staffers and lawmakers or helping them launch their own firms.[45] Every lobbying firm in Washington did that. But because of Abramoff's astounding success, he could offer former staffers something no other lobbying shop could match: $200,000 annual salaries. Therefore, ever hopeful Abramoff might hire them, staffers would claw one another to please him.

In December of 1999, Buckham resigned as DeLay's chief of staff to become a "political consultant."Buckham, who remained DeLay's private minister, needed a jump start. Any help Buckham received would implicitly please DeLay. So, on Abramoff's recommendation, Willie Tan hired Buckham and paid him a retainer of $100,000. Tan wanted Abramoff's contract renewed. So Buckham devised a plan to get Fitial elected speaker. In late December, Buckham and Michael Scanlon flew to the Marianas. Although Scanlon, who was still paying off his student loans and was about to start his own public-relations firm, was still DeLay's communications director, as well as his aide on the House Appropriations Committee. (DeLay would later claim that Scanlon was on an unpaid leave of absence when he went to the Northern Marianas. But payroll records reflect that DeLay paid Scanlon's staff salary through January 2000.)

In the Northern Marianas, Fitial told Buckham and Scanlon that two lawmakers, Alejo Mendiola and Norman S. Palacios, might be willing to switch their votes if Fitial demonstrated he had "clout" in Washington. Buckham promptly buttonholed Mendiola; Scanlon waylaid Norman S. Palacios.Each lawmaker seemed to have a legitimate request. Palacios wanted federal funds to renovate a crumbling breakwater on Tinian, the island he represented. Mendiola, who was from Rota, wanted his island's airport repaved. Buckham and Scanlon promised to see what they could do. As a result, Mendiola and Palacios switched their votes, and Fitial was elected speaker.

Why did they switch their votes? "The message was all that was needed: Fitial had the juice in DC to solve the [Northern Mariana's] problems," Abramoff says. "There was no need for any specific quid pro quo, which everybody knows is illegal. Buckham and Scanlon couldn't guarantee anything anyway. All they could do was promise to try."

Several months later both projects received federal funding from congressional committees on which DeLay served. Was this a coincidence? Federal prosecutors didn't think so. In 2005, they were able to persuade DeLay's former deputy chief of staff, Tony Rudy, as well as Michael Scanlon, to plead guilty to helping "secure certain appropriations projects for the [Northern Marianas] which [they] knew would help Abramoff's lobbying business and that had been sought by Abramoff."

Did Rudy and Scanlon sincerely plead guilty to bribery? That's highly dubious. Like most defendants threatened by federal prosecutors with omnipotent powers, Rudy and Scanlon undoubtedly felt coerced into pleading guilty for the sake of a much-reduced sentence.[46] When interviewed in 2005, Ben Fitial vehemently denied any connection between his getting elected speaker and the federal appropriations. "No! No! No! There was no—I give you something, you give me something," he insisted.

Willie Tan funded the Buckham-Scanlon trip to the Marianas, because a lobbying firm could not fund such travel. Abramoff instructed Tan to make the donation to the National Center for Public Policy Research, a nonprofit run by Abramoff's old College Republican chum, Amy Moritz Ridenour. Her group then reimbursed Abramoff who had paid for the flights and hotels on his Visa credit card. In an e-mail to his assistant, Susan Ralston, he wrote: "The tickets should not in any way say my name or the firm's name…if possible, say National Center for Public Policy Research."

Why the concern? "Because we weren't hosting the trip and it could be misconstrued. We were doing the bookings, and I didn't want an honest mistake made." Abramoff goes on to say that he took care of booking the trip as a favor to Tan. "A business man cannot just host and pay for a trip by congressional staffers," says Abramoff. "The trip either has to be paid for by governments, which is what we did for most of the years, or by an educational group, such as Amy's. The trip was in fact educational, so there was something to hang our hats on, but it was clearly—at least in retrospect—an improper use of a nonprofit."

The problem was that only Scanlon was an official congressional staffer at the time. Yet DeLay claimed he was on an "unpaid leave of absence." In the end, even Abramoff was forced to plead guilty to a bribery concerning Fitial's election as speaker. "He would have said he was guilty of anything," says a close friend of Abramoff's, "which is what he did." As newly elected speaker, Fitial launched a vigorous campaign to renew Abramoff's contract. On June 30, 2000, Fitial sent an e-mail to Governor Tenorio's top aides: "Please urge Teno to execute the agreement as we will continue to encounter problems…if the contract is not executed. We need [Abramoff] to help save our economy."

In early July, an editorial in *The Saipan Tribune*, which had once called Abramoff "our Michael Jordan," predicted "devastating" consequences without Abramoff as the Mariana's lobbyist. Two days later, the tourniquet was tightened. Fitial convened an extraordinary special session to pass a resolution urging the Governor to renew Abramoff's contract. A second one was passed on July 26. Finally, Gov. Tenorio relented. Two days later, he signed a contract with Abramoff that would eventually be worth $1.6 million. Later, when these shenanigans were brought to the attention of Rep. George Miller, Abramoff's nemesis, he weighed in with evident satisfaction: "This is starting to smell more like criminal activity —trading congressional appropriations for votes."[47]

Was this truly criminal behavior? If Rudy, Scanlon, and Abramoff had not pleaded guilty, would an impartial jury have convicted them of bribery? It seemed doubtful. If he and the others staunchly maintained that there had never been a specific quid pro quo, this kind of implicit horse trading would not have met the U.S. Supreme Court's 1999 definition of bribery. Nevertheless, their behavior would have fallen under the aegis of "honest-services fraud," a controversial—and perhaps unconstitutionally vague—law, which prosecutors creatively employ to circumvent the far tougher bribery threshold.

CHAPTER SEVENTEEN
CHOCTAW

Some of his Preston-Gates colleagues were envious of Abramoff's early success. For the new guy on the block—the zoo exhibit—scoring big with the Northern Mariana Islands had to be a fluke. It was beginner's luck. And since managing the Marianas account was all consuming, he would have no time to woo and pursue another major client. There simply wasn't enough time in the day. However, Abramoff appeared to be a conjurer, able to accomplish several things at the same time. He could wring out more than sixty minutes from an hour and more than 24 hours from a day, despite the fact that he was operating at a disadvantage: His work week was only six days long. As an Orthodox Jew, he had to sacrifice the Sabbath, during which he could not make a phone call, send an e-mail, drive in a car, fly on a plane, discuss business, or switch on a light bulb.

"It was frustrating to be sure. I'd work right up the final second [on late afternoon or early evening of a Friday] and I couldn't work again until 25 hours later. Three stars must appear in the Saturday night sky [to mark the end of the Sabbath]" Abramoff says. "But it forced me to take a day off and essentially meditate and recharge."

Abramoff's second big coup was the Mississippi Band of Choctaw Indians. This client would eventually pay his firms many millions of dollars. In the first half of 1999 alone, the Choctaws paid Preston Gates $2.3 million, far more than what Microsoft paid its 13 lobbying firms for the same period. Indeed, this tiny, obscure Indian tribe turned out to be the "top-paying single client of any lobbying" firm in the entire country.

When *The Washington Post* ran the first scandal story in February 2004, claiming that Abramoff was charging his Indian clients too much, it was hardly a secret. In 2000, the *National Journal* and the *Wall Street Journal* had run prominent stories about his exalted fees. And in 2003, *The New York Times* ran a similar story, in which the Choctaw chief, Philip Martin, declared, "Definitely we get our money's worth, or we wouldn't be doing it."

Once again, Abramoff's father was involved helping his son reel in another trophy client. In 1981, Frank had held a fund raiser at his Beverly Hills home for his son, who was seeking the chairmanship of the College Republicans. One of the invitees was attorney Marc Levin, a partner in a boutique securities law firm in Beverly Hills whose services Frank occasionally employed. The following year, Levin began dating Nell Rogers, the director of legislative planning for the Choctaws. Many years later, "in early 1995, prompted by the GOP revolution in 1994, and because the tribe is a political animal, Nell talked to me about needing a Republican lobbyist. I told her to give Jack a call. It was that simple and innocent," Levin says, as sits in his Malibu home overlooking the Pacific Ocean and the beach hundreds of feet below. "I've always been helpful about introducing people. I put them in touch." It was an introduction that would continuously bear succulent fruit for a ten-year period until it suddenly turned poisonous.

Native American tribes had always been closely allied with Democrat lawmakers, to whom most Indians made somewhat anemic contributions. Federally recognized tribes are considered sovereign nations within the United States. Therefore, Choctaw Chief Martin, who preferred to conduct a "government-to-government" relationship with the United States, would lobby Congress in person. Big changes were afoot, however. First, the Democrats no longer controlled Congress, and many of the tribe's legislator friends had vanished. Second, for the Choctaws—who had borrowed heavily to open its first gaming resort, the Silver Star Hotel and Casino—it was suddenly raining money. But the downpour was about to end. In early 1995, Rep. Bill Archer (R-TX), chairman of the Ways and Means Committee, announced plans to tax the "unrelated business income" [UBIT] of all Indian tribes. In other words, "[t]he tribe's Silver Star Hotel & Casino had barely opened and already legislation was moving forward in Congress calling for Indian casinos to be taxed in the same manner as Las Vegas gambling facilities."

The new Republican majority was not enamored of Native Americans, because, like blacks and other minorities, they rarely voted for or contributed to GOP candidates. But, thanks to Abramoff, that was about to change. Nell Rogers said, "…extraordinary alarms [went off] because that meant that the tribe's gaming…revenue could be taxed up to 34 percent, threatening [its] ability to pay off it debt and undermining it capacity to provide essential governmental services to the some-10,000 tribal members."Like the Northern Mariana Islanders, the Choctaws began having panic attacks. Rogers realized that the only prescription drug available was a Washington lobbyist with close ties to the Republican leadership. One day, she happened to be discussing her concerns with her ex-boyfriend, Marc Levin. He suggested Abramoff. Several days later, Abramoff and Meeds flew into Philadelphia, Mississippi, where they made a persuasive presentation to the Choctaws.

Rogers and Chief Martin were impressed. Abramoff would appeal directly to core conservative principles. He would pitch his fellow Republicans that the Choctaws did not occupy an Indian reservation, but a "free-enterprise zone,and that the imposition of any new taxes—

even on Native Americans—was anathema. To accomplish this, Abramoff would mobilize conservative think tanks and anti-tax groups behind the Choctaw cause. And it wouldn't hurt for the tribe to start making sizeable contributions—all perfectly legal—to Republican lawmakers and their pet charities.

"I came away thinking this is really different and unusual," said Rogers. "It was an unusual approach that you would engage other groups to help you in a campaign to say [about the Choctaws] 'these are good guys.'" Five years later in 2000, even *The Wall Street Journal* would sarcastically characterize Abramoff's tactic as nothing more than a "rain dance." This "GOP stalwart" had concocted an "anti-tax spin" to preserve the Choctaw's "lucrative perks," in order to pocket "hefty fees." So, for big bucks, the Choctaws and the Northern Mariana Islands ended up hiring the inexperienced Abramoff, who was suddenly the firm's biggest rainmaker. A right-wing, politically incorrect conservative was raking in millions by marshalling the ghost of Ronald Reagan for indigenous Micronesians and Native Americans. The irony was touching.

The world of Indian gambling—the industry preferred to call it "gaming"—was extraordinarily abstruse. It involved regulation and negotiation with various state, federal, and municipal agencies, as well as brutal intra-tribal warfare and politics, fierce competition from Indian and non-Indian casinos, not to mention racetracks.[48] A tribe that did not hire and pay top dollar for the very best lobbyist risked losing everything. "I worked on Indian matters for ten years," says Abramoff. "I had a PhD in this stuff. The intricacies are beyond belief. [*The Washington Post* and the McCain Report] took my life and made a cartoon out of it, and in the process destroyed my life. I wasn't the lazy lobbyist, drinking every night with pals, and having affairs. I was constantly working for my clients and the things I believe in."

The charges later leveled by *The Washington Post* and McCain claiming that Abramoff had ripped off his Indian clients seemed one-sided, biased, and oversimplified. Abramoff, pointing to a copy of the McCain Report, says, "I'd hate that guy too, the one that they've created. I'm just not that jerk." In addition, both the *Post* and McCain seemed to view the tribes paternalistically. The Indians were naïve victims of a super-slick snake-oil salesman. But these casino-operating Native Americans whom Abramoff represented were hardly sitting in teepees, trading wampum, and smoking peace pipes. They operated gambling parlors that raked in $300-500 million annually. They could afford to hire the best and brightest lawyers, accountants, and consultants…and lobbyists.

Nonetheless, in 1995, the Rep. Archer's 34% UBIT hung menacingly over Indian Country. The bill, vigorously supported by Speaker Newt Gingrich, passed in the House. "To Chief Martin, it looked like we were going to lose the UBIT fight," says Abramoff. "I told him how much money it was costing them. I felt bad about it. He told me, 'If you win, you're worth 20 times what you're charging us. If you lose, you're not worth a dollar.'" Even to Abramoff, the battle seemed doomed. The Archer amendment was attached to the House version of the Budget Reconciliation Act of 1995. The Senate's version did not include the Archer amendment. Differences between House and Senate versions of a bill are settled by a joint conference committee. Since the government was always hungry for new sources of revenue, the Archer amendment was all but certain to survive the final reconciliation.

"I got Grover [Norquist] to agree with me that this was a tax increase. We then quickly persuaded enough [conservative Republicans] on the [conference] committee to omit it from the final version," says Abramoff. "The reason Republicans didn't think about this is because Indians basically gave only to Democrats. At that time, no tribes were contributing to Republicans, only the Choctaws." During the next several years, at Abramoff's direction, the Choctaws made almost $350,000 in donations to Americans for Tax Reform, Norquist's anti-tax organization. The Choctaws were ecstatic. Chief Martin led his warriors in a victory dance around a roaring campfire for several days.

The battle had been won, but not the war. The legislation was re-introduced several times in the next few years. The Choctaw's lobbyist throttled it on every occasion. What was the UBIT victory worth? The amount is staggering. Over the course of the ten-year period from 1995-2005, casino revenues from hundreds of Indian gaming establishments have conservatively generated between $100 and $150 billion. Therefore, if Rep. Archer's tax had become law, it would have cost Indian Country between $33 and $50 billion in that 10-year period, not to mention that this tax would have continued in perpetuity. "Yup, I save them billions," Abramoff says, "That's how I first victimized Indian Country."

Many years later, the McCain report did not care to hazard a guess as to how much Abramoff had saved his client. Instead McCain faintly praised the monster victory with a muted, low-key sentence: "Abramoff and his colleagues at Preston Gates eventually succeeded in their efforts, and the UBIT tax failed…" Soon Abramoff's lobbying firm, already converted into a well-oiled travel agency for the Marianas, was firing on all pistons, parachuting dozens of lawmakers, staff, and conservative scholars into the Choctaw's reservation as well.

By coincidence, "nestled among the towering pines and stunning oaks…wrapped in over five miles of meandering spring-fed streams" was the award-winning 7000-yard Choctaw Dancing Rabbit golf course, "created by acclaimed golf course designer Tom Fazio and PGA great Jerry Pate." The first DeLay personnel to arrive and hit the links on a "fact-finding" mission were chief of staff Ed Buckham, an ordained minister, and press secretary Tony Rudy. Their two-day stay in March 1997 cost the Choctaws $3,000. Next year, DeLay, his wife, and Buckham's successor, Susan Hirschman, showed up for a "site review and reservation tour for a charitable event." That trip set the tribe back $6,935. Many of Abramoff's "fact-finding" tourists—including DeLay—traveled to both of Abramoff's all-expenses-paid destinations.[49]

Two of the usual suspects showed up as well: Doug Bandow and Peter Ferrara. In a syndicated column, Bandow hailed the Choctaws "for their entrepreneurial spirit…[who] offer a model for other tribes." Ferrara quickly dashed off a book, *The Choctaw Revolution: Lessons for Federal Policy*, in which he lionized Chief Martin and his accomplishments spanning his 30-year tenure as chief. Published by Grover Norquist's anti-tax organization, American's for Tax Reform, the book was promptly handed out to members of Congress. Certain disclosures were not made, however. Neither Ferrara nor Norquist revealed that the Choctaw's had made sizeable contributions to Norquist's Americans for Tax Reform. Essentially, Jack Abramoff had arranged for the tribe to pay to have the book self-published. For him, it was one of the many clever ways to get his ideological message across: "The Republicans did not understand Indian issues, but they surely knew tax reform," says Abramoff.

And how did he marshal so many right-wing Christian, adamantly opposed to gambling, behind the Choctaw cause? Abramoff had a ready answer. "Regardless of what you feel about gaming, what you are creating here is a tax on these people, and conservatives should never be in favor of new taxes." The attempted UBIT raid was only the first of many on Indian Country. Washington continued to seek other ways to exploit them. In 1997, Sen. Slade Gorton (R-WA) proposed a bill requiring all tribes to collect sales tax on goods and services purchased by non-Indians on reservation land. Abramoff stopped that too, also saving the Choctaws and all of Indian Country millions of dollars.

Abramoff also successfully "lobbied against legislation that would [have] restrict[ed] the tribe's ability to take its gambling operations online." Later that year, an amendment was quietly attached to the Interior Department's appropriations bill that would have prevented the Interior Secretary from forcing states to live up to their legally mandated requirement to negotiate in good faith with tribes that wanted to open casinos.[50] Abramoff fought off all attempted raids. Not a single one succeeded.

Flush with new wealth, the Choctaws were now eager to repossess land that they had been stolen from them. Such purchases—called "land into trust"—can be officially incorporated into the tribe's existing reservation—even if not contiguous—and used for the possible development of new casinos. However, Rep. Ernest Istook (R-OK) quietly introduced a subtle amendment that would have required the tribes to enter into a tax agreement with their states—which no tribe was currently required to do—if they wished to put any additional land into trust. That didn't slip by Abramoff either. "This was unprecedented," he says. "Forcing a tribe to enter a tax agreement with a state—otherwise the tribe would be barred from putting more land in trust. It's hard to quantify, but to Indian Country," he says, "it was clearly worth billions of dollars." Again, Abramoff prevailed. He shot down the Istook amendment. In 1997, Sen. Thad Cochran (R-MISS) slipped a 19-word sentence into a huge appropriations bill, which banned the National Indian Gaming Commission from levying fees on and regulating the Choctaw's casino operations.

Rep. Dale Kildee (D-MI), who led the Native American Caucus in Congress, called this exemption "unprecedented." Several published reports gave Abramoff all the credit.

Actually, "Cochran did this on his own," Abramoff says. "but then he protected the language in the Senate and we took care of it in the House. It saved [the Choctaws] $1 million a year forever."[51]

THE PERFECT VILLAIN

Another coup was the tribe's astonishing land expansion thanks to the efforts of its superman, but well paid, lobbyist. In June 2000, the House and Senate passed without debate, a bill sponsored by none other than Tom DeLay, which turned over more than 9,200 acres of land to the tribe. "The Choctaws had first applied for some of this land back in 1927. I remember that, because it's the year my Dad was born," says Abramoff. "The BIA [Bureau of Indian Affairs] had repeatedly 'lost' the application over the years. The Choctaws thought it was never going to happen. But we managed to get them that land. Naturally, McCain doesn't mention this, even though he was well aware of it." To the Choctaws, it was axiomatic. Keeping DeLay happy was worth every penny of political contributions to whatever charities Abramoff told the tribe to contribute to, notwithstanding their later, and somewhat self-serving, denials.

The next big threat facing the Choctaws was the proposed installation of slot machines in Alabama racetracks close to the Mississippi border. Since their casino essentially contained nothing but slot machines, Alabamans would stop flocking across the border to gamble. Abramoff and Scanlon came up with a brilliant tactic. They realized that the population around the Alabama race tracks was predominantly black, so they persuaded municipal and church leaders to pledge their support for installing slot machines at local racetracks, if the racetrack owners would donate five percent of the gross revenue to the surrounding communities for schools, parks, and other improvements. Five percent didn't really sound like much.

"We knew that because of taxes and other charges, this 5% [contribution] would have made it unprofitable [for the racetracks]," says Abramoff. "It was Scanlon who came up with it. You couldn't say no [to this proposal], because you'd be kissing off the African-American community, and they'd block it. And you couldn't say 5% was too much because no one would believe you. And you could say yes, because it would be unprofitable. So it killed the effort to put slots at dog tracks. We called it a 'gimme five,' the five percent that killed the slots."

"*Gimme Five*"—*Investigation of Tribal Lobbying Matters*—was the title of McCain's 373-page report. "Gimme five" was a phrase that occasionally appeared in Abramoff-Scanlon e-mails. According to Abramoff, McCain simply conjured up a definition to make Abramoff sound sleazy. Because Abramoff and Scanlon later asserted their Fifth Amendment privilege before the committee, McCain never had the chance to ask them what "Gimme Five" really meant. The report stated, "This appears to be the genesis of a partnership the two would infamously label later as 'Gimme Five', [which]…came to mean kickbacks to Abramoff from payments made by any of Scanlon's Tribal clients to Scanlon."

Abramoff says, "[Gimme five] was simply a synonym for a brilliant idea. It was something that we so enjoyed so much that we started to apply it to any clever way where everybody on our side of the table could win, including us. We were the best and we deserved to be paid a lot."

But Abramoff's e-mail exchanges with Scanlon—though selectively culled by the McCain report—made them sound like callous, ruthless businessmen. However, the "gimme five" did seem to have morphed into McCain's definition by September 10, 2001:

> Abramoff: Can you let me know how much more…we would each score should Coushatta come through for this phase, and Choctaw continue to make the transfers. I need to assess where I am at for the school's sake.
>
> Scanlon: Coushatta is an absolute cake walk. Your cut on the project as proposed is at least 800k … Total [:] 1.5. mil on top of the 660. For a toal [sic] of 2.1. Not bad :) :).
>
> Abramoff: How can I say this strongly enough: YOU IZ DA MAN.
>
> Scanlon: Ill [sic] take the man title for now—but not tomorrow, you return to being the man at midnight! Let's grow that 2.1 to 5!!! We need the true give me five!
>
> Abramoff: Amen!!

Yet years later, *The Washington Post* and the McCain report would rail against Abramoff for barely lifting a finger for his tribal clients and would accuse him of "defrauding them." Abramoff's alleged exploitation was repeatedly and publicly denounced. McCain posed this question to the Choctaw's Nell Rogers: "[You] had the most interface with Mr. Abramoff… If [he] were here right now, Ms. Rogers, what would say to [him]?"

It seemed she had practiced her reply, because she didn't hesitate: "Chief Martin asked me that same question. I told him that I am past anger and bitterness, but it is the act of betrayal, betrayal of the tribe's trust, betrayal of those of us who worked with him. It is an extraordinary story of betrayal, of deliberately building trust and then betraying it."

Saving the Choctaws billions of dollars was a bizarre way to betray them. Abramoff wishes he could have asked her: "Was I and my team betraying the Choctaws when I got them over 9,000 acres put into trust? We not only got them sovereignty over the land, but had it designated as original reservation land, which meant you could put casinos on it. And what about the tens of millions of dollars worth of earmarks and appropriations—all legitimate treaty obligations—that the [U.S.] government is always very reluctant to release—which we got for them?" And, he adds, "If you put on the scale what we did for the Choctaws, the scale would topple over. And they knew it. Every year we brought to them more than the total of the ten years we billed them." Federal legislative assaults alone seemed to have justified Abramoff's fees, but apparently that was only half of what he did. Other threats could literally vaporize the Choctaws casino revenues. Abramoff says that Nell Rogers and Chief Martin had apparently forgotten these victories as well.

Once again, most of the tribe's gambling clientele did not come from its home state of Mississippi, because there were an abundance of riverboat casinos on the Mississippi to the west, and along the Mississippi Delta to the south. Essentially, the Choctaws' casino clients were Alabamans, who drove across the state border about 40 miles away. In fact, many residents of Birmingham, the state capital, were eager to drive three hours to squander their hard-earned dollars to the Choctaws' slot machines and blackjack tables, because Alabama prohibited gambling. If the state of Alabama were to sink into the sea, the Choctaws' gaming revenue would shrivel up and die. And that is exactly what was about to happen, when the GOP candidate lost the gubernatorial election in Alabama.

In 1999, Democrat Don Siegelman became governor.[52] He had run his campaign on a single issue: the establishment of a state lottery that would raise $150 million to improve public schools, considered among the worst in the nation.[53] But, according to federal law, once a state allowed gambling, including a lottery, federally recognized Indian tribes must be allowed to open and operate casinos. There was only one federally recognized tribe in Alabama, the Poarch Creek Indians, who were very eager to cash in on the casino windfall.

"Eighty percent of the Choctaw's business comes from Birmingham, Alabama. When you lose 40% of your gross revenues, your fixed costs overwhelm you," says Abramoff. "It would have essentially put them out of business."

Stopping the lottery in next-door Alabama—polls showed that it was supported by a nearly 2 to 1 margin—would not prove easy.

CHAPTER EIGHTEEN
SNAKE EYES

Alabama was the heart of the Bible Belt. Gambling—the Scriptures were unequivocal—was a sin, and the Alabama constitution specifically forbade it. Nonetheless, the new governor pushed hard for a lottery. In March 1999, by an overwhelming vote, the Alabama Legislature approved his lottery plan. "This was a joint effort of Democrats and Republicans working together," Gov. Siegelman declared. "They are giving Alabama an opportunity to vote on the most important piece of education legislation in this state's history."

Unexpectedly, however, the Alabama House also passed by a single vote a bill allowing video poker and video blackjack at the state's four private dog tracks.[54] No doubt these games of chance would siphon off many Choctaw clients. "…because if you can drive only 15 minutes to gamble, you won't drive two hours to gamble," says Abramoff. "Our job was market protection. We wanted to stop the shrinking of our clients' business." The Choctaws' nightmare was about to come true and they were terrified.

At least, there was a little breathing room. First, the Senate was scheduled to act on the video-poker bill in early April; and second, voters would have go to the polls in October to decide if the constitutional ban on gambling should be lifted. The Choctaws' lobbyist would have to find a way to walk on water. Abramoff realized he could only accomplish this with "the right hand of God." Since their College Republican days, Abramoff had kept in touch with Ralph Reed, the 19-year-old summer intern who crashed on his couch for a year. Abramoff had admired and applauded Reed's meteoric rise to national prominence as the first executive director of the Christian Coalition, founded by Pat Robertson, a TV evangelist and insignificant candidate for President.

Many gave Reed credit for helping to put Republican majorities in both houses of Congress in 1994 by mobilizing Christian conservatives. So, in a sense, Abramoff owed Reed a debt of gratitude for his career change to lobbyist from film producer. In recognition of Reed's growing power, *Time* magazine had put him on its May 15, 1995 cover, calling him the "Right Hand of God." The subtitle must have widened his ego, not to mention his boyish smile: "Meet Ralph Reed, 33. His Christian Coalition is on a Crusade to Take over U.S. Politics—and It's Working." But God works in mysterious ways. Soon, federal prosecutors and the IRS were investigating Reed's organization, and in 1997, he resigned under a cloud.

Married with four children, he immediately launched Century Strategies, a political consulting firm, which offered advice to corporations and political candidates. Karl Rove—hoping to win Reed's support for a possible George W. Bush presidential run—arranged for the Enron Corporation to become Reed's first client. The $300,000 contract more than helped pay the bills. Reed would later become a Pioneer[55] fundraiser for Bush. In early 2001, Reed would go on to suggest that Susan Ralston, Abramoff's personal assistant, become Rove's personal assistant in the White House. And Reed would also become Abramoff's direct conduit to Rove.

Debt and gratitude, as Abramoff said, is what makes the world go round. Immediately after the November 1998 election cycle, Abramoff checked in on his old buddy by e-mail: "How did things go for you and your candidates. When are you next in DC? If on a Sunday, please be sure to join me for the Redskins' quest for imperfection." Reed responded four days later: "We won 7 and lost 5. Among our winners were… Steve Windom, who is now the first GOP Lt. Governor in the history of Alabama…"[56]

"Alabama" must have pulsated when Abramoff read the e-mail. It meant that Reed had fresh contacts in Birmingham that included the Lt. Governor. A few days later, Reed sent Abramoff another e-mail, which, years later, would prove embarrassing for the born-again Christian leader: "Hey, now that I'm done with the electoral politics, I need to start humping in corporate accounts! I'm counting on you to help me with some contacts…Let's chat."

Months went by. Suddenly, in March 1999, the Alabama legislature passed the lottery referendum and the House passed the video poker bill. Abramoff's early strategy stressed that the video poker and the state lottery would be a tax on the poor. Furthermore, the lottery would be run by non-Alabamans from New York who had allegedly unsavory connections. But these arguments weren't going to change the hearts and minds Alabama voters. "Our only chance was to somehow defeat this referendum with the help of the Christian Right," says Abramoff. "The only problem was that the wages of sin, an Indian casino, would be funding this anti-gambling drive." To kill the Alabama referendum and the video poker bill as well, Abramoff needed the help of a rock-star Jesus thumper with charisma and connections. That, of course, was Ralph Reed. But why in God's name would a Christian rabble rouser come to the aid of a smoke-filled heathen Indian casino? When he had been the leader of the Christian Coalition, Reed had repeatedly declared that an abhorrence of gambling was one of the cornerstones of family values. He viewed it as "a cancer on the American body politic…[like] stealing food from the mouths of children."

Abramoff says it was natural for Reed to work on this project, because it would stop gambling in Alabama, not start it. "Ralph readily agreed to help out," Abramoff says. "He was happy and excited to be getting the work and making the money. He just wanted it kept quiet." Almost immediately, Reed prepared a vague proposal with a $20,000 per month retainer and sent it to Abramoff, who forward it to the Choctaws. The tribe expressed concerns. He quickly forwarded them to Reed: "Ralph, I spoke with Nell [Rogers of the Choctaws] this evening. She wants much more specifics. They are not scared by the number, but want to know precisely what you are planning to do for this amount. They are very sophisticated, by the way. Let's chat on the phone so we can put together what she wants. They are hot to trot…"

The very next day, March 30th, Reed responded in greater detail. His marketing campaign would pull out all the stops. It would include a full panoply of the "grassroots" armory: direct mail, multiple editorials and letters to the editor in statewide newspapers, regular statewide conference calls with key pro-family activists, letters and constituent visits to key state senators, radio ads on Christian, country, and news-talk stations, newspaper ads, petition drives in evangelical churches, informational packets to 3,000 key evangelical pastors, and more—all railing against the evils of gambling. Moments later, without waiting for a reply, Reed fired off another e-mail to apply "subtle" pressure: "Jack, we have discovered since we got into the…project that the train [is] about to leave the station…We can still win, but it does mean…it will take a significant commitment." "Significant commitment" was jargon for big bucks. A good capitalist maximizes profits whenever possible. Abramoff replied 90 minutes later: "…I will call Nell at Choctaw and get [your budget and proposal] approved…"

But who would be writing the checks to Reed? Certainly not the Choctaws. Reed was wrestling with his reputation, not his conscience. If the Choctaws paid him directly, it could leak out. Some irrefutable document—an invoice or a cancelled check—would wend its way into the hands of atheists or the press. So Abramoff, always thinking outside the box, came up with a solution. He persuaded Jonathan Blank, the firm's managing partner, to "approve [a] subcontractor arrangement" for Reed. Essentially, the firm would act as a "pass-through." The Choctaws would pay Reed by writing a check to Preston Gates. The firm would then write a check to Reed. This pass-through device would later be exploited to extremes that appeared sleazy.

Almost immediately, Alabama senators were blitzed with a stream of derogatory information about video poker. It was "the crack cocaine of gambling." In Las Vegas, 90% of female gambling addicts and 66% of male gambling addicts were addicted to video gambling. As much as 11% of Louisiana's adult population and 14% of its college-age population were addicted to video poker, etc., etc. On April 4, the video poker bill was defeated in the Alabama Senate. Immediately, a pro-gambling senator threatened to introduce a new video-poker bill, which would require—like the lottery—voter approval in the fall. Two days after the video-poker defeat, Reed submitted a $100,000 invoice for the miracle he had performed.

Nell Rogers would later tell Sen. McCain that "Reed did not want to be paid directly by a tribe with gaming interests. It was our understanding that the structure was recommended by Jack Abramoff to accommodate Mr. Reed's political concerns." Another tribal official[57] said that

Abramoff told them Reed wanted it kept secret: "It can't get out. He's Christian Coalition. It wouldn't look good if [he's] receiving money from a casino-operating tribe to oppose gaming. It would be kind of like hypocritical."

Years later, Reed would tell *The Washington Post*, "While we were clearly aware that Greenberg Traurig had certain tribal clients, we were not aware of every specific client or interest." He would later tell McCain: "While I believed at the time that those assurances were sufficient, it is now clear with the benefit of hindsight that this is a piece of business I should have declined."

By May 10th, the Choctaws had paid Reed $1,353,903.26… and counting! The video-poker bill was all but dead, but the lottery referendum loomed less than five months away. Abramoff would wonder aloud whether Reed's invoices on behalf of Abramoff's tribal clients were a true reflection of Reed's efforts.

By late August, dark clouds still threatened the Choctaw's skies. Alabamans were still supporting the lottery referendum by 61 percent. But Reed kept hammering away. Finally, an unusual coalition of black and white churches persuaded voters that the lottery money—intended to help the state's dismal public schools—would come out of the pockets of its poorest residents. By October, the referendum was defeated by a margin of 54-46.

The Choctaws rejoiced…but not for long. "The threats never ended. We did our best to delay the inevitable [Indian casino in Alabama]. We went on to stop it for the next five years," says Abramoff proudly.

It should come as no surprise that the ubiquity of these threats was disputed. One congressional observer noted, "[Abramoff's] business strategy is to tell clients that if you aren't engaged…then you are going to lose. Eventually, someone is going to introduce legislation that will have a detrimental effect, so you have to be engaged constantly. It makes a degree of sense, but it also means…[Abramoff] can justify huge fees."

McCain sprinkled throughout his 373-page report doubts about the legitimacy of the hazards facing Abramoff's tribal clients: "squelching supposedly ubiquitous threats" … "Abramoff and Scanlon, on whom the Tribe relied as experts, persuaded the Tribal council that threats to the Tribe's gaming interests were everywhere" … "to battle the numerous threats—both real and imagined—that the Tribe faced" … "through alarming them, perhaps falsely, about threats to their sovereignty or gaming interests." There was some evidence of Abramoff trying to drum up additional business from his clients, but nothing close to the extent that the McCain report suggested.

In 2004, when McCain subpoenaed all of Abramoff's e-mails, Abramoff met with Reed to warn him. Reed said he had nothing to worry about. But Reed was foolish to hide behind the disingenuous claims that his Choctaw payments came from "non-casino" revenues:

"Ralph should have gone on the offensive and defended what he did. He should have said that he was opposed to gambling and wanted to stop it spreading to Alabama. Obviously, he couldn't do anything about gambling in Mississippi, but he could do something about it in Alabama. He tried raising money from the Christian groups, but they didn't have much, so he turned to the Choctaws to help him defeat it. He should have said that he is proud of what he did, and if he had it to do again, he wouldn't do anything different. Maybe if Ralph had taken that position, no one would be accusing him of hypocrisy or playing games with the truth, and today he'd be Lt. Governor of Georgia."

CHAPTER NINETEEN
DISCRETION

Ralph Reed was not alone in insisting on strict confidentiality. According to Abramoff, the Choctaw leadership also demanded it. They wanted no one to know—especially the Poarch Creek Indians and the wealthy owner of several Alabama racetracks—that it was they who were behind the multi-million dollar anti-gambling campaign in Alabama. The chief even felt he had to conceal it from his own tribal council. So when Reed asked for "conduits," the Choctaws were only too happy to comply. That admission, however, would not have served the designs of *The Washington Post* and Sen. John McCain, because it would have diluted the impression that American Indians—naïve and unsophisticated patsies of Abramoff's—were helplessly doing this solely at their lobbyist's behest.

Indeed, Indian tribes, which are often grouped together by non-Native Americans as members of a single entity, are not necessarily striving for the same goals. It would be like saying that the English, Germans, Greeks, and Albanians are the same because they are all Europeans. Abramoff explains that Native American tribes have different cultures, languages, customs, and histories. And they were often at war with each other long before the Europeans arrived. Today, those wars are over casino turf. Since most tribes were forced from their aboriginal land to new areas, many reside close to one another. The new inter-tribal warfare is over gaming territoriality. "With almost every tribal client, I was asked to go to war against a rival tribe," Abramoff says, "and it was usually done in secret. In Mississippi, it was to thwart the efforts of the Alabama Poarch Creek Indians, located near the main gaming market of the Choctaws in Birmingham, [Alabama]. For the Louisiana] Coushattas,[58] I battled against the Jena Choctaw and the Alabama-Coushatta. Both tribes had plans to open major casinos that would have crippled my client's revenue."

Abramoff says that Choctaw Chief Martin and his leading strategist, Nell Rogers, did not bring details of their political fights to the council, because they feared that if their enemies on the council leaked them out, the repercussions would not only prove embarrassing, but disastrous. "[Martin] didn't want the [Alabama] Poarch Creek Indians—he was on excellent terms with them—to know that it was he who had robbed them of their casino," says Abramoff. "So we let the lobbyists for the [Mississippi] gulf coast and riverboat casinos take all the credit. They were bragging to their clients and the whole world that they were one ones who had stopped all these gambling threats, which was both perfect and hilarious to Martin, Rogers, and me…Our opponents never knew who was beating them up."[59]

At first, these conduit payments to Reed went via Abramoff's firm, then via Norquist's Americans for Tax Reform, and finally via Amy Ridenour's National Center for Public Policy Research. But Rogers and Martin refused to corroborate Abramoff's claim that the Choctaws wanted secrecy. When Rogers testified before McCain's committee in June 2005, she was pointedly asked why the payments for grassroots work had been "washed through organizations in order to obscure and deceive the identity of the money?" In a careful response, in which she paused to consult with C. Bryant Rogers, the tribe's outside counsel who happened to be her ex-husband, Ms. Rogers replied, "We did not have a sense of an effort to obscure the money…[But it] is a common practice in this country by businesses and political and professional groups, to use intermediaries to get their message out. Jack Abramoff had structured that." Then she immediately contradicted herself: "I am sure there probably were concerns or public perception concerns about some of the recipients about not being associated with a gaming tribe." Later, in a private interview with McCain's committee, Rogers was more specific: "Ralph Reed did not want to be paid directly by a tribe with gaming interests. It was our understanding that the structure was recommended by Jack Abramoff to accommodate Mr. Reed's political concerns."

Abramoff alleges that there was an abundance of e-mail traffic between Ms. Rogers and him, regarding the Choctaws' own desire for secrecy, but McCain chose not to release them. "Nell specifically did not want so much money going to any one pass-through, because it would arouse questions from the tribal council, so we tried to divide it up into less conspicuous amounts at her request," says Abramoff. If Reed's reputation was the sole reason Chief Martin and Rogers were willing to conceal their payments, they did a remarkable job. His financial connection to the Choctaws remained unknown for nine years, until McCain subpoenaed Abramoff's e-mails in 2004.

"Nell [Rogers] was being evasive at best and possibly much worse. The tribe went to great lengths to keep it a secret, not just to protect Reed, but to protect themselves," says Abramoff. "She didn't tell McCain everything." Why was this omission so important? In late 2001, Abramoff started transferring the Choctaws grassroots work from Ralph Reed to Michael Scanlon. Yet the Choctaws continued to write checks to "conduits." With Reed and his reputation no longer germane, why would the tribe keep doing this? Scanlon wasn't a hypocritical Christian activist clandestinely using Indian casino money to stop the spread of gambling. He didn't have a reputation to protect.

McCain realized that this fly in the ointment required some kind of explanation. "In earlier grassroots efforts to protect its market share," he wrote, "the [Choctaws] had grown accustomed to sending payments through conduits at Abramoff's direction." In other words, the McCain report claimed that the Choctaws had become hooked. They couldn't help themselves. They couldn't stop sending their checks to conduits.

But then McCain slipped up. He included something in his report that undermined the very thesis he was so artfully manufacturing. He allowed Rogers to reveal—albeit inadvertently—why the Choctaws had continued to write checks to conduits after Reed's departure, which contradicted her earlier testimony. She stated that Abramoff had told her that even though Scanlon's fees were high—but no higher than Reed's—she understood that this was "the cost of operating under the radar." Even Donald Kilgore, the Choctaw's attorney general, seated at the table next to Rogers, confirmed that "…[Scanlon's] prices were high…[but] not out of line with other billings from other contractors for similar work that we have experienced."

So with Reed's reputation no longer on the line, why would the Choctaws continue paying such high fees clandestinely? The answer was obvious: The tribe wanted to keep "operating under the radar." And Chief Martin and Rogers were even willing to pay a premium to do so. The tribe wanted the conduits as badly as Reed. This confirmed what Abramoff had maintained. The tribe was delighted to keep paying "conduits" so that their enemies in Alabama would never know who was opposing them. Now, instead of writing checks to the former Abramoff-Reed conduits: Preston Gates, Americans for Taxpayer Reform, Toward Tradition, and National Center for Public Policy Research—the tribe began writing checks to Abramoff-Scanlon conduits: Capital Campaign Strategies, American International Center, Capital Athletic Foundation. In other words, if the Choctaws had paid the earlier conduits for the services that Abramoff-Reed had rendered and were now paying the new conduits for the services Abramoff-Scanlon rendered, what difference did it make to the Choctaws as long as gambling in Alabama was kept at bay?

What were Reed's profit margins compared to Scanlon's? Only Reed knows. Profits do not have to be disclosed and big profits are not illegal. Reed's profits may have even exceeded Scanlon's.

And if some of Scanlon's profits were sent to entities controlled by Abramoff as a referral fee, rather than in a single large and conspicuous check to Scanlon—(the Choctaws preferred smaller checks so as not to draw attention to the fact they were screwing their brethren, the Poarch Creek Indians)— what possible difference did it make? In many instances, referral fees do not have to be disclosed and are not illegal. Lawyers pay referral fees all the time, but are not required to disclose them to clients. A mortgage broker receives a referral fee from a lender, but is not required to inform the borrower, who may have fared better with another lender. Orthopedic surgeons routinely receive referral fees or stock options from the very companies that manufacture joint replacement implants that the surgeon uses without ever informing their patients.

McCain, *The Washington Post*, and federal prosecutors, however, insisted on calling them "kickbacks," a term that imputes criminality, because what Abramoff and Scanlon did somehow fell into something called "Honest-Service Fraud." This is a catch-all, constitutionally vague, selectively prosecuted statute, of which every person in the country is probably guilty. Failure to provide one's "honest services"—whatever that means—to your boss, your client, your wife, your friend is now a federally felony. In other words, all civil contract disputes are potentially a federal felony. Certainly, many lawyers, mortgage brokers, and orthopedic surgeons, who have accepted referral fees, are also guilty of this crime, which has given federal prosecutors magical powers to indict anyone they set their sights on. McCain—who was not exactly a templar of full disclosure—declared: "Abramoff owed the tribes he represented a duty, a duty to disclose his financial stake in the multimillion dollar contracts he was steering Michael Scanlon's way. That he and Scanlon did not speak up was immoral. It was unethical and ultimately it may have been illegal." In fact, Abramoff and Scanlon did nothing illegal. What's more, McCain knew that Abramoff was not alone in profiting or receiving a "finder's fee" from a vendor like Scanlon. McCain had tucked into a footnote deep in his report something that perhaps he hoped no one would notice. Reed, the report added, had apparently been doing the same thing:

> **Documents, however, indicate that at least with respect to one project, Reed received more than simply the management fee he itemized on his invoices: apparently, he…[received] additional commissions derived from profits that were built into costs charged by vendors (associated with Reed) to Preston Gates, which were likely expensed to the Tribes.**

Abramoff continued to defeat legislative attempts to tax the Choctaws out of billions of dollars on the federal level and to beat back all gambling efforts in Alabama that would have probably wiped out their casino. Essentially, the fee was the same. What the tribe had paid Reed, it was now paying Scanlon. Schmidt and McCain both asserted that Abramoff somehow defrauded or betrayed his Indian clients and implied that Scanlon's referral fees to Abramoff were illegal, despite the fact that undisclosed referral fees are not uncommon and legal in the United States. Did Scanlon defraud them by failing to perform all of the work Scanlon promised to do? If Scanlon were goofing off, how could Abramoff possibly know? As with Reed's grassroots operation, Abramoff had no first-hand knowledge of the nuts and bolts of Scanlon's grassroots operation. Abramoff did not monitor and never visited Scanlon's company. Even Abramoff's arch enemy, McCain, acknowledged this. At a public hearing in 2004, in which Scanlon also took the Fifth, McCain directly addressed the former public-relations whiz kid, who was seated across from him at the witness table: "…in reading all the testimony, and all the e-mails, it strikes me that you were working both sides of the street, if I understand this thing. You managed to not only con the tribe, but con Mr. Abramoff…When did you come up with this scheme to not only con the tribe but con your partner?"McCain was inadvertently letting Abramoff off the hook.

But to what degree did Scanlon defraud the Choctaws? What was the dollar amount? Certainly not a 100% fraud. Was it a 50%, or merely a 10% fraud? On this point there is much equivocation, perhaps because fraud can be difficult to quantify. But clearly, Scanlon was not just sunning himself on the beach, drinking pina coladas, and ripping off his Indian clients, which is what the McCain Report would lead us to believe. Indeed, there was documentary evidence that Scanlon's intervention might have actually saved the day for the Choctaws, which McCain may have deliberately tried to conceal. On October 17 and 22, 2002, the Republican Governor's Association received two political contributions from Scanlon's company, Capitol Campaign Strategies. Each was for $250,000.[60] Within days, that group contributed $600,000 to Rep. Bob Riley (R-ALA).[61] He was running against then-governor Democrat Don Siegelman. Like Ralph Reed, but unlike Siegelman, Riley was vehemently opposed to gambling and refused to accept any contributions from gambling interests. In a very controversial election and by a margin of only 3,120 votes—the narrowest in state history—Riley defeated Siegelman, much to the relief of the Choctaws, because for the next four years the tribe would not have to lose sleep over any renewed efforts to legalize gambling in Alabama.

THE PERFECT VILLAIN

McCain, however, may have taken steps to protect his GOP colleagues from the scope of his investigation. In his report, McCain omitted critical information on how Alabama Gov. Bob Riley was targeted by Abramoff's so-called influence-peddling scheme. Riley, a Republican, who won the election in November 2002, was reelected in 2006.[62]

In a December 2002 e-mail, Abramoff wrote to an aide what he would like to see Riley do in return for the "help" he received from Abramoff's tribal clients. The Chief of the Mississippi Choctaws "definitely wants Riley to shut down the Poarch Creek[63] operation…including his announcing that anyone caught gambling there can't qualify for a state contract or something like that." The e-mail showed that Scanlon's $500,000 contribution may have played the key role in tipping the scales in Riley's favor over Siegelman. Even though their contest was the closest and most disputed gubernatorial election in Alabama history, McCain failed to make this e-mail public even after the release of his report. Indeed, even Abramoff admitted that the Choctaws had spent $13 million "to get the governor of Alabama elected to keep gaming out of Alabama so it wouldn't hurt [the tribe's casino]." Abramoff later added, "Isn't it worth spending $13 million to save your $300 million business—at least for the next four years?"

Years later, in a 2008 interview, Siegelman maintained that Karl Rove who was responsible for corrupting the 2002 gubernatorial election. "Abramoff was, I think, Rove's bag man…[and by] following the money [and] Abramoff…a lot of [the money] came into Alabama…And it's also interesting that there has been no federal investigation of Ralph Reed's involvement, of Grover Norquist's involvement and the fact that they were used as conduits by Rove and Abramoff…to destroy me."[64]

What was truly unsettling was that McCain omitted from the appendix of his report Scanlon's entire ledger book. It could have been inserted with the click of a mouse. It required far more effort for McCain to release only "snapshots," his terminology for selective excerpts, from Scanlon's ledger. For example, regarding Scanlon's two crucial $250,000 contributions to Bob Riley's gubernatorial campaign, McCain made the following disingenuous statement: "During this period [around the fall of 2002], the [Scanlon] ledger also reflects a few incidental payments that probably provided little value to the Louisiana Coushatta or the Agua Caliente [two of Abramoff's clients], for example, a payment of $250,000 to the Republican Governors [sic] Association…" Fourteen pages later, the second $250,000 payment to the Governors' Association showed up. But in McCain's report, his "snapshot" of Scanlon's ledger came to a sudden stop in April 2002. The next "snapshot" resumed in January 2003. The critical period between April 2002 and January 2003—which includes Scanlon's two $250,000 payments on October 14 and 22, 2002—were omitted.

McCain made these omissions, despite the fact that the media had widely reported that Scanlon's two $250,000 payments had been made indirectly to Riley's gubernatorial campaign in the summer of 2004. Scanlon's $500,000 donation was the single largest that the Republican Governors' Association received in 2002. And yet McCain's report, released two years later in June 2006, did not mention this. McCain also failed to mention the possible affect these contributions had on Riley's victory or the definitive and beneficial affect Riley's victory had on the future prospects of the Choctaw casino. Why might McCain omit this? The answer was obvious. It would have undermined his claims that Abramoff and Scanlon, who had been so effective in defending their client's interests, had defrauded the Choctaws.

During her public testimony before the McCain committee, Nell Rogers was specifically asked to what degree the tribe had been defrauded. Had the tribe ever received any reports from Abramoff and Scanlon? "Yes, sir," she replied. "We received detailed reports. We know that the work was done. We also had independent means of determining that work was done." Of course, she didn't want to appear that the tribal leaders and its chief strategist had been asleep at the wheel while Scanlon was vacuuming millions of dollars out of the Choctaw treasury. Was she now saying that a certain portion of Scanlon's work had not been fraudulent? "The work was done," she repeated. "What appears to be fraudulent was the overcharges and the conspiracy…"

But that vague response proved less than satisfactory. What exactly did she mean? One of McCain's Senate colleagues pressed her for more details. She was asked how much would she attribute to fraud or overpayment or padding of the books? Kilgore, the tribe's attorney general, jumped in before Rogers could respond. "May I inject here?…[W]e are not able to give you the amount of harm in money terms. The reason is this. We are in very sensitive settlement negotiations with various parties…[and] it will jeopardize our ability to settle that civil matter with those parties." If the Choctaws were forced to admit under oath the dollar amount of the alleged "rip-off," the tribe would be unable to recoup an amount larger than what had been stated in these congressional hearings. In other words, the Choctaws preferred not to respond, because it wanted the option of overcharging—in essence defrauding—the "various parties" with whom the tribe was negotiating. And who were those parties? Abramoff's two former law firms—Preston Gates and Greenberg Traurig—to whom the Choctaws had paid his lobbying fees.

Marc Levin, Ms. Rogers' former boyfriend, says that over the many years that the two of them had spoken, the Choctaws had always been very pleased with the services Abramoff had provided them. Now, of course, Levin—a close friend of Abramoff's and Ms. Rogers'—must have been experiencing conflicting emotions, because it was he who had introduced the Choctaws to Abramoff. "Nell and the Chief are not dumb people. They are very sophisticated. They had long relationships with many politicians," says Levin. "There is no way they would have kept [Abramoff] on the payroll [for ten years] if he hadn't been providing them with great services."

Although Levin had not read Kilgore's testimony, he knew exactly why the Choctaws had turned against Abramoff. "It was good business," says Levin. "It allowed them to sue GT [Greenberg Traurig] for all of Jack's lobbying fees. GT later settled because they didn't want all of their e-mail traffic becoming public." Abramoff agrees with Levin. "It's a cynical world out there. The Choctaws won a huge settlement from Greenberg Traurig. They ended up getting all that work I did for them for free. And McCain and Schmidt want you to believe these people were defrauded and are stupid?"[65]

The evidence did seem to support Abramoff's claims that he provided the Choctaws with extraordinary lobbying services for nearly ten years. What was troubling was that *The Washington Post* and Sen. John McCain seemed to go to such lengths to oversimplify and distort the complex world of lobbying in Indian Country and to essentially omit anything good Abramoff had done on behalf of his tribal clients.

That doesn't mean businessman Abramoff was a saint. For example, he told a reporter in 2000 that "[I]t really bothers me to see them have to spend so much money...We want them to be able to spend this money on the reservation. I know that's hard to believe, coming from a lobbyist, but it's true."

McCain's report also raised the issue of the accuracy of Abramoff's billable hours. Although Abramoff was not a lawyer, the truthfulness of billable hours for many practicing lawyers in America would probably be a tender subject. The report claimed that one $5,000 payment was incorrectly billed, which gave "rise to concerns that Abramoff had defrauded the Tribe…"Abramoff's billing records were also examined and challenged that the House Government Reform Committee published on September 29, 2006.

Abramoff responded to these allegations by pointing out that the tribes, with the exception of the Choctaws, paid fixed monthly retainers to his firm: "The idea that someone could take the internal billing records of a law firm and deduce from them fraud and deception is absurd. Law firms routinely require their non-lawyer lobbyists—often working on fixed retainers from clients—to submit [time sheets.] While these are the normal tedium of those who have chosen the legal profession—along with filing briefs, reading statutes, and other forms of torture—the non-lawyer lobbyists in Washington uniformly hate this massive waste of time, and frequently will submit their [time sheets] in a manner so that they just get out of the work as soon as possible. [This leads] to inaccurate entries, but there is no consequence here, since it does not matter in the least to a fixed-retainer client, and since [these time sheets] are not created for public consumption—only to satisfy the arcane rules of America's barrister class."

CHAPTER TWENTY
THE GAME

In Abramoff's early days at Preston Gates, it became clear to his colleagues that their new Republican recruit was playing in a league of his own. He was a gifted fundraiser and schmoozer—the two linchpins of a successful lobbyist. Like anyone in his line of work, entertainment and fundraising events provided an opportunity to develop relationships with staff and elected officials. But Abramoff began orchestrating a crusade of ingratiation simply by employing the standard paraphernalia but with greater intensity: inviting a congressman, senator, or staffer to a sold-out football game at an exclusive luxury box sponsored by the Choctaws; to Scotland for a round of golf at the storied "Old Course," or to complimentary meals at Signatures—an upscale restaurant Abramoff would open in early 2002—not to mention providing a continuous flood of campaign contributions to politician's fundraising and charity events, as well as his pet PACs. Through these mechanisms, not only did Abramoff gain access to a congressman's ear so he could plead his client's case, but he utterly overwhelmed his intended victim with an irrepressible sense of gratitude. There was nothing illegal about all of this, as long as there was never any specific quid pro quo. The entire arrangement was implicit. Therefore, it never crossed the threshold of bribery.

"In the course of lobbying, a lobbyist regularly provides meals and gratuities and favors," says Abramoff. "They are seen as the way for people to do business with the decision makers, so that you can talk to them about an issue. Developing a social relationship obviously costs something—making legal contributions to their campaigns, PACs, and so forth. It's a tragedy of the system. And I am guilty of that. Are others guilty? Yes. Is everybody guilty of it? Yes. But they're probably not going to wind up in the cell next to me." Abramoff says he simply worked harder and succeeded better at the game that every single one of his competitors played.

What McCain's report did was to repeatedly minimize, deny, or ignore Abramoff's many victories and accomplishments. The report seemed to labor at underscoring Abramoff's defeats—what few there were—implying that Abramoff was a mediocre lobbyist, whose only goal was to defraud his clients. One typical example of alleged fraud was the infamous and widely reported golf trip to Scotland in 2000 for DeLay, his staff, and others. The Choctaws were allegedly duped into contributing $65,000 to this "educational" expedition. Nell Rogers told McCain that the Choctaws never intended for those funds to help finance this golf trip. "Rather, it was intended as a donation for some anti-tax and anti-NACS [National Association of Convenience Stores] work," she told McCain.

Another minor example was the $25,000 in consulting fees the Choctaws paid to Liberty Consulting Services, a firm set up by Tony Rudy, while he was still serving as DeLay's Deputy Chief of Staff. Rogers claimed Abramoff totally misled her into urging the Choctaws make this contribution. Abramoff smiles when he read that: "The tribe knew why they were doing this. I discussed the strategy many times with Nell [Rogers]. [The Choctaws] wanted to have every oar in the water vis-à-vis DeLay. Look at how much he'd done for them."

One of the conditions of his employment at Preston Gates had been that he would only represent clients consistent with his conservative ideology. What he did next was to take that concept to a higher power, by creating a loose federation of conservative interest groups that would come to the assistance of one another. It was a right-wing defense pact. These included think tanks, political charities, and other groups affiliated with, for example, Ralph Reed (right-wing Christians), Grover Norquist (anti-tax), Tom DeLay (Republican Party), Amy Ridenour (public policy), and Italia Frederici (conservative environmentalists), to name a few.

"Nell Rogers actually praises Abramoff in the [McCain] report," says Michael Goland, Abramoff's longtime friend. "She was fascinated by how Jack arranged for disparate groups to come together to support Choctaw Indian interests." These groups gave credibility and standing and support for Choctaw Indian initiatives when these groups had no apparent vested interest in or involvement with the Choctaw's primary objectives. This was a sea change in the way lobbying was done in D.C. It was group bonding for the sake of a conservative common cause.

"What Rogers and McCain failed to point out was that this mutuality had a reciprocity that required Choctaws to provide finance and political support and cover for these other groups," says Goland. "It was implicitly understood that everything has a quid pro quo and its lobbyists was the one who moved the pieces on the chessboard so that everybody can get their primary goals met. It is disingenuous for John McCain to claim not to have understood this, considering his close ties to lobbyists." In a short period of time, Abramoff formulated and assembled a potent, high-powered team that produced results for his clients that his colleagues and competitors could only dream of.

"Lobbying is very simple," says Abramoff. "A client comes to you. Someone has recommended you or has read about you. They tell you about this problem. If the government does this or that, it will hurt my business. Can you stop this legislation or can you get legislation passed to help me? As a lobbyist, first you determine if you can have an impact. Do you know people on the Hill who are in charge of this stuff? Do you know the players? Can you get to them? Can you get to the leadership: How do you stop this bill or get an earmark inserted?

"Everybody has relationships. You have to know people. First, you go to the people you know, usually the staff. You tell them here's what we're trying to do. Does it make sense? What do they recommend? Can they get this to their boss? You start to build an army to get them on your client's side. You're making friends all the time. You have a suite at the Redskins. You spend three hours with them. You play golf. You have dinner with them, so you can talk to them about the issue. The worst thing you can do is to approach someone the first time you meet them and ask for help. That not how human nature works.

"On top of that, members have fundraising issues. Congressmen [who run for reelection every two years] are paranoid about it. Do I have enough money to get reelected and keep my job? If you're already a donor or on their finance committee, you will get a hearing.

"Now, members of Congress do not want to do the work. They're too busy. The lobbyist does it for them. If you want a member to introduce something into the *Congressional Record* or write a bill, you'd better do it for them. They may change it, but you do the heavy lifting for them. You got to work the committee, the leadership, and both sides of the house, and you have to lobby both political parties…Most of the time, you can handle it through staff. It's the staff that wields the true power."

One of the very first things Abramoff did—which made the GOP leadership very happy—was to redirect the flow of tribal wampum from their traditional allies, the Democrats, into the pocket of the Republicans. For example, in 1999, the Choctaws donated $100,000 to the Republican State Elections Committee. By 2000, the Choctaws and Abramoff's other clients had funneled more than ten million dollars at his behest in unreported donations to a network of conservative groups. In 1995, the Center for Responsive Politics, a non-profit and nonpartisan research group, released a survey that demonstrated why Abramoff's clout was so effective and pervasive on Capital Hill. Since 1999, the study showed that Abramoff and his tribal clients had made political contributions to 210 members of Congress. Of the top 25 beneficiaries who received $21,500 or more, only five were Democrats and twenty were Republicans.

The top recipient was Republican Sen. Conrad Burns[66] from Montana, the longest-serving GOP senator in state history, who happened to sit on the powerful Senate Appropriations Committee. He was also the chairman of its Subcommittee for the Department of the Interior, the department that handled Native American affairs. Burns—who was once under federal investigation in the Abramoff probe, but was surprisingly cut loose—was the brightest light a lobbyist could possibly hope to find. Like Ohio Rep. Robert Ney, who was eager to help out Abramoff's fleet of floating casinos a thousand miles away in Florida, the Montana senator went out of his way to pamper the Saginaw Chippewa, one of Abramoff's tribal clients, whose Michigan casino is about 1000 miles from the voters that Burns represented.

Campaigning for reelection in 2006, in which he would soon be defeated because of his relationship with the disgraced lobbyist, Burns told an interviewer: "This Abramoff guy is a bad guy…I wish he'd never been born to be right honest with you, because he's done a terrible, terrible thing to our Native American community." Although saddened by Burns' comments, Abramoff says he was proud of the millions of dollars he had won for his tribal client, the Saginaw Chippewa: "Every appropriation we wanted from Sen. Conrad Burns' committee we got."

While Abramoff and his clients regularly gave the maximum amount allowed in personal campaign contributions,[67] the Center for Responsive Politics survey "did not begin to account for my real muscle in this arena. It was peanuts compared to the real money I raised money for the Republican Party committees," says Abramoff. These were the so-called soft money accounts of the 501c4s,[68] the so-called 527 groups, and the Political Action Committees or PACs.[69]

"I would respond to requests from senators for very large sums, including one insistent request from the venerable senior [Democratic] senator from Hawaii, [Daniel] Inouye," Abramoff says. "Senator Inouye, a paragon of senatorial virtue, who took every opportunity to berate and belittle me at [McCain's] Senate Indian Affairs Kangaroo Court [hearing], pushed his way directly to [Choctaw] Chief Martin to request $50,000 for the Democratic Senatorial Campaign Committee, of which he would be a major beneficiary, reminding both Martin and me that he was always there for the Choctaws whenever they needed him."

CHAPTER TWENTY-ONE
MOBUTU

As the fight was being waged in defense of the remote Mariana Islands and the humble Choctaw reservation, Abramoff managed to score a gaggle of other clients as well. In order to attend to their needs, he had begun hiring associates, mostly former congressional staffers, into a force majeure that became widely known as "Team Abramoff." Most members were former Capitol Hill staffers or lawmakers, which essentially was what all lobbying shops were composed of. As a reward, Preston Gates moved their budding Buddha into a bigger office. His hourly rate would soon soar to 500 dollars an hour.

Topping the list of his controversial clients was Mobutu Sese Seku, the diabolical kleptomaniacal dictator of the former Belgian Congo. In dozens of published reports, summarizing Abramoff's career, this incident was simply heaped on all the others without further elaboration. The implication was that evil Abramoff had no scruples. He would represent anyone, no matter how reprehensible. In fact, he seemed to go out of his way to find offensive clients to represent.

In 1995, the rule of Mobutu Sese Seku, a brutal and corrupt dictator who had led the Congo for over 30 years, was dissolving. From the neighboring country of Rwanda, rebel leader Laurent Kabila was preparing to lead an invasion that would eventually topple Mobutu at the cost of tens of thousands of lives. Abramoff was approached by Andre Soussan, a French journalist, who persuaded him that Mobutu, who knew his days were numbered, was ready to go into exile "and turn over the reins to the forces of democracy," says Abramoff. "Amazingly, Mobutu had agreed to do this, but only if he were able to come to the United States to announce that decision." To accomplish this, Mobutu needed a U.S. visa.

In July 1995, Abramoff told a reporter for *Influence*, a sister publication of *Legal Times*, "Everyone agrees that if something is not done soon, there are going to be millions of deaths in Zaire." On a pro bono basis, Abramoff lobbied several Republican members of Congress on Mobutu's behalf. Suspicious that the dictator was using this "announcement" as a ploy to cling to power a bit longer, President Clinton's State Department refused to grant him an entry visa.

Abramoff remained somewhat bitter about how the media exaggerated and portrayed his minor role: "The impression is that I'm immoral, that I will help anybody and everybody who will pay me. I have no conscience. I helped the apartheid government. I made a movie in defiance of UN sanctions. I even supported someone as evil as Mobutu Sese Seku… Unfortunately for me, reporters did not do their due diligence. All they had to do was dig up my letter to the editor to *The Seattle Times*, and they would have understood my motivations. Instead, reporters did what they do best. They stated that I had supported the effort, without giving me an opportunity to explain why, even when my explanation was in the public sector, available on Lexis-Nexis."

Abramoff believed that if his efforts had succeeded the resulting carnage from the 1997 invasion and overthrow of Mobutu would have been "dramatically reduced."

CHAPTER TWENTY-TWO
INTRIGUE

How was it possible that Abramoff could waltz into another cesspool about which the media would later trill? According to him, he was just doing his job—wooing a powerful and wealthy client for big profit and cementing his all-important relationship with House Majority Whip Tom DeLay.

"Usually the whip—the one in charge of lining up the votes—will not rise to prominence, but Tom did so because he was incredible at getting through legislation, despite razor-thin majorities. Not only did the conservative movement trust him, but his power really flowed from his ability to raise so much money to help out those in close congressional races," says Abramoff. "

Abramoff's single-minded strategy was to do anything and everything to please the DeLay, whose take-no-prisoners style of politics invariably produced stunning results for virtually every Abramoff client. Sure, he did what was obvious. Only a "troglodyte" couldn't figure out what every lobbyist knew: contributions buy access. He advised every client to contribute early and often to any and all political organizations and charities dear to DeLay's heart. But what could not be purchased, acquired, or imparted was Abramoff's blend of intellect, humor, and charisma. This allowed him to forge an ideological and philosophical bond so profound that many years later in 2007, when DeLay published his defiant memoir—*No Retreat, No Surrender*—he could still not bring himself to vilify Abramoff as had so many of his former friends and colleagues.

Nonetheless, eight years later, the media would excavate documents and draw unsettling inferences about Abramoff's involvement with the directors of NaftaSib—a powerful and well-connected Russian oil and gas conglomerate—and the controversial Tom DeLay. One published report called it "a corrupt deal brokered by Jack Abramoff [that] led Tom DeLay to sell a critical foreign-aid vote to the Russian mob." If true, Abramoff—a chest-thumping anti-communist super patriot—had sold out his country for profit.

Of course, DeLay and Abramoff contend that these allegations were absurd confabulations of liberal journalists yearning for a Ludlum thriller in order to sell more newspapers. And not unexpectedly, the dutiful Justice Department—taking its cue from the press—issued subpoenas in early 2006, seeking information on Abramoff's work with "any department, ministry, or office holder or agent of the Russian government."

As a cold warrior in the 1980s, Abramoff had cast himself in minor roles, performing on the periphery of the world stage, first with Col. Oliver North in Iran-Contra and then with anti-Communist "freedom fighters" at the Jamba Jubilee in Angola. Now, it would seem he was poised to take a supporting role in shaping world events in Russia after the collapse of the Soviet Union, and a leading role in "chang[ing] the whole dynamic of the Middle East."

Many books and articles have been written about the Russian economy's ensuing chaos after the sudden and largely unanticipated dissolution of the Soviet Union on December 25, 1991. Collusion between ex-Soviet security services and the new "oligarchs" led to the looting of virtually all state-owned assets. The Russian crown jewels were its vast oil and gas deposits, with proven reserves second to Saudi Arabia's. In order to protect their profits and avoid taxes, the new robber barons became proficient in creating corporate shells and illicitly chartered banks to move their billions of dollars offshore to the Bahamas, the Island of Jersey, and the Netherlands, where corporate ownership need not be disclosed.

The Cold War was over. Republicans, like Abramoff, were gloating. The Great Communicator, Ronald Reagan, had pulled off the impossible and deserved all the credit. Now the "end of history" could be etched in stone—in other words, the American political and economic system was the final word on the subject. However, there were a few loose ends. One of them was the former superpower's nuclear arsenal. Therefore, the United States launched a "strategic partnership" with Russia to encourage and protect its new democratic and capitalist "reforms," but most importantly to ensure that nuclear weapons and technology did not fall into the hands of terrorists or rogue nations. As a result, it was incumbent on America to pour foreign aid and International Monetary Fund loans into Russia to keep its fledgling democracy afloat.

In the early 1990s, Russia's public debt soared as its economy faltered and its tax-collecting abilities fizzled. Many ordinary Russian citizens, now far worse off than under Communism, were freezing and starving. It was no secret that Russia would soon be forced to default on its international loans, but the Republican-controlled Congress was reluctant to bail out its erstwhile foe yet again.

In 1997, Russian President Boris Yeltsin's Prime Minister, Viktor Chernomyrdin, would formally ask the United States for additional economic aid. But it would also be prudent for the Russian government to quietly cultivate access with the most powerful and influential members of the Congress. What the press and prosecutors later suspected was that there had been the desire to establish a discreet, backdoor channel. That was allegedly finessed with the utmost skill by NaftaSib[70], a low-profile Moscow-based oil-and-gas conglomerate. The company was run by two close friends of Chernomyrdin's, the shrewd and charming Alexander Koulakovsky and Marina V. Nevskaya.

"Alexander is about six feet tall and weighs about 250 pounds. He has silver hair, a broad and handsome face, and is very distinguished looking. Marina has dark hair and is in her early 40s. She's about four inches shorter and pretty. She is beyond brilliant, possibly one of the most brilliant people [I ever met] at any stage of all of my dealings. She speaks a dozen languages fluently. [During the Cold War] she wrote all the Russian-Vietnamese textbooks for the military," says Abramoff. Like many elite, Koulakovsky and Nevskaya traveled in bullet-proof cars and were protected by bodyguards armed with machine guns.

"NaftaSib's line of business is as shady as it is menacing," according to Mark Ames, editor-in-chief of *eXile*, a Moscow-based online magazine. "[NaftaSib] names as its biggest clients the Defense Ministry and the Ministry of Interior, and its top managers reportedly" are linked to Soviet-era internal security and intelligence agencies. Nevskaya is a former instructor at the Military Diplomatic Academy, a training school for Russian military intelligence agents. Steve Biegun, a senior Russia expert for the Senate Foreign Relations Committee in 1997, had similar misgivings about NaftaSib. At that time, he said he deliberately blocked a meeting that Nevskaya had sought with committee chairman Jesse Helms (R-NC). "Biegun had his own agenda," says Abramoff. "Others had them checked out by the NSA [National Security Agency] and said they were just fine."

The Russian conglomerate had the savvy to hire attorney Julius "Jay" Kaplan of the Washington office of Cadwalader Wickersham and Taft, one of the country's oldest and most venerated law firms, founded in 1792. Shortly before Chernomyrdin's official visit to the United States, Koulakovsky asked Kaplan whom else the prime minister should meet. Kaplan didn't hesitate—House Majority Whip Tom DeLay. But Kaplan didn't have the access, so he contacted someone who did. "In 1988, Pat Robertson ran for president. Ben Waldman, [one of Abramoff's future SunCruz partners], was his communications director, and Jay [Kaplan] was Pat's attorney," says Abramoff. "Ben introduced me to Jay and we became fast friends." Kaplan then introduced Abramoff to Koulakovsky, because he wanted to develop relations with U.S. politicians.

In February 1997, Chernomyrdin arrived in Washington and met with Vice President Al Gore. "[During this visit] I arranged a meeting between Tom and the prime minister," says Abramoff. "Tom gave Chernomyrdin a bull whip as a gift. They got along so well that he invited Tom to Moscow later that year, which I also helped arrange."

Abramoff was promptly rewarded. Several days after Chernomyrdin's departure, Abramoff notified the clerk of the House of Representatives that he was representing a new client—Chelsea Commercial Enterprises Ltd.—"to generate support for [the] Russian government's policies... [including] progressive market reforms" and bilateral trade.

In 1997, Abramoff received $260,000 in fees from Chelsea. What was Chelsea Commercial Enterprises? A shell corporation registered in the Bahamas, whose address later resurfaced at a post office box on the island of Jersey, a semi-independent tax haven off the coast of France.

On January 15, 1997, a month before Chernomyrdin's visit, "Nationscorp," a mysterious Russian entity, made a $49,975 contribution to the US Family Network[71], a "pro-family" and "moral fitness" political nonprofit, which Edwin Buckham had set up a few months earlier to provide money to evangelical Christian charities. Buckham—who would later pocket more than one-third of all contributions collected by the Network—was DeLay's chief of staff. Unfortunately, Buckham exercised poor judgment in appointing Chris Greeslin as titular head of the Network. This garrulous pastor would later make some extraordinary claims that would trigger the federal probe. "Nationscorp" funneled these funds to Buckham's Network through the London law firm of James & Sarch. In a promotional letter, DeLay would later praise the Network, even though it had only a single paid employee, as a "powerful nationwide organization dedicated to restoring our government to citizen control."

The Network purchased a Capitol Hill townhouse, located only a few blocks from DeLay's congressional office. The townhouse also served as the Washington office for DeLay's political action committee—Americans for a Republican Majority (ARMPAC). Buckham's nonprofit then did some extravagant things. It helped defray the cost of a few games at Abramoff's leased luxury suite at FedExField, home of the Washington Redskins. Greeslin later told *The Boston Globe* that Abramoff personally thanked him for paying for the suite, and now feels "duped" into heading Buckham's Network. "We had no idea it was just a shell operation for Abramoff," Greeslin said, referring to himself and other volunteer board members. The Network also paid for a few games at a leased skybox at MCI Center—home of the NHL Capitols and the NBA Wizards—"at the request of a donor," who turned out to be Abramoff. "These contributions came from companies in Europe which were related to Koulakovsky… and were generated at Ed Buckham's request," sources say.

Six months later in June 1997, Buckham flew to Moscow to smooth the way for DeLay's upcoming visit. Soon thereafter, an advance team from Abramoff's lobbying firm also arrived in the Soviet capital. Accompanying them were several conservative scholars and journalists,[72] whose itineraries Abramoff had arranged. This was a carbon copy of his strategy to promote other clients, such as the Mariana Islands and Choctaw Indians.

Buckham's trip and DeLay's upcoming trip to Moscow were funded entirely by the National Center for Public Policy Research (NCPPR), another conservative political nonprofit in Washington. Abramoff also served on its board, and DeLay was quoted on its website extolling the NCPPR as "THE CENTER for conservative communications." Amy Ridenour—Abramoff's old friend whom he had persuaded long ago not to run against him for Chairman of the College Republicans—was the Center's executive director. So where did Ridenour get the funds for these extravagance expeditions to Moscow? They came directly from Abramoff's mysterious Russian client, Bahamian-registered Chelsea Commercial Enterprises Ltd.

A few weeks after Buckham's return from Moscow, DeLay invited Koulakovsky, NaftaSib's chief executive, to Houston. On July 18, 1997, Koulakovsky attended a luncheon with nearly a dozen oil and gas executives, which Abramoff also attended. DeLay was delayed and missed his flight to Houston, so he arranged for his wife Christine and his deputy chief of staff, Susan Hirschmann, to be Koulakovsky's hosts. Years later, DeLay's spokesman would defend his boss as having "viewed [the luncheon] as a routine way to showcase Houston to businessmen interested in expanding trade."

What would later rivet the attention of reporters and investigators was that exactly six days later, Buckham's US Family Network received a second mysterious contribution—this one for $250,000—once again through the London-based law firm of James & Sarch.

Nearly three weeks after that, DeLay and his entourage jetted off in first class on August 5th for a six-day Moscow visit. He was accompanied by Buckham, as well as his deputy Hirschmann and her husband. Also tagging along were Kaplan and the executive director of the NCPPR—the organization that was "officially" funding the junket—Amy Ridenour and her husband. For Abramoff, this would be the first of many trips with DeLay: "[DeLay] was very gentlemanly and did not fuss over small stupidities," says Abramoff. "Some members of Congress can be bears on the road…He was just a nice guy. That was true on all our trips."

Even though he had been officially invited by Prime Minister Chernomyrdin, DeLay's primary motiveation for making this long journey was to persuade the Russian government to stop persecuting evangelical Christians. Apparently, a bill pending in the Russian legislature would have banned proselytizing by any Christian sect, other than the Russian Orthodox Church. DeLay buttonholed a number of government officials, including Chernomyrdin, and lobbied hard for greater religious freedom in Russia. "I remember we had breakfast with a number of Christian activists, and Tom was very moved by what they had to say," says Abramoff. One evening, DeLay and his crew dined with Koulakovsky and Nevskaya, NaftaSib's directors. "[During dinner] I remember DeLay telling us that on an earlier visit how at great risk he had snuck Bibles and prayer books into the old Soviet Union," says Abramoff. "Koulakovsky smiled and nodded with appreciation." NaftaSib was funding a new Christian school, the first since the Communist revolution in 1917, with an enrollment of 260 students. The school would conduct regular religious services.[73]

During that Moscow dinner, Koulakovsky allegedly wondered aloud what would happen if the DeLays woke up one morning and found a luxury car in their driveway. He was told that the DeLays "would go to jail and [Koulakovsky] would go to jail." Abramoff, who attended every dinner with DeLay in Moscow, insists that this conversation never took place.

As usual, DeLay's political enemies maligned the journey as an expensive golf junket. They did manage to play two rounds of golf at the Robert Trent Jones golf course at the Moscow Country Club. According to travel records filed with Congress, his and his staff's portion of the trip came to $57,238.

By early 1998, the unraveling of the Russian economy had begun to accelerate. Within six months, the Russian stock market tumbled 50%. By mid summer, the price of a barrel of oil, Russia's chief export, had bottomed out under $15. But the chief culprit of Russian's financial woes was that energy and manufacturing industries were paying only a fraction of the taxes they owed, largely by using a Byzantine blizzard of offshore shell corporations—including the Bahamas, the Island of Jersey, and the windswept atoll of Niue in the South Pacific—to siphon off and secrete its profits.

Whether or not to bail out Russia yet again became an extremely contentious and complex issue. President Clinton championed it because he wanted to prevent at all cost the reform-minded, booze-besotted Russian President Boris Yeltsin from being swept from power and replaced, say, by a karate-trained former KGB agent. On June 11, 1998, the GOP leadership, including DeLay, sent a letter to President Clinton demanding guarantees that future IMF loans to Russia be more carefully monitored; otherwise Congress would be less inclined to consider his request for an additional $18 billion for funding the IMF.

However, the very next day, international lenders, including the IMF, announced that they would lend Russia $22 billion, which it "desperately needs to make foreign debt payments and bolster its currency…[and in return Russia would pass] tough fiscal reforms to boost tax collection and cut government spending."

The problem was that the IMF's dwindling reserves badly needed replenishing. Exactly thirteen days later, Buckham's US Family Network received an extraordinary $1 million contribution, forwarded once again by James & Sarch.[74] Some investigative reporters would later claim that this was not a coincidence. A former director of the IRS's office of tax-exempt organizations later exclaimed to *The Washington Post* that "a million dollars is a staggering amount of money to come from a foreign source."[75]

On August 14, exactly $4.8 billion that the IMF transferred to Russia's Central Bank promptly vanished the day it arrived. This underscored Republicans' concerns about the IMF. Were American taxpayer dollars—which supply the largest share of IMF funding—being flushed down the drain because the IMF was handing money over to the Russia mob? Finally, on August 17—a day forever seared in the memory of the international financial community—the house of cards collapsed. The Russian government defaulted on its treasury bills[76] and devalued the ruble.

On August 30th, DeLay was interviewed on "Fox News Sunday." He said that the IMF refinancing bill was "unfortunate," because "[t]hey are trying to force Russia to raise taxes at a time when they ought to be cutting taxes in order to get a loan from the IMF. That's just outrageous," DeLay said.

Over eight years later—in late 2005 and early 2006—reporters for *The Washington Post* and *The Boston Globe* desperately sought a link between the large contributions from a mysterious Russian source to Buckham's US Family Network and the critical vote that Tom DeLay made "to replenish the IMF." This alleged link gushed from a single source—the garrulous Chris Greeslin, former head of Buckham's Network. In a December 2005 story, Greeslin told the *Post* that Buckham had told him the Russian contributions to the Network were meant to manipulate

DeLay's September 17, 1998 vote on legislation that helped the IMF bail out the deteriorating Russian economy. "Ed [Buckham] told me, 'This is the way things work in Washington,'" Greeslin said.

Greeslin's accusation could not be corroborated, because by 2005, Buckham was already under investigation and refused to comment. *The Washington Post* then went on to say in its December 2005 story: "In the end, the Russian legislature refused to raise taxes…and DeLay voted on September 17, 1998, for a foreign aid bill containing new funds to replenish the IMF account." Asked about the vote eight years later, DeLay's spokesman, Kevin Madden, said his boss "makes decisions and sets legislative priorities based on good policy and what is best for his constituents and the country." But the *Post* had failed to mention that DeLay's signature had appeared on the June 11th letter to Clinton, expressing concerns about the IMF. The *Post* also failed to mention that on September 10, DeLay had lobbied the House Appropriations Committee to deny Clinton's request for $18 billion for the IMF, which is exactly what the Committee ended up doing.[77] DeLay told *The New York Times*, "Instead of providing needed cash to basically sound enterprises, the IMF is now bailing out the bankrupt."

But the *Post*'s most serious transgression in its December 2005 story was not informing its readers that although the Republican-controlled Congress—including DeLay—did vote "to replenish the IMF account," it only approved a fraction—$3.5 billion (19%)—of the $18 billion Clinton had requested. If the newspaper had chosen to mention these three well reported facts, a stake would have been driven into the heart of its story. The $3.5 billion replenishment was hardly cause for celebration in Russia. If contributions to Buckham's Network had been intended to influence DeLay's vote, the Russians were disappointed, if not infuriated.[78] After that vote, however, the Network never received another penny from James & Sarch or any other mysterious Russian source.

After the Bahamian-registered firm of Chelsea Enterprises melted away, Voor Huisen, a firm in the Netherlands, materialized in its place and hired Abramoff. Voor Huisen seemed to be one of his best clients. According to the Lobbying Disclosure Act records, Abramoff billed Voor Huisen $2.1 million between 2001 and 2004, but he says he only received about $500,000. None of his former partners could explain what Abramoff did to justify the high fees. His official lobbying reports stated that Voor Huisen was promoting "private housing in the former Soviet Union and other projects in energy and economics," aviation safety, disaster preparedness and other issues "pertaining to defense and security."

Ronald Platt, one of Abramoff's former colleagues who worked on the Voor Huisen account, told *The Boston Globe* that he was later informed that it was highly likely that Koulakovsky and Nevskaya owned the firm. "I was told that they had an interest in developing moderate-priced middle-income housing in Russia," Platt said. "This would be a good thing to bring stability to Russia. The company, in order to pursue this," Platt added, "was hoping to get funds from the US government because it was theoretically in the interest of the US government. At the time, I said, 'I think this will never happen.'" In early 2006, a Dutch publication, Virj Nederlander, reported that Voor Huisen, which means "For Housing," had no assets, no activity, and listed no shareholders.

"[Koulakovsky] believed that Russia would not remain free until and unless there was a property-owning class, a large one, with people owning their own homes. The plan was to create a mortgage program for Russia, and with this in mind Voor Huisen was created," says Abramoff."

Nine days after *The Washington Post* ran its first story on the lobbying scandal in February 2004, Abramoff's firm forced him to resign. According to corporate records in the Netherlands, two days prior to his resignation, Voor Huisen was quietly dissolved.

CHAPTER TWENTY-THREE
JEWISH OIL

As an Orthodox Jew and ardent supporter of Israel, Abramoff dreamed of revolutionizing the Middle East by making the Promised Land an oil-producing leviathan. By giving it infinite wealth and clout, the tiny Jewish homeland would become stronger and more secure than ever. "The oil project was a chance to make a lot of money," says Abramoff. "I was, after all, in business and was not ashamed at the fact that I wanted to make money, even though I ended up giving most of it away."

When the Russians told him that they had satellite data that indicated there might be a significant oil field in Israel, Abramoff enthusiastically became involved. "First, I wanted to help Israel…If there were an oil field in Israel it would have changed a lot over there, especially as regards Israel's need to import oil," says Abramoff. "Plus, if it could become a net exporter, it would provide an interesting political situation. Would Israel be barred from OPEC? Of course, but it would have forced the OPEC nations to come out publicly with their anti-Semitism, something which would have set them back on their heels."

On February 6, 2001, Abramoff incorporated First Gate Resources, a drilling company, in the state of Delaware.[79] According to Abramoff's former lobbying partner Ronald Platt, who said he had seen the company's brochure, the First Gate's officers were listed as Abramoff, Koulakovsky, and Nevskaya. "They supposedly had some kind of technology for determining oil and gas resources," said Platt. "They had discovered vast oil and gas deposits in the Israeli desert, and [Abramoff believed that] if these were exploited it would change the whole dynamic of the Middle East." So he was eager to obtain a drilling permit from the Israeli oil commissioner, but he also needed a banker's letter certifying First Gate's financially viability.

Abramoff told an associate on November 4, 2001, that he needed this banker letter "Mega fast. This is something that Alexander [Koulakovsky] and Marina [Nevskaya] were supposed to get but have not done so. Our permit in Israel depends on it and we are running short of time." The bank letter would acknowledge, but not guarantee, that First Gate had the means to undertake a "project/transaction in the $5 million range," and would be sent to Yehezkiel Druckman, Israel's petroleum commissioner at the time. "The bank letter was a minor issue," says Abramoff. "If we had gotten the permit, we would have had no problem obtaining a bank letter."

In early 2006, Philip Mandelker, an Israeli oil expert, confirmed that "My understanding is that First Gate Resources had been in contact with the Israeli authorities in about 2001 about the possibility of acquiring petroleum exploration rights," but was unable to obtain the required permits. "There have been about 475 oil and gas exploration and development wells drilled throughout Israel, including the West Bank, both on- and offshore." But these efforts have yielded little. Mandelker did say that "[small amounts of] oil and gas have been discovered and produced both in the Negev and elsewhere in Israel, including an 18-million-barrel Heletz field[80] discovered in the northern Negev in 1955." This field still produces several dozen barrels of oil a day—an inconsequential amount.

"Alexander wanted to know if I had connections there to get permission for them to get a license. I had connections," says Abramoff, "through a very good friend of mine in the US, who represented the Israeli government on military matters. He brought us over there to meet with the commission in charge of granting licenses. They were not convinced that Alexander was correct, but they were impressed with what his geologists showed them."

Abramoff hoped to obtain a small grant of $2 million from the U.S. government to conduct an analysis. Koulakovsky believed that his being a Russian would make the Israelis skittish, but if the United States government were involved, then they might feel more comfortable. "We slowly made our way through the maze of the bureaucracy, but we were never able to get the permission we needed from the military to drill, so the project fizzled. We all suspected that the area where we wanted to drill was where the Israelis keep their nukes, but that was just speculation."

As for Platt's characterization about the effect such a discovery would have on the Middle East? "He is right," says Abramoff. "I did think that if we were able to find oil there, it would change the equation in the Middle East."

PART III
SUNCRUZ ARMADA

CHAPTER TWENTY-FOUR
RECONNECTION

Abramoff's next extravaganza—the SunCruz Affair—seemed to push the limits of audacity and controversy. After extensive interviews with the three partners involved in the purchase of SunCruz, and after reading virtually every news account, as well as thousands of pages of documents, both public and private, it can be said that a jury would have been hard pressed to find Kidan—never mind Abramoff—guilty of wire fraud and conspiracy to commit wire fraud, the charges to which both pleaded guilty and for which they were both eventually imprisoned.

Here are the overarching facts: On September 27, 2000, Abramoff and Kidan—along with Ben Waldman, a minor partner—purchased a flotilla of gambling boats in Florida worth $147.5 million from Gus Boulis, a volatile self-made millionaire. Without a single penny of their own money and with the collusion of Boulis and the primary lender, the buyers purchased this flotilla, in part, with a forged $23 million wire transfer. A few months later, Boulis—one of the most prominent and colorful businessmen in south Florida—was assassinated in a gangland-style slaying, allegedly committed by three mobsters, one of whom was a close friend of Kidan's.

While Abramoff was making a radical career move from film producer to Washington lobbyist, Kidan was reinventing himself as well. Soon after his mother's mob murder, he stopped practicing law to become a full-time businessman. In 1994, his stepfather, Sami Shemtov, filed a complaint against Kidan for embezzling $250,000, including the $15,000 reward money for the arrest of his mother's murderers. At that time, Kidan was representing Napoleon Barragan. Barragan was a Guatemalan immigrant who in 1976 had launched Dial-A-Mattress, a New York telemarketing bedding firm, which quickly delivered name-brand mattresses, box springs, and bed frames to people's homes. Eager to expand, Barragan persuaded Kidan to quit practicing law and open Dial-A-Mattress' first franchise. He was given the greater Washington D.C. area.

As the Republicans were being swept into power in Congress, Kidan launched his new business on February 14, 1994.[81] His press release promised to deliver a mattress within two hours and was stuffed with upbeat, but fatuous, puns and a chorus of exclamation points: "We knew the D.C. area was a great choice. This was a decision we didn't have to sleep on!" Like any shrewd businessman, Kidan brainstormed for ways to publicize his new bedding business. He soon stumbled on one. His somewhat banal on-air mantra, delivered with a Brooklyn accent—"Dial-A-Mattress: Leave off the last 'S'—that's for savings"—propelled him into the status of a minor celebrity.

Kidan says he wrote his own commercials, taping new versions every six weeks. His television spots ran on the four biggest furniture buying holidays of the years: President's Day, Memorial Day, July 4, and Labor Day. As the local "Mattress King," he became unofficial spokesman for the bedding business. For example, when a local radio station decided to deliver a bed to the door of independent prosecutor Kenneth Starr so that reporters covering the Monica Lewinsky scandal could take a nap, Kidan was quoted on Fox News. "We got national coverage on that," he says.

His appointment to the boards of various charities and political groups—including the Greater Washington Urban League, the D.C. Chamber of Commerce Political Action Committee, and Greater DC Cares—also gave his company invaluable exposure. He donated mattresses worth $25,000 to local charities.[82] "We like to help the shelters as often as we can," he told a reporter. "We do this on a regular basis."

And so what if he told some harmless—probably tongue-in-cheek—fibs, on which journalists would later pounce, illustrating his purported mendacity. For example at a charity ball, he told a reporter that when the Clintons first moved into the White House, they needed a new mattress. Kidan said he had one delivered within two hours.

"A funny thing about the Clintons," Kidan revealed. "The White House told us we could not use their purchasing a mattress from us for press purposes, and we agreed. But when six months went by and I didn't get paid I called the White House and said not only will I tell the press the Clintons bought our mattress, but that we didn't get paid. The next day I got a check." A few years later, as President Clinton was being attacked for permitting major political contributors to spend the night in the Lincoln Bedroom, Kidan did some embellishing. He claimed that he had sold the Clintons a queen-size Serta Perfect Sleeper for $549 in January 1993. "When the White House called our 800-number, they told us it was for the Lincoln Bedroom and Mr. Clinton's mom would be sleeping on it." Kidan then added that his Dial-A-Mattress's slogan "has always been 'Leave off the last S, that's for savings,' but maybe it should be changed to '"Leave off the last 'S,' that's for solicitations." What made the story apocryphal was that Kidan's Dial-A-Mattress franchise opened thirteen months after the Clintons moved into the White House.

Kidan expanded to six locations. Apparently, Barragan became jealous and—according to Kidan—began usurping some of his territory. In 1995, Kidan filed a 29-count lawsuit, charging Barragan with fraud, unfair competitive practices, and breach of contract. But Kidan lost in court. His lawyers advised him as a precaution to seek bankruptcy. They were afraid Barragan could retaliate by creatively interpreting a clause in the contract allowing him to rescind Kidan's franchise. Kidan put his business into bankruptcy as a business tactic. On his lawyers' advice, he also filed personal bankruptcy as well, because he had personally guaranteed all of the businesses' loans. And this claim was actually confirmed in a *Washington Post* story, in which Kidan filed for "bankruptcy protection"... to prevent a takeover by the parent firm."

However, soon thereafter Kidan told a reporter that the conflict had been settled "amicably." "It was just a blip on the screen that really did not affect our sales at all," said Kidan of the bankruptcy filing. If reporters had later included that inconvenient tidbit, it would have undermined their attempts to malign Kidan, and by extension, Abramoff.

In July 1999, Kidan finally agreed to sell the business back to Barragan. Both publicly "declined to disclose terms of the deal." Robert Isler, Barragan's assistant general counsel said, "It was an opportunity to get back a strong market that will be beneficial for the franchiser to operate directly." Despite repeated claims to the contrary in scores of publications years later, Kidan did indeed sell his "bankrupt" business. But for how much? This was a critical question because Abramoff would later allege that Kidan told him that he had sold Dial-A-Mattress for an "eight-figure payoff," an assertion that Kidan denies. (Barragan actually paid Kidan $800,000 in cash for the franchise.)

At least as far as Dial-A-Mattress was concerned, the evidence was clear that Kidan's business had not been a failure. And yet, for example, Matthew Continetti, both in *The Weekly Standard* and in his book, *The K-Street Gang*, labeled Kidan "a bold and unapologetic liar."[83]

Kidan claims that Abramoff must have heard Kidan's voice chanting his Dial-A-Mattress mantra on the radio: "One day I received a letter from Jack, which essentially said, 'I was driving in the car, heard your commercial. Let's get together,'" recalls Kidan. Abramoff says that he didn't write, but called his "800" number. Their friendship was rekindled. "We really enjoyed each other's company, golfing, going to the Redskins games," says Kidan. "It was strictly social. Occasionally, we raised money for Republicans."

According to Kidan, because Abramoff was so consumed by his lobbying work, he needed an outsider to talk to and "he would basically kvetch to me." Abramoff denies that: "I would not kvetch to him at all about anything. He was not part of my world in that way." In July 1999, "Jack saw the story [about selling Dial-A-Mattress]," Kidan says. "He called me up and asked what was I going to do now?" The then 34-year-old Kidan claims to have amassed "a large nest egg" and needed a break "from the bump and grind of business." He says he was driving a Range Rover, living in a lovely brick ivy-covered townhouse with a garage and garden, and was "engaged to a beautiful, but high-maintenance, woman." According to bankruptcy court records, Kidan was driving a 1995 Dodge.

Abramoff casually mentioned that he often came across business opportunities but lacked the time to follow through and would "try to feed me deals and I would work on them and we'd see if we could make money," says Kidan.

On December 1st, detectives in New York City call Kidan to say that his mother's four murderers have finally been arrested. One of them is Chris Paciello, a nightclub impresario on South Beach in Miami, whose friends include Madonna and Dennis Rodman.

CHAPTER TWENTY-FIVE
DEAL OF THE CENTURY

Their first venture was the underwhelming Potomac Outdoor Advertising, a startup company that hoped to place ads on taxis that plied the Potomac River in Washington, D.C. For some reason, Abramoff and Kidan brought in a third partner, Ben Waldman, an old College Republican friend. He had worked in the Reagan White House, twice run unsuccessfully for Congress from Virginia, and served as press spokesman for Pat Robertson's 1988 presidential campaign. "[Potomac Outdoor Advertising] never got off the ground, because we dropped it to do SunCruz," says Kidan.

In November 1999, Art Dimopoulos, a maritime lawyer at Abramoff's law firm, mentioned that a client was selling a fleet of eleven casino boats—with 2,300 slot machines and 175 gaming tables. They sailed from nine ports in Florida, as well as one in Myrtle Beach, S.C., into international waters, beyond the reach of state anti-gambling laws. Did Abramoff know anyone who might be interested in buying it? As a matter of fact, he did. Himself.

Abramoff had grown up in Atlantic City. His father had dreamed of owning a casino. Because one of Abramoff's best clients was the Choctaw Indians, who operated a casino that generated nearly $500 million annual revenue, he had acquired many contacts in the industry. And Adam Kidan claimed to have been the general counsel of his stepfather's casino down in St. Maartens and he also claimed to have a pocketful of cash.

"Kidan explained to Jack and me that he would be putting in the $20 million equity [for the down payment] from a mix of his father's money from the sale of the St. [Marteen] Casino and Beach Club and his sale of Dial-A-Mattress," says Waldman. "We had no reason to doubt this as Adam was well known in Washington, DC. His ubiquitous voice on the radio was an omnipresent reminder to all that he was a financial success. He hosted fundraisers and dinners, both political and charitable and hobnobbed with the rich and famous."[84]

At first, Abramoff did not reveal to Dimopoulos that he was the prospective buyer. Years later, reporters would criticize Abramoff for violating his firm's ethical rules by concealing his intentions from Dimopoulos. One published account, brimming with unnamed sources, claimed the firm "'could not represent a client in any matter in which an employee has a significant financial stake,' recalled a former colleague of Abramoff's." Another claimed that Abramoff did not inform Preston Gates for eight months. When Preston Gates did inform Boulis about Abramoff's involvement, Boulis told the firm he did not care.

"Art brought me this deal in December 1999. But I told [Dimopoulos] within a month that I might be involved. The reason I didn't right away was I wasn't sure we could really pull this off," says Abramoff. Besides, he added, another firm, not his own, was handling the sale of the casino boats. However, Preston Gates had represented Boulis on criminal matters, thus making him a client of the firm. Nonetheless, Abramoff claims his firm did not bristle when it learned of involvement in the possible purchase. "Preston Gates was excited that as an owner I would have the firm representing SunCruz," says Abramoff, "and I even had them help us on the maritime matters, including Dimopoulos. Everybody was delighted."

When Abramoff first broached the subject of their purchasing SunCruz, Kidan says he was stunned by its magnitude. "It was a lot sexier than selling mattresses," he says. "Hell, I had nothing to lose by taking a look. I told Jack to get me the basic numbers and a business plan, and if it looked good, we'd take the next step." Abramoff faxed him the information the next day. "You know what? These numbers are so good, that if they're real, this is a home run," Kidan says he told Abramoff later that evening. "And considering the asset level of the business, we could probably finance it pretty easily." The three partners signed a confidentiality agreement with the seller, and Kidan flew down to Florida in early January 2000, to take a look at the books and the business, and to meet the controversial and litigious Konstantinos "Gus" Boulis. But who had $150 million? And why did Boulis seem so eager to sell?

Gus Boulis was the archetypical, scrappy, rags-to-riches, Horatio-Alger immigrant American success story. He was born on April 6, 1949, in Kavala, a poor Greek fishing village on the Aegean Sea, about 80 miles north of Thessalonika. The ruins of a Byzantine fortress overshadow the village. Nicknamed Kosta, Boulis dropped out of grade school to work as a fisherman. Against his father's wishes, Boulis joined the merchant marines at age 16. Two years later, in order to avoid military service, Boulis slipped aboard a freighter heading across the Atlantic, and jumped ship at Halifax, Canada.

THE PERFECT VILLAIN

The five-foot seven-inch blue-eyed stowaway arrived in the New World penniless and friendless. His English was limited to "I love you" and "Yesterday." Years later, when Boulis was asked about his lack of education, he shot back: "Every day is an education." In Halifax, he got a job washing dishes. Within six months, immigration authorities were knocking on his door. He fled to the "hippie section" of Toronto and continued working as a dishwasher, then as a cook. He worked double shifts for $1.35 an hour, memorized the menu and could perform every job in the restaurant. The owners were impressed. They promoted him to manager.

He met Efronsini, the 16-year-old receptionist at a dry-cleaning store, whose family also came from Kavala. She was a Canadian citizen. That very same day, he was detained as an illegal alien. A week later, on July 24, 1971, Boulis and Efronsini were married, automatically granting him Canadian citizenship. Within four years, Boulis had fathered two boys with her, Christos and Panagiotis.

The restaurant owners soon offered the energetic Boulis a partnership if he would help them expand. Within a few years, their Mr. Submarine Sandwich Shop had become a chain of 180 stores. By 1979, the 30-year-old Boulis and his business partners were quarreling. They bought him out and he returned awash in cash to Kavala, Greece, with his wife and children. Within a year, however, he left his family behind in Greece and moved to the Florida Keys, but continued to support them in lavish style.

Within a few days after landing in the Florida Keys, he met Margaret Hren, an 18-year-old girl from Minnesota. Smart, pretty, and hard working, Hren agreed to help Boulis launch a restaurant business. With a $50,000 loan from a Canadian bank, they renovated a run-down restaurant in Key West. Two years later, using a $2.5 million overdraft from a local bank, Boulis constructed his first hotel in Key Largo. Soon, his portfolio was bulging with eight hotels and a chain of 192-franchised restaurants, called Miami Subs. His fast-food restaurants—known for their tropically colored neon décor—sold subs, Greek food, and $100 bottles of Dom Perignon.

At about the same time that Abramoff became a lobbyist and Kidan started peddling bedding, Boulis threw a party that would eventually lead to his murder. He entertained 300 of his Miami Subs franchisees aboard a gambling boat that sailed from Port Everglades into international waters. Beyond the three-mile limit[85], they were so enthralled by the Las Vegas style gambling that Boulis smelled an opportunity. Within a couple of days, Boulis had purchased for $2 million in cash the *Sir Winston*, a 100-foot long cruise ship, and quickly converted it into a gambling boat, which berthed at his Key Largo hotel. In its first week of operation, the *Sir Winston* was filled to capacity with 150 passengers a night. On his coast-guard application, he claimed to be an American citizen, which was a fib.

Within a month, Boulis had ordered a 350-passenger boat for $5 million. He then started assembling a fleet of hugely profitable offshore gambling boats, which he collectively dubbed SunCruz. Soon, his gambling boats were departing on "cruises to nowhere" from a dozen Florida ports, carrying tourists, high-rollers, conventioneers, and retirees. By 2000, SunCruz employed over 1,000 people and operated 11 boats, generating nearly $100 million in sales. These figures did not include skimming, common in a cash business, as well as perks for Boulis' family and friends.

Boulis' favorite was a 208-foot yacht, the *SunCruz VII*, moored near Cape Canaveral. While churning along for 45 minutes to reach international waters where gambling could legally begin, customers enjoyed live entertainment, a free buffet and cheap drinks. With the exception of frequent bettors, who boarded for free, customers paid a $15 entrance fee. Catering mostly to low rollers, the boat had the basics: blackjack, craps, roulette, three-card poker, mini baccarat, Let It Ride, Caribbean stud, and 437 slot machines.

One threat to the business was choppy seas, which made shooting craps impossible and patrons seasick. Another was Robert Butterworth, Florida's attorney general, who spent years trying to shut down SunCruz. Butterworth once declared, "This is a cash business and all the things that go along with that are potential problems. I'm talking about coming on a boat with a suitcase of money. No one is doing the books out there; no one knows what's going on out there."

The floating casino business was unregulated and untaxed—except in New Jersey and Hawaii—and highly profitable. But, there were only a handful in the entire country, because of several, but severe, limitations: A gambling boat was only profitable if located more than two hours from a land-based casino; the boat must depart from a location where international waters could be reached quickly; the boat must dock at waterfront property which was prohibitively expensive; a large parking lot was also essential, but expensive; and a sufficient nearby population density was required from which to draw customers. Because the SunCruz Casinos had crossed all of those entry barriers, it was a valuable cash business whose profits could probably be increased under better management. Employing the best lawyers and local lobbyists, Boulis had managed to fend off all legal attacks. According to rumors, he also bribed local officials. "When you have a lot at stake, maybe it's better to ask for forgiveness than to go through the bureaucracy," he said. "We don't take no for an answer. We hire lawyers if we have to."

One day, Butterworth raided his boats and seized all the slot machines. Boulis defiantly ordered another ship be brought down as a replacement, and business resumed the very next day. A few months later, due to a lack of probable cause, a judge ordered Butterworth to return Boulis' slot machines.

Finally, officials conjured up a way to shut Boulis down. In 1999, they invoked an obscure federal law—the 1916 Shipping Act, which barred non-citizens from owning ships registered in the United States. Its purpose had been to prevent foreigners from competing with Americans during WWI. The nearly century-old act was as obsolete as criminal laws against co-habitation by unmarried couples. Nevertheless, because Boulis had lied about his American citizenship on his coast guard license application for the *Sir Winston*,[86] punctilious federal prosecutors forced him to sell his gambling fleet and pay a $2 million fine. However, the agreement was kept confidential, even from Butterworth, so that the self-made immigrant millionaire could sell SunCruz for a fair price.[87] In early 2000, the government gave him 36 months to find a buyer.

Boulis didn't waste any time. He mentioned it to a Greek friend, a maritime lawyer in the Washington D.C. office of Preston Gates, whose name was Art Dimopoulos. But Boulis' reputation—as well as the tenuous legal status of the "cruise-to-nowhere" gambling industry in Florida— made the prospects of a sale uncertain. Republican-controlled Florida, led by Governor Jeb Bush, often mulled legislation that would have shut down the gambling boat industry. Any prospective buyer would not only have to be bold and wealthy but would be obliged to safeguard his investment by hiring a top Washington lobbyist to keep the government sharks, both state and federal, at bay.

Dimopoulos thought of the firm's star lobbyist, Casino Jack. With all of his connections, not to mention his Indian casino clientele, maybe Abramoff knew of someone who would want to purchase the business and would also hire the firm as its lobbyist.

CHAPTER TWENTY-SIX
BANKERS

In early January 2000, Dimopoulos flew with Kidan down to Miami, Florida to introduce him to the colorful, but volatile, Gus Boulis. "We really hit it off," says Kidan. "He was extremely charming." Boulis immediately took his guests onto one of the boats. During the tour, Boulis picked up garbage, hammered a nail, and even bused a table. This was not what the typical chief executive officer of a $150 million company did. What also impressed Kidan was that Boulis knew the names and faces of every employee on the boat. Later that day, Boulis flew Kidan on the SunCruz jet—a trinket included in the sale—to another boat on Florida's west coast. On the return flight, Boulis personally prepared a sumptuous meal for his important guest.

But Kidan says he was a bit perplexed. "Why was Boulis wining and dining me? Why was he selling something he clearly loved and was so personally invested in?" The question nagged him. "So finally, I asked him point blank," says Kidan. "'Why are you selling the business?' and for the first time, Boulis looked away. It was the first time he broke eye contract with me." Boulis explained that he was selling, because he wanted to concentrate on real estate and was tired of fighting the government, which was "out to get him."

Kidan was fully aware of Boulis' charm and ruthlessness. Despite his reputation for generosity in the Hellenic community in southern Florida, Boulis preferred handshake deals with his fellow Greeks, because it left room for ambiguity. "Boulis would show a financial statement for the restaurant claiming a low gross income for his own tax purposes, but telling prospective buyers the income was much higher to justify his price for the business," according to a report issued by the Florida Department of Law Enforcement. Boulis would then sell the restaurant without the liquor license or the land, forcing the new owner to pay him thousands of additional dollars. In October 1997, his longtime girlfriend and business partner, Margaret Hren, was forced to take out a restraining order against Boulis. She told the court, "He told me he was going to smash my head...[and then] kill him[self] and the kids so I would suffer for the rest of my life."

Kidan—who knew that Boulis' net worth approached $100 million, but was too cheap to buy an expensive hairpiece and rarely showered—prepared himself for the worst. As a precaution and without alerting Boulis, Kidan returned to south Florida several days later with Waldman. They secretly spent a week visiting all eleven boats. They noticed the many repeat customers, usually retirees, some who came to gamble every day. "[Boulis] was a great guy, gregarious, and interesting. He had a heart of gold, but bristled at being screwed," says Waldman.

According to Abramoff and Waldman, the original plan was for Kidan to put up most of the down payment; the remainder would be financed. Kidan had told them he was looking to invest his "eight-figure payoff" from the sale of his Dial-A-Mattress franchise. "This was why Kidan was the chief negotiator and why he was going to run the business," says Abramoff. "He was putting up his own cash and he and I would split the [up-front costs]."

Waldman agrees that was the understanding. "Jack and I deferred to Kidan on matters regarding the SunCruz acquisition because he was to put in the bulk of the equity and because Kidan represented that he had been the Chief Counsel at the St. Johns Casino and Beach Club." Waldman and Abramoff say that Kidan misled them from the very beginning.

Abramoff would receive regular requests from Kidan for cash infusions for legal, accounting, other costs involved in negotiating the purchase of SunCruz. "Adam used to send Jack a list of the expenses, which they were supposed to split," says Waldman, "but Kidan would double it, so that [Abramoff] ended paying almost all of the upfront expenses." In fact, Abramoff's out-of-pocket expenses amounted to approximately $700,000. Kidan's was only $50,000.[88]

Kidan repeatedly denies that he was supposed to supply the down payment. Abramoff was supposed to exploit his wide-ranging contacts—especially in the Northern Mariana Islands and in Israel—to help expand their new company into other markets. Furthermore, and more importantly, he would also neutralize any threats from local, state, and federal legislation that threatened to choke or extinguish the business. "From the beginning, we preferred to do this deal with no up-front money, or little of it," says Abramoff. "Like purchasing any asset, one wants to leverage it all the way if possible....Since I thought this was the deal of the century and that we would all make a fortune, I had no problem in going to friends...[but] if that could not work out, then, Kidan would put in the money—or so he led me to believe and so I did believe."

Kidan claims that Abramoff approached one of his Russian clients to fund the purchase. "I did approach Koulakovsky," says Abramoff, "[but] his priest was against it. He just did not feel comfortable doing a deal in gaming."

In late January 2000, to their surprise, Boulis signed a letter of intent to sell SunCruz to Abramoff, Kidan, and Waldman. The price was $145 million, subject to a $23 million down payment and an exhaustive inspection. Kidan quickly hired Arthur Andersen, one of the premier accounting firms in the world,[89] whose job was to confirm that SunCruz grossed $80 million and netted $19 million a year. Kidan figured that if he could increase efficiency and grow the net revenue to $25 million, it would allow them to refinance the debt on better terms. However, Boulis demanded that the exhaustive examination be done discreetly. He didn't want his employees to know SunCruz was for sale. Therefore, Kidan and his team arrived as "bankers," so that Boulis could claim he was refinancing. "We didn't look like bankers or drive cars like bankers," says Waldman. "We never wore ties."

Waldman and Kidan repeatedly visited all the boats, tested the books and revenues, interviewed the staff, secured new permits for alcohol and food, and ordered new surveys to confirm that the boats were seaworthy. "Adam was the prime guy, because he was putting up the down payment. I was the numbers guy. Initially, it was supposed to be an all-cash deal, without any seller [Boulis] financing," says Waldman. "Adam is actually very bright. At first, I really respected him and working with him was a lot of fun."

The partners agreed that that Abramoff and Kidan would each own 45% and Waldman 10% of the new company.

As weeks turned into months, Boulis kept demanding the $23 million down payment. Kidan says he became increasingly frustrated with Abramoff. His Russian client was always "on the verge" of coming up with the money. Kidan kept winning concessions that most sellers would have never agreed to. "Boulis kept compromising, which only added to my suspicions and concerns," says Kidan. Finally, Kidan announced that he didn't feel comfortable making the $23 million down payment.

"Well, give me two million," Boulis allegedly responded.

Kidan says to himself, "He's gone from $23 million to $2 million in exactly one second." Aloud, Kidan says, "Okay, that's reasonable. I'll go back to my partners and see what they have to say."

When Kidan informed him, a delighted Abramoff said he could easily raise the $2 million. (Abramoff claims "This is complete fiction. We never ever had such a conversation.") But several weeks went by and Kidan claimed that even that sum could not be dredged up. Finally, he informed Boulis that his partners concerns had not been mollified: "'Based on your litigious reputation, you'd file bankruptcy, you'd do something and we'll lose the $2 million."

"Okay," Boulis allegedly conceded. "Give me $100,000." Kidan says he was astonished and suspicious by the concessions that Boulis was making.

So, Boulis received a paltry $100,000 down payment, which was placed in escrow. "In fact, the escrow check bounced," says Waldman. "We were very embarrassed, but finally we made good on it."

CHAPTER TWENTY-SEVEN
WIRED

In March 2000, Boulis, who actually had no desire to sell SunCruz, began to develop a strategy that he would fine tune over the course of the next six months. Since it was likely he would end up lending the buyers the bulk of the purchase price, called "seller financing," this second mortgage might ultimately work to his advantage. Boulis could make money by charging interest, and—if the buyers defaulted—he could regain ownership of SunCruz. This would violate his agreement with federal prosecutors, but if an off-shore shell corporation—secretly controlled by Boulis—purchased it, none would be the wiser.

Boulis started making new demands. He increased the sale price and insisted that the buyers hire him as a $200,000-a-year consultant. He wanted to insinuate himself into the new company as much as possible in order to guide it into troubled waters. Kidan and Abramoff knew Boulis was still doing battle with Bob Butterworth, the Florida attorney general. Abramoff decided to respond with a counterattack of his own. He would have Boulis censured on the floor of Congress! From that Boulis would infer that Abramoff had the clout to pass legislation that would shut down the "cruise-to-nowhere" industry. "Federal regulations could put the industry out of business," says Waldman. "Why not scare Gus that we had pull if he didn't play ball."

On Abramoff's insistence, Michael Scanlon, Tom DeLay's former press spokesman, had just been hired by Preston Gates. Scanlon asked his good friend Neil Volz, chief of staff for Rep. Bob Ney (R-OH), if he would ask his boss to place a statement in the *Congressional Record*. "The reason they picked Ney and not DeLay" says Kidan, "was because Abramoff was too close to DeLay. Ney agreed to do it, because he wanted to get closer to DeLay and move up the ranks. He got a big contribution from us, which [Ney] then handed over to [the National Republican Congressional Committee]."[90] Abramoff says Kidan doesn't know what he's talking about. "[Ney] did it because Scanlon asked him [through Volz] to do it and he wanted to help me," says Abramoff. On March 30, 2000, Ney entered the following denunciation of Boulis—composed by Scanlon—into the *Congressional Record*'s "Extensions of Remarks," statements not actually made on the floor of Congress.

One Mr. Speaker, you hear many arguments surrounding the gaming industry in America. Some have merit, some do not...However, there are a few bad apples out there who don't play by the rules and that is just plain wrong....

One such example is the case of SunCruz casinos based out of Florida. Florida authorities, particularly Attorney General Butterworth, have repeatedly reprimanded SunCruz casinos and its owner Gus Boulis for taking illegal bets, not paying out their customers properly ...

Mr. Speaker, how SunCruz Casinos and Gus Boulis conduct themselves with regard to Florida laws is very

unnerving.... This type of conduct gives the gaming industry a black eye and should not be tolerated....

...I hope that steps will be taken...to weed out the bad apples so that we can protect consumers across the country.

A little shocked but impressed, Boulis wondered why a Congressman, who defended coal shippers on the upper Ohio River, would involve himself in an obscure business in south Florida, irrelevant to the interests of his constituents. What Boulis did not realize was that statements in the "Extensions of Remarks" of the voluminous *Congressional Record* were essentially meaningless and virtually never read. Congressmen inserted them to stroke the ego of a constituent, a campaign contributor, or a mistress.

Six days after Tom DeLay, his deputy chief of staff, Tony Rudy, and Abramoff returned from a golf junket to Scotland, Boulis received a flag that had flown momentarily over the U.S. Capitol, courtesy of DeLay. Less than a week after that, Abramoff and Kidan squired Joan Wagner, Boulis' chief financial officer—along with Tony Rudy—to watch Tiger Woods' record-breaking victory at the U.S. Open in Pebble Beach, California. Years later, federal prosecutors would bully Abramoff and Rudy into pleading guilty to bribery over this trivial trip, something Abramoff refused to discuss. On June 22, 2000, less than a week after the Pebble Beach trip, Boulis signed the formal agreement to sell SunCruz to Kidan, Abramoff, and Waldman. The new price was $150 million.

The next hurdle was daunting. They had to finance the purchase. Kidan approached Boles Knop & Co., an investment banking boutique, for advice in funding and structuring the complex transaction. Within a month, Kidan believed he was on the verge of closing the deal.

The following never publicly released e-mails in late July 2000 proved to be pivotal in Abramoff's later destruction. Here, Kidan was writing to Abramoff:

------original message-----

From: adam kidan [<malto:arkidan@prodogy.net>]
Sent: Saturday, July 22, 2000 4:40 PM

To: jacka@prestongates.com
Subject: CLOSING

…We had a rough day yesterday with all of the bankers. Now that we are in the final stages of closing we are reviewing the economic model. We spent six hours yesterday and a few today. I should become religious and avoid Saturday calls.

At this stage the banks are reviewing our free cash flow to determine operating covenants and amortization of the mezz[anine] loan. Once this stage is over the banks will negotiate their inter-creditor agreement. Gus must enter into that also. A lot of negotiating. We (me and Boles Knop) have a conf[erence] call with all of the banks and Arthur Andersen Monday late day. So far everything is working in our favor. The big negotiation will be with Gus. He is going to get less in terms of payments on his note (interest only for a while) and will hafe[sic] to increase the size of the note. I do not intend on broaching that with him until after the convention and right before closing. You and I need to review the shareholder agreement. Regards, Adam.

Boulis had already agreed to provide the buyers with substantial "seller financing," which was acceptable to the lenders as long as his loan was recorded in the "second position." Nevertheless, Abramoff and Kidan were still supposed to pay Boulis a $23 million down payment toward the purchase price.[91] Kidan had secretly and repeatedly informed Boulis that they were extremely reluctant to place into escrow such a large sum, because if problems arose during the closing, those funds could become entangled for years in costly litigation.

Clearly, Kidan didn't have $23 million in cash. However, he had discovered—for reasons he could not fathom—that Boulis was now so anxious to sell SunCruz that he had agreed to briefly and secretly lend them the down payment as well. The lenders would not be informed.

After the transfer of ownership was finalized, Kidan promised to hand over the $23 million to Boulis.

Although kept abreast by phone and e-mail, Abramoff was not involved in and did not fully comprehend the complicated negotiations. "The structuring was changing constantly and the [lenders] kept changing too," he says. When Abramoff learned that Boulis was going to lend them the down payment, Abramoff became concerned. He replied to Kidan's e-mail three hours later.

------original message-----

From: Abramoff, Jack (DC)
<mailto: jacka@prestongates.com>
To: adam kidan mailto:arkidan@prodigy.net
Sent: Saturday, July 22, 2000 7:47 PM
Subject: RE: Closing

Do you think we'll be OK? Also, are we going to be fine regarding the equity issue? Perhaps I have it wrong, but I thought you had told me that the banks did not know that our "equity" was from Gus. Will we be OK with this?

* * * * * * * * * * * * * * *

In 2005, nearly six years later, federal investigators were sifting through Abramoff's nearly five hundred thousand e-mails—subpoenaed from his former lobbying firms, Preston Gates and Greenberg Traurig—when they finally stumbled across the above e-mail. Kidan later claimed that his own attorney told him, "[Abramoff's] lawyer went to see the prosecutors to talk them out of indicting Jack, saying it was all me. When they showed him that e-mail, [Abramoff's] lawyer said, 'Oh well, I guess you'll be indicting Jack.'"

The pressure on Abramoff had been mounting. On September 29, 2004, he'd been publicly vilified when he'd taken the Fifth Amendment before McCain's Senate Indian Affairs Committee hearings, at which his racist-sounding e-mails had "coincidentally" been released. On August 18, 2005, he'd been publicly humiliated by his indictment, arrest, and jailing over night. His astronomical legal bills were mounting. For eighteen months, he'd endured a relentless media barrage portraying him as the most corrupt man who had ever lived. His wife and children were suffering. He wasn't sure he was guilty but if he was mistaken, he didn't want to spend the rest of his life in a maximum-security prison. Kidan and others had already pleaded guilty and had agreed to cooperate against him. The damaging e-mail—which Abramoff had completely forgotten about—put him over the edge. He concluded it was time to plead guilty—with sincerity and remorse—to the SunCruz charges in Florida—as well as to the conspiracy, fraud, and tax evasion charges up in Washington, D.C.

Federal prosecutors in south Florida were jubilant, because this infamous villain had first pleaded guilty in their jurisdiction. They had beaten their Washington D. C. colleagues to the punch. But far more importantly, these south Florida prosecutors would not have to risk taking to trial a case they had serious doubts they could ever win.

As a consequence, Abramoff's side of the story—and therefore a careful and comprehensive analysis of the scandal—would probably never take place.

"I couldn't believe I'd actually written it," Abramoff says. It was the "final-straw" e-mail that Kidan had talked so much about. Just before midnight, Kidan's response landed in Abramoff's inbox.

------original message-------

From:adam kidan [mailto:arkidan@prodigy.net]

Sent: Saturday, July 22, 2000 11:55 PM

To Abramoff, Jack (DC) [jacka@prestongates.com]

To further elaborate, our equity is in the form of a note from Gus. Andersen is going to provide an opening balance sheet showing that as equity. The note will be paid out of payments to Pegasus and Crew, the airplane company. We will refinance and avoid this issue in due course. It is slightly messy, but creative for getting in for free. Ass[sic] is carefully planned out. Regards, Adam

Abramoff says that the jargon and particulars of the deal were something he did not fully comprehend. Plus, he simply did not have the time to pay attention, because he was juggling so many things back in Washington. Waldman confirms that "Jack was never involved in the negotiations for the purchase of the company, nor did he ever visit Florida during this time. He completely and totally deferred to Kidan on all things financial."

Abramoff might have appeared willing to conceal from the lender that "our equity was from Gus." But clearly, it was a question, not a statement, one which Kidan had avoided responding to. And Kidan had written in his reply: "…creative for getting in for free. Ass [sic] is carefully planned out."

Abramoff tries to explain: "The structuring was changing constantly and the players kept changing, other banks, and there are plenty of deals like this in which no money is put down. The entire [leveraged buyout] industry is based on using the asset base in order to raise money" to purchase or refinance…All I knew was that Adam always said he had the money to make the down payment if we couldn't do it any other way."

The principal lender was Foothill Capital, a subsidiary of Wells Fargo Bank. Kidan tried hard to woo them. He pointed out how over-collateralized the purchase was. SunCruz's assets far exceeded the amount Foothill would be lending. He also tried to impress the lender with press clippings about his partner, the Washington uber-lobbyist. He showed them a recent front-page Wall Street Journal story that referred to him as "a Republican Stalwart."

The partners submitted financial statements. Abramoff listed his net worth at $13 million, including his lobbying practice valued at $7.5 million, as well as $1.4 million in parking lots in Atlantic City he shared with his father. There were a list of references, including one from Tony Rudy and Rep. Dana Rohrabacher (R-CA). "I don't remember it, but I would certainly have been happy to give him a good recommendation," Rohrabacher said. "He's a very honest man." However, Abramoff says that his financials were submitted by Kidan without Abramoff's knowledge or permission.

Years later, prosecutors claimed that in an August meeting in New York City "with representatives of Foothill…Abramoff falsely claimed to be a partner in the law firm of Preston, Gates…" Abramoff denies this: "I never told them I was a partner. I couldn't be a partner, because I wasn't a lawyer. I may have said I was a partner equivalent. As the head of their lobbying division, my combined business was 63% of the firm's lobbying revenue," says Abramoff. "I was the firm's biggest rainmaker."

He later explains that, "Kidan requested my financials for Boulis to see. I never gave Foothill my financials. Kidan gave it to them without my knowledge or permission." But wouldn't Foothill have wanted to see the financial statement of Kidan's partner?

The fact that Abramoff claimed a net worth of $13 million, reporters later maintained, was also fraudulent, especially the $7.5 million value of his lobbying practice. "I was contemplating leaving Preston Gates and taking my [lobbying] business public. Lots of little firms were doing it. You'd get a cap[italization] of five."[92]

Abramoff's financials might have been arguably valid. Kidan's were not. In his one-page financial statement, Kidan claimed his net worth was $26 million, alleging that all but $874,000 was in unspecified "closely held corporations." Apparently, this was intended to demonstrate to the lenders that the buyers had sufficient funds to make the $23 million down payment. In fact, Kidan had not finished paying off his bankruptcy obligations.

Foothill conducted a background check on Kidan and Abramoff. The 68-page report revealed that Kidan had "a string of liens, attachments, executions, as well as two bankruptcies."[93] Armed with this knowledge, why would any lender in its right mind loan a single penny to Adam Kidan, especially knowing he had submitted such a false financial statement? Incredibly, Foothill capital agreed to bankroll the deal. But it decided to persuade another specialty lender, Citadel Equity Fund of the Cayman Islands, to share the risk.

The final deal was structured as follows. The buyers would put up $23 million of their own cash, Boulis would grant a second mortgage to the buyers for $67.5 million, and Foothill and Citadel would supply the remaining $60 million as a first mortgage.

Thanks to its financial investigation of Kidan and Abramoff, however, Foothill had no clue where the buyers were going to come up with $23 million—information that it did not share with its partner, Citadel. But Foothill didn't care. It would be raking in millions of dollars in closing costs,[94] and the loan would be repaid at a generous rate of interest.

Furthermore, the value of the boats and the entire SunCruz operation exceeded the loan amount by $30 million. There was absolutely no risk.

When the closing began in late September 2000, "They kept shaking us down for more money," says Kidan. "It was simply going to be subtracted from the amount they were going to lend us. They even charged us for the meals brought in for their lawyers. It was ridiculous." Foothill would receive $750,000 from SunCruz in monthly principle and interest payments. It also insisted on a "lockbox."

"What that means," Kidan explains, "is they wanted our money put into a specific account [out of which] they would take their monthly mortgage payments. And for the privilege of doing this, there would be a $5,000 monthly processing fee! It was worse than the shakedown that I later had to deal with the mob."

But the lenders still weren't satisfied. "They also asked me and Jack to personally guarantee the loan," he says. "They knew we didn't have it. At that point, who cared?"

Greg C. Walker, a Foothill vice president, who approved the loan, was "a nice Irish guy, about six feet tall. The kind of guy you'd want to go to a bar with. He played football in high school and college. He's married with kids. They live on Long Island somewhere," says Kidan. "[Walker's] job was to bring in good loans that made money. Sure, he looked the other way about the [down payment], because he knew it was over collateralized. [His bosses] were so fat and happy about this deal." Years later, when *The Washington Post* asked him why he had taken a chance on someone like Kidan, Walker replied, "You had to be there." He refused to elaborate.

Waldman recalls, "Boulis' father had just died. He'd brought the body up to New York City to try to fly to Greece, but there was a problem getting the body out [of the country], and if he didn't leave right away, then there'd be a delay in releasing the body."

Boulis and Abramoff did not attend the five-day closing, which began in the midtown Manhattan offices of Foothill's lawyers, Schulte Roth & Zabel, on September 18, 2000, for which a team of lawyers had prepared a mountain of documents. Later that afternoon, Kidan and Walker rushed to the airport by limousine and flew down to Washington D.C. in a private jet. They attended a football game between the Washington Redskins and the Dallas Cowboys in Abramoff's skybox at Fedex Field. There, Abramoff introduced Walker to Tom DeLay, who just happened to be one of the guests. According to Kidan, Walker was quite impressed. Years later, when asked if meeting the House Majority Whip influenced him in any way, Walker replied, "The credit has to stand on its own." After the football game, Kidan and the Foothill vice president immediately flew back to New York City. The closing resumed the following morning.

The SunCruz transaction was complex. "Well, there was the transfer of leases in eleven locations, as well as the titles to all those ships," says Kidan. "Ship mortgages had to be perfected. The Coast Guard had to be notified who the new owner was. Boulis had so many entities. Each one had to have its own purchase-and-sale agreement. We had to negotiate the agreement with Boulis for his 10%, and for being a consultant. There were agreements between Jack and me and Waldman. And that doesn't even begin to include the reams [of paper] we had to sign with the banks."

And every day there were surprises. First of all, Kidan says that Walker demanded the buyers pay hundreds of thousands more than expected in closing costs to Foothill and Citadel. "There were six or seven lawyers [at their law offices in mid-town New York City]. There was a lot of yelling and screaming," says the mild-mannered Waldman. "I was eating at the buffet, stuffing myself. Adam looked up at me and said, 'What are you doing?' I had food in each of my hands. I couldn't take it. I got out of there."

Next, the Citadel lawyers suddenly announced that it was backing out of the deal, because Boulis had a criminal case still pending with the Florida attorney general's office. "Citadel was afraid that if Boulis lost the case, the state would seize the assets—slot machines and gaming equipment—involved in the criminal activity," says Kidan. Citadel was quickly mollified by a small holdback, equal to the value of the equipment.

The next morning, the lenders had changed their minds again. They were worried about political instability. The Florida legislature could pass legislation that would ban "cruise-to-nowhere" operations, or worse, would allow slot machines in Florida race tracks. The financial advisors at Boles Knop & Co. suggested a solution—insure against the risk that Florida will enact a law that would impair off-shore gambling. A $60 million insurance policy from Lloyd's of London would cost $1.4 million annually, an amount that would simply be subtracted from the loan. Foothill and Citadel quickly agreed. But then, the next day, Walker changed his mind. He told Kidan. "We'll assume the risk." In other words, the lenders would self-insure. "Instead of paying Lloyd's $1.4 million a year, they wanted us to pay them the money," says Kidan, shaking his head. "It was just another shakedown."

Kidan says he consulted with Abramoff—to whom he'd been faxing documents for him to sign every day. Abramoff agrees that it didn't make any difference. The additional $1.4 million insurance premium would simply be deducted from the loan amount. And more importantly, Abramoff and Kidan were planning to refinance the business as quickly as possible in order to pay off all lenders, including Boulis.

"[Abramoff] was so trusting of Kidan at that point, that he never received the actual guarantee agreement or the closing documents until weeks after the loan completion," says Waldman. "Kidan only faxed Jack the signature pages to be signed and sent to the closing officer. I know this because Kidan personally handed me the blank signature pages and told me to send them to Jack for him to sign. I asked if it wouldn't be better to send the entire document to Jack and Kidan told me that '[T]here isn't time.'"

Kidan claimed that that was not true. He says he had already faxed all documents in their entirety to Abramoff's lawyer in Baltimore, Maryland, for him to review in advance. Abramoff says that he had no lawyer in Baltimore: "The only thing he faxed to me was a draft of the personal guarantee, which I insisted on seeing and would not sign until I approved [to ensure that my wife was not liable]." The fact that Abramoff only signed faxed signature pages at the closing was a formality. But how could Kidan already have faxed all the documents when he only just received them at the closing?

Finally, it seemed there were no other hurtles. From that point, it should have been smooth sailing. Just a few perfunctory formalities remained. Under the final terms of the agreement, Kidan and Abramoff would pay Boulis $23 million in cash, Foothill and Citadel would loan the buyers $60 million, and Boulis would grant them a second mortgage of $67.5 million—which made the official sale price $150.5 million. In addition, Boulis would be hired as a paid consultant and would also retain a 10% share of the company.[95] His share would jump to 20%, if the second mortgage was not paid off in 90 days.[96]

Boulis, who had loaned the buyers the lion's share of the purchase price, believed that he would continue to have a major voice in the company's management. Indeed, he hoped the buyers would default so he could recapture SunCruz. The final day of the marathon closing was September 27.

The deal was all but done. Suddenly, Frederic Ragucci, one of the lawyers at the final meeting, turned to Kidan and dropped a bombshell. He casually informed Kidan that it was now time to put the $23 million down payment into the Schulte-Roth escrow account. "I remember feeling shock waves hitting my body and blood draining from my face when he said that," recalls Kidan. "Now, the deal was really dead." But Greg Walker jumped in and said, 'No, no, that's okay, Fred. They've already worked this out. They already have an arrangement between themselves,' meaning between Boulis and me."

Ragucci explained to Walker that the down payment was always put in escrow and that he'd never done it any other way. Walker insisted that this deal was different. Ragucci finally relented, but he demanded a copy of the wire transfer, "proving that we'd given Boulis the money. Walker looked at me and I looked back at him," recalls Kidan.

"Later that afternoon, I gave Waldman an old wire transfer. He took it to Kinkos, scanned it, and doctored it up. He even called the bank to get their fax numbers so he can make the heading at the top look like a real one," says Kidan.

Waldman says he had nothing to do with the fabrication of the wire transfer and that Kidan is being untruthful. What's more, Waldman points out, he was never indicted.

A "copy" of the wire transfer—dated September 23rd and faxed on September 28th to Ragucci—stated that $23 million had been transferred "by order of Adam Kidan" from his account in the Chevy Chase Savings Bank, to Boulis' account in the Ocean Bank in Fort Lauderdale. "Greg knew it wasn't real. He knew I was broke. But he didn't care. He just needed paper for the file," says Kidan. Years later, Kidan admits that Abramoff had no involvement in or knowledge whatsoever of the phony wire transfer.

Kidan and Boulis had secretly substituted two promissory notes totaling $20 million. Not only had Kidan refused to pay the $23 million until after the closing, but he had actually driven down the sale price by $3 million to $147.5 million.

With a simple phone call, Walker could have determined that Kidan's Chevy Chase bank account had, in fact, been closed for 15 days and that it never had a balance greater than $200,000. "Even Gus didn't know about the fake wire transfer," says Waldman, "because he thought he was going to get the money after closing when he returned from burying his father. Only Foothill and Adam knew about it."

Kidan says that Walker and he had an implicit—but never explicit—agreement, which might explain why Walker was never indicted. It was a wink-and-a-nod understanding. "Did [Walker] know about it? Of course," says Kidan. "Was there a conversation, like 'Hey, we know you don't have the money'"? No, but did they ask for tax returns? No. Did they ask for bank statements? No. Did they escrow the money, which is what every lender in the world does? No. Did they have a 60-page report from one of the best private investigation firms in the world showing that I had no money and that I was broke? Yes. Did I commit a crime by submitting false financials? Yes, and I will pay the price."

Foothill later claimed that the buyers and sellers knew that the secret arrangement was fraudulent and tried to conceal it. Foothill cited a fax to Kidan at his hotel from Joan Wagner, Boulis' chief financial officer and his representative at the closing. The fax included copies of the two promissory notes and the hand-scrawled instruction: "Please review and if 'ok' sign and give to Jimmy in a sealed envelope."

"Jimmy" was another Boulis lawyer, according to Foothill. The lender said in a court filing "the clear implication of this directive was to hide the very existence of the substituted notes from the lenders."

Foothill had a confidential side agreement with Kidan, requiring him to resolve the liabilities in his personal bankruptcy within 45 days, to which a Citadel lawyer wondered: "…who are we hiding these items from & why?"

Years later, Kidan's criminal attorney, Martin Jaffe, would point out why federal prosecutors would have been reluctant to prosecute this case, which in turn made them so desperate to squeeze out guilty pleas. "You can't be defrauded if you [Foothill] know what's going on and are a party to it," he said.

Kidan agrees. "How could Foothill think I had $23 million in the bank when they knew I still had a few thousand [dollars] outstanding in my personal bankruptcy to pay off to people!"

One additional and possibly damning fact is that Phyllis Glait, an employee of Foothill's attorney, notarized Kidan's signature on the $20 million in promissory notes to Boulis, which were secretly substituted for the $23 million wire transfer. Furthermore, Foothills attorney requested that Ms. Glait attend the closing.

Because of the strong evidence that Foothill was a party to the fraud, it is doubtful that the government would have been able to persuade a jury to vote unanimously beyond a reasonable doubt that Foothill had been deceived or defrauded. Therefore, it is highly unlikely that Kidan—and especially Abramoff—would have ever been convicted of wire fraud, especially when Abramoff had no knowledge whatsoever of the forged wire transfer.

Despite the fact that Abramoff and Waldman castigated Kidan years later, when the ownership of SunCruz was officially transferred to them on September 27, 2000, Abramoff and Waldman were dazzled by Kidan's accomplishment. Of course, supposedly unknown to Abramoff and Waldman, was the $20 million question. What was Kidan going to do when Boulis returned from Greece—after burying his father—and demanded his money? The new managing partner of SunCruz Casinos didn't seem fazed. "Kidan thought three or four steps ahead of the rest of us," says Abramoff.

CHAPTER TWENTY-EIGHT
OFFSETS

The owners of SunCruz boarded their new acquisition with great fanfare and media attention. Only Kidan and Waldman actually showed up at the Ft. Lauderdale headquarters—located in the soon-to-be infamous Broward County—to celebrate and take charge. Abramoff, who stayed behind in Washington, D.C., had never even seen the business or met Boulis. "Waldman was in charge of community relations and politics," says Kidan, but "he didn't do much, [although] he was a good sounding board and travel partner."

The salaries and perks they gave themselves would later be criticized. CEO Kidan's $500,000 salary with bonuses could reach $1 million a year. Vice-president Abramoff also earned $500,000 annually. And president Waldman, who only owned 10% of the company, took home $100,000 a year. At company expense, Kidan leased a $4,300 apartment and purchased the Summer Wind, a $34,000 motor boat. "[The media] made a big deal about this boat. I bought a 5-year old boat to give myself some peace of mind. I worked seven days a week, so occasionally I took the boat out and enjoyed myself," says Kidan. He also authorized the payment of $310,000 to defray the cost of Abramoff's leased sports boxes at Fedex Field, the MCI Center[97], and Camden Yards—a partial repayment for his partner's upfront acquisition costs. Later, the company's controller told investigators that in less than nine months, Kidan spent "somewhere close to a million dollars" in company funds on items that appeared "personal in nature." But as one federal prosecutor pointed out, "This was a privately owned business. They could do whatever the hell they wanted as long as they paid the interest on the loans."

For Kidan, assuming the helm of SunCruz was the climax of his life, a day he would recall as his proudest. The 36-year-old CEO had masterminded the impossible purchase of a $147.5 million business with over 1,200 employees. His plans were to expand it throughout the country and around the world. The sky was the limit.

As for Abramoff, one published account claimed that he yearned to be a billionaire and that SunCruz was the vehicle. It "dominate[d] much of the year and led to major frictions with his colleagues [at Preston Gates]." One former associate said, "Jack was totally focused and consumed with owning a gaming company…He talked about it a lot." According to another former associate "…SunCruz promised to be his ticket to riches and his exit from hourly fees."

Abramoff bristled at these claims, which, he pointed out, came from two unidentified sources. "I tried to help Adam where I could—Ben could confirm that—but it was basically Adam's show…I was incredibly overwhelmed and busy with so many other things. I was looking into starting my own firm, because I was not happy at Preston Gates. Also, there were so many Indian and [Northern Mariana Islands] issues, plus the [Bush] election that I worked day and night on. I went to Scotland twice—once with DeLay. There was the eLottery campaign. To say I devoted long hours [to SunCruz] is ridiculous. I wish I had spent more time. Unfortunately for me," Abramoff says, gesturing at the prison visitor lounge where he sits on a purple plastic chair, "I didn't. Obviously, [these sources] didn't know what the hell I was doing that year."

Nevertheless, Abramoff had gambled $700,000 of his own cash on a risky venture with little chance of success, which suggested he was far more committed to its outcome than he cared to recall. "At first, Adam told me it would only be $100,000. Then he asked me for another $50,000. Then a little more. Pretty soon, at $300,000, he says if I didn't put in another $35,000, I'd lose it all," says Abramoff. "If I'd know it was going to cost me $700,000, I would have never done it in a million years."

On the very first day, Kidan deftly handled his press interviews like a pro. He wisely "lauded the remarkable accomplishments of Gus Boulis, who started the SunCruz operations initially just six years ago with a single boat." He handled controversial issues gracefully, promising that he would "steer SunCruz clear of run-ins with state agencies and communities where the ships dock," calling the company a "political fixer-upper."

"We will reach out to reasonable people," said Kidan. "If we're doing something wrong I want to change it." Even Boulis' nemesis, state attorney general Bob Butterworth, chimed in. "It's good news he (Boulis) is going," said Butterworth. "He cut every corner, violated every environmental rule." And finally, Kidan crowned his public-relations day by promising that SunCruz would be "earmarking a minimum of $1 million in charitable contributions annually."

But in the late afternoon—exhausted from eight months of negotiations and the nail-biting seven-day closing—Kidan blundered. First, he made the mistake of telling a reporter that Boulis would only be a consultant "on an as-needed basis." The Greek tycoon would surely resent being relegated to the role of a minor factotum. After all, it was he who had provided $87.5 million—nearly 50% more than the lenders—in loans to the new buyers. In fact, he was somehow under the mistaken impression that Kidan and Abramoff would remain in Washington, D.C., and that Boulis would continue running the business on a day-to-day basis.

But Kidan's second mistake was more serious. He told a *Miami-Herald* reporter that Boulis was "a walking controversy. His problem is that he did not address the problems with the community. He was not a good corporate citizen."

One thing Boulis did not cotton to was public humiliation. If only Kidan had massaged—just for the first three months—Boulis' volatile ego, SunCruz might have grown into a billion-dollar business. The new owners had already set into motion the mechanism to refinance the loans within ninety days, in which Foothill, Citadel, and Boulis would all be paid off. Once accomplished, Kidan knew that the fraud would have been entombed forever.

A couple of days after arriving at his new offices, Kidan's phone rang. Assistant U.S. Attorney Christina Davenport was on the line. She asked to see a copy of the closing documents. She told him that Boulis had violated the 1916 shipping act. He had paid a large fine and been forced to divest himself of SunCruz. As a part of the agreement, he could retain no ownership interest in SunCruz and was banned from owning any off-shore gambling company. The implications, Kidan says, blew him away. First of all, it explained why Boulis had been so uncharacteristically accommodating throughout most of the negotiations.

"Does Boulis retain any interest in the company?" the assistant U.S. attorney asked.

"Well, Ms. Davenport, yes, he does. Ten percent. Actually, it jumps to twenty percent, if we can't refinance in 90 days."

"I need to see those documents."

"Look, you know Boulis. I don't want to tick him off. Why don't you subpoena the records and I'll happily provide them." After receiving the subpoena, he sent her the documents without ever informing Boulis.

But what really infuriated Kidan was that Abramoff "had to be privy to that information from Dimopoulos." says Kidan. After that he says he stopped trusting Abramoff. "…Since Dimopoulos knew that Jack was forbidden by ethical rules from purchasing SunCruz, he must have told him." But Kidan was making an assumption. He had no proof. Furthermore, if Abramoff had known, why wouldn't he have shared this information with his negotiating partner in order to drive down the sale price? "Jack is very, very smart," says Kidan, smiling. "He didn't care what the purchase price was, because we weren't putting any of our own money into it. He was getting $500,000 a year [salary] for doing basically nothing, plus the use of the company jet. His firm was getting $300,000 as a retainer for doing nothing."

But Kidan's explanation made no sense. A lower purchase price would have decreased monthly mortgages payments, increased profits, and eased refinancing. However, a published account made the same assertion—without any attribution. "Dimopoulos…told Abramoff…that Boulis was being forced by the government to sell…SunCruz." Abramoff denies it: "Art Dimopoulos did not tell me that Boulis was being forced to get out. It's simply not true."

Even before the closing, Kidan's financial advisors had already submitted applications to a battery of investment bankers and bond underwriters. If SunCruz went public, they might be able to raise $100 million in junk bonds. Not only would the loans to Boulis and the lenders—including the $20 million down payment—be retired, there would be over $10 million in operating capital leftover.

"We were getting close to signing a deal with Jefferies and Company," says Kidan. And he had already made inquiries about purchasing two Long Island-based gambling ships and began planning to install a new boat in the Marianas Islands, where Abramoff was the lobbyist.

But refinancing proved to be more complicated and time consuming than anticipated. In the meantime, Kidan needed to devise a strategy to rebuff Boulis' demand for the $20 million. The buyers had always wanted to pull all eleven boats out of the water to inspect the hulls, but Boulis had refused, saying it would have disrupted business. Built into the agreement, however, were "offsets," designed to cover the cost of unanticipated repairs that "were known or should have been known." Kidan claimed that in early October, the Coast Guard seized a SunCruz boat because it had failed inspection. What's more, boat captains had begun telling him that Boulis had forbidden them from making repairs, because the company was being sold. "For example, I found cracks in the hull [of a boat] below the water line that had been covered over with a skim coat of concrete," says Kidan. "That boat had to be pulled out of the water and repaired at a cost of $450,000, and that doesn't include the loss of income." Waldman disputes these claims. "We never lost a [boat] license," he says. "There was a minor crack or two, but there were hold backs for these kinds of things."

After burying his father and brawling with his wife, whom he threatened to evict from her seaside home because she had recently launched divorce proceedings against him, Boulis was in no mood to be conned when he finally returned to Florida in mid October. The first thing he did was to demand his money from Kidan.

Often, the best defense is a vigorous offense. Kidan calmly pulled out a list of boat repairs that totaled $30 million. Not only would he refuse to pay the $20 million, but the company would not make any loan payments to Boulis until these "unexpected" costs were calculated and subtracted. "First, Kidan told me that Boulis had actually concurred," says Abramoff, "which I realized later was just another lie."

Boulis went ballistic. He sent Kidan several letters threatening to reveal to the lenders that Kidan had not made the equity contribution. Kidan was nonplussed. Not only had Boulis been a part of the fraud, but Foothill had acquiesced to it. But when Boulis threatened to take legal action, Kidan became alarmed. A lawsuit could chill the prospects for refinancing. He briefed Abramoff, who once again, through Michael Scanlon, turned to Congressman Bob Ney. They asked him to insert remarks praising Kidan into the *Congressional Record*. These appeared on October 26.

> ...Since my previous statement, I have come to learn that [the]...new owner [of SunCruz Casinos] has a renowned reputation for honesty and integrity. The new owner, Mr. Adam Kidan, is most well known for his successful enterprise, Dial-a-Mattress, but he is also well known as a solid individual and a respected member of his community.
>
> While Mr. Kidan certainly has his hands full in his efforts to clean up SunCruz's reputation, his track record as a businessman and as a citizen lead me to believe that he will easily transform SunCruz from a questionable enterprise to an upstanding establishment....

Reporters would later howl at Ney's tribute, because Kidan was a failed businessman, a bankrupt, a disbarred lawyer, and mob-connected. Soon thereafter, SunCruz and Scanlon made $10,000 donation to the

National Republican Congressional Committee—which was credited to Ney and $4,000 to Ney's own reelection campaign.[98] And when Ney's remarks were brought to the attention of Boulis, it seemed to infuriate him even more. But in fact, he was secretly delighted. Kidan's ploy was seamlessly playing into Boulis' hand. Obviously, the last thing Boulis wanted the new owners to do was to refinance his loans. If he could delay them until December 27, his stake in the new company would double to 20%. And if he could continue to harass, bleed, and disrupt the new owners with lawsuits, they might actually default, which would allow him to foreclose and recapture SunCruz. However, he had a formidable and truculent foe, named Adam Kidan. Without him in charge, Boulis believed he could have more easily regained control.

Kidan had only himself to blame by falsely promising to pay the $20 million to a businessman with a reputation for ruthlessness. Kidan says he expected Boulis would try to turn Abramoff and Waldman against him, but he was stunned when he heard rumors that Boulis had also put out a contract on his life. Kidan took the threat seriously. He immediately engaged Seraph Inc., a security firm, to conduct a "threat assessment" on Boulis. Kidan also hired bodyguards and leased an armor-plated Mercedes Benz. According to the Seraph security report, Boulis "has a long history of violent behavior dating back to his life in Canada and Greece. Boulis grew up in a culture of violence."

Kidan decided to seek additional protection from his old mobster friend, Anthony "Big Tony" Moscatiello, caterer from Howard Beach, New York. He asked him to come down to south Florida and make contact with "everyone—you know, the Italian, Greek and Spanish [mobsters]— and let them know he was my friend—and an associate of [crime boss] John Gotti—and that if Boulis [were to] hurt me, there would be serious consequences." Kidan figured that if word got around that he was "protected," Boulis would not be able to hire a local hit man. However, Kidan would later testify that he was "unaware of Moscatiello's legal troubles or alleged Gambino affiliations."

In return for this assistance, Kidan hired Moscatiello as the wine vendor for SunCruz.[99] When he could not obtain a state beer-and-wine license, Kidan retained him on a "short-term basis as a food-and-wine consultant" for a salary of $145,000 over a four-month period. At Moscatiello's behest, Kidan later hired another mobster, Anthony

Ferrari, at a cost of $105,000. Those astronomical sums would come back to haunt Kidan.

"If [Kidan] had given that $250k to Gus, it would have gone a long way toward smoothing the situation, so that he'd think that he was going to get paid," says Waldman. "Maybe then we could have paid off the banks, as well as Gus, and we'd still own the company today."

And yet of all the strange events that would soon unfold in the SunCruz Armada, there was one that would end up being the most bizarre of all. Years later, *The Washington Post* would report that "Moscatiello had been indicted on federal heroin-trafficking charges in 1983 along with Gene Gotti, brother of John Gotti, the boss of the Gambinos...After Gotti and several others were convicted and sentenced to prison, charges against Moscatiello were dropped. The story helped to further besmirch Abramoff's reputation by linking him—via Kidan—to a mobster once arrested for heroin trafficking. Most readers would have inferred that Moscatiello was guilty, but the charges had probably been dropped due to a technicality or insufficient evidence.

Gotti's lawyer, Ronald Fischetti, was also surprised when Moscatiello was "cut loose." He says the government had incriminating wiretaps and an abundance of evidence. "I thought it was unusual," Fischetti says. "[Moscatiello] was involved with them because he was their financial guy. He did their taxes and handled their real-estate ventures."

As far as Kidan was concerned, it would prove to be another amazing example of the small-world department. One of the federal prosecutors in that case was Robert P. LaRusso. In 2004, he retired from the Justice Department to enter private practice as a criminal defense attorney. In August 2005, Kidan hired LaRusso, along with Joseph Conway, to defend him against the SunCruz fraud charges. "I actually called up Tony [Moscatiello] and asked him what he thought of him," says Kidan. "He said LaRusso was a nice guy."

Curious why Moscatiello's heroin-trafficking charges had been dropped, Kidan asked his new defense attorney to explain. "LaRusso told me he had to go in front of the judge and sheepishly ask that [Moscatiello] be released," says Kidan. "It was a case of mistaken identity. They'd arrested the wrong guy." The fact was that LaRusso could not reveal the real reason to Kidan, because it was top secret.

CHAPTER TWENTY-NINE
HONEST HANDS

Meanwhile, the acrimony between Kidan and Boulis rapidly came to a boil. The Greek tycoon finally told Waldman that Kidan had never paid him the $20 million. At the closing, Waldman did fax a copy of the $23 million wire transfer, but claimed he didn't know it was a forgery. Kidan maintains that Waldman, because of his computer skills, had actually fabricated the wire transfer and therefore knew perfectly well that Kidan had not made the down payment. Shortly after Boulis' return from Greece, Waldman claims that "…Boulis told me first [about the $20 million] and, after confirming the facts independently[100] Kidan denied it and said that Gus was having seller's remorse. Of course, I immediately told Jack," says Waldman.

Abramoff informed his personal secretary, Susan Ralston, to alter his busy schedule. After casting his ballot in the 2000 presidential election, he would have to fly down to the company headquarters in Broward County,[101] Florida, on an emergency diplomatic mission to keep SunCruz afloat. His goal was "to try to mediate their differences for the good of the business," says Waldman, adding that they worked "out a procedure by which we took power away from Kidan [in order to] return the management of the company to honest hands." After arriving in Florida, Abramoff, who had never met Boulis, listened to his complaints and supposedly learned for the first time that Kidan had never made the down payment. According to his lawyer, "Abramoff was flabbergasted by this news."

The "procedure" to placate Boulis was the formation of a management committee, which would run the company. It was composed of all four owners: Abramoff, Boulis, Waldman, and Kidan. Unfortunately, Waldman's assertion that he and Abramoff were returning the company "to honest hands" was contradicted in the weeks and months ahead, by their continued support of Kidan. In fact, the committee quickly fell into abeyance. In the hubbub swirling around the most disputed presidential election in American history, which hinged on "chads"[102] in Broward County, there were other dramatic, but secret, developments.

On November 13, 2000, Kidan was quietly, but officially, disbarred from the practice of law in the states of New York and New Jersey.[103] A few miles away, an Arab resident of Hollywood, Florida—seething with hatred—was quietly completing his flying lessons at the Huffman Aviation International flight school. His name was Mohammed Atta. The fury and frustration of Gus Boulis, who happened to be living a stone's throw from Atta's apartment, was increasing. In fact, on November 5, Kidan's fears were reconfirmed when he learned that Boulis had allegedly threatened to have Kidan "beaten and/or killed."

Back in late September, following the sale of his company, Boulis had vacated the SunCruz office and had conveniently leased another down the hall, because he believed he would remain intimately involved in the company's management. As a result, Boulis and Kidan bumped into each other and traded insults almost daily.

In late November, Boulis received word that Kidan was "protected." At a community meeting in Mayport, where SunCruz docked one of its boats, a Boulis ally publicly accused Kidan of having Mob ties. Embarrassed, Kidan threatened to sue.

On December 5, Waldman decided to play the role of peace maker. He invited Boulis and Joan Wagner, Boulis' chief financial officer, to a meeting with Kidan in his office. "[Wagner] is heavy, blond, of medium height. She was always dogged in her defense of Gus and his interests," says Waldman. The meeting quickly deteriorated. Kidan told Boulis to stop interfering in the way the company was being run.

"What do you mean 'stop'? I'm the guy who lent you the $90 million to buy my business. I can do anything I want. I can take the fucking thing back if I want."

"Gus, you can't interrupt the business. You can't harass employees. It's enough. It can't go on."

"Don't tell me what I can do,"

"Gus, we've tried to accommodate you, but nothing is working. Enough already. I can't live with these threats. I can't live with this intimidation. If you're not happy, sue me. We'll work it out in the court system if we can't work it out here."

"I'm not going to sue you. I'm going to fucking kill you." Boulis then ran around the desk and stabbed Kidan in the neck with pen, drawing blood. Kidan's bodyguard came rushing into the room and pinned Boulis to the floor. Boulis screamed at the bodyguard, "I'm going to kill you. I'm going to kill your wife and children." Moments later, the police arrived and arrested Boulis.

Convinced that his adversary had put out a contract on his life, Kidan immediately hired two additional bodyguards at $5,000 a week. Two days later, he obtained a temporary restraining order, forcing Boulis to move out of the office building they shared and "ordering him to stay at least 500 feet from Kidan and any SunCruz operations."

Boulis' lawyer, Stephen Stalling did not agree with Kidan's version of events, declaring that "[His client] will have his day in court." But when Boulis failed to show up in court, the restraining order became permanent.

Kidan's side of the story was supported by an e-mail Waldman wrote to Abramoff later that day. Scanlon also claimed to have witnessed the attack, implicitly supporting Kidan's version. Waldman later changed his position. On further reflection, Waldman, who had witnessed the attack, later realized that Kidan must have staged the whole thing: "Kidan said provocative things to Gus to upset him. Finally, Gus lost it and there was a scuffle. Gus happened to have a pen, but I never saw any blood...I think Kidan did this to make him seem violent, so that Jack would change his allegiance back to Kidan."

Abramoff agrees: "After the Boulis violence, I told myself that maybe Kidan's been telling me the truth, so I continued to support him."

In the meantime, Moscatiello persuaded Kidan to hire Anthony Ferrari, who owned Moon Over Miami Beach, a local security firm, to protect the boats from sabotage at a cost that eventually totaled $105,000. "Ferrari isn't his real name. It was something Hispanic, but he wanted it sounding Italian so he could claim to be John Gotti's cousin. [Ferrari's] about 5'7", fat, sloppy, disheveled. He always wore sweatpants. A real stupid, two-bit crook. The guy was always surrounded by these big bouncer types. One of them was this black guy by the name of Dwayne Nicholson. I shook hands with him a couple times, but we never spoke," says Kidan. "All Ferrari's security firm really did was bouncer type work. I don't think he'd ever protected boats before." In fact, Ferrari and Moon Over Miami Beach were never licensed to provide security services, according to documents at the Florida Department of State Division of Licensing.

A few days later, Kidan concerns increased. He had learned that Moscatiello had brought several other mobsters down from New York City to beef up Kidan's protection. In an e-mail to Abramoff, Kidan wrote, "My friend in NY is acting out of concern for my safety. By sending security I am afraid it will make things worse and I will ask him today to remove them. I appreciate his efforts, but the situation is at a critical point."

It dawned on Kidan and Abramoff that Boulis' strategy was to wrest back control of SunCruz. They decided to counterattack by painting him negatively in the press. "I was the victim of family violence before. Let's use that in our favor (my mother wouldn't mind) to show how we can't tolerate violence and the likes of criminals," Kidan e-mailed Abramoff. Abramoff immediately e-mailed one of Boulis' attorneys: "Gus and Adam need to resolve the issue of what Gus is owed and Gus needs to move on out of the company."

But Boulis, who ownership percentage of SunCruz had now doubled to 20%, was not about to move out. On January 19, 2001, he filed a lawsuit, seeking to bar Kidan from operating the SunCruz and forcing him to make his loan payments. Kidan quickly countersued, accusing Boulis of stealing slot machines from one of the boats. The following day, Kidan and Scanlon witnessed President Bush's inauguration and attended a reception at DeLay's Capitol Hill office. Several days later, Boulis suddenly found himself under attack on another front. Federal prosecutors sued him for contempt because he had retained a 20% interest in SunCruz. Boulis' lawyers replied that their client could continue to retain ownership in the company, because 13 months remained on his deadline to sell SunCruz.

A week after the inauguration, Abramoff leased a corporate jet to ferry congressional staffers down to Tampa, Florida, for the Super Bowl game, followed by a night of gambling aboard a SunCruz boat. Kidan provided Abramoff's guests with complimentary chips. "Abramoff was very big with the staffers. You don't have to be a rocket scientist to know that they're the ones who get things done. Some are very powerful. Sometimes they don't have to recommend something to the Congressman or Senator they work for. They just do it," says Kidan. The Super Bowl was in our backyard, and we had a boat nearby...Ney was supposed to come down with his two sons, but he had to cancel at the last minute because one of them was sick."

On January 31, the SunCruz mêlée finally hit the front page of *The Florida Sun-Sentinel*. Kidan was quoted extensively. He described the pen attack and repeated that Boulis had threatened to kill him. "This guy is violent. He's sleazy," Kidan said, adding ominously, "This man has finally met his match. We're not taking this lying down."

However, because of mounting legal fees, the payments to Moscatiello and Ferrari, not to mention the money to pay for Abramoff's sky boxes in Washington, D.C., Kidan had been unable to make his loan payments to Foothill and Citadel. More importantly, because of the lawsuits and countersuits pending, refinancing SunCruz was now out of the question.

Despite its financial precariousness, SunCruz continued to expand. On January 30, Kidan christened the *SunCruz XI*, berthed in Fort Meyers. Early the next morning, he flew to London and then on to Tel Aviv, where Abramoff met him at the airport. Not only were they prospecting for new casino locations, but Abramoff was hoping to discover oil in the Negev with Alexander Koulakovsky's new-fangled technology. "Jack was going to get some legislation pushed through Congress to provide the [exploration] money [for Koulakovsky]," says Kidan. "They were going to make a killing." But the project fizzled, along with their efforts to expand SunCruz into the Promised Land. Two Israeli generals informed them that a gambling boat would be too easy a target for terrorists.

After spending the night in London, Kidan and Abramoff were about to depart from Heathrow Airport on a flight to Hong Kong, where they were thinking of installing a gambling boat. It was then that they received a phone call that would change everything.

CHAPTER THIRTY
GANGLAND SLAYING

Abramoff was in the first-class lounge, checking his e-mail. Kidan in a duty-free shop, purchasing Hermes ties. Suddenly, his bodyguard's cell phone rang. It was his wife calling from Ft. Lauderdale. "Boulis has been shot. He's dead." When the bodyguard told his client, Kidan was stunned. "I couldn't stop saying, 'Holy shit! Holy shit!'" The news transported him back to the moment he learned that his mother had been murdered. "The first thing I thought about were his kids," says Kidan.

He ran to the first-class lounge and told Abramoff, who was also stunned. "At the Wailing Wall I'd prayed for Boulis to go to jail," admits Kidan. "But never this." Several minutes later, as the initial shock began to wear off, they thought about the implications of Boulis' death. Abramoff decided that Kidan should fly back to Fort Lauderdale immediately and reassure SunCruz employees that the company remained strong and the future secure. Abramoff would continue to the Far East as planned.

As they were about to board separate planes, Kidan says he told Abramoff, "Well, I don't want to sound like a schmuck, but now we can run SunCruz our way. No more interference."

From Heathrow, Kidan flew to New York, where the SunCruz corporate jet was waiting to whisk him to Fort Lauderdale Airport. He contacted Michael Scanlon, the company spokesman, and instructed him to issue a condolence statement: "SunCruz executives are shocked and saddened by the death of Gus Boulis." But Kidan himself declined to comment "out of respect for the family."

The south Florida media called the murder "a gangland-style slaying." The Boulis family offered a $100,000 reward for information leading to the arrest and conviction of his killers. Kidan knew it wouldn't be long before reporters learned of his mob connections. The court of public opinion would instantly try and convict him. And a feeding frenzy would be unleashed when they learned than Kidan's mother had been also slain by the mob, ignoring the fact that it had been just a botched home invasion. He was certain a brace of detectives would be waiting to pepper him with questions the moment he stepped off the plane in Florida.

Instead, it would be a month before police first questioned him. When they did, Kidan told them, "I didn't kill him. I didn't order it. I had absolutely nothing to do with it." He conceded that he had been embroiled with Boulis in a bitter business dispute. But the police already knew that. They knew that Boulis had stabbed him in the neck with a pen and had threatened to kill him, and that he had a restraining order against Boulis. But they wondered if Kidan had struck first. But it was also clear that the hot-tempered tycoon had many other enemies.

"He didn't seem to have too many friends," said Attorney General Butterworth. "If you had to say who the suspects [were], it would have been anyone who had done business with him. He was just not a good person."

An editorial lauded Boulis for his remarkable business savvy but faulted him for an "impatience with laws, rules, and codes [which] cast a dark shadow over an admirable achievement. His conduct stands as a warning that a reputation for honor still should count in business."

Hollywood Mayor Mara Guilanti chimed in, "He was a person who liked to play by his own rules."

The police sensed that Kidan was not "being completely forthright." They were correct. Several days after he returned to Ft. Lauderdale, he learned who had murdered Boulis, but he was not about to tell police. Otherwise, he too would be murdered. He also knew that, if worse came to worse, this information might prove to be an ace in the hole.

According to Kidan, it was Moscatiello, his "food and beverage consultant," who told him that the Gambino crime family had ordered the hit. Moscatiello then described with some obvious embellishments what happened on the evening of February 6.

Boulis had emerged from the rear entrance of his four-story Ft. Lauderdale office building at 910 S.E. 17th St. The darkened parking lot was empty, except for his car. He was dressed in a rumpled shirt, khakis, and loafers with no socks. He had just finished a contentious meeting about a controversial real-estate deal on city-owned land called Diamond on the Beach, which, due to his heavy Greek accent, he always called "Diana the Bitch."

He opened his car door with a keyless remote and eased into the brand-new BMW 740Li He slipped a Mikis Theodorakis CD into his car stereo, exited the parking lot, drove through a back alley, and turned left on Miami Road. On the dimly lit street, there were no traffic cops, only warehouses and small apartment buildings. He sped along, heading for a tryst with a former Trump casino model in her late 20s.

At 9:17 P.M., several blocks from his office, he had to reduce speed behind a slow-moving black Chevy Blazer with dealer plates. For no apparent reason, the car suddenly stopped in the middle of the road. Annoyed, Boulis leaned on the horn. The Chevy refused to move. Suddenly, a dark-gray Mustang with temporary paper plates came from the opposite direction and pulled up next to Boulis, their doors almost touching.

Johnny Gurino, a Gambino capo, was behind the wheel of the Mustang. He lowered the window and shouted to Boulis: "Hey, why you been avoiding us? All we wanna do is fucking talk to you."

Boulis was furious. "Fuck you! I don't have to talk to you scumbags."

"Oh yeah? Fuck me? No, fuck you." Smiling, Gurino produced a semiautomatic pistol.

Obviously, this hit had been carefully planned. They'd been watching him for days. Nothing had been left to chance. They knew his route. The killers would ditch the cars and vanish. Gurino squeezed the trigger. Four hollow-point bullets pierced Boulis' throat, cheeks, and chest. He screamed. The killers sped away in opposite directions.

Bleeding profusely, Boulis raced toward the hospital, only minutes away. There, the doctors could stop the bleeding and save his life. He turned onto busy Federal Highway, jumped a landscaped median strip, and crashed into an oak tree across from one of his "Miami Subs," the restaurant chain he had founded. Boulis, a Greek, would have appreciated the irony.

Still conscious, he was rushed by ambulance to the Broward General Hospital, several blocks away. At 10:20 P.M., he was pronounced dead.

A few days later, and half a world away, to the strains of the traditional clarinet music he had loved, wafting over the rugged mountainside that overlooked the impoverished Aegean fishing village of his youth, Boulis' cold, bullet-riddled body was laid to rest in a platinum casket.

Life continued. SunCruz' eleven gambling boats, weather permitting, sailed twice a day, seven days a week, on schedule. The profits kept pouring in. Two weeks after the murder, Kidan and Abramoff applied to Foothill and Citadel for short-term loan because the company had a temporary cash-flow problem. The request was denied. Kidan hired Abramoff's new firm, Greenberg Traurig, as its new Washington lobbyist, and they keep pushing forward with their planned $100 million junk bond offering so they can retire their debt and expand the SunCruz operations.

At the end of February, Kidan flew up with his bodyguards to New York City for the day to join his sisters in a courtroom. One of their mother's killers was about to be sentenced to 50 years in prison. When it was Kidan's turn, he stood and told the judge, "We're not here to incarcerate a defendant. We're here to sentence an animal…He walked into a person's home and shot her at point-blank range. He killed my mother!"

In early March, Kidan and Abramoff attended a fundraiser for Rep. Ney at Abramoff's skybox at the MCI center in Washington. And two weeks after that, Kidan launched the new *SunCruz IV* in Panama City with great fanfare. By then, media reports about the murder had subsided, but pressure on Kidan continued to mount. He began having trouble sleeping.

First, the Boulis heirs—in part to determine the value of his estate, which included 20% of SunCruz—wanted to examine the company books. Kidan refused, but he knew the court would eventually force him to make them available. Next, the Boulis heirs filed several lawsuits against him for breach of contract and fiduciary duty. Their strategy was to launch an all-out assault to force Kidan, whom they suspected of ordering Boulis' murder, from the company. The problem with lawsuits was they would result in depositions under oath. What would he do if asked about the $23 million down payment? What if Moscatiello's name came up?

Fearing for his life, Kidan continued to pay Moscatiello $25,000 a month for "food and beverage services," which he did not perform, and Ferrari for boat security, which he did not provide. Kidan claimed that Moscatiello doctored a $6,000 SunCruz check into one for $16,000. Kidan didn't dare contest it. He says he had no choice but to allow the shakedown and extortion to continue.

Large payments that Kidan had made to two known organized-crime associates—before and after Boulis' murder—would be difficult to justify if the SunCruz books were ever scrutinized. They could be construed as disbursements for a mob hit.

Finally, Kidan was worried that if prosecutors discovered that he had never paid Boulis a single penny of the down payment, they could indict him for conspiracy and fraud. Kidan and Abramoff could face many years in prison.

On April 10, a film crew from the TV show *America's Most Wanted* arrived in Fort Lauderdale to film a segment on Boulis' murder. Detectives were delighted that the case would receive national exposure. "It's always good to stir up a story," says detective Mike Reed. Kidan was contacted by the show but declined to be interviewed.

In the middle of April, Circuit Judge Mark Speiser appointed an independent accountant to examine the SunCruz books so that the company could be appraised. The proverbial can of worms was about to be opened. Kidan feared that someone was going to wonder what had happened to the $23 million Boulis never received, not to mention substantial payments to Moscatiello and Ferrari.

A few days later, Kidan met with Abramoff in Washington. "I told [him] about who murdered Boulis as we were standing on the balcony of his office [at Greenberg Traurig]. We were within view of the White House. He was surprised but not surprised. I think he was a little titillated," says Kidan. Why did he tell Abramoff? "I wanted him to know that I had muscle and not to fuck with me," adds Kidan. When asked about this meeting, Abramoff calls Kidan a pathological liar and denies this meeting ever took place or that Kidan ever told him the identities of Boulis' murderers.

In early June, Kidan's world began to unravel. Always unflappable, he fought back. The Boulis estate filed another lawsuit against Kidan, claiming that he had misappropriated $30,000 in company funds by paying that sum to the daughter of Anthony Moscatiello, a reputed Gambino crime family associate, just before Boulis' murder. Kidan angrily denounced the implications, calling them a bad work of fiction. He conceded that he had had a long friendship with Moscatiello, but denied any wrongdoing.

"The Boulis people are on a scorched-earth campaign to smear me. That's what's going on here," says Kidan. He vowed to seek sanctions against the Boulis estate lawyers for defamation and slander, because they implied that he arranged for Boulis' murder and that the murder of his mother might have been related to his association with Moscatiello. "[Moscatiello's] a very nice man," Kidan told a reporter. "He's given me a lot of great advice over the years." He admitted that he paid Moscatiello $30,000 for consulting on "food and beverage." He had requested that the three $10,000 checks—on December 13, 2000, January 23 and January 31, 2001—be paid to his daughter. "Look, this is a cash business," Kidan explained. "If I'm going to give Tony Moscatiello illegal money, why would I write him a check, or write it to his daughter? It doesn't make sense, does it?"

It would only make sense if Kidan never thought the SunCruz books would be audited. Or if Kidan thought that by saying that no one in his right mind would pay for a hit by writing checks, he might as well let the company pay for it.

Lawyers for Boulis' estate asserted that these questionable payments, as well as other expenses, were just "the tips of the iceberg....in other words, there are likely many more similar transactions yet to be discovered." They were right. In fact, Kidan was still paying Moscatiello $25,000 a month.

The local police did not consider Kidan a suspect. "If Kidan in some way benefited from [Boulis' murder], I wish somebody would tell me how," said detective Jack King, one of the two homicide investigators working full-time on the case.

The negative press notwithstanding, SunCruz revenues remained somewhat robust. Table revenues had increased more than eight percent a month and slot machines had grown by 23 percent each month since Kidan and Abramoff acquired the company. Nonetheless, Kidan warned that with the company hemorrhaging $500,000 a month in legal fees, it might be forced into bankruptcy. On June 20, Kidan did just that, saying the Chapter 11 filing would consolidate the eight pending lawsuits. "[This will allow] a judge [to] decide if there's any validity [to them]," Kidan told a reporter. "I am sorry that it has come to this, but we have to stop the onslaught of nonsense lawsuits."

Abramoff and Waldman decided to wash their hands of the entanglement by assigning their shares in the company to the Boulis estate without compensation.[104] Later, Abramoff told a reporter, "I was fortunate to get out of that financially better off than when I entered it. I was lucky it did not damage me. But it's not something I would repeat."

When asked why his partners had turned against him, Kidan shakes his head and says bitterly, "Jack was always looking after himself…He jumped sides, because the Boulis people had threatened to sue him, and he didn't want the bad publicity."

Again, Abramoff disputed this: "I sold my shares because this guy had destroyed the company…They had my name on a personal guarantee of [the Boulis estates'] loan, which [Kidan] was not paying and was going into default…If he considers that my looking after myself, then yes."

Bankruptcy, however, was the only viable way Kidan says he could extricate himself from the Gambino shakedown without getting fitted with cement shoes. He could now legitimately tell Moscatiello, who in turn would tell the Gambinos that SunCruz was under the control of the federal bankruptcy court, not Kidan.

Moscatiello actually confirmed the shakedown years later to the Fort Lauderdale police, after his arrest for Boulis' murder: "It's a company doing $147 million a year. If you can't skim a few dollars off $147 million a year, ha ha, you shouldn't be in the business."

Despite the bankruptcy, Kidan announced that SunCruz would continue to operate and would continue trying to refinance its debts.

Privately, he was relieved. He knew his days at SunCruz were numbered. Now armed with Abramoff's and Waldman's shares, the Boulis estate immediately voted to oust him from the company.

Kidan knew it was important to give the Gambinos the impression that he was putting up a fight. He had his lawyers point out in court that SunCruz's operating agreement, negotiated last fall with his now-disgruntled partners, allowed him to maintain managing control of the company unless he died, became incapacitated, or resigned. On July 2, U.S. bankruptcy Judge Paul G. Hyman agreed, denying the request for Kidan's ouster.

Seven days later, Kidan "reluctantly" agreed to surrender his 35 percent interest in and managerial control of the company to the Boulis estate for $200,000 in "walk-away" money. More importantly, the Boulis estate promised to drop all lawsuits—past and future—against him. According to Kidan's calculations, the agreement exempted him from liabilities exceeding $3.4 million. Creditors were vigorously opposed to the settlement, however, because a conflict of interest had been created. The Boulis estate, the company's largest creditor, would be less concerned with the welfare of other creditors, such as Foothill and Citadel. The decision was appealed. Kidan breathed an enormous sigh of relief. He immediately vacated his SunCruz offices and fled back to New York.

But on August 10, company accountants announced that Kidan had paid mobster Moscatiello, not $30,000, but $145,000. In addition, he had paid another mobster, James Ferrari, $105,000. The total now stood at $250,000. They immediately turned this information over to the police.

When a reporter contacted him, Kidan defended the payments as legitimate business expenses. He paid Moscatiello for food and beverage consulting and Ferrari for security against dockside sabotage of SunCruz boats. "There was never any secret about these payments," said Kidan, without explaining why he hadn't ever mentioned them before. Lawyers for the Boulis estate pointed out that these payments were made to organized-crime figures before and after Boulis was murdered, which, they claimed, was exactly why Kidan had initially refused to hand over the company books.

America's Most Wanted aired a nine-minute segment on the Boulis murder. Though not stated explicitly, the producers left no doubt that Kidan had ordered Boulis' assassination. He now realized that he had erred by declining to appear on the show. A vigorous denial would have created at least some doubt.

Two days later, an unanticipated development badly rattled Kidan. He feared the dominoes might be about to fall. He had always figured that since the forged $23 million wire transfer involved the collusion of Boulis and some of his closest associates, it would be very unlikely for the Boulis estate to raise the issue at all. What no one anticipated was that one of Boulis' ex-partners, H. DeWayne Williams, a minor creditor in the SunCruz bankruptcy, suspected that the down payment had never been made and that the lenders had been deceived. Because some of the same Boulis associates were now running SunCruz, the bankruptcy court should not allow the Boulis estate to be in charge of running the company. It would be equivalent to leaving the fox in charge of the hen house.

Williams' allegation triggered some academy-award performances. Claiming it knew nothing about the nonpayment of the down payment, the Boulis estate went through the motions of combing dozens of Boulis bank accounts in search of the $23 million wire transfer. To its amazement and shock, it discovered that no transfer had ever taken place.

The next thespian was Foothill. Its lawyers issued subpoenas for Boulis' and Kidan's bank records to confirm or refute the alleged $23 million wire transfer. Kidan, who was no longer in touch with Abramoff, realized that this development could result in criminal prosecution for both of them, as well as for Waldman.

Unbeknownst to Abramoff and Kidan, Martin Steinberg, one of the lawyers for the Boulis estate, was a former assistant U.S. attorney. In August, he decided to alert his former colleagues that Kidan and Abramoff appeared to have committed bank fraud. The U.S. attorney's office in south Florida, swamped with drug-related prosecutions, often could not become excited about bank fraud in which the lender has not yet been harmed. The Boulis estate, which had assumed the loans, was making its monthly payments. Nevertheless, federal prosecutors decided to look into this particular case because of its possible ties to the sensational organized-crime slaying of one of Florida's most "notorious" businessmen. Abramoff didn't interest them. Boulis' murder did.

Near the end of August, several Muslim men were captured on SunCruz security cameras gambling on one of its boats. Nearly two weeks later, these men would hijack and fly four commercial passenger planes into the World Trade Center, the Pentagon, and a field in rural Pennsylvania. "They acted just like normal guests of ours and they were courteous," a SunCruz spokesman would later say. "There were no issues."

In the meantime, like the proverbial cat, Kidan had somehow landed on his feet. He had embarked on a new venture, SecureCar Worldwide. His new company leased chauffeured "protected" luxury cars to high-profile foreign and American businessmen who feared assassination, kidnapping, or just wanted to impress their girlfriends. Kidan had already quietly incorporated a company called Sun Coast Casinos. By the spring of 2002, he hoped to be operating a "cruise-to-nowhere" gambling boat out of Gloucester harbor, on the north shore of Massachusetts. A week after the 9-11 terrorist attacks, Kidan was interviewed by *Forbes* magazine. Sounding undaunted and unrepentant, he mentioned his third, somewhat brash, venture. "I'm writing a book," he said by the pool at his Hamptons rental, his bodyguard lurking inside. "It's called *Three Miles Out*."

By December, he had signed a contract with a literary agent. They quickly prepared a press release:

> This stranger-than-fiction true story involves a volatile self-made millionaire, a high-powered Washington lobbyist, a well-known businessman, murder, high finance, the mafia and its associates, casinos, beautiful and exotic women, wealth, jet-set lifestyles, and lots of cash....
>
> **Adam Kidan is a respected businessman with an incredible story to tell. His experience with his many businesses have brought him recognition as a man who knows how to effectively promote his book. As well, he knows how to make his book profit from the many close relationships he has established through his business dealings.**

Kidan had omitted a few biographical details.

PART IV

ICARUS

CHAPTER THIRTY-ONE
SMEAR CAMPAIGN

Only with a crystal ball could Abramoff have foreseen that the year 2000, would set the stage for his downfall. Life as he knew it would be destroyed forever. It would hinge, in part, on two unrelated events. The first was the $23 million counterfeit SunCruz wire transfer Abramoff knew nothing about. The second was the 2000 Republican South Carolina primary.

On February 2, 2000 the under-funded underdog, Sen. John McCain, defeated Texas governor George W. Bush in the New Hampshire Republican primary by a surprising 19 points. Right-wing conservatives—most of whom loathed McCain—panicked.

Perhaps the most visible and notorious McCain bashers were the unholy trinity of Ralph Reed, Grover Norquist, and Jack Abramoff. They were joined by Rep. Tom DeLay[105] and televangelists Pat Robertson and Jerry Falwell. They believed that the traitorous McCain had to be stopped at all cost. In fact, Norquist would later call McCain "a nut job." To some, the methods mattered not. The end justified the means. Nothing less than the future of mankind—not to mention the Republican Party—was at stake.

The morning after McCain's 2000 New Hampshire victory, Abramoff's cell phone rang. It was Ralph Reed. "'Jack, we need to beat this guy,'" Abramoff recalls that Reed said, adding that he was almost hyperventilating. "'We need to raise money; we need a massive grassroots effort. I can get the churches, but this is a bad guy. He's going to beat Bush.'"

Abramoff, who agreed that Bush "was on the ropes and had to be saved," tried to mollify Reed, his close friend. Abramoff told Reed, whom he considered "the cocky and smart political assassin" not to worry. He'd handle it. "And I did," says Abramoff. "I raised about $3 million. It took me a day, day and a half. This money all went to a non-campaign entity controlled by Reed."

Reed certainly had a high opinion of himself as the ultimate stealth warrior. He once told a reporter: "I want to be invisible. I do guerrilla warfare. I paint my face and travel at night. You don't know it's over until you're in a body bag. You don't know until election night." At the time, Abramoff says he believed this would be a wise investment for his clients, many of whom made the contributions, and for the most part they agreed: "Little did I realize that, less than four years later, this investment would help to bring me to ruin."

Maverick McCain—also known as the heretic—was despised by conservative Republicans for many reasons. "And he was the darling of the mainstream media to boot, which made matters worse," says Abramoff. In addition to McCain's co-sponsorship of campaign reform—which limited political contributions and was viewed by the rightwing as an obscene violation of the Constitutional right to free speech—he was too independent, too liberal, too arrogant, and too cozy with liberal Democrats such as Ted Kennedy, Tom Daschle, and John Kerry.

In the ensuring years, McCain would further infuriate conservative Republicans by supporting immigration reform, objecting to Bush tax cuts, and opposing drilling for oil in Alaska. Perhaps his most subversive sins were acknowledging the severity of global warming, criticizing the use of tough interrogation techniques, and refusing to support a constitutional ban on same-sex marriage.

There were other disturbing aberrations. McCain actually had the gall to invite Democratic Minority Leader, Tom Daschle, to his Arizona ranch for a weekend visit. In 2001, McCain even contemplated switching to the Democratic Party. In the spring of 2004, conservative Republicans were appalled when McCain toyed with accepting John Kerry's offer to be his running mate on the Democratic presidential ticket.[106] And the final straw was McCain's collusion with Democrats to kill the "nuclear option," which was an effort by the Republicans to eliminate the age-old Senate filibuster and ease the approval of pro-life, Bush-nominated candidates to the Supreme Court.

McCain's arrogance had also become intolerable. "[McCain] doesn't just challenge other Republicans, he acts as if he is morally superior to them," said *The Weekly Standard*. Some right-wing Republicans, including Anne Coulter and Rush Limbaugh, hated McCain so much that they actually said they preferred Hillary Clinton over McCain for president in 2008.

After McCain's huge 2000 New Hampshire victory, the next GOP primary was only 17 days away, in South Carolina. The polls showed McCain was in a dead heat with Bush. McCain was confident that his momentum—along with his support from the state's sizable population of fellow veterans—would carry him to another decisive victory. However, he did not anticipate the fervor of the state's evangelical Christians and that percentage of the population whose bigotry could be exploited. Because Abramoff had raised so much money so quickly, Reed—who was Bush's southern chairman—was able to muster the Christian Coalition storm troopers on a moment's notice.

"The money [that I raised] was given to the groups through Ralph. I'm sure he buried it, since that's the way he did things," says Abramoff. "I did not care for any credit at the time, in particular, since I only did this as a favor to Ralph. I was supportive of Bush, but he did not excite me. I did this because [Reed] asked me."

Apparently, Bush never knew of Abramoff's involvement in South Carolina. But Abramoff was sure that Reed would inform those who needed to know. And that meant Karl Rove. "Rove did not ask me directly [about the money I raised in the 2000 South Carolina Republican primary campaign]. I did not speak with him about this. I don't recall ever speaking with him about it, actually," says Abramoff. "I can say this, though, that the money which was spent by Ralph on getting the churches out to vote did not include any effort which was tied in any way to the nasty stuff." But, upon further questioning, Abramoff conceded that there was no way for him to be certain about that. What was crucial, however, was not whether Abramoff's money ended up funding the smear campaign, but whether McCain believed it had.

For political junkies, the South Carolina smear campaign would achieve legendary status. Overnight, McCain found himself bombarded by widespread anonymous and scurrilous phone calls, flyers at campaign events, faxes, and postcards. The most infamous smear involved an eleven-year-old black girl who repeatedly appeared on stage with McCain throughout the South Carolina campaign.

"Push pollers"— people who claimed to be conducting a nonpartisan poll, but were in fact planting seeds of doubt in the minds of voters—had begun making calls statewide. The question they asked was this: "Would you be more likely or less likely to vote for John McCain for president if you knew he had fathered an illegitimate black child?" Some flyers claimed he had sired the child with a black prostitute,[107] echoing similar assertions during the 1992 presidential campaign that Bill Clinton had fathered a black son. These efforts pandered to the registered voters of the only state in American history to elect a U.S. Senator—the staunch segregationist Strom Thurmond—on a write-in ballot.

The fact that McCain had clumsily mishandled questions about the appropriateness of the Confederate flag flying over the South Carolina statehouse may have contributed to his defeat. But what stuck in McCain's throat for months and years to come were the allegations about Bridget, his then 11-year-old black daughter. In fact, what made this smear particularly unconscionable was the fact that Bridget's presence in McCain's life and (on the campaign podium with him) had resulted from an extraordinary act of compassion. McCain and his wife had actually adopted her as a baby from an orphanage in Bangladesh, established by Mother Theresa, no less.[108]

Six months later, New York Times columnist Maureen Dowd claimed that the McCains were "still seething about Bush supporters in South Carolina spreading [false accusations about]…their dark-skinned…daughter."

But the smear campaign didn't end with Bridget. It was just warming up. Next in line was McCain's wife, Cindy. She was labeled a "weirdo" and a drug addict, because she'd had an earlier dependency on prescription pain medication. The Bush supporters were relentless. They began circulating flyers calling McCain the "fag candidate," because he was the only GOP contender to have met with members of the Log Cabin Republicans, a gay group. These fliers were handed out at McCain campaign events, "even as Bush subtly reinforced that message by indicating he wouldn't hire openly gay people for his administration."

THE PERFECT VILLAIN

Finally, McCain's war-hero status—he'd been shot down and held prisoner for nearly six years in North Vietnam—was assailed. His famous "temper," not to mention his frequent use of profanity in private, was used to suggest that he was unstable due to his nearly six years in captivity and his possible post-traumatic stress disorder. Would America want a commander in chief with a "screw loose" making the decision about launching nuclear weapons? Did America dare elect a "Manchurian Candidate" for president?[109]

According to *The New York Times*, "Literature began to pepper the windshields of cars at political events suggesting that Mr. McCain had committed treason while a prisoner of war in North Vietnam." Some blamed Karl Rove, the king of push polling, for spreading these smears. Rove had heard of these allegations of treason, because some of McCain's fellow POWs—many of whom still refuse to talk to him—had been spreading the word. The POWs believed that McCain did not deserve to fall under the "war hero" rubric.

McCain's critics suspected he had something to hide. In 1992, the House of Representatives had unanimously passed a bill that would have authorized the release of all American POW/MIA documents held by the Pentagon. When the bill reached the Senate, McCain essentially blocked it, citing privacy concerns for the families and too much work for the bureaucrats. Some claim he did this because the records contained evidence that he had collaborated with the North Vietnamese. McCain would repeat this tactic 14 years later when he released less than 2% of the Abramoff documents obtained by his Senate Indian Affairs Committee.

In a 2005 documentary, *Missing, Presumed Dead: The Search for America's POWs*, narrated by Ed Asner, startling claims were made against McCain. Tracy Usery, former special investigator for the Senate Foreign Relations Committee, said, "…[McCain] made over 32 tapes of propaganda for the Vietnamese government." Dr. James Lucier Sr., Sen. Jesse Helms' former chief of staff added, "…[W]e do know that…[McCain]… cooperated with the communist news services in giving interviews there, ah, not flattering to the United States."

In fact, only two months after his release from captivity, McCain wrote a first-person account of his ordeal, published by *U.S. News & World Report* on May 14, 1973, in which he admitted that he was ready to aid and abet the enemy. In the first instance, he told his North Vietnamese captors: "O.K., I'll give you military information if you will take me to the hospital," because he feared that the blood pooling in his leg could kill him. McCain said they initially turned down his offer but returned soon after, when they realized his father was "a big admiral," and then took him to the hospital. In this account, McCain did not then mention what, if any, "military information" he'd given to the enemy in return.

McCain later wrote in his 1999 autobiography, *Faith of My Fathers*, a slightly different version. The first part essentially remained the same: "Take me to the hospital and I'll give you the information you want." This time McCain added something he'd somehow "forgotten" to mention 26 years earlier: "I didn't intend to keep my word, reasoning that after my injuries had been treated, I would be strong enough to deal with the consequences of not holding up my end of the bargain." McCain then revealed the alleged content of "the military information" he had shared with the enemy:

> I gave them my ship's name and squadron number, and confirmed that my target was a power plant. Pressed for more useful information, I gave the names of the Green Bay Packers' offensive line, and said they were members of my squadron. When asked to identify future targets, I simply recited the names of a number of North Vietnamese cities that had already been bombed.

In his initial account, McCain had also written in the 1973 *US News & World Report* that he had been tortured:

> They wanted a statement saying that I was sorry for the crimes that I had committed against North Vietnamese people and that I was grateful for the treatment that I had received from them…I held out for four days. Finally…I said, O.K., I'll write for them. They took me up into one of the interrogation rooms, and for the next 12 hours we wrote and rewrote. The North Vietnamese interrogator…wrote the final confession, and I signed it. It was in their language, and spoke about black crimes, and other generalities.

In *Faith of My Fathers,* his signed confession became slightly more specific:

> **I am a black criminal and I have performed the deeds of an air pirate. I almost died and the Vietnamese people saved my life. The doctors gave me an operation that I did not deserve.**

In his 2004 bestseller, *Why Courage Matters: The Way to a Braver Life,* McCain seemed to be reflecting on his own disgrace as a POW. "Cowardice is often a secret affair. Usually no one knows of our failure," he wrote, and "that 'the cover-up is always worse than the crime.'" A few pages later, he revisited his ordeal in Hanoi, but provided no new information. "In prison, I was not always a match for my enemies… my courage ran out much earlier than I had expected." Moments later, he added, "Remarkably, no more than a mere handful of us returned without our honor, having lost the courage it demanded." The repetition of this theme was intriguing, if not telling, when, near the end of the book, McCain wrote, "Their examples [the bravest of his fellow POWs] encouraged the rest of us to resist as best we could, though my best was considerably less than theirs." Finally, still speaking about his captivity, he seemed haunted "by the shame I felt when I didn't measure up."

The fact that McCain broke under pressure was understandable and forgivable, and he has repeatedly admitted his shame and remorse. But McCain seemed to be holding something back. His behavior suggested that he may not have provided the American public with a full, accurate, and detailed account of his collaboration with the enemy while a prisoner in North Vietnam.

Are there documents—in Hanoi, Moscow, or the Pentagon—that should be released which would allow the American electorate to make a more fully informed decision before the ballots are cast in the 2008 presidential election—perhaps one of the most pivotal in the nation's history?

At least four documents surfaced in early 2008, either declassified by the Pentagon or otherwise leaked, that suggest McCain may have more to reveal.

The first document was a transcript of a broadcast in Havana, Cuba, intercepted by US intelligence on November 9, 1967, in which the newly captured POW John McCain was being interviewed:

> A reconnaissance officer…showed me photographs of my target and marked out the paths to be followed by the [USS] Oriskany [aircraft carrier] at this point. They pointed out to me a number of antiaircraft positions near Hanoi and a number of possible rocket positions, the position of our rescue ships, the radio frequency… upon our arrival near the target, our formation, with six bombers, would mount the attack according to the following order: I would be number three, and the chief of the formation, number one. Each pilot would have to approach the target from a different direction… While moving toward the target we stumbled over a very dense network of fire…a few rockets were seen, our chief turned to approach the target and I followed him at a distance. At the time when I was preparing to drop my bombs—I did not know whether or not I could drop them because things were happening too fast—I heard a terrible explosion, which shook my plane and sent it toward the ground…You [the North Vietnamese] are excellent artillerymen…For me there is no longer any doubt…the United States seems to be standing alone, so much is its isolation.[110]

This statement seemed to provide a bit more than just the name of his ship and his squadron. The second document was a transcript of an "exclusive" interview of newly captured POW John McCain, conducted by French TV reporter Francois Chalais in early 1968:

> McCain: I was carrying out a bombing mission, my 23rd raid, over Hanoi. It was then that I was hit. I wanted to eject but while doing so I broke both arms and my right thigh. Unconscious I fell in a lake. Some Vietnamese jumped into the water and pulled me out. Later I learned there must have been about 12 of them. They immediately took me to a hospital, in a condition

> two inches from death. A doctor operated on my thigh. Others at the same time dealt with my arms…

Chalais: How have you been treated?

McCain: Very well…Everybody is very nice to me.

Chalais: How's the food?

McCain: This isn't Paris, but it is alright.

This account certainly did not square with McCain's later claims that he was not taken to the hospital for three or four days. The third document was a transcript of a broadcast from Hanoi beamed into South Vietnam on June 2, 1969, reportedly quoting the voice of John McCain. He was responding to a recent plea on May 19th by Defense Secretary Melvin S. Laird calling for the North Vietnamese to treat American POWs according to the Geneva Convention:

> McCain: I was a U.S. airman engaged in the crimes against the Vietnamese country and people. I had bombed their cities, towns, and villages and caused more injury, even death, for the people of Vietnam. After I was captured I was taken [to] a hospital…where I received very good medical treatment. I was given an operation on my leg, which allowed me to walk again, and a cast for my right arm which was badly broken three places. The doctors were very good and they knew a great deal about the practice of medicine. I remained in the hospital for some time. I regained much of my health and strength.

McCain had never mentioned in any of his books or accounts that he had made taped statements or confessions—which could have been subsequently broadcasted.

The fourth document was the transcript of an extensive interview conducted by Spanish psychiatrist Dr. Fernando Barral with American POW John McCain during his incarceration. This interview was published in Havana, Cuba on January 24, 1970:

Barral: Could you tell me your name, serial number, and rank?

McCain: My name is John Sidney McCain and I am lieutenant commander in the U.S. Navy—serial no. 624787…I understand and speak some Spanish. I studied it in school and I have been in Spain several times. On one of those occasions I visited the Naval Academy and met with Prince Carlos…

Barral: Immediately afterward I asked him about the date and circumstance of his capture.

McCain: On 26 October 1967 I was overflying Hanoi in an A4E based on the carrier Oriskany when my plane was hit by a ground-to-air missile. I bailed out, colliding with the remains of the plane, and I landed in one of the lakes in the center of Hanoi, in the middle of the water. On landing I tried to get free of my parachute, but I could not move, and I did not realize why I could not move my arms and legs, but it was because of my injuries.

Barral: Injuries?

McCain: Yes, as a result of colliding with my plane, I fractured my right leg at the knee, and both arms, the right one in three places. Moreover I dislocated both shoulders.

Barral: [When he told me this I superficially examined his ability to move his arms, which is almost unrestricted (only he has some difficulty bending his arm all the way). Also his grip is normal. Aside from this, he uses a crutch on the right side only, which shows normal functional ability of the extremity most affected by the traumatism.] What happened next? That is, what was the capture itself like?

McCain: Well, many people gathered around since it was the center of Hanoi and at midday.

Barral: Soldiers, militiamen, or civilians?

McCain: I could not determine exactly, because they had removed their clothing in order to take me out of the water.

Barral: Well, go on.

McCain: From there, they took me to a military hospital in Hanoi, a large hospital where they operated on me and attended to the multiple fractures. I understand I received more than a liter of blood…

Barral: Were you the object of any physical or moral violence?

McCain: No, although at the time of capture I could sense the people's hate or indignation, there were no insults or violence of any type. On the contrary, you have seen how I am recovering from my injuries.

Barral: But were you not afraid of being the object of violent treatment if you were captured…?

McCain: Actually, I never thought I would become a prisoner; therefore those fears never came up.

Barral: Did you ever think of the possibility of being captured?

McCain: No. I was traveling at a high altitude. I felt completely safe in the plane…I am considered one of the best pilots.

Barral: Why were you a member of the U.S. Navy?

McCain: There is a family reason, since I have many relatives in that branch of [the] service. In particular, my grandfather was outstanding in World War II; he was one of those who [witnessed] the Japanese sign the act of surrender, and a Naval destroyer bears his name. And my father is also an admiral; he is chief of the Pacific Command of the U.S. Armed Forces. Actually, it is a matter of military tradition. One of my forebears was a colonel in Washington independence forces. Another was a general in the war of secession. Thus it was only natural for me to follow a military career. Of course, my father was not always an admiral; during World War II he was the commander of a submarine. He has been in the Navy since 1927 and has been an admiral since 1965. He holds the highest rank in the Navy. If I had not been downed, I would have become an admiral at an age earlier than my father. Theoretically, Gen. Abrams [commander of all American troops in Vietnam] is his subordinate.

Barral: Theoretically?

McCain: Yes, although in practice, because of the importance of this war, Gen. Creighton Abrams receives his orders directly from Washington…

Barral: I do not understand this about "in theory and in practice." I thought that in military life everything is standardized in an inflexible manner.

McCain: Well, look, in fact Abrams is his subordinate but since the Tet offensive of 1968[111] in view of the gravity of the situation, Abrams, instead of asking for instructions from my father, who is in Honolulu, so that he in turn would ask for them from Washington, went directly to Washington for them because the war is here in Vietnam and my father also has Okinawa, Korea, and so forth under his command. That is why, since the war is so important, he receives his instructions directly from Washington. It is a political problem also, not only military.

Barral: Well, let us leave these things about political and military aside. They are too complex. At any rate I do believe that your father likes the situation very much; that his subordinates receive orders directly from above.

McCain: Look, my father is a very intelligent person, but…when the bombings of the north began, [U. S. President] Johnson asked Abrams' opinion, not my father's because Abrams [was] in Saigon, in the war… Now I am going to speak about my wife…she is not in the armed forces…I saw her the last time in August 1967.

At that time I was on the aircraft carrier Forrestal when a fire broke out which damaged it heavily and it had to be sent for repairs to the United States. At that time I miraculously escaped with my life because I was in my airplane and the two pilots on my left and the two on my right were killed.

Barral: How did that happen?

McCain: A plane caught fire and one of its rockets went off. This in turn caused other explosions. There were

135 deaths, almost all the airplanes were destroyed, and the ship was seriously damaged. As a result of the fire I became famous on TV.

Barral: As one who miraculously escaped death, no?

McCain: Yes, but in addition I was able to see my family and stay there nearly a month. I then returned this time to the aircraft carrier Oriskany and 1 month later I was shot down.

Barral: You said you were going to talk to me about your wife, but you continue on the subject of war.

McCain: She is very pretty. Before marrying me she was a model for magazines and on TV. We have a 3-year-old girl. When I saw her she was still a baby. She also has two children from a former marriage. She has now returned to work as a model on TV.

Barral: How did you find this out?

McCain: I had a letter from her after I became a prisoner…[My captors] authorized me to receive a letter and presents on Christmas Eve and I was able to send greeting cards.

Barral: Would you like me to relay a message for you?

McCain: If you would be so kind. Tell her I am well, that I wish her happiness, and not to worry about me.

Barral: The address?

McCain: Her name is Carol McCain, Mrs. Carol McCain. She lives in [He writes with his left hand]..553 Patio Lane, Orange Park, Florida, USA.

Barral: What schooling did you have?

McCain: I went to the Naval Academy. I took two university majors, electrical engineering and naval architecture. The courses were very difficult; 1,200 of us began and only 400 graduated. Disciple was very strict also….When I finished I had two choices: to be a naval officer or a pilot. I chose to be a pilot. I had to study another year and a half and I graduated in 1958. I trained intensively. I flew many hours in training to become a jet pilot.

Barral: Many?

McCain: Yes, 4,000. They really only demand 200 but I flew 4,000 hours.

Barral: Why?

McCain: I want to be a test pilot. It is fascinating to test the new models.

Barral: At any rate the difference between 200 and 4,000 seems to be great.

McCain: Well, look, it was because I wanted to be a[n] astronaut. That is why I also engaged in a great deal of sports: boxing, wrestling, swimming, camping, and so forth.

Barral: And what happened?

McCain: I had to come to Vietnam.

Barral: What is your religion?

McCain: I am a Protestant.

Barral: Being in captivity, has your faith increased? Do you have hopes for the future?

McCain: My beliefs have always been more or less of the same intensity. As long as the war lasts I do not have much hope for the future.

Dr. Barral then made the following observations: "[McCain] showed himself to be intellectually alert during the interview. From a morale point of view he is not in traumatic shock. He is neither dejected nor depressed. He was able to be sarcastic, and even humorous, indicative of psychic equilibrium. From the moral and ideological point of view he showed us *he is an insensitive individual without human depth, who does not show the slightest concern, who does not appear to have thought about the criminal acts he committed against a population from the almost absolute impunity of his airplane, and that nevertheless those people who saved his life, fed him, and looked after his health, and he is now healthy and strong. I believed that he bombed densely populated places for sport. I noted that he was hardened, that he spoke of banal things as if he were at a cocktail party* [emphasis added]."

McCain's comments seem decidedly more extensive than simply reciting name, rank, serial number, and the lineup of the Green Bay Packers.

Ted Sampley, a former Green Beret who fought in Vietnam and is a vocal and colorful critic of both McCain and Sen. John Kerry, said: "I have been following John McCain's career for nearly 20 years. I know him personally. There is something wrong with this guy and let me tell you what it is—deceit."

* * * * * * * * * * * * * *

Back in 2000, George W. Bush, the soon-to-be Republican nominee for president, tepidly disavowed the South Carolina smear campaign, even though he was its chief beneficiary. Most campaign strategists, however, believed they knew who had engineered it. According to *Salon*, "Although Rove and Reed left no visible fingerprints in those attacks, they have been universally suspected...of responsibility for the anonymous leaflets and telephone 'polls' that accused McCain of fathering a black child out of wedlock, smeared his wife, Cindy, as a 'drug addict,' and insinuated that the senator had been driven to insanity and even treason during his wartime imprisonment by the North Vietnamese communists." Abramoff's close friend Grover Norquist was one of McCain's most outspoken critics in the 2000 presidential primary, condemning him for co-sponsoring the McCain-Feingold campaign finance law.[112] Norquist held press conferences in New Hampshire and South Carolina and ran ads calling McCain "the only candidate approved by the liberal *New York Times*" and accusing him of advocating the policies of "Big Labor."

The smear campaign, among other factors, ended up kneecapping McCain. He lost South Carolina by 11 points. Less than three weeks later, he dropped out of the race. Bush went on to capture the Republican nomination and the presidency. Since it was safe to assume that Bush would seek a second term, it meant that McCain would have to wait until 2008 for his next White House bid. But by then, he would be 72, the oldest man ever elected to a first term as president. Therefore, back in 2000, it appeared that his South Carolina defeat would be McCain's political Waterloo, intensifying its sting.

McCain was well known for his temper tantrums. His staff referred to them as "McCain moments." Some of his colleagues referred to him as "Senator Hothead." He probably experienced a "McCain moment" soon after the loss in South Carolina when Bush excused the vicious smear campaign with a shrug, explaining to McCain just prior to a debate: "It's just politics, John. It doesn't mean anything."

Despite this defeat, McCain's ambitions never wavered. He refused to allow his presidential aspirations to fade. If he were to have any shot at the 2008 presidency, he would have to come to a politically expedient "reconciliation" with Bush. This would mean campaigning for his rival "through gritted teeth." As a result, McCain met for 90 minutes alone with Bush in a Pittsburgh hotel room in May 2000, and they emerged "with smiles and pledges to work together." McCain never really got over the South Carolina attacks, however. Despite his public denials, his anger and loathing simmered.

Four years later, however, McCain would find that *The Washington Post* had given him a shot at political payback. Along with McCain's other most vociferous enemies—Ralph Reed, Tom DeLay, and Grover Norquist—the head of Jack Abramoff had just been handed to McCain on a silver platter.

There were several intriguing questions about the motives behind McCain's Senate Indian Affairs investigation. How much did McCain know or infer about Abramoff's involvement in the 2000 South Carolina primary? Was McCain hell-bent on settling old scores when he launched the Abramoff probe the morning after *The Washington Post* ran its first story in February 2004? More importantly, why was McCain's 373-page report—despite his repeated claims that it was fair and neutral—so one-sided and misleading? Why did McCain only publicly release less than 2% of the 750,000 pages of subpoenaed Abramoff's e-mails, memos, schedules, and billing statements? Why did McCain refuse to release *all* of the Abramoff documents—just as he had refused to release his own POW documents? As a result, investigators and researchers could not possibly conduct a thorough review of the evidence in order to confirm McCain's conclusions.

Finally, if McCain purposely produced such a deceptive document—funded with taxpayer dollars—couldn't that be construed as a breach of the public trust, as well as honest-services fraud?

A few political observers did express concern about the lack of even-handedness in McCain's report, but their voices were drowned out by the ubiquitous outrage against Abramoff. What's more, Sen. John "Straight-Talk-Express" McCain was considered too honorable and principled to produce something so biased.

Two months before McCain's report was released, *Vanity Fair* reported that lobbyists for Native Americans had begun to question the accuracy of the portrait painted by McCain and Schmidt. "The Mississippi Choctaw, the Louisiana Coushatta, the Saginaw Chippewa—they are very wealthy tribes with big casinos," one lobbyist told to the magazine. "They knew they were spending money on him and they had an agenda which was to shut down other, poor tribes…but the idea that they didn't know they were spending $30 million to kill a rival's casino…Well, let's not pretend the Indians are stupid."

Even the Native-American media seemed to agree. "There is some suggestion Jack Abramoff victimized unwary tribes and politicians, but this is more a case of unbridled greed [by the tribes] than people taking advantage of powerless tribes and corrupting innocent politicians," wrote the former editor of *The Native American Times*. "It would be easy to play the victim card, but that would be avoiding the responsibility many tribes had in their unrelenting drive to protect and obtain more gaming opportunities."

* * * * * * * * * * * * * *

McCain had to try to appear neutral—not transparent—if he was going to go after Abramoff as political payback. Thus, when *The Washington Post* ran its first story in February 2004, and McCain immediately launched his probe, McCain's staff claimed that the senator had never met or heard of Abramoff. "Mr. Abramoff flatters himself," said Mark Salter, McCain's chief of staff and frequent co-author. "Senator McCain was unaware of his existence until he read initial press accounts of Abramoff's abuses, and had never laid eyes on him until he appeared before the committee."

This claim certainly stretched credulity. Had McCain directed Salter to say this because the ex-POW was afraid that his true motives would become apparent? It seemed inconceivable that McCain did not know Washington's well-known super lobbyist. Abramoff was a legend in GOP circles. Abramoff maintained that he had met McCain on several occasions before the story broke. "As best I can remember, when I met with him he didn't have his eyes shut," says Abramoff. "I'm surprised that Senator McCain has joined the chorus of amnesiacs."

It was equally inconceivable that McCain would not have known of, much less loathed, the infamous right-wing triumvirate—famously hatched in the crucible of the College Republicans—of Ralph Reed, Grover Norquist, and Jack Abramoff. They had openly and vocally despised McCain for many years. "McCain's 2000 campaign had great on-the-ground intelligence," says Abramoff. "There is no way in the world McCain did not know that I was the funder. He certainly knew about Reed and Norquist. Whenever Reed was doing something, everyone knew I was funding it, because I was his only major funding source."

During the 2000 and 2004 Bush campaigns, fund raisers were assigned numbers with the goal of achieving the status of a "pioneer" or a "ranger." A reliable source says: "Much of the money that Abramoff raised in 2000 [for Bush] went through Reed's number. Ralph asked him to do this and Abramoff was certain that Rove knew. His access to Rove was through Reed." In August 2003, Abramoff was one of the "pioneers" who had earned an invitation to a ho-down with Bush at his ranch in Crawford, Texas, but couldn't attend because the event fell on the Sabbath.

"In 2004, I was on my way to Rangerdom," says Abramoff, "when I had a bit of a train wreck."

CHAPTER THIRTY-TWO
MUSIC, GOLF, LUCK

In early April, 2000, with McCain knocked off the yellow brick road to the White House, the right-wing Republican cohort—DeLay, Norquist, and Abramoff—could relax and bask in the cherry blossoms that briefly enchanted the nation's capital. They no longer had to fear that "wacko" McCain, a Republican in Democrat sheepskin, would run the country into the ground.

Of course, the people's business always came first, but what was the harm if an elected official occasionally listened to good music or played a round of golf, especially at someone else's expense. A little recreation only helped sharpen the congressional mind grappling with so many legislative challenges. After all, federal lawmakers, who could earn far more in the private sector, deserved to be rewarded with trivial pursuits to compensate for their many sacrifices. For example, on the evening of May 7, 2000, House Majority Whip Tom DeLay—an opera buff—arranged a special treat for major contributors to his political action committee—Americans for a Republican Majority. Although the concert was sold out, they were ushered into the plush seats of a coveted skybox at Washington's MCI Center, where they enjoyed a command performance by the world's top three operatic tenors—José Carreras, Plácido Domingo, and Luciano Pavarotti.

Although lawmakers were barred from accepting gifts of $50 or more, they could accept—and did not have to report[113]— hand-outs of food, transportation, and lodging at a political or educational event so long as a political committee or campaign footed the bill. Indeed, virtually any lobbyist worth his salt regularly made available these innocuous perks to lawmakers and clients for the sake of bonding. In this case, the lobbyist who donated his skybox on that particular occasion to a certain political action committee—which DeLay accepted as its chairman—happened to be the indefatigable Jack Abramoff.[114] But this paltry political gift paled in comparison to the European junket that Abramoff would arrange for DeLay & Co. three weeks later. This was the infamous golf trip to Scotland in May 2000, the one that the press and federal prosecutors would later scrutinize. They suspected that its true purpose was to persuade DeLay to vote against the Internet Gambling Prohibition Bill, which would have put eLottery, Abramoff's client, out of business.

This episode—dazzling in its inscrutable, labyrinthine nuance and complexity—once again demonstrated Abramoff's luck and genius in defending the interests of a high-paying clients. The paradox was that McCain, *The Washington Post*, and federal prosecutors wanted to have their cake and eat it too, a pattern that repeated itself throughout the probe of this scandal. On the one hand, they wanted to characterize Abramoff as defrauding his clients by not doing enough; on the other hand, whenever he delivered a virtuoso performance, they accused him of underhandedness. They would have better masked their bias if they had simply praised him when he deserved it and bashed him when he allegedly broke the law.

In the final analysis, the Scotland golf trip and the eLottery battle were not directly connected at all. Like DeLay's 1997 trip to Moscow and his subsequent IMF vote, the press moved heaven and earth to eke out a direct link between the 2000 Scotland trip and the eLottery battle in Congress. Perhaps something criminal did take place, but at best it was minor, technical, and probably inadvertent. Furthermore, the government would have been hard pressed to explain to a jury—never mind persuade them to convict—that something nefarious had really gone on. Of course, the Justice Department—which could famously find a way to "indict a ham sandwich"— knew it would never have to face a jury, because it could always terrorize a defendant into pleading guilty. Abramoff, however, refused to discuss or listen to any presentation of this analysis.

THE 2000 GOLF TRIP TO SCOTLAND

"The truth is that I was just interested in finding funds for the golf trip, since it was something we all wanted to do, and I felt that the more time I spent with members [of Congress] the better it was for my clients," says Abramoff. "Not once did I discuss with DeLay on that trip any legislation, much less [eLottery]."

Abramoff didn't have to become a contortionist to navigate his way through the complex laws that prohibit lobbyists from paying for congressional junkets. Indeed, what he did was hardly the exception. Thanks to well-established legal loopholes, thousands of such "educational" trips are funded every year. For example, between January 2000 and June 2005, lawmakers and their staff enjoyed more than 23,000 junkets—all "financed by private sponsors, many of them corporations, trade associations and nonprofit groups with business on Capitol Hill," according to the Center for Public Integrity.

Once again, the press omitted that this was a humdrum phenomenon, known to the greenest Washington reporter, when it asserted that DeLay's Scotland trip smacked of egregious corruption.[115] Using a typical loophole, Abramoff once again enlisted his old College Republican friend, Amy Ridenour, head of the National Center for Public Policy Research. As she had done for DeLay's Moscow trip in 1997, Ridenour agreed to sponsor his travel for "educational" purposes to Great Britain. It made perfect sense. Abramoff sat on her board, many of his clients made significant contributions to her organization, and DeLay had publicly endorsed and praised her nonprofit organization.

Abramoff persuaded two clients—the Choctaws and eLottery—each to pony up $25,000 to Ridenour's group. Even though Abramoff had carefully explained to his clients the axiomatic political principle that one hand washes the other, both would later claim they had no idea their donations were going to fund a golf trip for DeLay, the powerful House Majority Whip, who just might decide to influence legislation that might later serendipitously save them millions. The date that their checks were written "coincided with the day that DeLay departed on the trip," according to *The Washington Post*. Ridenour would later say, "This trip was going to be paid for by the National Center, regardless of whether we got the donations from the Choctaw or eLottery." After that, however, she started backpedaling, telling McCain that because she was about to give birth, she had paid scant attention to the trip's itinerary and was surprised when she learned that they had done a frolic and detour to the links at St. Andrews.

The cost of the trip ballooned to nearly $120,000 for DeLay and his entourage—well over the contributions from the Choctaws and eLottery. The press would later rip into Abramoff because he had used his American Express credit card to pay for some of the expenses. However, for logistical and practical purposes, he was merely advancing the funds for which he was later reimbursed.[116] Whether his doing so was a nominal violation of the law was debatable.

Roger Burchfield, DeLay's lawyer, later claimed that as a member of Ridenour's board, Abramoff could pay expenses for the sake of convenience, as long as they were promptly reimbursed. "[The press] made a big deal about [the 2000 trip], because it was DeLay and Abramoff," says a reliable source. "Members take these trips every year. DeLay did do a lot of work while in the UK and spoke at a few venues. If there were violations, they were minor and technical. DeLay was careful not to break the rules."[117] Nevertheless, the press did have a point. The trip appeared to be a golfing vacation with a few meetings thrown in as window dressing. According to the *U.S. House and Senate travel disclosure forms*, these privately sponsored trips should not be "substantially recreational in nature." DeLay would later maintain the junket was perfectly valid: "I went to London to meet with conservatives in England and Scotland and talk about the things we had been doing in the Republican, conservative House. They wanted to dialogue to see if they could adopt some [of] the things we had done."

The ten-day journey began at Dulles Airport on May 25. DeLay and his wife, Christine, flew in business class. Their itinerary included stops in London, Edinburgh, Glasgow, and St. Andrews in Scotland. There, DeLay golfed where all avid golfers dream of making the hajj—to the storied Old Course.[118] His officially stated purpose for this jaunt was "educational" and to consult with "conservative leaders" in the British Isles. He did meet with former British Prime Minister Margaret Thatcher.

After a round of golf at St. Andrews, Abramoff threw a dinner party for everybody, including a handful of Scottish parliamentarians, at a nearby historic mansion. The participants were Ed Buckham, DeLay's former chief of staff, who had become a lobbyist. He had been kind enough to hire DeLay's wife as a consultant and would end up paying her $115,000 over a three-year period. Buckham had received $1.3 million in contributions from NaftaSib, Abramoff's Russian client, later accused by the press of trying to influence DeLay's 1997 vote on replenishing the IMF to save the Russian economy. What prosecutors later found so intriguing was that Alexander Koulakovsky, head of NaftaSib, was also one of the dinner guests. "I don't think there was an agenda on [Koulakovsky's] part, and there was none on mine," Abramoff later says. "It was just that Tom [DeLay] was in Europe and so was I, and it was not much effort for [Koulakovsky] to join up with us. He had taken up golf and wanted to play, and there were probably not many places to play in Russia. It was more social than anything else." Sitting next to him was Terry Martin, chief of the Louisiana Chitimacha, who would hire Abramoff a few months later as the tribe's lobbyist, an event that would have far-reaching consequences. Also in attendance were Susan Hirschmann, DeLay's chief of staff, and her husband—who had also dined with Koulakovsky on DeLay's 1997 trip to Moscow.

Tony Rudy—DeLay's press secretary, policy director, and deputy chief of staff—also showed up. A few months later, Abramoff would go out of his way to help Rudy's wife find a job. He arranged for two clients, eLottery and Magazine Publishers of America, to each make a $25,000 contribution to Toward Tradition, a nonprofit run by Abramoff's friend and spiritual advisor, Rabbi Daniel Lapin, the one who had first introduced Abramoff to DeLay back in 1995. Lapin used the $50,000 contribution to hire Rudy's wife as a "consultant." "[Rudy] was basically my best friend at the time," says Abramoff, "so I did everything I could to help him. Same for him for me...I saw a bunch of needs. Lapin's need to have someone who could get things done for his conference in D.C., Lisa's [Rudy's wife] need for work, the client's need to be helping the guy who was helping them, and I came up with a bad solution to the problems. [Rudy] was a government employee and I had his wife hired. I just was not thinking and didn't realize it was illegal at the time." Abramoff even listed Rudy as a personal reference on the Foothill loan application to purchase SunCruz Casinos.

Nearly six years later, in his plea bargain Abramoff would admit that the $50,000 was a bribe so that Rudy would help stop the Internet Gambling Prohibition Bill and slow down postal-rate increases. Rudy

THE PERFECT VILLAIN

would also be forced to plead guilty, admitting that he advised "members of Congress, while still employed by [DeLay]…to vote against proposed legislation limiting gambling on the internet, without disclosing that he gave this advice in part because Abramoff asked him to oppose the legislation and provided him with things of value." One of those "things of value" included a trip Rudy had taken on the SunCruz jet to the U.S. Open at Pebble Beach—even though it was several months before Abramoff purchased SunCruz. The fact that the prosecutors cited this example suggested they were scraping the bottom of the barrel for supporting evidence.

Was there a specific quid pro quo between Abramoff and Rudy? Of course not. There didn't have to be. It was implicit. They were best friends. They never had the following conversation: "Hey, Jack, if you get a job for my wife, I'll help your clients in Congress." Assistant U.S. attorneys have made friendship a felony, but only selectively prosecuted. Hundreds of thousands of examples of such friendships exist in Washington and in every state capital and affect the delivery of "honest services," whatever that is.

For example, *The New York Times* reported in the spring of 2008, that Sen. McCain "had used his influence and special position" to help out his friend, Donald K. Diamond, a wealthy real-estate developer, "snap up some prime California coast"—even though McCain was a senator from Arizona. Diamond, who made a cool $20 million profit on the deal, thanked McCain by becoming a frequent and generous and contributor to McCain's campaigns, including $250,000 for his 2008 presidential bid. In fact, Diamond essentially characterized what he did as bribery. Candid about his expectations as a fund-raiser, he said, "I want my money back, for Christ's sake. Do you know how many cocktail parties I have to go to?" This sounded like crossing the "bright red line." In another example, McCain placed a $14.3 million earmark in a 2003 defense bill which provided a windfall "for [SunCor] an Arizona developer whose executives were major campaign donors." During his 2000 presidential campaign, McCain, who was head of the Senate Finance Committee, talked about finance campaign reform as he flew around the country in private jets owned by corporations that had business before his committee. In these instances, McCain's behavior seemed far more serious than giving away a few meals at a restaurant, but for McCain there would be no consequences.

Abramoff would never dare agree with the following statement and, for obvious reasons, must continue to maintain that his guilty pleas were sincere, and that he feels profound remorse for the many crimes he has committed. But ironically, the true criminals—shielded by limited "sovereign immunity"—were the federal prosecutors themselves, who bullied terrified defendants into committing perjury by forcing them to admit to crimes they knowingly did not commit. (It is important to note that this charge does not necessarily apply to the line prosecutors in the Abramoff probe or to the political appointees to whom they report, but to the increasing and unfettered power that the Department of Justice has unconsciously bestowed upon itself over the past few decades.)

SAVING ELOTTERY (AND INTERNET GAMING)
PART I

The Washington Post later claimed that DeLay went on this all-expenses-paid Scotland trip so that "two months [later] DeLay [could help] kill legislation" that would have destroyed the business of eLottery, Abramoff's client. The bill's defeat had little to do with Tom DeLay. It had to do with the arrogance and stupidity of the bill's chief sponsor, Robert W. Goodlatte (R-Va.). Otherwise, nothing could have stopped the passage of legislation that enjoyed such widespread support. "Goodlatte was not the most worthy of opponents," says Abramoff. "It's a good thing, since if they'd had someone really smart, they would have beaten us."

Edwin McGuinn, president of eLottery, which hoped to make millions by selling state lottery tickets online, agreed that if the law had passed banning their proposed business, "We wouldn't have been able to operate." Founded in 1993, the company, which had essentially never made a dime, was becoming frantic. ELottery's lobbyists had been employing the "it's not fair" approach, which wasn't working. Since the House vote was only a couple months away, they turned in desperation to Abramoff. "As was often the case, I was brought in at the last minute by a client, who wanted me to pull a rabbit out of the hat," says Abramoff. "In this particular case, I lacked the rabbit and the hat. The battle was so far gone I didn't really think there was much I could do."

According to federal lobby disclosure requirements, Abramoff's firm, Preston Gates, registered as eLottery's lobbyist on June 3, exactly one day before the end of DeLay's Scotland junket. The company agreed to pay Abramoff a monthly retainer of $100,000, not including the costs of the grassroots campaign. Since the vote was slated for a July 17 vote, Abramoff only had 44 days to work his magic.

The bill that Rep. Goodlatte was sponsoring in the House, dubbed the Internet Gambling Prohibition Bill, had already passed by a wide margin in the Senate six months earlier, in late 1999. The legislation would have made virtually all internet betting a federal offense. Its passage in the House was considered a shoo-in, thanks to the support of right-wing Christian groups, including the Moral Majority, the Christian Coalition, and Focus on the Family.[119] DeLay, who was opposed to the spread of gambling, supported the bill. However, it did contain an exemption that concerned him.

"We studied the bill and realized that it actually favored internet betting on horse [and dog] tracks and made it, for the first time, legal!"[120] says Abramoff. "We also found out that this provision had been critical to the Senate passage of the bill. I believe it was [Diane] Feinstein in California and [Mitch] McConnell in Kentucky—obviously big horse [racing] states—who had said that if this were not included, they would have filibustered and put a hold on the bill." In other words, eLottery would have made it easier for individual states to sell their lottery tickets online, which would have benefited their public school systems, hardly a reprehensible prospect. However, liberal Sen. Feinstein and conservative Sen. McConnell preferred to promote online betting on horse racing nationwide, rather than augment public school financing.

Abramoff says he had to somehow persuade conservatives to oppose the legislation, because contrary to its purported purpose, it would actually expand gambling. He says he used this to drive a wedge on the right. His approach was that the internet gambling bill should either ban gambling for everyone or for no one. It was hypocritical to allow horse racing to slip through. "We made an ad showing a kid at home on his computer betting on the horses," says Abramoff. "We also circulated posters throughout the Hill, quoting the bill's language. It was entitled 'Three Washington Whoppers,' as in lies: The check is in the mail, I did not have sex with that woman,[121] and the Internet Gaming Prohibition Act prohibits internet gaming."

Abramoff's contention that Goodlatte's bill actually expanded gambling was not without merit. Therefore, he was able to persuade several prominent socially conservative leaders to oppose the passage of the bill. Of course, a little financial lubrication helped motivate them. He arranged for eLottery to pay $25,000 to Traditional Values Coalition, a southern California anti-gambling group with links to nearly 50,000 churches across the United States. The coalition was run by Reverend Louis. P. Sheldon, an old Abramoff friend.

He also turned to his steadfast superstar friend, Ralph Reed, who once again preferred anonymity. Even though the effort was a legitimate anti-gambling campaign, Reed was uncomfortable receiving funds from pro-gambling forces, so eLottery employed the same conduit used by the Mississippi Choctaw Indians. The company sent $160,000 to Grover Norquist's Americans for Tax Reform, which opposed the bill on libertarian grounds. He kept a $10,000 administrative fee and sent the remainder to Faith and Family Reliance, a company controlled by Reed.

As the head of Traditional Values Coalition, Sheldon held news conferences and telephoned several congressmen, but Abramoff realized the effort was futile. He e-mailed his lobbying team: "I just chatted with Ralph. We are going to have to go on the air nationally on radio. We must get the conservatives back on this or we are doomed." Four days before the vote, even DeLay was still undecided. Sheldon privately buttonholed the Majority Whip in a private meeting: "I told him I strongly opposed the bill." Abramoff also threw in his two cents. "As a good lobbyist, I had access to [DeLay] and made a case consistent with his ideological approach to life, and he sided with us. He was subsequently beaten up by Dobson, but he did the right thing. That bill was a travesty."

Finally, DeLay announced his opposition. His lawyer would later maintain that DeLay's votes were always "based on sound public policy and principle." As the vote neared, the bill's passage seemed so certain that Rep. Goodlatte, its House sponsor, exploited a parliamentary trick. He had become concerned about his opponents' ability to outfox him. He feared that during the protracted floor debate several amendments might be slyly tacked onto the bill making it so unpalatable that it would trigger President Clinton to veto it. Instead, Goddlatte decided to preempt this by placing the bill "on suspension," which would severely limit debate and preclude all amendments. However, the bill would now have to pass by a super majority of two-thirds, not a simple majority. Goodlatte didn't even bother to count noses before making this decision. A member of his staff later claimed, "We were told [by House leaders] to bring it up on the suspension calendar so you won't have to deal with all those amendments."

Did Abramoff ask DeLay to suggest the suspension to Goodlatte? "I wish I had," says Abramoff. "It would have been a brilliant move. The truth is I got lucky."

On July 17, after 40 minutes of debate, ballots in the House were cast and counted. Exactly 245 voted in favor of the bill—43 more than a simple majority—and 159 had voted against it—25 votes shy of the two-thirds majority needed to pass it.[122] For the moment, the bill had failed. Despite Goodlatte's unexpected last-minute parliamentary maneuver that no one could have possibly predicted, the *Post* would later accuse Rudy of helping to "scuttle the bill in the House" and would credit Abramoff with somehow anticipating Goodlatte's ill-fated tactic so as to have "eroded just enough votes" to defeat the bill.

SAVING ELOTTERY (AND INTERNET GAMBLING)
PART II

The war was not over. The bill's supporters were stunned but not unbowed. The legislation would simply have to be rescheduled for a vote by amending it to another bill. Next time it would easily pass by a simple majority. Realizing this, Abramoff had only one option—prevent the bill from ever being scheduled for a re-vote. But how to accomplish this? The *Post* would contend that because Abramoff arranged the May golf trip to Scotland, DeLay was able to prevent the bill from reaching the House floor later that year. If that had been the case, Abramoff could have simply sat back, collected his hefty retainer, and twiddled his thumbs.

Five days after the bill's defeat, Rudy received an e-mail from a fellow DeLay staff member: "Goodlatte and [Billy] Tauzin (R-LA) [another ardent supporter of the bill] asked Tom [DeLay] what they needed to do to get his vote, and Tom said to talk to you!"

The answer was obvious. Eliminate from the bill the exemptions for horse-racing and jai lai and DeLay would vote for it, but Senators Feinstein and McConnell had made it clear that that was non-negotiable.

Rudy forwarded the e-mail to Abramoff, who knew that DeLay was under additional pressure from the right. James Dobson, for example, had recently complained that he was "sick about what the Republican leadership is doing with regard to gambling." He exhorted his millions of radio listeners to implore GOP leaders, including DeLay, to put the bill to another vote.

Abramoff knew that there was no way for DeLay to prevent the bill from being rescheduled. The media would later claim that to save his client's business, Abramoff was reluctantly forced to craft a gutsy strategy that could have cost DeLay his job as Majority Whip! Abramoff would try to keep the bill off the House floor by exploiting the GOP's razor-thin 13-seat majority. He was playing chess at a level where few could compete.

With the November elections only a few months away, Abramoff would direct his grassroots attack dogs to target ten vulnerable Republican congressmen, who were locked in tight races and had supported Goodlatte's bill. They would be accused of supporting the expansion of gambling, because they had voted *for* the bill! In turn, this would make the House leadership fearful that another vote on the bill could cost ten seats in the upcoming November election, which would hand back control of the House to the Democrats.

In mid August, Abramoff directed eLottery to ship Reed more money. "I have chatted with Ralph and we need to get the funding moving on the effort in the 10 congressional districts," wrote Abramoff. "Please get me a check as soon as possible for $150,000 made payable to [one of Reed's companies]." A few days later, Abramoff contacted Reed, who confirmed receipt of the funds and announced that "Yes, all systems [are] go."

And indeed, that seemed to be the case. Correspondence from Sheldon's organization—paid for by Reed—soon began appearing in the mail boxes of Republican constituents of Alabama Rep. Robert Aderholt, Oklahoma Rep. J. C. Watts, California Rep. James E. Rogan, and North Carolina Rep. Robin Hayes. All were accused of being soft on gambling, because they had supported Goodlatte's bill. Of course, their Democratic opponents immediately exploited these attacks. Later, Sheldon would claim that he was completely unaware of Abramoff's or eLottery's involvement in funding his organization's attacks on the Goodlatte bill. "This all tied to Jack? I'm shocked out of my socks," said Sheldon. And Reed would do the same. Taking the same position as he had done with the Choctaws, he claimed that Abramoff had reassured him that his anti-gambling work had not been funded by gambling interests.

"Our mailings into the Republican districts were not done to beat them. We were very gentle, trying to get people to lobby them to vote the right way, but still make the point that the member [of Congress] best support our position," says Abramoff. "The people we crushed later came out and said that we mailed to defeat Republicans. We did not do that. I would not have put the Republican majority at risk over this issue. That would have been insane, since it would have killed all my other clients and my business."

However, what the *Post* and federal investigators would later zero in on with some justification was the appearance of an incestuous arrangement. Near the end of August, at Abramoff's direction, eLottery made a $25,000 contribution to Rabbi Lapin's Toward Tradition—of which Abramoff was a board member. Almost immediately, Lapin hired Rudy's wife to organize an interfaith conference in Washington, D.C., held in mid September. Speakers included Tom DeLay, Grover Norquist, and Louis Sheldon. Later, Lapin claimed that there was no connection between his hiring Rudy's wife and the $25,000 contribution for eLottery. Nevertheless, Rudy made sure to remind DeLay that several Republican congressmen in tight races had become even more vulnerable because of their vote on Goodlatte's bill.

All the while, Goodlatte and Tauzin had been importuning the Republican leadership to affix the bill to some year-end legislation. Finally, the House Republicans caucused to fine tune their strategy two weeks before the November elections. What occurred at the meeting clearly demonstrated that Abramoff's daring strategy had worked. David Safavian, a lobbyist, who attended the meeting, immediately shot Abramoff an e-mail, describing what had just occurred: "[DeLay] spoke up and noted that the bill could cost as many as four House seats. At that point, there was silence. Not even Rep. Dick Armey (R-Texas—our previous opponent—said a word."[123]

In July, Goodlatte's gambit had backfired. And by the end of the year, he simply found himself outmaneuvered. In Washington, D.C., that's how politics works every day of the week. The *Post* exploited a golf trip to Scotland in order to make highly speculative imputations. By omitting from the story that congressional junkets were extraordinarily routine, the newspaper implied that the Abramoff junket was an aberration of a corrupt lobbyist. The scandal was not Abramoff. The scandal was the plethora of junkets, as well as the press trying to ascribe to a golf trip legislative hanky-panky.

Three years later, a similar congressional bill was revived with exemptions for horse racing. Once again, Abramoff was hired to defeat it. "I defeated it pretty much the same way, though this time, I made a poster based on Seabiscuit," says Abramoff. "The film was all the rage at the time. [The poster] showed a slimy guy riding the horse representing the tracks and we called the poster 'Air Biscuit,' which is a euphemism for flatulence."

CHAPTER THIRTY-THREE
THE STARS LINE UP

In September, 2000, Abramoff landed the Chitimacha Indians,[124] his second Native American client. The tribe operated a small casino in southern Louisiana on the Gulf Coast. At first Abramoff worked for free and later charged them a pittance. Because there were many Gulf Coast and riverboat gambling operations nearby, he could do little to augment the miniscule market share of their casino. However, the Chitimacha would indirectly prove fabulously profitable for Abramoff, which, in turn, *The Washington Post* and Sen. McCain would subsequently manipulate to drive the final nail into the lobbyist's coffin. Chitimacha lobbyist, Terry Martin, had attended boarding school on the Mississippi Choctaw reservation. There, he befriended Philip Martin—no relation—who would later become the Choctaw chief. In the late 1990s, Philip had introduced Abramoff to Terry. For some reason, the two hit it off. Hence, it made sense for Abramoff to invite Terry—his long-standing friend, an excellent golfer, and friend of DeLay's—to tag along on the Scotland golf junket.

"[In September,] the Choctaws called and asked me a favor. Would I help out the Chits, who were about to renew their compact [contract to operate a casino within the state of Louisiana]? So I renegotiated their deal," says Abramoff. "The governor and his staff liked them, deservedly so, and frankly I really wasn't needed, but maybe they felt the need to show the government that they had a Washington player in the room." Later, McCain did not list the Chitimacha as one of the tribes Abramoff had allegedly defrauded. "It was not sexy to include tribes that we did not charge a lot of money to—like the Chits and the [Massachusetts] Mashpees," says Abramoff. McCain would have undoubtedly contended that these tribes had not been included in the probe because they were too poor to defraud.

"To my knowledge the Chits never attacked me. In fact, Terry was a good friend through most of the [scandal], though once the FBI came to interview him I did not hear from him again," says Abramoff. The Chitimachas would fade into the background for several months, until early 2001. In the meantime, as Abramoff continued juggling his usual array of balls—defending his many demanding clients, launching a private school for Orthodox Jewish students, and dealing with the SunCruz shenanigans—he had been nominated for membership in the prestigious Cosmos Club in Washington, D.C. Members have included Alexander Graham Bell (who launched the National Geographic Society as a club function), Woodrow Wilson, Herbert Hoover, Nelson Rockefeller, Carl Sagan, Henry Kissinger, and Sandra Day O'Conner. But there was a problem. Abramoff's membership seemed doomed. Most candidates had received awards and he had none. So in mid September, he contacted his friend Rabbi Daniel Lapin.

> **Abramoff:** I hate to ask you for help with something so silly…but I was wondering if I could put [in the Cosmos application] that I have received an award from Toward Tradition with a sufficiently academic title, perhaps something like Scholar of Talmudic Studies?…Indeed, it would be even better if it were possible that I received these in years past, if you know what I mean….Anyway, I think you see what I'm trying to finagle here!
>
> **Lapin:** I just need to know what needs to be produced. Letters? Plaques? Neither?

Abramoff: Probably just a few clever titles of awards, dates, that's it…Do you have any clever titles…or shall I dip into my bag of tricks?

Lapin: "Let's organize your many prestigious awards so they're ready to 'hang on the wall.'"

McCain would later parade these e-mails to embarrass Abramoff, but also to drive home an imputation of Abramoff's intrinsic duplicity. Even though the subject had nothing to do with Native Americans, they were read aloud at one of McCain's hearings.

Lapin would later claim that the whole matter was blown out of proportion and that he never produced the awards, because "[f]rom my side it was tongue-in-cheek." Later, he would elaborate: "Anyone familiar with Abramoff's jocular and often fatally irreverent e-mail style won't be surprised that I assumed the question to be a joke," said Lapin. "The very notion that an exclusive social club would regard a meaningless award from Toward Tradition to be adequate credentials for admittance was ludicrous. I responded in similar style offering to 'wallpaper his office with awards.'"

Abramoff has a different explanation: "Jay Kaplan was the new head of the [Cosmos] recruitment committee and they wanted to bring down the average age from deceased to something around 80, so he asked me to join. I had no interest, since I couldn't eat there, but Jay was a friend and an important business associate, so I said 'Sure.' When I submitted my application, Jay said I needed some awards… and asked me to get some. I made some calls, including to Lapin, and rounded some up. To be consistent, I added them to my website, in case anybody checked, and then never joined the club. After that I forgot all about it. It was only after McCain raised it that it became an issue. This became another proof that I was a fraud and a charlatan, of course."

On the Greenberg Traurig official website, two of his awards did hail from organizations controlled by Rabbi Lapin: The 1999 Biblical Mercantile Award from Cascadia Business Institute, and the 1994 Scholar of Biblical and American History from Toward Tradition. His friend

Amy Ridenour also pitched in. Her organization, the National Center for Public Policy Research, which had sponsored DeLay's junkets to Moscow and Scotland, honored Abramoff with the 1998 Outstanding Public Affairs Professional Award, and the 1997 Winston Churchill Award.

In the fall of 2000, what concerned Abramoff most was the upcoming presidential and congressional elections. The outcome would have a direct effect on the influence he could wield on behalf of his clients. As right-wing Republicans bit their nails and crossed their fingers with Election Day approaching, Abramoff forwarded an October 31 e-mail to Rove. It pointed out that whenever the Redskins had lost their last home game of the season, it guaranteed a change in party control of the executive branch. Therefore, Bush was destined to be the country's next president. Rove, also a former two-term College Republican chairman, responded: "Jack—I will rest much easier between this and the Halloween mask test."

Obviously, a lobbyist's access—even the perception of access—to the president's closest advisor would be invaluable. Indeed, federal investigators would later attempt to uncover just how valuable, and more importantly, if these contacts had risen to the level of criminal activity. "My job was to get to know powerful people to help my clients. Yes, I'm guilty of asking Karl Rove for help. There's nobody I wouldn't have asked for help," says Abramoff. "All these people were shocked that there's gambling at Café Rick's, but I was in the business of lobbying. That's what lobbyists do…Wouldn't it be great if people could cure their own illnesses, grow their own food, and walk into court and say 'I didn't do it.' But businesses with millions of dollars on the line have to hire people like me to save their businesses. I charged what the market would bear, which my clients were happy about…"

In 2006, federal investigators would discover that Abramoff and his lobbying team had had nearly 500 e-mail contacts with the White House, including 82 contacts with Rove's office. This did not include Abramoff's many visits to the executive mansion—just how many the Secret Service would later refuse to disclose.[125] And this did not include his many private meetings with Rove at private dinner parties, in Abramoff's exclusive sports boxes, and at Signatures, the restaurant that he would open in early 2002. "Karl and I were the only two-term chairmen of the College Republicans, at least in the recent era," says Abramoff. "Rove would later come to view me as one of his top outside contacts and advisors, but both of us knew better than to publicize this fact."

In September 2006, Abramoff received a $1500 check in the mail from Rove, belatedly reimbursing Abramoff for free meals Rove had enjoyed at Signatures three years earlier.[126] When asked if that reimbursement was sufficient, Abramoff rolls his eyes and says he cannot discuss it, presumably because of the ongoing investigation of Rove.

Years later, when asked about Rove's relationship with Abramoff, a White House spokesman said, "Mr. Rove remembers they had met at a political event in the 1990s...Since then, he would describe him as a casual acquaintance." Former Bush press spokesman, Scott McClellan, who would publish a controversial memoir in 2008, wrote that "top White House officials...including [Karl] Rove...allowed me, even encouraged me, to repeat a lie."

Back on election night—November 7, 2000—Abramoff and his family were anxiously awaiting the results at the ESPN Zone in downtown Washington—along with DeLay and approximately a thousand of his supporters. "My wife and I spent a good part of the evening viewing the results in a private room with Tom [DeLay] and Christine [his wife]. [Ed] Buckham and his wife were also there," says Abramoff. "Later as the networks [mistakenly] called Florida for Gore, we went home to bed."

Although at first it appeared that Gore had won the election, it soon became evident that the vote in Florida—and therefore the election itself—was too close to call, triggering a bitter recount. "I didn't go down there for the recount effort, but I did send a number of my staff, including Shawn Vasell, Duane Gibson, and Todd Boulanger" says Abramoff. "The fact that Greenberg Traurig had turned over their offices in Tallahassee to the Bush campaign helped me clinch my decision to jump ship from Preston Gates."

Shawn Vasell and Todd Boulanger would later boast that they had been team leaders in disrupting the vote recount in two important Florida counties. Best friend Tony Rudy, whom Abramoff would hire as a lobbyist a couple months later, also fought in the trenches. They all did their part in Florida to prevent a fair and timely recount. But Abramoff claims they were just trying to prevent the Democrats from stealing the election. However, the infamous Brooks Brothers Riot—in which Duane Gibson proudly participated—would start a chain of events that would lead directly to Abramoff's future destruction, or as he described it, "[to his] being killed on the battlefield."

On November 19, hundreds of furious Republicans—"[wearing] loud madras shorts and pinstriped suits"—stormed the Miami-Dade polling headquarters, demanding that the hand recount of 10,750 remaining ballots be halted. The disruption caused such delays to the recount that they were not be completed in time to meet the strict deadline set by Katherine Harris, Florida's Republican Secretary of State, who was also happened co-chair of Bush's Florida campaign. Since Bush officially won the state of Florida by only 537 votes, those ballots in Miami-Dade's heavily Democratic country might have made the difference. Directing the "riot" with a walkie-talkie from within a van across the street was Roger J. Stone, Jr., a notorious Republican dirty trickster. Former Secretary of State, James Baker, Bush's post-election strategist, had personally selected Stone for the job and was quite pleased with the results. Stone would soon be amply rewarded. He would help select the new chief of Bureau of Indian Affairs, among other appointments, which would allow him to earn millions of dollars as a consultant for Indian casino developers often in direct competition with…Jack Abramoff. But the man who would later prove to be a key in this Shakespearean drama was Stone's good friend and business partner, lobbyist Scott W. Reed.

On December 12, the Supreme Court declared that Bush was the president-elect by the margin of a single vote. Abramoff immediately sent Rove an e-mail: "… I just wanted let you know that, although I do not want to enter government, I am at your disposal for anything you need here in DC. I have a lot of resources at my disposal and am happy to place them at your service if need be… Please do not hesitate to ask me for anything you might need… Regards, Jack." Abramoff says later, "Karl and I exchanged e-mails, but not frequently. I only e-mailed him when I had something I could not pass to him through someone else. Susan [Ralston, Abramoff's secretary, hired by Rove a month later] eventually become that person of choice."[127] McCain would later imply that Abramoff improperly used his Rove connections to secure a position on the Interior Department's transition team, allowing Abramoff to lobby for appointees who would be more sympathetic to his clients, especially the Northern Mariana Islands.

As he was in the process of leaving Preston Gates and moving his team of lobbyists to Greenberg Traurig, the eighth largest law firm in the world, Abramoff wrote an e-mail to Ralph Reed on January 2, 2001, asking him to contact Rove and suggest that he, Abramoff, be named to on the Insular Affairs transition team for the Bureau of Indian Affairs. Reed immediately replied: "[Be] happy to." Abramoff was actually appointed to the transition team's honorary advisory board. "I was put there because I was a donor," says Abramoff. "My whole role was to go to one meeting and give my big-picture ideas as to how the administration should give territories more freedom to develop their economies and that the tribes' sovereignty should be strengthened." But that didn't stop Abramoff from pushing for the appointment of his friends and allies to the Bush Administration. "'Personnel make policy' was the slogan of the Reagan administration and one that I learned well," says Abramoff. Although most of his recommendations met with scant success, one failure later resulted in criminal charges.

On January 11, Abramoff wrote to Reed again, asking him to ask Rove to appoint Mark Zachares as head of Insular Affairs. Reed quickly responded: "It never hurts to ask." Zachares, Abramoff's friend and ally, was the former Secretary of Labor and Immigration for the Mariana Islands. He was so determined to win Zachares' appointment that on March 6th Abramoff went to the White House to meet with Rove to discuss it. An internal White House e-mail exchange several months later indicated that Abramoff had won support from Rove on the Zachares appointment: "Karl and Susan have shown much interest in Zachares." But it didn't pan out.[128] E-mails—released years later—indicated that both the White House and the Interior Department requested that Abramoff meet with and sign off on their choice, David Cohen, before he was approved for the position.

Zachares struggled to find work. By 2002, he was out of cash. In desperation he asked Abramoff for a loan. "Mark was in financial trouble, so I helped him out," says Abramoff, who arranged a wire transfer of $10,000 from his charity, Capital Athletic Foundation, into Zachares' bank account. "The idea was he would do some legal work for [Abramoff's charity]…but we forgot about it, as usual, but not on purpose." The loan was never repaid. In June, with Abramoff's help, Zachares was finally hired by Rep. Don Young (R-Alaska), who served on a committee that monitored Native American and territorial affairs, matters dear to Abramoff's clients.

For Zachares, bagging groceries would have been better. Five years later, he would be forced to plead guilty to a single count of conspiracy for having provided valuable information to Abramoff "in exchange for the promise of future employment, a 2003 golfing trip to Scotland, free meals and drinks at Abramoff's restaurant, Signatures, and approximately $30,000 worth of tickets to sporting events and concerts."

Although later trumpeting Abramoff's allegedly corrupt—but largely failed—insinuations into the newly installed Bush administration's Department of the Interior, McCain was mum about other Indian entrepreneurs, whose insinuations proved far more fruitful. These included Roger Stone and his close business associate, lobbyist Scott W. Reed, a longtime friend and supporter of McCain. Reed—former windsurfing instructor and campaign manger of Bob Dole's failed 1996 presidential bid—and Stone had been friends for years. Unfortunately, Reed had to briefly distance himself from Stone—an unpaid Dole advisor—when "the tabloids got hold of photos of Stone and his second wife, Nydia, striking come-hither poses in swinger's ads, putting out the call for bedroom playmates with exacting specifications: "no smokers or fats please."

What McCain omitted from his report was that Stone and Reed successfully influenced the make-up of the Bureau of Indian Affairs. In a prospectus, "Indian Gaming Opportunities," the boastful Stone claimed to have "served on the Interior Department's "Presidential Transition" committee and "was involved in selecting appointees for that department for the present administration." Although Stone was not officially listed among the 38 members of the transition committee, which never met but was contacted by phone and by e-mail, he was consulted. Tom Sansonetti, asked by Vice President Dick Cheney to run the committee, later admitted that "We built a network of advisers that helped us put together the transition briefing books, and Roger [Stone] was one of those…[who was] very helpful," said Sansonetti, adding that Stone may have made job recommendations for the Bureau of Indian Affairs as well.

Stone next used the Bush-Cheney Presidential Foundation letterhead to mail letters to a number of tribal leaders across the country, urging them to support Neal McCaleb for the top post at the Bureau of Indian Affairs. Stone and Reed helped install Aurene Martin, the third most powerful person at the Bureau of Indian Affairs, as well as Chuck Choney to the three-member board of the powerful National Indian Gaming Commission.

When Wayne Smith was appointed to the number two position at the Bureau of Indian Affairs, McCaleb informed him that Scott W. Reed was "very important to the White House" and someone who should not become "upset with you." Reed informed Smith that the Democrats had been "making money off of the Indian gaming for too long…[and now] it was 'our turn'" for Republicans to receive campaign contributions from the wealthy Indian gaming tribes. Smith also claimed that Reed said he was going to "take out" Abramoff and became "the king of Indian gaming." Reed later denied saying this. By 2004, Scott Reed had signed up about a dozen Indian gaming clients. But his biggest competitor and thorn in his side remained Jack Abramoff. So, according to several sources, Reed decided to take action. Never in his wildest dreams did he think it would meet with such spectacular success.

The Washington Post ran its first story on February 22, 2004, stating that Abramoff had charged his Indian clients enormous fees. What made the story so poignant was that unnamed "lobbyists and congressional staff" claimed that Abramoff had charged these gullible Indians such high fees when there were "no major new issues for gaming tribes on the horizon." One of those unnamed lobbyists, perhaps jealous of Abramoff's success and high fees, was his competitor, Scott Reed, a lobbyist with close ties to McCain.

Reed, who did not respond to requests for an interview, did nothing wrong by feeding this information to a reporter, and Schmidt did nothing wrong by including his views, which she did without attribution. But should she have at least mentioned that one of her sources was a rival lobbyist of Abramoff's? Not necessarily. Nonetheless, in one fell swoop, Reed hit the Trifecta. He eliminated his most prominent Indian-lobbyist competitor, vaporized one of McCain's arch enemies, and grabbed one of Abramoff's tribal clients, the Saginaw Chippewa. What the *Post* reporter and its typical reader could not possibly fathom was that the phrase—"no major new issues"—was irrelevant. In the Byzantine world of Indian Country, the real threats—some vague and opaque—to a tribe's casino revenues usually came in minor shapes and sizes. It was the job of an eternally vigilant lobbyist to stop all threats—major and minor—on a moment's notice.

CHAPTER THIRTY-FOUR
ADJUSTMENTS

The year 2001 would prove to be a truly extraordinary year for Abramoff. His power and influence grew exponentially. Everything he touched turned to gold, with the glaring exception of SunCruz. Conservative George W. Bush was about to succeed the liberal Bill Clinton as president, which meant that the Republicans would now control all three branches of government, as well as the Supreme Court.[129] Abramoff was a member of Tom DeLay's kitchen cabinet. Among GOP lawmakers and conservative groups, Abramoff's popularity would soar thanks to his uncanny aptitude in raising huge sums of money. Abramoff would add two big-ticket casino operators to his tribal headdress—the Louisiana Coushattas and the Saginaw Chippewa in Michigan. He would solidify his reputation as a mensch for his generosity. His ever expanding galaxy of friendships would soon rival President Clinton's. Most importantly, he believed in and loved what he was doing: implementing the conservative agenda that he insisted was good for the country and the world, fiercely defending his clients, making a ton of money, and giving much of it away to his religious community. If someone had whispered in his ear that he was destined for prison as a convicted felon, he would have thought it a sick joke.

His disenchantment with his firm, Preston Gates, had been growing. The feeling was mutual. The liberal Seattle-based firm seemed increasingly uncomfortable "that I even worked there," says Abramoff. Recent articles in *The Seattle Times* about his lobbying for the Mariana Island "sweat shops" had added to the firm's embarrassment. "At some point I had 62% of the [the firm's] lobbying business and I was a huge gorilla and this generated a lot of jealousy," says Abramoff. But there were those at the firm who believed "he was moving too fast and being careless." Manuel Rouvelas, who had founded the firm's Washington branch, met with Abramoff and said prophetically: "If you're not careful, you will end up dead, disgraced, or in jail."

Abramoff says he bears no ill will toward Rouvelas: "Manny was right. I was moving at such a speed that I wasn't careful. I didn't delegate properly. I didn't follow up on what people were doing. I made rash decisions, and all of these things ultimately cost me. [On the other hand], Manny was not used to dealing with lobbyists like me. He was used to staid, passive, typical lobbyists. My win-or-die mentality rubbed him the wrong way. He thought I worked too hard, was too aggressive, and would burn out…His comments, however, really shook me, and it was the thing which started me to think about leaving the firm."

On December 14, managing partner Jonathan Blank, the friend and former across-the-street-neighbor who had hired him six years earlier, officially announced that Abramoff and Preston Gates would part company on December 31. Abramoff—and his ten-member team—would be joining Greenberg Traurig, along with his major clients, including the Choctaws, the Mariana Islands, Channel One,[130] and SunCruz Casinos. Greenberg Traurig's chairman of the national government relations practice, Fred Baggett, who would later testify against him at the McCain hearings, said that Abramoff "gives us critical mass [and] we're heavy into substance lobbyists. Jack is heavy into the relationship side"

The ranking of Preston Gates, which in 1999 had been listed as the 5th largest Washington lobbying firm, plummeted. It instantly lost 50% of his lobbying revenue. Greenberg Traurig immediately "vaulted" into the upper tier. Abramoff's spill-your-blood-for-your-clients lobbying philosophy seemed to mesh with his new firm. Ronald Platt, a Democrat who had worked for the Gore presidential campaign and was credited with persuading Abramoff to join Greenberg Traurig, agreed: "Jack brought a huge amount of business with him, but the other thing is synergy. Let me come back and say first of all, we don't expect to ever lose. Period. That's the reputation we want to have." The first two people Abramoff hired at his new firm would later be among the first to plead guilty in the scandal: Tony Rudy and Michael Scanlon.

However, two events in the first week of February shocked Abramoff. He was in Israel—prospecting for oil in the Negev Desert and exploring with Adam Kidan the possibility of launching casino boats off the coast of Israel—when he received a phone call from Susan Ralston, his long-time trusted executive assistant. She told him that Karl Rove had called. "I instructed Susan to tell him that I was traveling in a car to Jerusalem and would call him back at the first opportunity," says Abramoff. He had misunderstood. Rove hadn't called to speak to Abramoff, but to Ralston. Rove had offered her a job at the White House as his executive assistant and she told Abramoff that she had decided to accept it immediately. "I know [Ralston] well," says Kidan. "She is very bright, conscientious, hard worker, and very cute. She's in her mid 40s, medium height, dark skinned, almost Filipino looking. I remember the look on Jack's face. He turned to me and said, 'I've just been screwed by my best friend, Ralph Reed. He got her the job.'"

Perturbed that this had taken place behind his back, Abramoff figured that if he had to lose her, better that she went to the President's closest advisor. Abramoff immediately called Reed, who admitted he had recommended her to Rove, because, as Abramoff's gatekeeper, she'd had great experience and exposure: "Even though I thought what Ralph [Reed] had done was really rotten," says Abramoff. "I quickly forgave him, but I reminded him that, since most of his business came from me, he should be mindful not to disrupt his golden goose again."

Abramoff denies ever telling anyone that he had gotten Ralston the job. He says he was polite in his e-mail announcing her departure "to make it not look as though she had bolted in the most rude fashion possible—while I was on an overseas trip." A confidential source noted: "perhaps out of guilt for the way that [Ralston] continued to do stuff for Abramoff's staff, and kept requesting tickets from Abramoff for events." Six year later, the House Government Reform Committee released a report that detailed 485 contacts Abramoff and his team had had with the White House. These included 69 with Ralston, who in 2005 had been promoted to Special Assistant to the President.

Ralston's preexisting relationship with Abramoff apparently exempted her from the official ban on gifts over $20 that White House officials can accept from those doing business with the government, but clearly his gifts to her were worth thousands of dollars. Indeed, she appeared to be the most frequent recipient of free tickets to the four luxury boxes that Abramoff leased. An ardent sports fan, Ralston preferred choice seats at the games played by the Washington Capitals, Washington Wizards, and Baltimore Orioles, as well as Bruce Springsteen and Andrea Bocelli concerts. For example, in December 2001, Ralston asked Abramoff for four Wizards tickets worth $1,300.

Allen Stayman, an official in the office of Insular Affairs, had long been a thorn in Abramoff's side in the Mariana Islands and he wanted Stayman fired. On July 9, 2001, Ralston informed her former boss that the State Department had "worked out a deal." Stayman would "be out in 4 months." He was doomed anyway, because he was a controversial, super liberal Clinton holdover.

In the fall of 2001, Benigno Fitial, then speaker of the House in the Northern Marianas, was running as a third-party candidate against Juan Babauta, a Republican. Back in 1999, Fitial had captured the Speaker post—thanks to the assistance of two former staffers for Tom DeLay, Michael Scanlon and Ed Buckham. As a result, Fitial subsequently helped renew Abramoff's lobbying contract with the Northern Marianas. On October 30, Ralston wrote that Rove had "read your memo [on why Babauta's candidacy should not be supported by the Bush administration.]" Three days later, she told Abramoff: "You win :). KR said no endorsement."[131]

Despite Sen. McCain's later claims that Abramoff had defrauded his Indian clients, another e-mail surfaced, showing Abramoff's willingness to waste a chit with Rove over a minor tribal matter. On January 17, 2002, Abramoff asked Ralston if he could meet with her boss because the Choctaws were "getting screwed" by the administration over "funding for their jail project." He added that his client had "been one of the party's best helpers, and this is totally incredible." Ralston quickly replied that Abramoff should meet with Ruben Barrales, the director of the White House Office of Intergovernmental Affairs, who, "works directly under Karl."

Rove also was a sports freak, evident from several e-mail exchanges. For example, in March 2002, Abramoff e-mailed his former secretary about tickets in one of his private suites at the MCI Center for the NCAA basketball tournament that he was giving to Rove. There were many examples of free sports tickets and free meals at Signature's, Abramoff's restaurant, that Abramoff provided to Rove, members of his staff, and other White House officials. On October 6, 2006, a week after the House Government Reform Committee released its report, Ralston resigned her $122,000 a year position, "becoming the first official in the West Wing to lose a job in the [Abramoff] influence-peddling scandal."

CHAPTER THIRTY-FIVE
COUSHATTA COMPACT

Like the Mississippi Choctaws, the Louisiana Coushattas would also turn against their trusted Washington lobbyist during the McCain investigation. In terms of self interest, it was the savvy thing to do. First, it could be catastrophic for a tribe to defy McCain, the powerful head of the Senate Indian Affairs Committee, who had an excellent shot at becoming the president in 2008. And second, there was the prospect of a financial windfall. They could sue Abramoff's former law firm, Greenberg Traurig, for fraud, which would feel obliged to refund most—if not all—of what the tribes had shelled out in lobbying fees. In effect, the tribes would now enjoy the benefits of Abramoff's stunning achievements without its costing a dime.

For example in April 2002, William Worfel, the Coushatta's vice chairman, proclaimed to *The New York Times*, "I call Jack Abramoff, and I get results." However, later he would jump ship, telling McCain: "...these thieves [Abramoff and Scanlon] took every opportunity...[to rob] us." A careful examination of Abramoff's lobbying efforts for the Louisiana Coushatta—who once subsisted on pine-needle basket weaving before opening their fabulously successful casino in 1993—suggested that his accomplishments were quite staggering.

In addition to his many smaller victories, Abramoff could take credit for three major triumphs that literally saved the Coushattas from financial ruin. First, Abramoff twisted the governor's arm into renewing the Coushattas' compact with the state of Louisiana. Without it, the tribe would have been forced to shut down its casino. Second, he warded off the threat posed by another Indian tribe, the Jena Band, which was determined to open its own nearby casino. And finally, since much of the Coushattas' clientele came from Houston and southeastern Texas, Abramoff was able to shut down a casino which a Texan tribe (confusingly called the Alabama-Coushattas) had opened between Houston and the Louisiana-Texas border.

These victories went unmentioned, hardly mentioned, or were minimized in McCain's report, even though McCain had access to hundreds of thousands of pages of Abramoff's e-mails and memos that discussed the strategies that went into these victories. Instead, McCain chose to suppress them.

In the winter of 2000, the Louisiana Coushattas were getting nervous. Its seven-year compact—the agreement that allows the tribe to operate a casino in state of Louisiana—would expire later that summer. It would have to be renegotiated. Their 107,000 square-foot Grand Casino Coushatta—located in Kinder, Louisiana, which is only 50 miles from the Texas border—was one of the most lucrative tribal casinos in the country. As William Worfel, the tribe's former vice-chairman, would later tell McCain, "From 2001 through 2004, most, if not all, of the Louisiana Coushatta's revenue came from its casino profits."

At that time, every tribe with a casino was envious of the Cherokees, who had just hammered out a 25-year compact with the state of North Carolina. The Louisiana Coushattas wanted the same. They didn't want to have to worry every seven years. But their prospects looked dim. Republican Gov. Mike Foster was running for reelection that year and was desperately seeking additional revenue. The tribe was expecting a "very vigorous fight." And they were concerned that their portly lobbyist, former U. S. Sen. J. Bennett Johnston—who was only charging the tribe $152,000 a year—might not be up to the task.

It just so happened that two tribal council members—William Worfel and Bertney Langley—had recently attended a regional Native American convention and bumped into Terry Martin.[132] He was a member of the tribal council of the Chitimacha, another Louisiana tribe operating a casino on the Gulf of Mexico. With the help of its Washington lobbyist, the Chitimacha had just successfully renegotiated its compact with Gov. Foster. But during the process, the governor's staff had mentioned in passing to Terry Martin that this would not be the case with the Coushattas. Martin felt compelled to pass along this information to Worfel and Langley. It confirmed the Coushatta's worst fears. They asked Martin for the name of his lobbyist. He was prominent and well-connected. His name was Jack Abramoff. Martin happened to mention that he also represented the Mississippi Choctaw, "viewed in Indian country as very respected and as a sophisticated business-oriented tribe."

"The Chitimachas were not in a position to pay the large sums that I charged the other clients, but I was very fond of [Terry] Martin and we became close friends. When the time came to for them to renew their seven-year gaming licenses, Martin sought my advice and help. The non-Indians in the state—who were used to dominating the tribes over history and killing them if need be—had become progressively more jealous of the huge profits being generated by the tribal casinos," says Abramoff. For example, Mississippi riverboat casinos, which pay a 21.5 % state tax, were putting lots of pressure on the governor, because they were the ones always being hit with tax increases. Indian casinos pay no state tax.

"Martin was concerned that there might be some difficulties on the road to renewing [the Chitimacha] compact and asked me to join him for meetings with…[Foster] and his staff," says Abramoff. "At one meeting, Foster said something which caught Martin's attention. [The governor] noted that while he was fine with extending the compact for the Chits—he was from the same parish [county] as they were—he was not under any circumstances going to renew the compact of those 'damn' Coushattas." At the time, the Chitimacha casino was a small operation. However, the Coushatta's was huge. With over 4000 slot machines, it raked in nearly $400 million a year. "Plus, unlike the Chits who were friends with everyone around them, the Coushattas were in a constant state of warfare with their non-Indian neighbors—particularly the parish council and local police," says Abramoff. "For these reasons, and the fact that they were also known to have called the governor a racist and bigot, things did not look good for the Coushattas."

With Martin's permission, the Coushattas invited Abramoff and his public-relations specialist, Mike Scanlon, to meet with the tribal council in early March 2001. When they arrived at the council chambers located in the tribe's modest headquarters, Abramoff and Scanlon were introduced to the five council members, including the chairman, Chief Lovelin. "The Chief was a soft spoken man, often almost inaudible because of his low, gentle voice," says Abramoff. "That quality was not shared by the main activist on the council, William Worfel. 'Hi I'm William Worfel, and I'm a pit bull with AIDS' were the first words out of his mouth," recalls Abramoff. "Scanlon and I smiled to each other. Finally, we had found the tribal council member in Indian Country who best resembled our take-no-prisoners approach to lobbying. Scanlon and I would not accept defeat, and neither would Worfel. [It would be] a marriage made in heaven…or perhaps hell."

Six years later, *Time* magazine would put Abramoff on its cover and report that he had flown down to meet the Coushattas "on a private jet, shared some of their fried chicken…then waited for them to turn off the tape recorder that they used for official business." Shaking his head, Abramoff says that this was a typical example of sloppy reporting. "The first time we went, we had to take several connections and drive hours just to get there. We later determined it was not the smart way to get there, so we started going by chartered jet. Shared fried chicken? How could I? It would not have been kosher," says Abramoff. "And they taped all of their tribal council meetings. The tape rolled until we left the room, since we never stayed through the end of any of their meetings, and it was never turned off for any reason, as far as I know."

The first meeting, however, couldn't have gone better. The tribal council members were impressed by Abramoff's credentials, connections, and knowledge of Indian Country. They were also moved when he told them that he could empathize with their plight, because as an Orthodox Jew, "his people, the Jews, had also been…mistreated, been misled," said Worfel. But the tribe was particularly impressed with Abramoff's new-fangled strategy, the same one he had pitched to the Choctaws: Gain influence by carefully targeting political contributions to various Republican organizations and lawmakers. For example, he recommended that the tribe participate in an upcoming charitable golf event sponsored by House Majority Leader Tom DeLay. This would give them real "stroke" in Washington.

Scanlon then pitched himself as a "bulldog…the one who puts out fires…did the groundwork, like on the ads, the radio blitz, the phone banks." He also promoted the creation of a customized political database so they could, for example "flood the offices of policy makers with calls." But Abramoff didn't come cheap. He demanded a hefty monthly retainer of $125,000. And Scanlon would need $534,500 to kick off his grassroots crusade to save the tribe's casino.

Years later, during the Senate Indian Affairs hearings, these tribal officials would complain that Abramoff had never told them that he would receive a cut of what the tribe paid Scanlon. Imputing that what Abramoff did was illegal, McCain failed to disclose in his 373-page report that Abramoff was under absolutely no legal obligation to inform the tribe of his "referral-fee" arrangement with Scanlon. For example, a contractor, who charges $6,000 for an extensive plumbing upgrade, would never inform the homeowner that the subcontractor was actually doing the job for $3,000. The same is true of mortgage brokers, orthopedic surgeons,

THE PERFECT VILLAIN

and lawyers, who are not required by law to disclose their referral fees. Profit-making—whose scope is rarely revealed—is the keystone of the free-market capitalistic system. And yet if one's "honest services" have not been fully provided when raking in those profits, then a federal felony has been committed.

On March 20, 2001, the Coushattas signed the contract. Abramoff got right to work on the compact renewal. "I convened my team and we examined the situation. There was little or nothing we could do to help on the federal level, since it was almost impossible to conceive of a situation whereby the Republican Bush Interior Department would not override the wishes of a GOP governor, Foster in this case, to grant a license for casino gambling. No, the effort was going to have to come from the state level," says Abramoff. In other words, it would require a grassroots effort. He met with Scanlon and they crafted an approach. "It was clear that the only way to get the Foster's signature on their compact renewal was for Scanlon and me to force the pen into his hand," says Abramoff.

They decided to raise an army, which would march on the state capital, Baton Rouge. But whom could they enlist? The tribe only had about 800 members. There was no way for Ralph Reed to cast a spell over the Christian Coalition to help an Indian casino renew its license in a state saturated with gambling. There was only once solution. "I asked [the Coushattas] how many vendors they dealt with. The answer was astonishing—8,000. We got the list and phone banked them," says Abramoff. "All of them of course supported us, because they sell to the Coushattas. And in many cases [these vendors] were even [political] donors of Foster."

Scanlon arranged for nearly 30,000 individual letters to flood into Gov. Foster's office. Abramoff says that the governor let it be known that he would sign the compact if the Coushattas agreed to pay the state a 25% tax on revenues, instead of the 8% "in lieu of taxes"[133] that the tribe was currently paying. "We shut down [the governor's] phone system; we had people picketing his home; and this was the guy who had said he'd never give them their compact," says Abramoff.

Pressure from Washington—real or implied—couldn't hurt. A few days after the Coushatta's signed the contract with Abramoff, he wanted to impress his clients that he was worth every penny they were paying him, so he arranged for Chief Poncho to meet with the President of the United States. Several days later, Chief Poncho signed a $25,000 check.

On April 19, the Coushatta chief met with President Bush in the White House—with Abramoff and Norquist in attendance, something that Gov. Foster was made aware of.

Additional Washington pressure on the Louisiana governor also wouldn't hurt. In July, Abramoff told a tribal official that he hoped that "our guy Steve Griles"—the deputy Secretary of the Interior, who in effect was the department's chief operating officer—as well as his boss, Secretary Gale Norton, would send some "positive signals" to Gov. Foster about his renewing the Coushattas' compact. Apparently, he got the message loud and clear. "[Foster] finally capitulated and [the tribe] only ended up paying 6%," says Abramoff. "I basically went to war with a Republican governor at the beginning of the Bush administration, which was not the usual thing. I saved their existence and at least a $400 million a year. And we established them as a big political player in the state. Now the Coushattas could proudly proclaim: 'If you screw with us, we will bring in the bulldogs.'"

In his report, McCain had to concede that Abramoff and Scanlon had succeeded. "[The tribe] did see evidence that Scanlon's strategy was implemented. In July 2001, Governor Foster signed the compact."

In addition to the donation to Norquist's organization, the Coushattas had wisely followed many of Abramoff's other recommendations in making strategic political contributions. For example, 0n March 22, 2001, the day after signing up its new lobbyist, the tribe made a $50,000 contribution to the Council of Republicans for Environmental Advocacy (CREA), an obscure nonprofit in Washington that critics claimed actually lobbied for and was funded by mining and oil companies. CREA had been founded by Gail Norton—former Colorado Attorney General, who was the current Secretary of the Interior. She had handed CREA over to Italia Federici, who had worked on Norton's political campaigns.

In September, Federici arranged a fundraising dinner party for CREA on September 24 at the home in Embassy Row of a wealthy Republican. There, Coushatta Chief Poncho met with Secretary Norton—along with Steven Griles, her deputy. The introduction was probably far more valuable than when the chief met with the President of the United States back in April. Engineering the meeting between Chief Poncho and the Secretary of the Interior would have been a coup for any lobbyist. As a result, Abramoff was all "jazzed" up and told Federici that the "event last night was outstanding."

Even though *The Washington Post* would later mislead its readers—by claiming that Abramoff had exploited his Indian clients by charging them huge sums when "there [were] no major new issues for gaming tribes on the horizon"—any unbiased Native American lobbyist fluent in the complex affairs of Indian Country knew that just a few words slipped into an obscure bill could siphon off millions of dollars from an Indian casino and that a good lobbyist had to be eternally vigilant and prepared for unexpected threats.

Therefore, Abramoff was effusive in thanking CREA's Federici for what she had just pulled off. "I have fantastic box at the Redskins stadium," he wrote to her in an e-mail. "How about you come this Sunday and see it (invite Steve [Griles] to come with his family too) and we'll discuss my doing a fundraiser for you guys? Let me know as soon as you can…I think Attorney General John Ashcroft and his guys will also be there."

Obviously, Federici was close to Interior Secretary Norton, but Federici was also a close friend of Deputy Secretary Griles. Federici wrote back to Abramoff, "[In] the glamorous world of nonprofit work, [you are] about one half step above beggar." Her message was clear. One hand washed the other. She had access to Norton and Griles. Since the affairs of Indian Country were controlled by the Department of the Interior, Abramoff wisely urged the Coushattas to contribute generously to Federici's organization.

Federici would later tell McCain's committee that CREA—whose annual budget was $250,000—had received nearly $500,000 from Abramoff's Indian clients. Most generous of all were the Coushattas who gave her $150,000. It was money well spent. And it was all perfectly legal. The argument was that this was not bribery. It simply provided an opportunity for the Coushattas' concerns to be fully heard at the Department of the Interior.

Even though nearly seven years later Federici would plead "guilty to tax evasion and lying to" McCain's Senate committee, she was not forced into pleading guilty to receiving illegal contributions from Abramoff's tribal clients, nor for making illegal inquiries on their behalf. Her sentence of sixty days in a halfway house and four years probation was considered relatively mild. In addition to fudging her tax returns,

Federici's gravest error was her decision—probably against her lawyer's advice—to respond to any questions posed by McCain during his committee's investigation.

CHAPTER THIRTY-SIX
JENAS

Because federally recognized Indian tribes are considered sovereign nations, they are state-tax exempt. In other words, they pay neither state income tax nor sales tax on goods and services sold on the reservation. However, as has been done countless times in the past, the U.S. government can blithely supersede Indian sovereignty (such as nullifying or ignoring treaties) by passing legislation that would tax Indian casino tribes. On the several occasions when it attempted to do so, Abramoff managed to step in and block it. But there are other subterfuges that had to be guarded against. For example, a state governor could demand a huge "in lieu of tax"—equivalent to an income tax—for signing a compact to allow a tribe to open or continue operating its casino.

Nevertheless, these Indian tax exemptions created much resentment. Other gambling operations—such as racetracks and non-Indian casinos—had to pay taxes, which cut into their profits and made goods and services more expensive—and less competitive—than those on Indian reservations. What was also irksome was that smokers flocked to Indian casinos, lounges, and restaurants because these don't have to abide by state and local smoking bans.

Non-Indian gambling establishments applied continuous political pressure to change state and local regulations. One of the major threats that Abramoff had to ward off to protect his tribal clients' casino revenue in Mississippi, Alabama, Louisiana, and later in Michigan was the installation of slot machines at race tracks, which required municipal approval. For the Coushattas, one threat was from nearby dog race tracks, which yearned to install slot machines and video-poker games in order to remain financially viable. "After renewing their compact" says Abramoff, "our mission was to kill slots that would impact the [Louisiana] Coushatta's' casino." But there were bigger threats. What if another tribe opened a casino nearby?

THE PERFECT VILLAIN

In his report, McCain would later claim that Abramoff was bamboozling his client by exaggerating these threats: "Abramoff and Scanlon, on whom the Tribe relied as experts, persuaded the Tribal council that threats to the Tribe's gaming interests were everywhere—state-sponsored gambling, slot machines at horse tracks, the possibility of Texas' legalizing gaming, and competing casinos possibly being built by other tribes." Coushatta tribal councilor William Worfel, formerly Abramoff's staunchest defender, seemed to agree. "It was always one crisis after another. There were real threats and some not so real, looking back with hindsight," said Worfel, "Texas gaming was one of those oversold threats. In 2001, we were told by Abramoff that Texas was one vote away from allowing casino gambling. I have since learned that legalized casino gambling was far from being approved by the Texas Legislature."

It is astonishing that McCain would allow Worfel's statement into his report. There was no question that the Texas legislature was about to pass legislation that would have allowed two illegal Indian casinos—which were about to be shuttered by the Texas Attorney General—to remain open. And one of those casinos—operated by the confusingly named Alabama-Coushattas tribe and located between Houston and the Louisiana border—would have killed the Louisiana Coushattas' casino!

"We didn't make these [threats] up. They're all in the newspapers. They brought some of this stuff to us," says Abramoff. "There is so much evidence in Louisiana newspapers. For example, if Texas gets a casino near Houston, it will wipe out the [Louisiana] Coushattas' business. Worfel was doing what every other tribal member was doing—trying not to get indicted and trying not to get sucked into my side of the table, so he could be on McCain's side."

At the very end of 2001, the Coushattas were shocked to learn that they had been stabbed in the back by a good friend: the Jena Band Indian tribe.[134] Former tribal councilor Bertney Langley later turned against Abramoff, claiming that their lobbyist had failed to anticipate that Gov. Foster would secretly sign a compact with the Jenas. It had been Langley—along with William Worfel—who had first talked to Chitimacha's Terry Martin about hiring Abramoff. Even though the impoverished Jena Band, a small 200-member tribe, had no reservation, federal courts had declared that Indians could go "reservation shopping." Because the entire United States had once belonged to them, federally recognized tribes could purchase land wherever they wanted—which was usually in location where they thought a casino would be most profitable.

Actually, the Coushattas and the Jenas had been on excellent terms until the moment the Jenas announced its decision to construct the casino in Vinton, an hour closer to the source of most of the Coushattas' clientele in Houston. Gov. Foster had happily signed the Jenas' compact because the tribe had promised to pay a hefty 15.5% in lieu of taxes, allowing him to increase teachers' salaries without a tax hike. Behind the scenes, however, Scott Reed's partner, Roger Stone, was working against Abramoff. Stone had brought an investor to H. K. Stanley, whom the Jenas had hired to build their casino.

The next step for the Jenas was to win the approval of the Bureau of Indian Affairs at the Department of the Interior. Langley claimed it was the tribe, not Abramoff, who got it quashed. Ironically, there was ample evidence—supplied by *The Washington Post*—that Langley was mistaken or forgetful. It was Abramoff who once again saved the day for his client. But the *Post*'s story put the worst possible light on what Abramoff had accomplished. As Abramoff's lawyer would later point out, "The effort to stop the illegal placing of a Jena casino in a position to destroy the economy of Abramoff's tribal client, the Louisiana Coushattas, was extensive and successful." Abramoff couldn't win. Either he was vilified for defrauding his tribal clients, or he was vilified for saving them.

With its state compact in hand, the Jenas formally applied to the Bureau of Indian Affairs on January 22, 2002. By law, the review had to be completed in 45 days. Therefore, Abramoff had little time to waste. This particular war was different from the one he had waged on behalf of the Mississippi Choctaws, in which he had blocked the Alabama state lottery. To save the Louisiana Coushattas, he needed to quickly mobilize his artillery both on the state and federal level.

Statewide, he once again hired his old College Republican buddy and former Christian Coalition leader Ralph Reed to shepherd his religious infantry. Reed persuaded one of the most famous evangelical Christian leaders in America, James Dobson, to help stop the pernicious spread of gambling in Louisiana. Dobson's organization—based in Colorado, Interior Secretary Gale Norton's home state—produced a daily radio show, Focus on the Family, which was purportedly broadcast to 7,130 radio and television stations to over 220 million people worldwide.

Dobson, who viewed gambling as the work of the devil, was a man whose minions could shut down the phones at the Department of the Interior and possibly cost Norton her job. Thomas Minnery, Dobson's right hand man, notified Norton by mail that Louisiana was already awash with gambling. Enough was enough. What Minnery did, at Reed's suggestion, was to let Norton know that the letter would be forwarded to Andrew Card, President Bush's chief of staff.

On February 20, 2002, a delighted Abramoff wrote to Scanlon that Reed "may finally have scored for us! Dobson goes up on the radio this next week! We'll then play it in the [White House] and Interior." Apparently, Card quickly contacted Doug Domenech, Secretary Norton's liaison to the White House. "Doug came to me and said, 'Dobson's going to shut down our phone system. He's going to go on the air and tell everyone who listens to Focus on the Family to call Interior to oppose the Jena compact,'" an unidentified former senior Interior official later told *The Washington Post*. That Dobson had weighed in "really scared Interior officials." This was confirmed by Michael Rossetti, Norton's legal councilor.

At this point, Abramoff says most Washington lobbyists would not have accomplished so much so fast, and if they had, they would have kicked back and relaxed. But Abramoff was well aware that the driving force behind the Jean's casino bid was a group of sophisticated and tenacious non-Indian entrepreneurs, who were just as determined to win as Abramoff was to stop them. The man that McCain would later accuse of defrauding his Indian clients brought relentless pressure on Norton from every imaginable direction.

Next, Abramoff enlisted Federici's help. On February 21, 2001, she informed Eric Ruff, Norton's press secretary, that Reed "had been bending the ear of Karl Rove and possibly even the president about land-in-trust and gaming issues. I am also hearing that Ralph has involved James Dobson…[who] is planning to run ads and they mention [Norton] by name." Federici then added that House Republicans "have been asked to sign a letter to [Norton] and the President slamming [her]."

What Federici was referring to was the fact that Abramoff's well-paid subcontractor, Ralph Reed, had also persuaded Louisiana GOP Congressman David Vitter[135] to coordinate 26 other congressmen into signing a letter urging Norton to reject the Jena Band's bid for a casino.

Reed arranged for one of his organizations, The Committee Against Gambling Expansion, to inundate Vitter's office with mail, applauding his opposition. "[Vitter is] feeling the love," Reed told Abramoff in an e-mail.

The two Republican senators from Mississippi, Thad Cochran and Trent Lott, even sent letters to Norton opposing the Jena Band bid. Soon thereafter Cochran received $68,500 and Lott received $27,000 in political contributions from Abramoff and his Indian clients. Finally, Louisiana Democratic Sen. John Breaux forwarded to Norton scores of letters he'd received from constituents who were against the Jena's casino. Breaux also was the beneficiary of $14,250 in political donations from Abramoff's clients. In a word, Abramoff pulled out all the stops. He played to win. His goal was to crush the opposition beyond recognition. "My team and I were willing to shed our blood for our clients," says Abramoff.

Norton got the message loud and clear. Her staff became concerned that her Jena Band decision could mushroom into a monster. "Norton didn't want a spectacle involving the department, especially involving [Indian] gambling," said a former senior Interior official. Norton was quite cognizant of "Wampumgate," in which Bruce Babbitt, her predecessor, had been accused—but eventually cleared after a two-year probe—of perjury in connection with his decision to deny an Indian casino license. Just to drive the last nail into the coffin, Abramoff persuaded the Coushattas to launch a final broadside of guided missiles. The day before Norton's decision, he persuaded Lovelin, the tribal chief, to cut "61 checks to members of Congress and their political action committees...[including] a $100,000 check to CREA." On March 7, Norton announced the rejection of the Jena's application for a casino, but she needed something compelling to justify her decision. Anti-tax guru, Grover Norquist, provided her with the perfect excuse.

While the department's press spokesman insisted that the decision was not "influenced by any kind of outside pressure," assistant secretary of the Interior, Neal A. McCaleb, declared that Gov. Foster's insistence that the Jena Band pay a 15.5% in lieu of tax on its casino revenue was nothing more than an unacceptable income tax on a sovereign Indian nation. Despite later claims by tribal council members Langley and Worfel that Abramoff had little to do with stopping the Jenas, the evidence was clear that he had gone to extraordinary lengths on their behalf.

Abramoff's vigorous effort to save his client's tribal client's casino from destruction was completely ignored in McCain's "fair, neutral, and factual" report. In Part One of the report, which is called "Fact Summary by Tribe," McCain went into great narrative detail about Abramoff's dealings with each of his six Indian clients. In the twenty pages devoted to the Coushattas, McCain never once mentioned Abramoff's success in scuttling the Jena's attempt to open a casino.[136]

However, the war was not over. The Jenas had contracted with a new highly sophisticated and wealthy non-Indian developer—the Las Vegas-based Pinnacle Development, Inc.—to build and operate the Jena Band's casino. It realized that it needed to sign up lobbyists on par with Abramoff. Again, quietly working in the shadows, Roger Stone became a paid consultant to Pinnacle Development as well. In early 2003, Pinnacle—on behalf of the Jenas—hired Patton Boggs, perhaps the best lobby shop in Washington, one that was not particularly enamored of Abramoff. Perhaps even more adroitly, the tribe also hired Wallace Henderson, former chief of staff for lawmakers, Louisiana Sen. John Breaux and Louisiana Congressman W.J. "Billy" Tauzin. Henderson was able to persuade both of his former bosses to switch sides and support the Jenas new bid for a casino.

This coup caught Abramoff off guard. In February 2003, he wrote to Federici in a state of panic. Abramoff asked her to inform her friend, Steven Griles, about this development. Two months later, he asked her if Norton was having a change of heart on the Jena casino. "Any way to see if this is something coming from the top?" he asked Federici.

"[I'll] see what I can find out," she quickly replied. Now came the implicit quid pro quo. "I hate to bother you, but is there any news about a possible contribution…"

As he tried to ascertain if there was any policy shift at the Interior, he applied strong political pressure from the outside. By June, Abramoff pulled another rabbit out of the hat. In an unprecedented coup, he had persuaded all four House leaders—Speaker Dennis Hastert, Majority Leader Tom DeLay, Whip Roy Blunt, and Deputy Whip Eric Cantor—to sign a joint letter, urging Norton once again to reject the Jena Band's bid for a casino. A week before this letter was signed, Abramoff just happened to throw a fundraiser at his restaurant, which raised $21,500 for Hastert's political action committee. Keep our Majority (KOMPAC). Hastert later denied any link to the letter he signed.

Patton Boggs was not pleased. "It was very unusual to see four House leaders weigh in on any Indian issue, let alone one that on its face involved only a small poor tribe in Louisiana," said Heather Sibbison, a Jena lobbyist, no doubt with a tinge of envy. It should also be duly noted that these four House Republican leaders were weighing in on matters concerning an obscure Indian tribe located in a state that none of them represented.

Abramoff even persuaded other non-Louisiana lawmakers—both Republican and Democrat—to join the anti-Jena crusade with letters to Norton. These included GOP Congressmen John Doolittle and Dana Rohrabacher from California, and Democratic Senators Harry Reid[137] of Nevada and Byron Dorgan of North Dakota—all of whom received generous political donations from Abramoff and his tribal clients. But for some mysterious reason, his hard work was not having the desired effect. This time it appeared that the Jenas were going to succeed, so Abramoff redoubled the effort. Although he rarely had any dealings with Indian Country, Griles, Federici's special friend, was persuaded to become more involved. Unfortunately for Abramoff, this improper meddling was not particularly successful.

Norton's legal counselor, Michael G. Rossetti, immediately became concerned. He wanted to protect his boss from potential charges that she had somehow intervened on a lobbyist's behalf by subverting the department's standard review process. "[Griles] had a very keen interest [in the Jena's application]," Rossetti later told McCain, and made "constant requests to be involved in [Jena] meetings."

Suspecting Griles of doing Abramoff's bidding, Rossetti finally confronted the Deputy Secretary in front of other Interior officials. "I wanted Mr. Griles to know I had my eye on him, because I was worried about it—whether founded or not, I was worried about it," Rossetti testified. He said he asked Griles "whose water he was carrying."

Griles took strong exception to the implication, later claiming that he did not "recall intervening on behalf of Mr. Abramoff, ever," adding "there was no special relationship with Abramoff in my office." However, outside of Griles' office that may not have been the case. In September, he dined with Abramoff and Fred Baggett, the managing partner of Greenberg Traurig. They offered Griles a job as a lobbyist. Was this an implicit bribe seeking help for Abramoff's tribal client? Apparently not, because he realized that Griles would have to recuse himself.

Later that evening, Abramoff sent out an e-mail to his lobbying team: "This cannot be shared with anyone not on this distribution list," he wrote. "I met with [Griles] tonight. He is ready to leave Interior and will most likely be coming to join us...I expect he will be with us in 90-120 days." The following day, Griles immediately notified and sought advice from an ethics official at the Interior Department. Griles decided not to accept Abramoff offer.

Nonetheless, the machinations were not yet at an end. At the end of 2003, just as Norton was about to make the final decision on the Jena's second casino application, Griles handed Rossetti a carefully organized anti-Jena binder that contained, among other things, letters from many congressmen and senators from both sides of the aisle. Rossetti claimed that Griles wanted to be sure that Norton was aware of "all sides of this issue."

Rossetti would later claim that "after a series of questions that took much longer to...answer that I would have thought necessary," Griles reluctantly admitted that the binder had come from a congressman's chief of staff by way of a lobbyist "who turned out to be Mr. Abramoff." Griles strongly disputed Rossetti's recollection. "I did not say it came from Mr. Abramoff. I did not say it came from Congress. I speculated that it could have come from any of those sources," said Griles. "I do not know and did not know where it came from," Griles later told McCain

The binder, which had no title, but was addressed to Griles, had been delivered by courier to the Interior's front desk. He decided to "just [flip] through it," and realized it was a packet of information about the Jenas. "[It] looked like it had letters—congressional letters, it had studies or something in it." He asked Sue Ellen Wooldridge, one of Norton's legal advisors, what he should do with it. She informed him it was now a federal document and that he had "no option except to give it to...Michael Rossetti." In fact, the binder had been prepared by Abramoff's team, which then anonymously delivered it to Griles.[138]

Abramoff still did not give up the fight to stop the Jenas, however. He helped Louisiana Sen. Vitter draft a provision that was inserted into a Congressional conference report, which recommended that the Jenas be barred from opening a casino unless it was located within the confines of their traditional tribal lands. In other words, permit the Jenas to open a casino, but not where it would threaten the Coushattas' sole source of revenue. Vitter's recommendation was ignored. In December 2003, Norton approved the Jena's application. With help from Roger Stone, Pinnacle Development had won. Reporters would later describe this as one of Abramoff's biggest defeats, citing the millions the Coushattas had squandered.

Abramoff reassured the Coushattas that there was no cause for alarm. Norton's decision would not impact their casino revenues at all. "The 'loss' to the Jenas was not a loss at all," says Abramoff. "I had used a variety of tactics and strategies to counter the full court press of the Jenas. First I thwarted them at the federal level, then at the state level."

Anticipating that there was a good chance Norton might approve the Jena's second application, Abramoff says someone on his staff was close to and worked with the Democratic gubernatorial candidate, Kathleen Blanco, who was then elected governor of Louisiana.[139] Even though she was a Democrat, Blanco had been very vocal about her opposition to the expansion of gambling. "I knew when it was sent back to the state for reaffirmation, [Blanco] would kill it and she did," says Abramoff. "To this day, no Jena casino is open in any of the states—Mississippi, Louisiana, Texas—in which they sought permission to operate. This contradicts the claims of [McCain] that I did nothing for the Coushattas. I 'defrauded' them right into a renewal of their compact and 'defrauded' them right in saving their annual income from being decimated."

CHAPTER THIRTY-SEVEN
BIN LADEN

One of the criticisms of Abramoff was that he had no scruples. In spite of his professed and deeply held religious beliefs, the only god he worshipped was money. "The range of his clients and associates was breathtaking even by Washington standards," declared Jason Isaacson of the American Jewish Congress. Abramoff's claim that he would only take on clients consistent with his political ideology appeared to be a crock, especially when the Orthodox Jew signed up a client with alleged ties to Osama bin Laden.

Right after the terrorist attacks on the United States on September 11, 2001, Abramoff agreed to represent the General Council for Islamic Banks. The chairman of this Bahrain-based consortium of Muslim banks—operating under the code of Sharia or Islamic law—was Saudi businessman Salh Abdullah Kamel. He wanted the United States to know that his bank consortium did not shelter any funds for any terrorist networks and hoped not to be restricted by any new anti-terrorism banking legislation that Congress was about to enact. The problem for Abramoff was that it later emerged that Kamel, worth about $2.6 billion, had "been a major investor in a Sudanese bank that was used heavily by Osama bin Laden." In June 2002, the consortium's representatives dined at Signatures, Abramoff's restaurant. In attendance were Abramoff, Mike Williams, Neil Volz, and Bob Ney. Later, a spokesman for Ney said that it "should surprise no one" that Ney attended this dinner with Islamic banking officials, because he served on the House Financial Services. Ney had also once taught school in Iran and was fluent in Farsi.

"Mike Williams[140] from my staff landed this client thanks to Khaled Saffuri,"[141] says Abramoff. "I was not thrilled about it, but did not stop it. I even met these guys when we dined at Signatures. The reason I was dragged into this was that I signed all the client intake forms and the LDA [Lobbying Disclosure Act] forms, since I was the head of the [firm's] lobbying practice. I was then pilloried unfairly in the press as if this was my client. I came out hard at that point and demanded that the firm get rid of the client, which they agreed to do. This was a very unfair attack."

CHAPTER THIRTY-EIGHT
SAGCHIPS

The trials and tribulations on the Saginaw Chippewa reservation in Mt. Pleasant, Michigan, were typical of an American Indian tribe blessed with a lucrative casino. Inter tribal warfare—which was what led gaming Indians to hire lobbyists in the first place to stop their nearby brethren from building their own casinos—was only outdone by intra tribal warfare. For many years, but especially since tribal gaming had brought real economic power to tribes with casinos, its members—some with barely a drop of Native American blood in their veins—had employed notorious and sometimes deadly methods to secure their power and to ensure a rival's failure. Abramoff ventured into a cauldron.

"Scanlon and I were hired to protect the [Saginaw Chippewa's] market as we'd done for the Choctaws and Coushattas. But their competition—the Gun Lake Band—had an advantage," says Abramoff. "They had an insider helping them—[tribal councilor] Bernie Sprague. He was not merely interested in the welfare of the tribe that elected him and to whom he owed a fiduciary duty, he wanted to make sure that the Gun Lake also had a major casino, notwithstanding that this casino would take money right out of the pockets of his own members. The reason? Bernie's uncle was an official of the Gun Lake Tribe."

Susan Schmidt of the *Post* quoted Sprague in her first story, but didn't mention these machinations. If she had, her readers might have had a fuller appreciation of the story's complexity, which would have undoubtedly caused their eyes—or any reader's eyes—to glaze over. Schmidt could profess ignorance of these Native-American civil wars. But McCain, as head of the Senate Indian Affairs Committee, could not. When it became evident in carefully reading his report how deliberately biased McCain had been, one had to wonder about the integrity and motivation of a man who'd so publicly proclaimed the report's fairness and neutrality.

In that report, the Saginaw Chippewa was just another one of the six tribes that Abramoff had routinely ripped off for millions of dollars. Essentially, the tribe's sole source of income was a smoke-filled, slot-machine warehouse, called the Soaring Eagle Casino, one of the most successful tribal casinos in the country.[142] According to a Bureau of Indian Affairs 1999 Labor Force Report, no Saginaw Chippewa tribal members lived below the poverty guidelines and there was no unemployment. In 2006, its casino's estimated annual revenue was $400 million and the tribe employed over 4,000 people. Thanks to the casino's revenues, each registered member of the tribe—every man, woman, and child—received a "per capita" of about $2,400 every other week, or nearly $60,000 a year. This stipend was above and beyond what each tribal member could additionally earn, for example, by working as a blackjack dealer at the tribe's casino. It was not uncommon for candidates—who had just won seats on the tribal council, as well as their supporters—to work at the casino in various well-paying capacities. Those who had lost the election—and their supporters—often found themselves unemployed.

This patronage—not uncommon in non-Indian country—created such ill will and resentment in the tribe that it concerned Abramoff.

McCain found a way to exploit Abramoff's concern in order to marshal a case against Abramoff by taking selected e-mails taken out of context and leaking them to the media. These were widely reported as evidence of Abramoff's racism. In one such e-mail, Abramoff wrote to Scanlon: "[The newly elected tribal council] spent the whole time discussing the firings of late. I like these guys…but they are plain stupid…Morons."

Years later Abramoff explains that he was afraid the wholesale dismissal of so many fellow tribal members would create "tremendous harm and upset….I thought their actions were moronic and I called them morons and jokingly called them troglodytes too. This was not aimed at all Indians, but it was aimed at my friends on the tribal council. This was inside-the-family talk."

It all began back in late 2000. The tribe's chief lobbyist was Democrat Larry Rosenthal, a former Bureau of Indian Affairs official under Clinton, and one of Abramoff's "keenest competitors." Rosenthal's lobbying firm, Ietan Consulting, focused almost exclusively on Native American issues. Maynard Kahgegab, Jr., a council member and future tribal chief, described Rosenthal as a pleasant fellow, but a run-of-the-mill lobbyist. Kahgegab said he kept asking Rosenthal why he wasn't able to obtain "what the Choctaw are getting. His response was because you're rich. [Rosenthal] just kept showing us one-page briefings, basically stuff you could get off the internet on Indians.com."

Once Bush was elected, the tribe realized it needed a Republican lobbyist with strong connections to the new administration. It hired Abramoff. But then, the tribal council had to decide whether to keep Rosenthal. Abramoff, who considered Rosenthal lazy, was annoyed because "Rosenthal has been badmouthing us non-stop." Abramoff informed the tribal council—whose majority liked the personable Rosenthal—that if he were retained, Abramoff could not work for the tribe. When Abramoff quit, he predicted that the tribe would reconsider. He wrote, "[G]iven the animus of our Hill and new Administration friends…[when] the Saginaws are told by our friends how dead they are, and after their appropriations are zeroed out, they'll be back."

A number of tribal members were unhappy that Abramoff had resigned. They knew how effectively he had defended the gaming interests of the Choctaws and Coushattas. What deeply concerned the dissident tribal members were the ambitions of the Gun Lake tribe,[143] only two hours south of the Saginaw Chippewa. Gun Lake was determined to open its own casino. Since most of the Saginaw Chippewa casino clients came from the more heavily populated south, the Gun Lake casino would devastate the Soaring Eagle's business. This would cause a precipitous plunge in each member's "per capita" pay out.

Bernie Sprague, one of the council members that McCain later relied on so disproportionately in his report, claimed that the Gun Lake casino would "only affect a small percentage of the Saginaw's market, between 10 and 17 percent." Sprague also declared that he was not opposed to the Gun Lake casino, because "they have their right to gaming just as we do"— a valid and seemingly altruistic, but self-destructive, point. He did concede that his uncle, D.K. "Richard" Sprague, was a Gun Lake tribal official, but claimed that he was not assisting his uncle's tribe to obtain a casino. This denial was much disputed by his critics in the tribe.

According to Kahgegab, Sprague's uncle "came up from Gun Lake and wanted to borrow $120 million from us. Bernie supported the proposal, but we turned it down. Why would we help fund a casino that was going to rival us?"

Other dissident tribal members concurred. "We loathe Bernie Sprague. He is a traitor to SagChips for selling us out to Gun Lake," says Delores Jackson, a former council member. "He used our status and our money to help his uncle, D.K. Sprague. We believe the reason is that Bernie will switch tribes, because Gun Lake only has 300 members and therefore the distribution of [the per-capita] money from the casino will be much greater [for him]."

Velma Lytle-Kyser, the first baby born on the newly established reservation in 1939, pipes in: "Bernie wanted to get his uncle's tribe going at our expense. And Jack Abramoff was in the way." Patricia Peters, who operated a dissident Saginaw Chippewa website, says that as long as Abramoff was the tribe's lobbyist, Gun Lake was stopped. "Once he was gone, Gun Lake got their federal recognition and now they're on their way to getting a casino." Indeed, after clearing many hurdles, the Gun Lake casino was poised to open in 2009. Even though Sprague did speak for many members of his tribe, McCain avoided mentioning this contentious background in his report.

During 2001, at the urging of dissident tribal members, Chris Petras, the tribe's legislative affairs director, and tribal member David Otto pursued hiring Abramoff. In October 2001, Petras met with Abramoff in Washington, D.C. According to the McCain report, an evil scheme was hatched. A group of candidates—called "The Slate of Eight"—would run in the upcoming tribal election, and Scanlon would help them win. If they had a majority on the tribal council, they would hire Abramoff and Scanlon to fight off all threats to and preserve the market share of the Soaring Eagle Casino.

Scanlon pulled out all the stops. On behalf of the "Slate of Eight" candidates, he drafted flyers and mailers, as well as personalized letters from the eight candidates that were mailed to all tribal members. For example, one stated: "[We] are asking the tribal members to vote for us so that we can put the scandal-plagued politics of this tribe in the past." Scanlon devised campaign strategies and also helped to organize a "candidates' night" and even recorded a radio ad. As the November 6th election neared, Scanlon told Abramoff that three of his employees were on the reservation "for the final push." He said, "If we don't win after all this, we never had a chance!" Abramoff replied: "Looks like you have it well in hand. I smell victory! I smell gimme five!!!," their private term for a brilliant move. Later, Abramoff added that he couldn't "handle losing two elections in the space of 4 days."[144]

The McCain report would later point out that Scanlon was never reimbursed, implying that his working for free was highly inappropriate. One of the Slate-of-Eight candidates, David Otto, who would later turn against Abramoff, admitted that there was no *quid pro quo*, only a "non-verbal understanding that Scanlon would like a chance to work for the Tribe." McCain must have known that this was neither illegal nor sleazy. In the business world, it's called "on spec"—doing work without being paid in hopes of winning a future contract. Seven out of the eight "Slate-of-Eight" candidates won seats on the 12-member tribal council. Maynard Kahgegab, Jr. was elected Chief, and David Otto was elected Sub Chief. Unfortunately, the Chief and sub Chief soon had a serious falling out. Two days after the new tribal council was sworn in, Abramoff was hired on a $150,000 monthly retainer.[145] This was far more than Larry Rosenthal, who was immediately fired, had ever been paid by the tribe.

"[Rosenthal] was pissed. He kept saying he'd be back. He'll be back in two years," says Kahgegab.

The popular, but controversial, Bernie Sprague did not lose his council seat, but did lose his influence. He claimed that because of his continuing criticism of Abramoff and Scanlon, he eventually lost his longtime job as commissioner of parks and recreation and was unemployed for six months. Of course, he did not lose the nearly $120,000 annual per-capita tribal payment that he and his wife received that year. Sprague, who declined to be interviewed, would later tell McCain that non-Indians' interference in tribal elections was "unheard of." Apparently, this was not the case. Tribal candidates occasionally use political consultants, who are neither tribal members nor Native Americans.

McCain declined to credit Scanlon for being honorable when the next tribal-council election rolled around. When Scanlon was approached by a tribal official who asked for assistance in the upcoming election so that the same members would retain their council seats, Scanlon refused, saying that because his firm was under contract with the tribe "we… cannot use tribal funds to conduct campaign activity…"

Sprague also told McCain that just before the tribe hired Abramoff, he questioned the lobbyist about his relationship with Scanlon. Sprague said that Abramoff told him that he knew Scanlon and that he was a professional. Later, Sprague also told a reporter that he had telephoned Abramoff because he'd heard rumors that the lobbyist was going to sue him for libel. According to Sprague, "[Abramoff] said I was spreading rumors that he had somebody killed in Florida…[and] said he had reputation to protect." Sprague said Abramoff denied the charge and then backed down.

Abramoff remembers it differently. Several council members had told him that Sprague had been defaming him as a mobster and a murderer because of Gus Boulis' assassination. One day, Abramoff got a call from Sprague, whom Abramoff says he had never before spoken to or met. Sprague asked about the status of the federal appropriations for a new tribal school. "I politely answered his questions and then asked him if he had been slandering me," says Abramoff. "Sprague became very embarrassed and denied it, but I had too many sources. I told him that if he ever repeated such a lie, I would turn the matter over to my attorneys. Not waiting for a reply, I ended the call."

It appeared that Abramoff's victories, such as that tribal school, were also used as a tire iron against him. Abramoff would later wrangle $3 million for a new school for the Saginaw Chippewa, even though such federal funds were only supposed to go to poorer tribes. He scored that coup with the help of Sen. Conrad Burns (R-Mont), chairman of a key Senate appropriations subcommittee, who slipped in a last-minute earmark before the final vote on a massive appropriations bill. Later, Abramoff would boast that "every appropriation we wanted from [Burns] we got." And as a result, no other member of Congress received more contributions from Abramoff and his clients than Sen. Burns. His total take was over $140,000. "Our staffs [Abramoff's and Burns'] were as close as they could be," Abramoff says. "They practically used Signatures [Abramoff's restaurant] as their cafeteria."

In 2006, the tribe decided not to accept the school funding, because it had become "too much of a political embarrassment," and because it did not want to pay for the operational costs of running the school. According to Abramoff, this version had no bearing on reality: "One of the top priorities of the [Slate-of-Eight] council was to get school funding…I suggested the tribe offer to match, dollar-for-dollar, the grant…forthcoming from the federal government. The tribal council was elated, and we got them the funding. In the end, under Sprague's control, the tribal council refused the grant. While they mumbled that they were rejecting it because of the scandal, the truth was widely known. The reason they turned the money back—money for which I and my team had spilled many gallons of blood, sweat, and tears—was that the finances of the tribe had been so mismanaged by the new council that they could not meet the match."

After an annoying delay, in February 2002, the tribe finally hired Michael Scanlon for $4 million to develop a political "database" and to protect the tribe's casino revenue from threats that included slot machines at race tracks, as well as competing tribal casinos. The tribe eventually paid Scanlon an additional $6 million for other grassroots activities and political consulting, such as trying to get Michigan to pass a law banning all public smoking state wide, which would drive smokers to the Soaring Eagle Casino.

Ten million dollars was a lot of money. It was very difficult to confirm the McCain reports's analysis and calculations of the profits that Abramoff and Scanlon reaped from their tribal clients, because of McCain's refusal to release Scanlon's financial ledger in its entirety. But McCain contended that in general Scanlon spent one-third on the tribes, while the other two-thirds went into the pockets of Abramoff and Scanlon as profit. McCain characterized these 200% profits as "brazen" and "deceptive."

Simply put, huge profits are not illegal. And in many instances, they are not uncommon. In the world of free-market capitalism, of which McCain and Abramoff are proud paladins, profit margins are notoriously proprietary and complex to calculate. Nonetheless, here are some unnerving examples. A former designer for a Ralph Lauren home-furnishing store says that his mark-up was 900%. For example, the store would purchase a $100 item and sell it for $1,000. At auto dealerships, the new-car buyer is always offered a dazzling array of tempting extras. Unbeknownst to the consumer, the mark-ups are often staggering. For instance, the mark-up on rust proofing is 2,000%; on fabric protector, 6,000%; on paint sealer, 3,000%; and detail and pin-striping, 1,000%. At a fancy restaurant, the diner probably does not realize that the mark-up on hard liquor falls between 200% and 300%. For smaller-sized diamonds, jewelers make as much as five times more (500%) than what they paid. One can only hazard a guess as to how much profit a Windows upgrade puts into the pockets of multi-billionaire Bill Gates and the legions of other billionaires spawned by Microsoft.

Therefore, McCain's claims that Abramoff and Scanlon illegally or immorally charged their tribal clients too much was a canard. Besides, they were under absolutely no obligation to inform them what their profit margins were or that there was even a referral fee.

When former Chief Kahgegab was later interrogated by the FBI, he says he told them that "Jack did a way better job than Larry did. Well, [Abramoff] got us 34 parcels of land into trust; he got us the $3 million for the construction of a new K-12 school; he got $1.2million from the feds for a road….As for [the referral fee], it didn't bother me, because we got our money's worth. We paid $4 million for that database but we saved the tribe $100 million by stopping a bill that would have allowed [2,500 slot machines into a nearby race track] and the tribe's still using [that the database] today."[146]

Everything about McCain's report seemed to insult the reader's intelligence. He implied that there was something nefarious going on because "the Slate of Eight [was] keenly interested in assuring its incumbency." What incumbent, including McCain, doesn't want to keep his job? According to McCain, Abramoff's philosophy on client management revolved around "keeping our people in power." And what were those reprehensible measures that Abramoff took to achieve this unsavory goal? Scanlon drew up a public-relations plan "to provide the Saginaw Chippewa Tribal Council with the tools and resources necessary to successfully and *proactively* promote their agenda and improve their image among tribal members, the media and legislators."

One would suppose that every public-relations firm and every political consultant—including the many lobbyists that worked on McCain's presidential campaign—were equally guilty of such dastardly manipulations. And what businessman wouldn't want to retain his clients, especially when a change in the tribal-council composition could result in the return of Abramoff's much-loathed competitor, Larry Rosenthal?

But what was so blatantly untrustworthy and unjust about McCain's report was that the 49-page Saginaw Chippewa section contained interview excerpts and/or prepared statements from only two tribal members—both highly critical of Abramoff. They were Bernie Sprague, who was cited 27 times, and David Otto, 25 times. But Otto actually didn't say anything critical about Abramoff in the report; his contributions were merely factual and informational. Hence, Sprague's was the only Saginaw Chippewa voice heard. McCain allowed only Sprague to speak on behalf of the entire tribe. The views of all the other members—nearly 3,000-members strong—did not find their way into his report. It was as if McCain had declared that he would write a "fair and balanced" monograph on the Israeli-Palestinian conflict, but would allow only two fervent Zionists—or two members of Hamas—to testify.

Other tribal members insisted that they had notified McCain of their desire to be interviewed, but they were ignored. "We hand delivered four letters to the Senate Committee on Indian Affairs, letting the committee know our views and that we were waiting to hear from them, but there was no response," says Patricia Peters. "And we waited at the hearings, hoping to talk to someone, but no one approached us. The only people they wanted to talk to were [David] Otto and [Bernie] Sprague."

One letter sent in August 2004 to McCain on official tribal stationery stated: "We would like to make clear that Sub Chief Bernie Sprague does not speak for our entire tribe." The letter was signed by six tribal members, including Gary Sprague, Bernie's brother.

Former Chief Kahgegab says that he also wrote an urgent letter to McCain informing him that he was ready to testify: "He never contacted me and never invited me to the hearings...That report doesn't give both sides of the story. He allowed Bernie Sprague to testify on behalf of the entire tribe. That was completely ridiculous."

On December 2003, a new tribal council was swept into power and sworn in. Most of the Slate of Eight was out. Abramoff and Scanlon were fired at once. Larry Rosenthal was rehired. Three months later, all tribal councilors flew to Washington. Rosenthal squired them around town. According to then council member Delores Jackson, one of the people to whom Rosenthal introduced them was another lobbyist that the tribe—unbeknownst to Jackson—had officially hired. His name was Scott W. Reed of Chesapeake Enterprises.

At a videotaped tribal community meeting two years later, Rosenthal stood up at the podium, castigating the evil Abramoff and promising to "never do anything to embarrass the tribe." Rosenthal then introduced his new lobbying partner, Aurene Martin. She was the former Acting Assistant Secretary of the Bureau of Indian Affairs, for whom Roger Stone and Scott Reed had successfully lobbied for the Bush administration to hire.

None of this political warfare and in-fighting was improper or unusual. In fact, it was basically ho-hum. But what these distortions implied was that McCain's presentation of a black-and-white version of a complex narrative was hardly objective and reliable. Abramoff believes that McCain simply wanted payback. Furthermore, he wanted to knock out of the box his most powerful and vocal right-wing critics—Abramoff, Tom DeLay, Ralph Reed, and Grover Norquist.

"McCain figures most prominently in a very bad way—for him as well—in this scandal," says Abramoff, seated in the visitor's lounge at the satellite camp of the federal prison in Cumberland, Maryland. "By his taking selected e-mails from me and leaking them in a way which so villainized me, he set in motion a course which could not help but cause tremendous damage to the GOP. McCain focused his fire entirely on Republicans...By bringing down the Republican control of [Congress], McCain eliminated in one fell swoop the most anti-McCain elected officials from power, primarily DeLay, which gave [McCain] a clear path for the [Republican] nomination. By eliminating me—along with Ralph and Grover—he removed the one lobbyist activist who could have raised the money needed to stop him in the primaries, as I helped to do in 2000. While attacking me as a corrupt lobbyist, his own lobbyist pals—Scott Reed, Roger Stone, and others—were able to swoop down and grab my business."

It's doubtful that this grand conspiracy had been neatly planned out in advance and then coolly executed, and the only client Reed snagged was the Saginaw Chippewa, but in retrospect it's easy to understand why the traumatized Abramoff might have reached this conclusion.

CHAPTER THIRTY-NINE
MORE TRIBES

It was an inconsistency that the press did not question or bring to the attention of John McCain. While Abramoff was allegedly defrauding his tribal clients, they seemed quite satisfied with his representation, kept renewing his lobbying contracts, and were more than happy to recommend him to other tribes. One explanation for this paradox was that Abramoff had cast a spell over these wealthy, but defenseless and naïve, Native Americans, not to mention their sophisticated lawyers and accountants. The more compelling reason was that the charges—elaborately embroidered and politically motivated—spun a simple, but misleading, narrative. In the final analysis, it should be said that the public was just as guilty as Schmidt, McCain, and the Department of Justice in persecuting Abramoff, because of our inherent and unquenchable thirst for such narratives. The need for the epic myth—imprinted upon our collective unconscious long before the first cuneiform inscriptions were etched in clay—clouded our judgment and skepticism.

Two other tribes that Abramoff represented—the Agua Caliente in Palm Springs, California and the Pueblo of Sandia in New Mexico—also underwent the withering and tendentious McCain analysis.

THE PUEBLO SANDIA
For the Sandia Indians, the overarching issue was not slot machines and blackjack. It was lucre of a different sort: A sacred mountain. The

ability to purchase and place "land into trust" was complex and frustrating. Delays could take decades. Abramoff had pulled off a coup for the Choctaws by obtaining nearly 9,000 acres, placed into trust, portions of which the tribe had originally applied for in 1927. This had required Congressional approval, which, thanks to Abramoff's wining and dining of DeLay, was finally accomplished. For the Sandia Indians, a clock was ticking on a land issue of paramount importance to the tribe. The Sandia Mountain had served "as [the tribe's] church and…spiritual sustenance for hundreds of years." Because of an erroneous 1859 survey and because of its location on the northern city limits of Albuquerque, developers had begun encroaching on the mountain's foothills. After protracted litigation, a time-sensitive settlement was reached, incorporating the mountain into the tribe's reservation. The agreement, however, would expire if not ratified by Congress before November 16, 2002.

With the deadline only nine months away, the tribe's anxiety was growing as its confidence in its lobbyists was diminishing. The Sandia needed a lobbyist with muscle in Washington to make it happen. They met with Abramoff and Scanlon in February 2002. Abramoff told them that although there were never any guarantees, they rarely lost, which happened to be true. But the tribe balked at Scanlon's $2,875,000 fee for a database and a grassroots effort. Later, a tribal lawyer told McCain that that Abramoff had insisted that Scanlon was "part of the package" and essential to success. Abramoff reduced Scanlon's fee to $2,750,000, and to sweeten the deal, halved his firm's $125,000 monthly retainer. The reason was that "Abramoff [was plotting] with Scanlon to split the…Sandia profit as part of their 'gimme five' scheme," wrote McCain. "The… elements of deception are much the same. However, the financial loss to the… Sandia and the subsequent financial gain to Abramoff and Scanlon were, relatively speaking, on a scale considerably smaller than what the other Tribes experienced. This fact was not lost on Abramoff and Scanlon early in their relationship with the [tribe], as [seen in] the following e-mail exchange on March 7, 2002:"

> **Scanlon:** [$]2.75 [million from Sandia] is chump change!!! What [t]he hell were we thinking?
>
> **Abramoff:** No kidding….

> Scanlon: Hey – it's still a W[in]—and I will take the W[in] any way we can—now a [$]4.5 [million] W[in] would be nicer—but wait till Thursday when COush [Coushatta] comes to town!

Abramoff remembers it differently: "Their other lobbyists had failed them and it was the 11th hour, but the lawyer who was negotiating for them didn't like Mike [Scanlon]. For reasons I don't want to go into, the guy hated him. It was uncomfortable doing the pitch meeting." The lawyer claimed the tribe was poor and had no money, but Abramoff knew the tribe had constructed a dazzling casino, golf course, and resort. "Finally, I put my foot down and figured they'd walk away, but I didn't care. They came back and said yes, but this guy had so poisoned the atmosphere that Scanlon was reluctant to do it, although the profit on this was good. Negotiations over the fees for [the firm] and [Scanlon] were parallel but separate. I agreed to $50K per month, down from our usual $150K a month, and Scanlon agreed to lower his fee a bit."

There appeared to be little doubt that the tribe was unhappy with Scanlon—either because of interpersonal conflicts or because Scanlon's work was not up to snuff. Later, McCain did not equivocate. He insisted that the eventual Congressional ratification of the Sandia Mountain agreement came about due to the "support from the New Mexico Congressional Delegation and a homegrown grassroots effort…"

Abramoff laughs: "That homegrown grassroots effort was Scanlon!"

In the final sentence of his concluding remarks of the Sandia section of his report, McCain stated unequivocally, "Success was achieved for reasons wholly unrelated to the extraordinarily expensive pretensions of Abramoff and Scanlon." What incontrovertible evidence did he have to make such an unqualified statement? But it was telling that McCain omitted something that would have undermined his declaration. Soon after the Sandia Indians got their mountain, the tribe renewed its contract with Abramoff.

Of course, once McCain launched his investigation, the Sandia quickly—and some would say expediently—ganged up on and turned against their lobbyist.

THE AGUA CALIENTE BAND OF CAUHILLA INDIANS

The Agua Caliente reservation—located on hot springs, hence its name, which means "hot water"—operated two very profitable casinos in the southern California desert near the forests of towering wind turbines surrounding Palm Springs. For Abramoff, the tribe happened to be conveniently located a couple miles from the retirement community where his parents lived.

Why McCain even bothered to include this tribe in his report was unclear, except to repeat his monochromatic litany. He criticized Abramoff and Scanlon for helping re-elect two candidates to the tribal council, who were dissatisfied with the tribe's current lobbyist and wanted to hire Abramoff. But attempting to snag a new client or luring one away from a competitor was standard operating procedure in the business world, hardly unseemly, never mind criminal. McCain condemned Abramoff for not proclaiming from the rooftops that he and Scanlon had provided these candidates with assistance. McCain denounced Abramoff for not mentioning the payment of two confidential "finder's fees" and for not informing the tribe that Scanlon was paying him a referral fee—both rather common business practices. McCain belittled Scanlon's database and his grassroots efforts and demeaned him for hiring subcontractors, something extraordinarily routine. As usual, McCain peppered his Agua Caliente section with a choice e-mail or two, ripped out of context, to showcase Abramoff's callous and wicked soul. And finally, McCain used language freighted with innuendo. For example, when Abramoff cited another tribe as a reference, McCain hissed that "Abramoff *traded* on the name of the...Choctaws." And when Abramoff and Scanlon discussed an upcoming tribal election and its effect on the renewal of their contract, McCain snarled that they "continued *to conspire* about how to increase their influence over the Tribal Council."

In January 2002, Abramoff flew to California to marry a little pleasure with business. He arrived in Palm Springs and visited with his parents, who lived in Rancho Mirage, and then met with Virginia Silva and Candace Patencio, two long-term council members of the Agua Caliente tribe. Each expressed concern about the tribe's upcoming compact renegotiation with the state and their dissatisfaction with and a desire to terminate the contract of the tribe's lobbyist, Pace-Capstone. Both had political ambitions. Silva wanted to be the tribal Chairman and Patencio,

Vice-Chairman. Later, they met with in Washington with Abramoff and Scanlon, who eventually helped them prepare for the tribal elections in March. Silva, however, lost; Patencio retained her seat.

Nevertheless, at Patencio's invitation, Abramoff and Scanlon flew back to Palm Springs to make a formal presentation to the full council. They made their usual pitch, describing what they could do to secure and increase the tribe's power base. Abramoff explained his strategy of guiding the tribe's political contributions to "targeted" lawmakers "who may [seem to have] nothing to do with what [the tribe is] doing, but we know that that Member will be able to control or influence a bill…" Scanlon pitched his database and grassroots expertise. The council liked what they heard and hired them. They agreed to pay Abramoff's firm a fixed-retainer of $150,000 a month, with no expenses. They agreed to pay Scanlon a total of $7,400,000 to help them get their compact renewed.

Next, McCain then snatched a few nasty- or heartless-sounding e-mails and sprinkled them in his narrative for effect. For example, one day when Abramoff was feeling down in the dumps, his partner shot him an e-mail.

> **Scanlon:** Hey—good day all around—we wrapped up the Sag Chip crap—We hit Coush—I think for 3 mil—and we are working [on] Acaliente [sic] presentation—should be tight.
>
> **Abramoff:** Thanks so much! You are a great partner. What I love about our partnership is that, when one of us is down, the other is there. We're gonna make $ for years together!
>
> **Scanlon:** Amen! You got it boss—we have many years ahead!

When Abramoff thought the tribe was close to hiring them, he e-mailed Scanlon: "Can you smell the money?" A year later, when Scanlon was feeling overworked in general and vexed with Patencio in particular, Abramoff sent a wisecrack e-mail to Scanlon hoping to wrangle a smile out of him: "I think the key thing to remember with all these clients is that they are annoying, but that the annoying losers are the only ones which have this kind of money and part with it so quickly."

Abramoff says that almost every lawyer and certainly every lobbyist has had moments when they just didn't want to work for their clients any longer. "Whether it's the constant phone calls inquiring about the status of their situation…it can get on your nerves," says Abramoff. "But this was not a reflection of how I felt about my clients…And never in my life did I think that anyone other than the people to whom these [e-mails] were addressed would be reading them. Never."

Despite assistance from Scanlon in her campaign, Patencio lost her council seat in the next tribal election. And what did McCain have to say about this? "In the [March] 2003 elections…Patencio lost her race. Within months, the [McCain] Committee would start its investigation, and the Tribe would learn the truth about Abramoff and Scanlon's assistance to…Patencio and Siva in their elections. It would also learn about their secret partnership." Once again, McCain omitted an inconvenient tidbit. Despite Patencio's absence on the council, the Agua Caliente retained the services of Abramoff and Scanlon, not for "months," but for more than a year.

The mendacity of McCain's report seemed to know no bounds. But the mother of all lies lay in the section on the Tigua, a gaming tribe in El Paso, Texas. The timing of this lie would indelibly trash Abramoff's already devastated reputation and effectively seal his fate.

CHAPTER FORTY
QUADRUPLE BOGEY

Of all the junkets Abramoff organized, the Scotland golf holiday in August 2002 would prove to be the most problematic. Four of the seven adult participants would end up convicted felons.

In May 2002, Abramoff sent Ralph Reed an e-mail about organizing the boys' annual golf picnic to the celebrated links of St. Andrews: "The package on the ground is $4K per person. that [sic] covers rooms, tee times and ground transportation. One idea is that we could use one of my foundations for the trip – Capital Athletic Foundation – and get and make contributions so this is easier." The problem was that the stated purpose of the Capital Athletic Foundation (CAF) had nothing to do with paying for middle-aged men to play golf. The nonprofit's stated purpose was to help inner-city youth with education and sports.

Even though nationally known nonprofits, such as the Red Cross and the Nature Conservancy, have been publicly scolded for serious IRS violations, no one in either organization was indicted, jailed, or even investigated. Abramoff later admitted that he shouldn't have used the charity he founded and funded to pay for any portion of the trip. "Probably 98% of the money—much of it contributions from me—that CAF spent was used for charitable purposes," says Abramoff. "Some of the rest was used for that Scotland trip…[which] was supposed to be part golf and part education, but turned out only to be golf. And that was wrong. I shouldn't have done it."

Abramoff then set into motion an effort for his tribal clients to make contributions to fund the trip, claiming it would please the powerful Bob Ney and the even more powerful Tom DeLay. Half of this claim was deceptive. He e-mailed one of his wealthy tribal clients, asking for a contribution, saying that Ney had requested the trip and "if we could help (as in cover) a Scotland golf trip for him and some staff." He then shot an internal e-mail to his fellow lobbyist, Tony Rudy, DeLay's former deputy chief of staff: "Hi Tony. Did you get the message from the guys that Tom wants to raise some bucks [for] Capital Athletic Foundation? I have six clients in for $25K. I recommend we hit everyone who cares about Tom's requests." Abramoff followed up with Rudy later that month: "Please hit them both [Stoli and Sag Chip] to get checks for the Capital Athletic Foundation asap. we [sic] need to get this cash in hand. I am pushing Tigua and Choctaw. We are still short of full cost coverage (which is around $115K)."

Next, Rudy asked Todd Boulanger, manager of the Saginaw Chippewa account: "Can you ask…whether they can make a contribution [to Capital Athletic Foundation]? We asked for 25k."

> **Boulanger:** What is it? I've never heard of it.
>
> **Rudy:** It is something our friends are raising money for.
>
> **Boulanger:** I'm sensing shadiness. I'll stop asking.

Rudy: Your senses are good. If you have to say Leadership is asking, please do. I already have.

Poor Tony Rudy. He didn't even get to go on the trip. Yet he would later have to plead guilty over it because he had sought contributions from one of Abramoff's tribes "by falsely claiming that a public official [DeLay] requested them to solicit funds for the charity [CAF] from their clients." Abramoff too had to later plead guilty for soliciting from one of his tribes a charitable donation that he used "for his personal and professional benefit to partially pay for a golfing trip to Scotland for himself, public officials, members of his staff, and others."

Even after their return, Abramoff continued to seek contributions to defray the trip's costs. On September 18, he complained to a Saginaw Chippewa tribal official about their promised, but long-overdue, donation: "I saw the CAF guys this morning and we are getting into a bit of an embarrassing situation." A couple of weeks later, he sent another e-mail: "I am getting serious pressure on the Capital Athletic Foundation. Please let me know if this is going to happen, and if not, I need to try and find a replacement. I am really out of time on this and am getting called daily." Well, that was a bit of fib, because the "CAF guys" consisted of only one guy—Abramoff.

The trip actually ended up costing $150,225, or about $18,788 per person. This proved problematic for David Safavian, a public official. He was legally barred from going on the trip if Abramoff had any business pending with Safavian's agency, and was also barred from traveling as Abramoff's guest. In other words, he had to pay his own way. Safavian wrote a check for $3,100—the exact amount that Ney reported paying—to reimburse Abramoff for the trip, a sum which federal investigators later determined fell a little short. At that time, Abramoff was trying to lease two properties controlled by the Government Services Administration, where Safavian was the chief of staff, and had been asking for his help.

Abramoff seemed to have made his motives perfectly clear for including Safavian on the junket. In a 2002 e-mail, one of his colleagues asked Abramoff: "Why Dave? I like him but didn't know u did as much. Business angle?" Abramoff replied: "Total business angle. He is the new COS [chief of staff] of GSA [Government Services Administration]." Abramoff felt badly when this e-mail was made public: "Todd was a bit jealous that I was bringing David and not him, so I was trying to make him feel better. The truth is that I was bringing David because he is a friend."

On October 5, 2005, Safavian would also be indicted and arrested, in part, for allegedly lying to McCain's Senate Indian Affairs Committee about this trip to Scotland. Safavian proved to be the exception. He was the only person in the scandal who has thus far opted to go to trial rather than allow himself to be intimidated by the government into accepting a plea deal. He was then tried and convicted of four felonies, and, on October 26, 2006, sentenced to 18 months in prison. However, he appealed his conviction. The judge allowed him to remain free on bail, pending appeal, which usually occurs when the judge believes the appeal has merit. On June 17, 2008, declaring that prosecutors had overreached, the US Court of Appeals for the District of Columbia overturned Safavian's conviction.

On the night of August 3, 2002, as a limousine transported a band of eight merry golfers to the airport in Frederick, Maryland, no one had any idea what a disaster this junket would turn out to be. Neil Volz—Rep. Bob Ney's former chief of staff, but now a lobbyist at Abramoff's firm—stood on the tarmac, waving goodbye to those boarding the chartered Gulfstream II jet. Bound for Scotland were Jack Abramoff and his son, Alex; Ney and his chief of staff, William Heaton, as well as Paul D. Vinovich, a lawyer on the House Administration Committee that Ney chaired; David Safavian, the chief of staff of the General Service Administration; Michael Williams, a lobbyist at Abramoff's firm; and Ralph Reed.

Even Volz would end up a convicted felon.

After a refueling stop in Newfoundland, they landed the next day at 11 am in St. Andrews, Scotland, where they were met by Jason Murdock, the golfing organizer, who drove them to the Old Course Hotel. Apparently, Bob Ney was not much of a golfer and had borrowed his son's clubs. And for some reason, he refused to cover his head or apply suntan lotion to his face. Five hours later, they were teeing up on the Kingsbarns links. The next day, they played the glorious Carnoustie, and the day after that, the legendary Old Course—famous, among other things, for the Swilcan Bridge, an iconic stone overpass, meandering across the 1st and 18th fairways. In all, a grueling seven courses in five days. The package deal included the $400 fee per person per round of golf. Only Abramoff and his son shared a $500-a-night room.

On their second day, they were all slated to dine with some Conservative Party members of Scottish Parliament. This "educational" event would have lent some legitimacy to the trip, but the dinner was cancelled at the last minute. On August 9th, they all flew to London—some for one night, others for two—on their way back to the United States.

But Bob Ney and the 23-year-old William Heaton—the youngest chief of staff on Capitol Hill—had arranged a business meeting in London, which Ney did not mention to anyone, including Abramoff. "Heaton was a nice, quiet young man, very well mannered and respectful. I think he was probably a bit intimidated by the others in the group, since he was the youngest, except for my son Alex. He was more like a personal valet for Ney than a traditional chief of staff," says Abramoff.

At a private casino, Ney and Heaton met up with Fouad al-Zayat, known as "the Fat Man." In fact, this would be their third meeting that year with the Syrian businessman and would-be arms merchant. On each occasion, al-Zayat, blessed with Middle-Eastern courtesy, had provided the congressman and his aide with several thousand dollars in free casino chips. As they drank and gambled, they continued to discuss how best to dissolve a pesky problem that al-Zayat was having. He wanted to sell millions of dollars of American-made airplanes and spare parts to Iran, which was prohibited. The Fat Man hoped that Ney could help persuade the State Department to lift the ban.

Less than a month later, Ney and Heaton were back in London—again at al-Zayat's expense—to continue their discussions on how Ney could help the businessman circumvent the ban. On this occasion, al-Zayat was in a particularly generous mood. He made Ney a gift of $52,000 in casino chips, which Ney and Heaton subsequently cashed and brought into the United States. Ney claimed that with an initial bet of only $100, he had played a couple hands of cards at a casino and won $34,000 of the cash in his possession. On his official disclosure forms, he also "substantially under reported the costs [of the August 2002 Scotland golf trip] paid by Abramoff…and mischaracterized the purpose of the trip." Indeed, Ney claimed that Amy Ridenour's nonprofit, the National Center for Public Policy Research, had funded the trip, and that he'd given a speech to the Scottish Parliament, even though it was in recess at the time.

THE PERFECT VILLAIN

When the scandal broke two years later, reporters and investigators began scrutinizing Ney, in light of his seemingly incongruous *Congressional Record* statements about Gus Boulis and Adam Kidan. But Ney insisted he had done nothing wrong. Then the noose started to tighten. Mentioned in Michael Scanlon's plea agreement on November 21, 2005 was a "Representative No. 1," who had been given "things of value… "in exchange for a series of official acts;" Ney admitted that this referred to him, but insisted that he'd been "duped" by Abramoff and Scanlon. "Representative No. 1" was named again when Abramoff pleaded guilty on January 3, 2006. Twelve days later, pressured by the GOP leadership, Ney "temporarily" relinquished his chairmanship of the powerful House Administration Committee, but then eleven days after that announced that he was running for reelection. At the end of March, Ney's name popped up once again when Tony Rudy, DeLay's former chief of staff, pleaded guilty. Suspecting that even Neil Volz, his former long-time chief of staff, was cooperating with authorities, an infuriated Ney started leaving rants on Volz's voice mail. These were turned over to the prosecutors as evidence. Despite incessant bad press, the popular Ney remained outwardly confident and defiant. Back in Ohio, he won the Republican primary for his congressional seat on May 2nd by a landslide with 68% of the vote. He confidently told his constituents: "I have a healthy campaign account, in contrast to the Democratic Party, which is deeply divided and has a candidate with almost no campaign cash." For Ney, the ultimate betrayal seemed to come when Volz pleaded guilty on May 8, 2006. But Ney was mistaken. Preparations for the ultimate betrayal—the coup de grace—were already underway.

Ney continued to protest his innocence. His conscience was clear. He knew—and he knew the prosecutors knew—that there had never been any specific quid pro quo—not a single one—involving Jack Abramoff. There didn't have to be. Every congressman and senator—alive or dead—had played the same game. What's more, it was perfectly legal. His only vulnerability was the $52,000 in casino chips. Bribery, perjury, and money laundering were serious offenses. But he had nothing to worry about, he thought. The fact that he had not won the money playing cards was known only by himself and his trusted chief of staff, William Heaton, who was more like a son to him. The kid was unshakably loyal and worshiped his boss. What Ney never suspected was that all of his recent conversations with Heaton, some of them incriminating, had been recorded. The FBI had fitted Heaton with a wire.[147] Still oblivious, but under increasing pressure from Republican leaders, Ney finally announced on August 7th that he would not run for reelection in the fall, explaining that his family had to come first: "I can no longer put them through this ordeal." Soon thereafter, federal prosecutors confronted him with the evidence—his own words.

On September 15, 2006, Ney announced that he had signed a plea agreement, admitting to his involvement in an influence-peddling enterprise whose ringleader was the notorious, convicted felon Jack Abramoff. Miami-area newspapers rushed to point out that the corruption case had south Florida roots. In October, 2000, Ney had lauded Kidan in the *Congressional Record* as a businessman with a "'renowned reputation for his honesty and integrity'...Law enforcement officials said that just weeks after the controversial SunCruz sale, Abramoff and Kidan took $10,000 from their gambling business and donated the money to the National Republican Congressional Committee on Ney's behalf....Although Ney did not receive the $10,000 directly, U.S. officials said SunCruz's donation in his name to the GOP campaign committee was improper."

Actually, that particular crime sounded like a bit of a stretch. But those newspapers were only playing up the local angle, which would explain why they had to highlight such a lame example. So what sinister machinations did Ney's plea agreement reveal? Well, it mentioned three free or partially subsidized trips—including the 2002 Scotland golf trip—that he had taken, which had been arranged by Abramoff. It didn't mention, however, that the trips had been funded by nonprofit organizations. Nor did it mention that thousands of "fact-finding" congressional junkets every year were usually orchestrated around an award-winning golf course. Nor did it mention how sumptuous political fund-raisers were constructed around golf. The indictment declared that Ney had frequently nibbled for free at Abramoff's upscale restaurant. And in return for all of this, Ney had sold his soul by placing a few remarks in a document that no one read. Okay, so he had helped one of Abramoff's clients land a contract to install wireless routers throughout the Capitol building. Maybe that client's proposal turned out to be the best. (That paled in comparison to Sen. McCain's having helped one of his biggest political contributors to obtain California coastal land that turned a profit of $20 million.) To cap it off, federal prosecutors forced Ney to admit that he had accepted tens of thousands of dollars in campaign contributions. These charges were at best tenuous, and at worst, ridiculous. Didn't the prosecutors have anything better to do with their unlimited powers and resources?

After Abramoff's sensational guilty plea in January 2006, the probe seemed to sputter. Poised to pounce on the next victim, the media would soon grow weary of waiting for the big heads to roll in what they had called perhaps the biggest congressional corruption scandal in the nation's history. But these corruption probes took time. The tireless prosecutors plodded along. The evidence had to be carefully gathered, weighed, sifted, and marshaled on the remote chance that the case might actually go to trial. But it was invariably preferable—especially for the sake of "judicial economy"—for the lawmaker's staff to turn against their former boss. Prosecutors could dangle powerful incentives to induce a staff member to plead guilty and cooperate with the investigation. High-value cooperation—like telling prosecutors what they wanted to hear—might result in a much-reduced sentence, even an ankle bracelet or probation.

The media wanted DeLay so badly. Hastert would have been a worthy substitute. Karl Rove would have been the ultimate dream come true. But at least for now, they could hold aloft the ruddy head of Congressman Bob Ney.[148] In the final analysis, the only thing that had brought Bob Ney to his knees was the cash bribe from the Fat Man. That charge, unfortunately for the press and prosecutors, had nothing to do with Abramoff. However, once federal prosecutors had caught Ney red handed, they could threaten him with a life sentence with violent offenders, unless he was willing to plead guilty to other crimes—which he had not necessarily committed, and which prosecutors would have been hard pressed to persuade a jury to find Ney guilty of.

Not surprisingly, Ney pleaded guilty to all the charges brought against him by the prosecutors. It was imperative that Ney's guilt and remorse be expressed with sincerity. He wisely followed Abramoff's example, who, earlier that year, had told the court: "Your honor, words will not be able to ever express how sorry I am for this, and I have profound regret and sorrow for the multitude of mistakes and harm I have caused."

As a result of his plea bargain, Ney was only sentenced to thirty months in prison. However, because of his alleged alcohol addiction, which qualified him to enter a drug rehabilitation program in prison, a year was shaved off his sentence. That, along with a little "good-behavior" reduction, meant Ney ended up spending less than a year behind bars.

Actually, there were no bars. He served his sentence in a minimum-security prison camp and was released on February 19, 2008.[149]

Neither Ney nor Abramoff could have dared to hint about—never mind admit to—doubting their guilt for the crimes they had pleaded guilty to. There could not be the slightest suggestion that they had been coerced into pleading guilty. Even if inwardly insincere, their guilty pleas had to be expressed with the utmost earnestness. Equivocation, or a lack of remorse, would have enraged the judge.

Since so few public corruption cases ever went to trial, judges typically rubberstamped the prosecutors' recommendations for a sentence reduction. Ironically, by usurping the role of judge and jury, prosecutors had subverted due process—especially for white-collar crimes—by single-handedly investigating, indicting, coercing, condemning, and sentencing the defendant.

Judge and jury had become relics.

Any attempts to discuss these views with Abramoff met with only one response. He refused to talk about it.

CHAPTER FORTY-ONE
CALM BEFORE THE FIRESTORM

In the two-year period leading up to *The Washington Post* story that launched the scandal in February 2004, Abramoff's world couldn't have been sweeter. His was a rich life—financially, spiritually, socially, and politically. What's more, a beautiful and devoted wife and five healthy children awaited his arrival at his multi-million-dollar home every evening.

At work, he was a rock star. His hourly fee was $750. Team Abramoff consisted of a dozen smart, highly paid, well-connected, and highly motivated lobbyists, mostly former Senate and House staffers, who revered their boss.

On the spiritual front, he continued his study of the Talmud and Hebrew, in which he had become haltingly fluent. He was still personally funding the Eshkol Academy, a Jewish yeshiva and prep school that he had founded in 1991, and which required continuous infusions of cash. His often-anonymous generosity toward those in need only seemed to increase. At one point when he was experiencing a severe shortage of cash, he sucked all the equity out of his home. And Hotel Abramoff continued welcoming long-term guests, including seven Eshkol students from around the country whose parents could not afford to pay their living expenses. In most cases, Abramoff ended up paying for their medical and dental care as well. His plan, in the not-too-distant future, was to build a dormitory for the school a few doors down the street from his home.

On the political front, things were virtually perfect. Following the mid-term elections in 2002, Abramoff's dear comrade, Tom DeLay, would become the 24th Majority Leader of the House of Representatives, perhaps the most powerful ever. And Abramoff continued to cement his relationships with Karl Rove, House Speaker J. Dennis Hastert, and scores of other influential officials, both elected and appointed, particularly those who chaired committees and subcommittees critical to Abramoff's clients.

As for his many tribal clients, they gladly continued paying his huge monthly retainer and renewing their contracts with him. They were delighted that his aggressive take-no-prisoners representation protected their casinos' all-important revenue, which, in turn, preserved their cherished "per capita," something Abramoff privately frowned upon as a Socialistic.

On the recreational front, Abramoff continued to play racquetball and golf at the elite clubs to which he belonged. In fact, he was so determined to reduce his ten handicap that he purchased and installed an expensive high-tech golf simulator in a large room in his finished "basement," which fortunately had ten-foot ceilings. This expensive toy allowed him to tee up, take a full swing, and drive a real golf ball caught by a large screen a few feet away. Monitored by a computer and a series of video cameras, the speed and angle of his stroke was digested and analyzed. Moments later, it calculated the distance the ball would have traveled down a real fairway—and if it had hooked or sliced—and displayed it on a monitor.

But it was on the gastronomic front that Abramoff reigned supreme. He owned and operated not one, but three, restaurants: the upscale Signatures, as well as Stacks and Archives, the only kosher delicatessen and restaurant in Washington, D. C. (Stacks and Archives shared the same kitchen.) This gave him great panache in the political arena, and "koved" in the Orthodox Jewish community.

On February 21, 2002, after months of round-the-clock preparation, Signatures—located at 801 Pennsylvania Avenue, eight blocks from the White House—was ready for its gala opening. "I invited several hundred Washington players…as well as the 'foodies,' whose word of mouth would ensure that the restaurant was viable," says Abramoff. "The place was packed…all feasting on the free hors d'oeuvres and fine wine…[and] many stayed until the late hours…Several members of Congress were there, including Phil Crane and his wife Arlene."

Signatures—which quickly became the symbol of his power, influence and affluence—promised to bestow "Liberal portions in a conservative setting." Place settings consisted of Villery & Boch chargers, Christorfle utensils, and lint-free cloth napkins. For those who preferred to store their own favorite vintages, private wine lockers were available. After-dinner cigars could be purchased from the establishment's humidor. The restaurant's name came from the wall decorations—signed historic documents, which were for sale. These may have been intended as subtle blandishments to remind its patrons of the significant—and soon-to-be historic—nature of their contributions in shaping the republic. Perhaps as an unconscious warning, there was a copy of Richard Nixon's pardon—price tag $5,000—signed by his successor, President Gerald Ford. The carte de jour, which received mixed reviews from food critics, included a $74 steak, a $36 beef filet, a $140 tasting menu, and a lunchtime cheeseburger for $14 that came with custom-made ketchup. There were also two private dining rooms with separate entrances in the rear, perhaps for those who preferred discretion.

Later, Sen. McCain, *The Washington Post,* and the Justice Department contended that Signatures became the hub of Abramoff's influence-peddling schemes. But he was not the only one to own a restaurant. Two prominent Washington lobbyists, Democrat Thomas H. Boggs, Jr. and Republican Haley Barbour, were the principal owners of The Caucus Room, a steak house. "It's a downtown waterhole and a place to make deals," said Boggs when the restaurant opened in August 2000." One of his lobbying partners added, "You are billing them for your time, and they pay for the meal. In that way it's sort of a sweetheart deal."

Barbour, the former GOP National chairman, was famous for reportedly inserting a $50 billion tax break—perfectly legal—for the tobacco industry while assisting congressional staffers draft a portion of a 1997 appropriations bill. At least he has never been accused of high crimes and misdemeanors for giving away meals at his restaurant.

For the conservative politicos running the world's most powerful village, Abramoff's quickly became the fashionable place to nosh. From his corner perch at Table 40, Abramoff—constantly making calls or sending e-mails from his Blackberry—usually sat decked out in a dark double-breasted suit, a black yarmulke, and a silk tie dotted with small red-and-blue elephants. As he chowed down on sushi and sashimi, as well as delicacies prepared in a special kosher kitchen, he also savored the hit parade of repeat, high-profile patrons: President Bush's closest advisor Karl Rove, House Speaker J. Dennis Hastert, and House Majority Leader Tom DeLay, as well as other top presidential advisors, Senators, Congressmen, their staff, and other Washington elite. Even "Kindergarten Cop" Gov. Arnold Schwarzenegger, himself the proprietor of several restaurants, showed up. The mostly conservative clan enjoyed lunching or dining, seeing and being seen, talking shop and striking deals. "It was a who's who, and that's the way they wanted it,'" said Michael Rosen, a sous-chef at the restaurant. "Jack loved the attention of everybody being there."

And because he was genetically generous, but shrewd, at heart, he would "comp" many meals, particularly for his many "FOO,"— Friends of the Owner—who also happened to be politically powerful. Later, McCain would criticize him for transferring $200,000 from Capital Athletic Foundation, the charity he ran, to help open the restaurant, even though Abramoff repaid those funds within two weeks.

"I was raised by a father who almost never let anyone pay for his meals, or their own when they dined with him," says Abramoff. Indeed, most of his friends and colleagues agree that even before the launch of his restaurant, he was very generous about picking up the tab. "[At Signatures] people who dined with me were almost always treated to their meals by me," says Abramoff. "The ironic exceptions were David Safavian, who would always insist on paying for his own food, and Steven Griles, the much maligned Deputy Secretary of the Interior, who, [notwithstanding being] my friend, never let me pay for his food. Almost everyone else, however, was my guest."

With the start-up cost and the first year of operation setting him back about $3 million, not to mention his giving away too many free meals, the restaurant was a financial drain, but worth every penny. Many GOP politicians held fundraisers at Signatures, including House Speaker Hastert, Louisiana Republican Sen. David Vitter, and Oklahoma Republican Rep. Ernest Istook. A year after the scandal erupted, Hastert and Vitter scrambled to reimburse it. Apparently, Istook never got around to it.[150] Another example of largesse was a private dinner party for 18 that Robert Ney hosted, for which Abramoff picked up the $1,900 tab. A few weeks later, Tom DeLay and four guests were also "comped" for dinner. Said Laura Clifton, one of the former managers, "[People] would come in for lunch with Jack and they wouldn't get a bill. It was a showplace and it was for business…all the time." Lawmakers were not supposed to receive anything of value from lobbyists, except small gifts, unless they were friends. Of course, friendship is an abstraction difficult to define. But in the case of Rep. Dana Rohrabacher and Abramoff, their camaraderie went back 20 years to the Jamba Jamboree. "Just because you are a member of Congress doesn't mean you have to give up your friendships," said Rohrabacher, who added that he reciprocated often by taking Abramoff out to dinner. "[I was having] dinner with a friend and I didn't think of it as a gift."

Over an 18-month period between 2002 and 2003, Signatures "swallowed" about $180,000 of what it should have charged its not exactly impecunious patrons. Of that total, about $65,000 were free meals for the owner and his guests. "The fact is I rarely dined with a member of Congress at Signatures," says Abramoff. [More than a year after the restaurant opened], I began a rigorous diet routine and lost 80 pounds. [The only way to accomplish this] was to eat every meal—breakfast, lunch, and dinner—seven days a week specially prepared by my chef…so when the comp accounts were calculated, since none of these meals were on the menu, the assigned price was well above cost, which is a technique frequently used in restaurants."

But at least he could expense his clients whenever business was discussed, which was not infrequently. One published account claimed that some of his tribal clients received bills—above and beyond their monthly retainers—for expenses "that included hefty tabs for meals…One striking example was a huge lunch bill for $4,000 at Signatures…

[another was a] charge of $2,500 for a Super Bowl party at Stacks,… [his] delicatessen." Abramoff denies ever improperly expensing any of his tribal clients.

At the end of the day, federal prosecutors would later demand that defendants—which included Abramoff, Neil Volz, Tony Rudy, and Bob Ney—admit to bribery over offering and accepting a "stream of things of value," essentially what can only be described as small potatoes: free meals, sports tickets, and partially subsidized golf junkets. These were the typical things that lobbyists did, which were not illegal, unless when terrorized into pleading guilty.

A snapshot of Abramoff's finances in the first nine months of 2002, revealed that his tribal clients had paid $12.2 million in fees to Greenberg Traurig, not including expenses. There was additional income streaming in from his many other clients. And, of course, it did not include the giant referral fees he was quietly pocketing from Michael Scanlon for steering grassroots business his way. In those nine months, he spent $232,000 on personal travel, mostly by chartered jet—his preferred mode of travel, including an eight-day Passover family vacation at a Jewish spa in Arizona. He also purchased a $134,000 BMW 745Li that included nearly $50,000 in extra goodies. At his firm's insistence and expense, he hired a personal driver for $69,000 a year. "It took me half an hour to drive from my home [in Silver Spring, Maryland] to my office [in downtown Washington]," says Abramoff, "and the firm said it didn't make sense for me to squander an hour of potential work time driving myself back and forth to work." Charges against his credit cards from January to September came to $103,000; he paid his accountant $36,000; and he personally made $28,000 in campaign contributions.

Now in his early forties, the still beefy Abramoff was in his prime and the sky was the limit. He was flying so high that he didn't notice or was indifferent to the jealousy his visibility might be provoking. As for his old SunCruz business partner, he hadn't spoken to or communicated with Kidan since the summer of 2001, and essentially never thought of him. But unseen clouds were gathering on the horizon.

There would have been no reason for Abramoff to know this, but shortly after the 2002 mid-term elections, *The Boston Herald*, a Rupert

Murdoch tabloid, ran a "double-truck" expose on Sun Coast Casinos, an obscure "cruise to nowhere" gambling boat that was sailing into international waters twice a day from Gloucester harbor. The story revealed that the man running the show, Adam R. Kidan, had mob connections, a string of bankruptcies and failed businesses, and was a disbarred attorney. It also accused him of mishandling the $15,000 reward money offered for his mother's mob murderers. The story's crowning jewel was the revelation that Sun Coast Casino's corporate officers were Rose Marie Russo and Anthony Russo, the daughter and son-in-law of Anthony "Big Tony" Moscatiello, a reputed associate of the New York Gambino crime family, who would soon be indicted for Boulis' murder.

The effect was so devastating that a few days after the story ran, the operation shut down and went out of business. Kidan's literary agent and the freelance writer[151] hired to pen his "as-told-to" book, who had never been informed of these unsavory biographical tidbits, decided to suspend the writing project indefinitely.

"There was nothing remotely true about the articles in the [*Boston Herald*]. I told [the reporters] that, but they said they were going to write it anyway," says Kidan. "I had [incorporated Sun Coast Casinos] when I was still at SunCruz and I needed someone to be a shill. [Moscatiello] did it as a favor to me, but he wasn't involved in any way. My partners were two doctors. Moscatiello had nothing to do with it."

The Boston Herald stories ran on a Thursday and Friday in November 2002. Kidan's long-planned wedding took place the following day. "When I returned from my honeymoon the following Saturday, there was a business card from an FBI agent stuck in my door. That Monday, he showed up with a subpoena for bank fraud in the SunCruz case. I said to myself, 'Holy shit, I'm going to jail,'" says Kidan.

Soon thereafter, he flew down to Ft. Lauderdale to be interviewed by federal prosecutors. "I met in the U. S. Attorneys Office with two assistant U. S. attorneys-- Lawrence LaVecchio and Paul Schwartz. Also, there [were two FBI agents], one was handling the bank fraud and the other guy was handling the organized crime connection. My lawyer…did not prep me at all for what to expect."

Held in a somber room with the curtains drawn, the meeting ought to have proceeded like a typical calm, casual, cordial question-and-answer session. "The first question was 'How long have you been an associate of the Gambino crime family?' I got annoyed right away," says Kidan. "I said, 'Your question is wrong.' 'What do you mean?' asked LaVecchio. 'It's not a question of how long,' I said. 'It's a question of if.'" Kidan says they proceeded to tell him that he was a suspect in his mother's murder: "I looked at the guys and said, 'Are you fucking kidding me? The people who are responsible are in jail. It's been solved. They confessed. What are you talking about?' Then Schwartz piped in. 'You've always been a suspect. You know that.' And it kept going downhill from there."

Even though a federal grand jury had been empanelled to look into the SunCruz matter, Kidan can't remember if Abramoff's name came up, probably because the prosecutors didn't know or care who he was. Except in Washington political and lobbying circles and a handful of Indian reservations, he wasn't that well known. The prosecutors also realized how difficult it could be to prove bank fraud, especially when the lender wasn't a bank, and the lender and the seller had colluded in the fraud. But if the prosecutors could use SunCruz to squeeze Kidan into helping them nail the killers of Gus Boulis, why not give it a try? At that time, Kidan was "the big fish," not some obscure lobbyist in Washington.

With much trepidation, Kidan finally admitted that he knew their identities. The killers, two of whom had worked at SunCruz as Kidan's employees, had told him in great detail how the murder had been carried out. Finally, after a series of meetings, the prosecutors agreed to cut him a deal. They would let the bank fraud charges slide if he would wear a wire.

"I had to sit down and talk to Moscatiello and get him to talk about the murder," says Kidan. "After a lot of hand wringing, I agreed. The FBI got me all wired up, and then literally the day before I was supposed to do it, they cancelled. They gave me no explanation whatsoever." (Kidan would not hear again from the prosecutors until after *The Washington Post* stories broke in February 2004.)[152]

In the spring of 2003—Abramoff's final year at the pinnacle of power and prestige—he granted a long interview to The Hill, a newspaper geared to Washington insiders, in which he offered a primer on lobbying in the administration of the second President Bush. Even though Abramoff was referred to as a "Republican power broker" and "one of Washington's most sought-after lobbyists and political strategists," his observations were carefully tempered and restrained. If he was so arrogant and brash, as some have maintained, it didn't come across in the interview. Abramoff was careful to extol the Bush administration and GOP congressional leaders as paragons of virtue, immune to the influence of lobbyists. "[The Bush administration goes] out of [its] way to make sure that they are not courting special favors to lobbyists and to special interests. They'll only agree to things on strict merits," he said. "From a good government point of view, that's very refreshing. From a lobbying point of view, it's obviously more of a challenge." He also praised House Speaker Dennis Hastert for creating a "confident, very organized and even-tempered…stable environment;" and complimented Tom DeLay for his "very mature ground operation."

He did tell a fib, however. He implied that he had made a noble sacrifice by switching careers. After mentioning that he used to be a motion-picture producer, he said, "I'm the only lobbyist who took a 90 percent pay cut to join the lobbying field."

But at the end of May 2003, Boulis' ghost suddenly reared its head. Foothill and Citadel, the two lenders, notified Abramoff that they were suing him in civil court, along with 15 other defendants, for $60 million, claiming they had been misled and defrauded them regarding the $23 million down payment in the purchase of SunCruz. Boulis had told Abramoff back in November 2000 that the down payment had never been made. But Abramoff thought that when he'd transferred his SunCruz shares to the heirs of the Boulis estate, who had contractually absolved him of all liability, that he was free and clear of any SunCruz entanglements. His own firm offered to represent him in this civil lawsuit.

"Greenberg Traurig came to me and asked to represent me, since they wanted to make sure I did not have any problems which would disrupt the work I was doing for them and told me I'd only have to pay the hourly fees of the associates…not the partners," says Abramoff. "I just wanted to settle this thing and move on. I gave [Greenberg Traurig] access to all of my financials, including my tax returns."

A couple of weeks later, the 11th Circuit Court of Appeals rendered a stunning decision. It tossed out the original 2001 bankruptcy settlement, which had placed the Boulis heirs, who had been running the company ever since, in control of SunCruz. The court stated that because of their dual role as manager and major creditor, the Boulis heirs might favor their own interests over those of other creditors, among them Foothill and

Citadel. As a result, management hypothetically reverted to Kidan, who says he toyed briefly with taking back the reins of the gambling-boats. The Boulis heirs quickly struck back by suing Foothill, the principal lender, for colluding with Boulis and the buyers—Kidan, Abramoff, and Waldman—because Foothill had failed to confirm that the wire transfer ever occurred. And then to top off this mad spiral of litigiousness, Citadel, the secondary lender, also sued Foothill for the same thing—colluding with Boulis and the buyers to hide the forged $23 million wire transfer.

Abramoff remained unconcerned. The able lawyers at his firm, Greenberg Traurig, were handling the matter on his behalf. The $23-million-wire-transfer forgery had been done behind his back in concert with Boulis and the lender. Abramoff had had absolutely nothing to do with it, with the exception of affixing his name to the final signature page, as Kidan had instructed, acknowledging that the transfer had been made. The possibility that this would eventually result in a criminal prosecution seemed remote.

As the New Year dawned, Abramoff was still flying high. The Republican president had been reelected to another four years. According to secret service records, Abramoff visited the White House on January 20, 2004. He and Chitimacha Chief Terry Martin met with an environmental lawyer, but did not see Rove. That evening, Abramoff was Rep. Ralph Regula's guest at President Bush's State of the Union speech.

A week later, however, Abramoff received an unsettling call from an investigative reporter from *The Washington Post*. Her name was Susan Schmidt. She wanted to ask him some questions about his lobbying for Native American tribes. Alarm bells didn't go off, but he knew that declining the interview would be ill advised. "No comment" was the worst possible response. It was imperative to confront and blunt whatever lies and false allegations his competitors had been feeding her. Indeed, Schmidt, 41, just a couple of years younger than Abramoff, would recall later that she had been tipped by a rival lobbyist, who had contacted her in the fall 2003. That lobbyist was most likely Scott Reed. Schmidt had also chatted with Saginaw Chippewa Sub Chief, Bernie Sprague. Perhaps her most invaluable source was Emily Miller, Scanlon's ex-fiancée, a former assistant press secretary with the State Department,[153] who in the course of performing her duties had struck up a friendship with Schmidt. Miller and Scanlon had been planning an extravagant wedding at Shutters on the Beach, a chic hotel favored by celebrities, in Santa Monica, California. At the last minute, Scanlon had jilted Miller for a waitress he'd met in a seafood restaurant, whom he later married. A woman scorned was about to make sure that Scanlon's wedding would end up costing him millions and earn him the sobriquet "convicted felon." For Miller, like McCain a few weeks later, it was payback time. From pillow talk, she knew all about Scanlon's arrangement with Abramoff. She was intimately familiar with Scanlon's $4.7 million ocean-front mansion in Rehoboth Beach, Delaware, and his $17,000-a-month rental at the Ritz Carlton in Washington as well.

On Tuesday, February 3, 2004, Schmidt arrived at the offices of Greenberg Traurig in downtown Washington. She was met by Jill Perry, the firm's director of marketing, and press spokesperson. Perry escorted Schmidt, whom Perry later described as "very cold," to a small fifth-floor conference room near Abramoff's office. There, they awkwardly waited for Abramoff's arrival. The short, dark-haired Schmidt made small talk. She asked if Marvin Rosen, the former chairman of the Finance Committee for the Democratic National Committee, still worked for the firm. Perry politely told her that he was now "of counsel." Next, Schmidt inquired if the firm had offices only in Miami and Washington. Perry explained that Greenberg Traurig had been founded in Miami but now there were 21 offices nationwide, the largest in New York City. As Perry later reported to colleagues in an e-mail, "It was not easy to make conversation with her."

When Abramoff finally walked in, he was accompanied by four people. Apparently, Schmidt seemed slightly taken aback that so many others would be present. Introductions were made. She shook hands with Abramoff, litigator Allen Foster, and three members of Team Abramoff—Kevin Ring,[154] Todd Boulanger, and Jon van Horne.

All sat down. Schmidt and Perry turned on their own tape recorders, and the cat-and-mouse interview began. Except to consult her two pages of notes or to glance at the others when they spoke, Schmidt essentially never took her eyes off Abramoff.

"As I'm sure you know, I'm working on a story about your work with some of these gaming tribes and your relationship with Mike Scanlon and his company, and the work that [the] two of you have done in tandem…," said Schmidt. "Basically, the thing that I have discovered…is that you guys are...making an unprecedented amount of money from the tribes, mostly, the lion's share to Scanlon's company..."

Abramoff inwardly cringed. This reporter seemed to know a lot of strictly confidential information. To her next few questions about Scanlon's role, his relationship to the firm, and why Abramoff recommended him so often, he responded longwindedly by essentially declining to discuss his "confidential dealings with...clients."

Finally, Schmidt stopped circling: "Do you have an ownership stake in [any of Scanlon's firms]?" Abramoff replied, "No. No, I don't..."[155]

"So you don't have any ownership stake in any..." Abramoff remained cordial: "I've answered that...I said I don't. I don't have any."

Both the McCain report and a book by journalist Peter H. Stone[156] would later call Abramoff's response a lie. But it was mistaken. The next question Schmidt posed seemed to confirm what Jon van Horne would later observe: "I had the impression she is a neophyte in Indian Country...I think she envisions the reservation as some sort of migrant workers camp. I'd like to know if she actually talked to any Indians, even dissidents. She also did not seem savvy about lobbying in general..."

Schmidt said, "Okay, all right...Because you are a big connected Washington lobbyist that goes out to these tribes, unsophisticated people often, and you are selling your access...and they're buying that for a very large fee and then you're recommending [Scanlon who then charges] three or four times what you're charging, which is already pretty high... [and that's] what I'm going to be writing about, so anything you want to say about that..."

Abramoff told her that he helped his tribes renegotiate their compacts with the state and ward off threats to their casinos. He told her about how he had stopped the UBIT [Unrelated Business Income Tax], which had "saved all tribes 30% of their revenue," but neglected to mention that it had saved them tens of billions of dollars and continues to save them more with each passing day. He continued a dry exposition on the minutiae involved in his work.

Finally, she asked him the question that would later appear in her article: "Are there big pressing issues right now before Congress...?" Abramoff replied that there were "somewhere between 20 and 40 bills that are meaningful to the tribes." He explained what some of them were. His colleagues joined in and did their best to explain the arcana of their business. But Schmidt still didn't understand: "So…this is the biggest thing going right now?"

At this point, Team Abramoff made an egregious blunder. They failed to realize that Schmidt believed the only way for Abramoff to justify his huge fees was if he were thwarting major legislation. Otherwise, he was simply bilking "unsophisticated people" out of millions of dollars. Even though Abramoff and his colleagues proceeded to explain for several tedious minutes what they did, undoubtedly Schmidt's eyes glazed over. They should have made it clear that "big pressing issues…before Congress" rarely threatened the tribes. It was a host of seemingly minor and obscure issues that really had the potential of destroying a tribe's casino, and that this demanded constant vigilance.

Schmidt's next two series of questions also must have made Abramoff cringe. Clearly, she was more than well prepared. She asked whether environmental groups or the Christian Coalition had helped muster public opinion "against…[a] casino proposed by a rival tribe." Even Ralph Reed's name came up. Several minutes later, her questions were freighted with greater specificity: "So, can you then tell me a little bit about some of the groups that you recommend tribes to donate to, in addition to political parties…[Scanlon's] Council of Republican Advocacy…[Federici's] Coalition of Republican Environmental Activists, [Abramoff's] Capital Athletic Foundation, [Norquist's] Americans for Tax Reform." Abramoff could only respond as before: "Well, again, I'm going to defer in terms of the specific advice we give to the clients."

The interview dragged on. Abramoff tried to tell Schmidt that "it's just very important to make sure you get a wide picture among the various [warring] factions within the tribes…[because] you'll wind up with varying views [about] the validity and value of the work [being] done… right down to the people providing them with tissue paper probably."

Several minutes later, she even brought up Signatures: "Well…I've heard [complaints]…that some tribes get one to two thousand dollars a month in bills [from] Signatures…as though they're floating your restaurant…" Abramoff denied the accusation, blaming it on tribal dissidents.

Finally, ending the nearly two-hour interrogation with a sledgehammer, Schmidt inquired about SunCruz: "I'd just like to know a little bit about the $23 million wire-transfer issue and what's going on with that." Abramoff declined to talk about "an ongoing [legal] matter."

Moments later, the endless interview ended. Jill Perry, who escorted Schmidt to the elevator, reported that "[Schmidt] was much more conversant…almost friendly, and said she would be in touch."

Although everyone agreed that Schmidt seemed poised to publish something dreadful, Abramoff was fairly nonplussed. He asked for reactions and impressions. Todd Boulanger believed that "she has a well thought-out agenda. She has been programmed by our competitors and has used them to make contacts with our enemies within each client." Kevin Ring, who would later decline to testify before McCain's committee, was convinced that Schmidt was "prepared to do an old-fashioned hatchet job…[and] seemed to hate everyone in the room."

Later that day, Abramoff wrote to Candace Patencio, his ally at the Agua Caliente tribe: "[Someone at the tribe] has been feeding *The Washington Post* a hit piece about Scanlon and me. It's going to be terrible…Can't wait to see you on the 23rd." Two days later Todd Boulanger e-mailed Abramoff and Kevin Ring: "Someone on the [Saginaw Chippewa Tribal] council trashed us, our work, and Scanlon…We're going to get smoked here." He wondered if Abramoff should file a lawsuit for slander. Boulanger added: "Going to bed. I'm really in a terrible mood." Abramoff replied: "Me too."

Nonetheless, Abramoff went about his business but he couldn't get the interview off his mind. On February 6, *The Miami Herald* and *The Sun-Sentinel*, south Florida's two major dailies, let the third anniversary of Boulis' murder pass without mention. On the first anniversary, Ft. Lauderdale detective Art Carbo had said about the murder, "We just keep coming back to SunCruz." But Abramoff, who didn't remember the grim anniversary, had been composing a letter to Schmidt, which he mailed a few days later: "I am extremely upset by your characterization of my clients and other Native Americans as "unsophisticated people" who, because of their naïveté, your thesis is, are being taken advantage of. It is precisely this kind of elitist, condescending attitude which has underlain the deprivation of equal treatment for Native Americans…."

Schmidt did not contact Abramoff again: "When a reporter does a hit piece on you, you're the last one interviewed," he says. All Abramoff could do was stay busy and distracted. Ten, twelve, fifteen, seventeen days drifted by. Nothing appeared in print.

On February 20, Abramoff sent his friend Grover Norquist a flippant e-mail: "FYI, the *Post* is going to do a major hit on me, probably coming this weekend. It's on our tribal representations. Oh well, I guess I won't be welcome at the ACLU meetings any longer."

Nineteen days after the interview, Schmidt's front-page story, headlined—*A Jackpot From Indian Gaming Tribes*—was published in *The Washington Post*'s Sunday edition on February 22, 2004. It was actually available online Saturday night. Someone sent the story to his Blackberry. After reading it, he thought: "This isn't so bad." He forwarded it to one of the top partners in the law firm, who responded by e-mail and agreed. Abramoff considered putting it "on my website to advertise how much I charge."

He was clueless.

PART V

THE LONG FALL

CHAPTER FORTY-TWO
OPENING SALVO

The full title of Susan Schmidt's first article was "*A Jackpot From Indian Gaming Tribes: Lobbying, PR Firms Paid $45 Million Over 3 Years.*" No one had any idea of the impact it would produce. Unlike McCain, she included interviews from both sides. There was praise for Abramoff and Scanlon from two Saginaw Chippewa officials, former Chief Maynard Kahgegab, Jr. and Chris Petras, as well as commendation for Scanlon from Coushatta tribal council member William Worfel. Nevertheless, she reported that Abramoff and Scanlon had charged their clients $45 million in a three-year period. Later, it would turn out that the amount was closer to $60 million.

These kinds of stories can generate strong responses. If the mighty ravages the puny, there is outrage. Nevertheless, some sensational news stories inexplicably wither, while others become Godzilla. So many intangible factors affect the outcome—timing, psychology, pent-up resentment, the need for a scapegoat, and perhaps most significant, the creation of a simple, black-and-white, easy-to-digest narrative. That last one is never easy. There's always that inconvenient "other side of the story," which usually mucks things up. In this case, there was none.

During Schmidt's interview with Abramoff earlier in the month, she had mentioned her belief that the tribes were "unsophisticated people." She infused that belief into her story by quoting a man who seemed to be a tribal authority with no agenda: Saginaw Chippewa Sub-Chief Bernie Sprague. He declared: "Tribes are gullible." The implication was clear.

Abramoff had been stealing candy from a baby, a baby who had been ruthlessly oppressed by European invaders for the past five centuries.

Indeed, eight months later during the first Senate Indian Affairs hearings, McCain would take up this sword with all the righteous indignation he could muster. "Etched in the history of our great nation is a long and lamentable chapter about the exploitation of Native Americans," he said. "Every kind of charlatan and every type of crook has deceived and exploited America's native sons and daughters...What sets this tale apart, what makes it truly extraordinary, is the extent and degree of the apparent exploitation and deceit."[157]

If her story was going to have any traction, Schmidt needed to keep driving this point home, so she added: "The fees are all the more remarkable because there are no major new issues for gaming tribes on the horizon, according to lobbyists and congressional staff." The fact that these unnamed lobbyists were Abramoff's competitors was not revealed by Schmidt until two years later. In a *Washington Post* article she co-wrote in December 29, 2005, she said: "Rival lobbyists, including some Republicans, were comparing notes about what they considered Abramoff's outrageous conduct. One of [those lobbyists] contacted the *Post* in fall 2003."

Of course, just because they were Abramoff's rivals didn't mean that their allegations weren't valid. Nevertheless, what they implied was that even "major new issues for gaming tribes"—of which there were allegedly none at the time—could not justify such huge fees for a tribe's lobbyist. Furthermore, they implied that "major new issues" were the only real threat to a tribe's casino that might justify such high fees. For good measure, Schmidt underscored these competitors' claims by noting that Abramoff's fees were "10 or 20 times what the tribes paid their former lobbyist." Her implication was that the services of all lobbyists were roughly on par, even though a public defender, for example, might be paid as little as $75 an hour while a top defense attorney might command as much as $1,000 an hour. Finally, Schmidt characterized Abramoff and Scanlon's fees as outrageously high by comparing them to what the largest corporations in America had paid to their lobbyists: "General Electric Co. paid more than two dozen lobbying firms $30.4 million over the same three-year period...The nation's top four pharmaceutical companies paid dozens of lobbying and law firms $34.8 million [in a one-year period]."

No reader—no matter how savvy—could have pierced the veil of this story and understood its potential flaws.

Apparently, Schmidt didn't bother to ask Sprague, Kahgegab, or Worfel—three Native American tribal officials whom she had just quoted in her story—what factors might threaten the revenue of a tribal casino. Perhaps she didn't ask, because she assumed these Indians had just tumbled off the turnip truck and were simply too "unsophisticated" to know what was going on. That omission was certainly unfortunate for Abramoff, because later Worfel would tell McCain: "As council members, we all know that competitive threats of expanded gaming were happening *all the time* [emphasis added]. State-sponsored gambling, slot machines at the horse racetrack, and the possibility of Texas legalizing gaming and the casinos being built by other tribes were consistent threats to our market share... [as well as] local governments that are always trying to gain something off your casino revenues."

What Worfel then said to McCain would have torpedoed the main thrust of Schmidt's article: "What should you spend to save a $300-million-a-year business when the lawyers who work for you tell you that it could all be gone if we do not act now? Our tribe has one and only one business. We made tough decisions and we acted always in the best interests of our tribe."

Schmidt's next move was brilliant, as she shoved the knife deeper into the heart of Abramoff's alleged perfidy. She questioned why he always seemed to recommend to his tribal clients the public relations and grassroots know-how of Michael Scanlon, who charged them many millions of dollars. She asked Abramoff if he were a part owner of Scanlon's company: She wrote: "Abramoff said in an interview that he does not have an *ownership interest* [emphasis added] in any of Scanlon's firms...." She seemed to cast doubt on Abramoff's credibility by adding: "Scanlon's companies are incorporated in Delaware, where privacy laws shield corporations from disclosing ownership."

If Schmidt could suggest that Abramoff's fees or activities might be criminal, it would give her story more gravitas. Fortunately, she could report: "...the FBI has stepped up an investigation into alleged spending irregularities by one of Abramoff's clients [Louisiana Coushatta]...

[and] FBI agents in Michigan [last week] also interviewed members of the Saginaw Chippewaws." And if Schmidt could somehow link this to some other potentially criminal behavior in Abramoff's past, it would go a long way toward further sullying his reputation and undermining his denials. She wrote: "Abramoff's work for the tribes is not the first time he has encountered controversy in connection with gaming interests. In 2001, a federal magistrate ruled that a $23 million down payment put up by Abramoff and a partner as part of the $147 million purchase of Florida-based SunCruz Casinos was never actually paid. Abramoff declined to comment on SunCruz, citing ongoing litigation."

With this story, Schmidt hit a grand-slam homerun. But for Abramoff the perfect storm had just begun.

Monday, the day after the story appeared, there was a flurry of activity in the offices of both Abramoff and John McCain. Fellow Team-Abramoff lobbyist, Neil Volz, e-mailed Kevin Ring, who had participated in Schmidt's interview, wondering what effect her story would have. Ring responded: "Lots of damning facts in there." Abramoff e-mailed friends and clients a copy, calling the story a "hit piece," and the reporter "a real racist and bigot." A few hours later, Marc Schwartz, a consultant for the Tigua Indians of El Paso, Texas, one of Abramoff's clients, wrote back: "Well, it wasn't pretty. It sure looks like Scanlon was living a little large, huh! Call me when you get a chance." Abramoff replied: "Don't you love Washington? I'll try to call you later today." Todd Boulanger, who had also participated in the Schmidt interview, then contacted Abramoff, telling him that he sensed the need for a swift counterattack: "[A]l our leadership press people (our friends) think we need to do something. Like op-eds from our clients saying they get what they pay for. Also, DeLay's office is not happy with this article AT ALL. They are considering issuing a statement that says Scanlon is not an ally or friend..." Abramoff replied: "We need to strike back with letters from the tribes. We need to organize this internally and quickly." McCain would later call this an attempt by Abramoff to obstruct justice, rather than calling a spade a spade: Abramoff was simply exercising his constitutional right to defend himself.

A few blocks away, McCain had also been busy that morning. In fact, he hadn't wasted a minute. As a top-ranking member of the Senate Indian Affairs Committee, he had called Pablo Carrillo, his best investigator, and told him to come right over. When Carrillo walked in, McCain was smiling devilishly. It was payback time. He handed Carrillo a copy of Schmidt's story and said, "Hey, boy, here's your next project." McCain also immediately began meeting with one of Abramoff's rivals, Scott W. Reed. A few days later, McCain wrote a personal letter to the new chief of the Saginaw Chippewa, in which he stated: "I appreciate your Tribe's willingness to assist in the Congress' investigation into alleged misconduct associated with Indian lobbying activities. We have met with Scott Reed, who was very helpful on this issue."

On February 25th, McCain made the official announcement that he was launching an investigation of Abramoff: "It's disgraceful," declared McCain, adding that his focus would be on whether "this [was] improper behavior," especially in light of so many Native Americans "still living on [a] subsistence level." McCain was slanting the truth from the very beginning. He was hardly ignorant of the fact that most of Abramoff's tribal clients received a generous "per capita" payment. For example, Bernie Sprague and his wife took home over $120,000 a year without lifting a finger. "If Senator McCain wants a hearing on it, we'll do one," stated Sen. Ben Nighthorse Campbell, chairman of the Senate Indian Affairs Committee.

"The reason McCain could come in and take over was because Campbell would have never held hearings. How could he? I [and my clients] had been a big donor of his," Abramoff says. "It was only after it was clear that I would not be responding to any questions at the hearing [in September] that Campbell decided to jump on the bandwagon and attack."

Campbell, who had recently undergone treatment for prostate cancer, had been in the hospital when the story broke and was readmitted a few days later with chest pains. Soon after, he announced that he would not be running for reelection for health reasons. In effect, he did agree to hand over the Abramoff investigation, and later that year the committee chairmanship, to McCain. Therefore, McCain would be in charge. He would run the investigation and write the report. This was a gift from the gods. McCain had just been handed all the power he needed to railroad Abramoff.

The second phase of the perfect storm had just swept into place.

Within the first two weeks, subpoenas were issued, calling for all of Abramoff's e-mails from both law firms he had worked for—Preston Gates and Greenberg Traurig. Eventually, the committee would obtain about 750,000 pages of documents, hold five public hearings and conduct about 60 depositions and witness interviews, culminating in the production of a 373-page report two years later.

Several of Abramoff's tribal supporters had contacted McCain at the onset of his investigation. Coushatta council member William Worfel wrote that the attacks on Abramoff and Scanlon has been "completely unfair and unwarranted," that he was displeased with the "clearly anti-Indian slant" to Schmidt's article, and that McCain's investigation would be "viewed as an attack on tribal sovereignty." Former Saginaw Chippewa Chief, Bernard Kahgegab, also wrote to McCain praising Abramoff. Kahgegab steadfastly stood by the lobbyist. He even asked to testify before the Committee, as did several other members of the tribal council. Incredibly, not one of Abramoff's Indian supporters was allowed to testify. McCain was hell bent on producing a report that was hardly "factual and neutral."

In the meantime, Tom DeLay, the powerful House Majority leader, had quickly distanced himself from Abramoff. "If anybody is trading on my name to get clients or make money," he declared, "that is wrong and they should stop it." Abramoff refused to speak to reporters, but not Scanlon. "Public relations and public affairs spending by Indian tribes is rapidly growing into a billion-dollar-per-year industry," he said. "I look forward to sharing my experience in the field, both good and bad, and putting to rest some of the critical questions that have been raised by recent news reports." Obviously, Abramoff didn't dare contact DeLay, so he e-mailed DeLay's wife: "I am sorry I have not been in touch in the past week or so to let you know that Tom and you are in my prayers… Unfortunately, for me I too am under a horrific assault by a combination of leftists, jealous lobbyists, and renegade members of tribes…as [even] my own firm [leaves] me twisting a bit in the wind. I hope I am reading it wrong."

He was reading it dead right. Nine days after the story broke, three senior partners in his firm—two from Florida and one from New York—flew to Washington. A few hours after his e-mail to DeLay's wife, they met with Abramoff to inform him that he would have to resign at once.

Abramoff reportedly broke into tears. Abramoff says he was shocked, but not crying: "I stared back at the partners in disbelief, not sure what to say." That evening, Greenberg Traurig executive Richard Rosenbaum announced that the firm had accepted Abramoff's resignation, because he had "disclosed…for the first time personal transactions and related conduct which are unacceptable to the firm." According to Abramoff, this was not what they had agreed the communiqué should say. He accused his former employer of "overreacting" to Schmidt's story and issued his own statement: "It is regrettable that Greenberg Traurig would indicate that my resignation was based on anything other than our mutual decision to ensure that recent events did not interfere with the representation of our clients." Schmidt published three more stories, including one on Abramoff's forced resignation, in which she repeated that he had denied having "any ownership interest" in Scanlon's companies.

In the meantime, Abramoff realized he should retain legal counsel. Oliver North recommended Brendan Sullivan. Abramoff spoke to Sullivan, who agreed to take the case, but then had to withdraw several hours later when he learned that someone in his firm was representing Greenberg Traurig on another matter. Eventually, Abramoff hired Abbe Lowell, another top defense attorney.

"G[reenberg] T[raurig] firing me not only shocked me, it shocked my team, the rest of the firm, and the whole city," says Abramoff, but he figured his life would resume once things quieted down. "I calmly moved some of my team to Cassidy and Associates [another lobbying shop in Washington] and planned to bring my clients with me, much as I had when I'd left Preston Gates and moved to GT."

In a March 30th story, Schmidt cited a letter that McCain had sent to Abramoff, asking him to produce documents. This angered attorney Lowell, because Abramoff himself hadn't yet received the letter. How had Schmidt gotten a copy of it? Lowell filed a complaint with the Senate Ethics Committee, charging "improper collaboration" between McCain staffers and Schmidt. The complaint went nowhere.

But a subtle change had taken place in her story. Apparently, Schmidt's editors expressed concern over her use of the term "ownership interest." Did she have any proof contradicting Abramoff's denials? No, she didn't. They decided to make a slight modification. From now on, she would only report that Abramoff had a "financial stake" in Scanlon's firm.

McCain, however, didn't have an editor lording over him. His claim that Abramoff had an ownership interest in Scanlon's firm was based on a single e-mail exchange nearly three years earlier between Abramoff and Scanlon, back on June 18, 2001, in which the two had speculated on the possibility:

> **Scanlon:** "A few weeks ago you mentioned something to me—I took the concept and have put together a plan that will make serious money. We also talked briefly about it in the beginning of the year but I think we can really move on it…I have been making contacts with some larger Public Affairs companies in town for a few months. I have two solid relationships that will seriously consider acquiring Capitol Campaign Strategies [Scanlon's company.] The problem is that there is not much in CCS right now…However, if we build [it up] enough I can get it acquired by a large firm by the end of next year at 3x the firm['s] revenue. Bottom line: If you help me get CCS a client base of $3 million a year, I will get the clients served, and the firm acquired at $9 million. We can then split…up the profits. What do you think?"
>
> **Abramoff:** Sounds like a plan, but let's discuss when we are together.

Abramoff later says it quickly became apparent to him that the value of Scanlon's company's value would rest solely on his willingness to refer clients to it. If Scanlon sold the company, Abramoff says he would have never referred business to the new owners. The idea of co-owning Scanlon's firm was quickly discarded, and, as far as Abramoff could recall, never discussed again. Indeed, McCain was never able to produce another e-mail in which this was discussed. And yet when McCain excerpted Schmidt's interview of Abramoff in which she had asked him if he had an "ownership interest" in any of Scanlon's companies, his report said: "[Abramoff's denial] of course was a lie."

McCain insisted on asserting this with good reason. If Scanlon had defrauded his tribal clients, and if Abramoff had had an ownership interest in Scanlon's company, then Abramoff would be equally guilty of fraud. But the claim was never substantiated. In fact, in 2005, when Scanlon agreed to plead guilty and cooperate with federal investigators, he denied that Abramoff had any "ownership interest" in his business. In the "Factual Basis" for his guilty plea, Scanlon was forced to say that he had defrauded tribal clients by failing to disclose financial interests—meaning the perfectly legal referral fees to Abramoff. And furthermore, "The prices [Scanlon] charged for [his] services were significantly in excess of [his] costs." That statement was rather curious. On what statutory basis did prosecutors define "significantly in excess of [his] costs?" They failed to cite a statute that quantified an amount regarding which profits are permissible and which are significantly excessive and illegal.

Undoubtedly, all prosecutors would do was fall back on honest-services fraud, the highly dubious and constitutionally vague catch-all statute. There were two reasons why basically honorable and well-meaning, but out-of-control, prosecutorial crusaders could take such liberties with the law. First, Scanlon had pleaded guilty to whatever they told him to plead guilty to. Second, because this case was never presented to a jury. Any jury in its right mind would have said, "Huh? Wait a minute."

The point was that the prosecutors were able to force Scanlon to confess to a clutch of wicked deeds, but they did not require him to admit that Abramoff had ever had an "ownership interest" in his companies, because the simple fact was that this was not the case. Yet it no longer mattered. For Schmidt and McCain, Abramoff's "ownership interest" had already served its purpose.

A troubling question remained. If Abramoff was so wicked, why did Schmidt and McCain have to cross the line so frequently to make what appeared to be such an air-tight case?

* * * * * * * * * * * * * * *

After his ouster from Greenberg Traurig, Gerald Cassidy, one of Washington's premier lobbyists, met with Abramoff.

"I had never met [Abramoff]," said Cassidy. "There were a lot...of people who were friends of [his who] were very nice people...[and] he had made a lot of money for Greenberg Traurig and that they had made a very bad decision about not defending him, and that what he was doing was defendable and defensible, and that he had a story to tell and that it would come out...He was very charming...[and] impressive on how he would approach things, so we hired him [on March 23] on a consulting basis."

For nearly three months, Abramoff had a place to hang his hat. But in mid June, Hawaii's Sen. Daniel Inouye, vice chair of the Indian Affairs committee contacted Cassidy and told him that if he didn't fire Abramoff "[Y]our people do not come in to my office [anymore]." Cassidy said that Inouye actually told him, "Get rid of him today." In July, the *Post* reported that Abramoff and Cassidy & Associates had parted company.

A few weeks later, Abramoff launched Margate productions, a film and real-estate development company, but his new venture essentially never got off the ground. "At some point, it must have dawned on me that I wasn't going to recover from all of this," says Abramoff.

In June, however, *The Washingtonian* published a piece, probably the only one that expressed concerns about Schmidt's initial story:

> The *Post* article oddly failed to mention two lobbyists who have earned nearly as much in tribal fees as Abramoff: Scott Reed, a former aide to Bob Dole, and longtime DC power player Roger Stone. According to sources at the Bureau of Indian Affairs, Reed once told then-BIA chief Wayne Smith that he was going to "take out" Abramoff and become "the king of Indian gaming" himself. Reed denies this but has been actively signing up tribes as clients. Chief among them is the Saginaw Chippewa tribe of Michigan, which Abramoff previously represented.

In early September, Abramoff was served with a subpoena, requiring him to testify in person before the Senate Indian Affairs Committee and his arch enemy, Sen. John Sidney McCain.

CHAPTER FORTY-THREE
THE SECOND CASINO

Three days before Abramoff's scheduled appearance before McCain's committee, Susan Schmidt ran a truly devastating story on September 26, 2004. She portrayed Abramoff as the ultimate scumbag swindler. This lobbyist psychopath—with his pretensions of religious piety, his gentle demeanor, his expressions of sensitive concern, his attachment to lofty ideological principles, his devotion to his wife and five children—was nothing more than a sinister monster preying on the vulnerable. He deserved far more than just a long prison sentence.

Schmidt had single-handedly exposed an apparent political corruption scandal that went far beyond a few obscure Indian tribes. She had triggered a wide-ranging criminal investigation that would implicate many elected and appointed federal officials and reach into the highest levels of the White House. It seemed that her reporting had already done a great public service and that she had a good shot at winning a Pulitzer Prize.

But no one realized that Schmidt's September 26th story contained an egregious omission. Why would she write such a story, risking her reputation, her job, and her possible Pulitzer? What was more amazing was that Schmidt got away with it. Readers, bloggers, pundits, and seasoned journalists—who should have been able to grasp the problem with her story—had become so intoxicated by this artfully spun yarn that they got swept away by the lynch-mob, Salem-witch-trial mentality. They had stopped thinking. They stopped questioning. They'd become like a fly in a spider's web.

What got lost in the brouhaha surrounding Abramoff's alleged duplicity was the true duplicity—Schmidt's story. Of course, Abramoff's refusal to defend himself at the hearing three days later didn't help. In fact, it only reinforced the image of his incontrovertible guilt. This absolute clarity—which rarely exists in a confusing, complex, troubling, and an often bitterly divided world—provided an oasis of comfort. There were no shades of gray, no grainy images, no distortions of any kind in this story. This was evil of the black-hole variety.

On September 26, 2004, the headline on Schmidt's story read: "*Insiders Worked Both Sides of Gaming Issue: E-mails Suggest Men Tried to Exploit Closure of Casino for Huge Fees From Tribe:*"

Washington lobbyist Jack Abramoff and public relations consultant Michael Scanlon quietly worked with conservative religious activist Ralph Reed to help the state of Texas shut down an Indian tribe's casino in 2002, then the two quickly persuaded the tribe to pay $4.2 million to try to get Congress to reopen it.

Dozens of e-mails written by the three men and obtained by *The Washington Post* show how they built public support for then-Texas Attorney General John Cornyn's effort to get the courts to close the Tigua tribe's Speaking Rock Casino in El Paso in late 2001 and early 2002. The e-mails also reveal what appears to be an effort on the part of Abramoff and Scanlon to then exploit the financial crisis they were helping to create for the tribe by securing both the multimillion-dollar fee and $300,000 in federal political contributions, which the tribe paid.

Ten days after the Tigua Indians' $60 million-a-year casino was shuttered in February 2002, Abramoff wrote a tribal representative that he would get Republicans in Congress to rectify the "gross indignity perpetuated by the Texas state authorities," assuring him that he had already lined up "a couple of Senators willing to ram this through," according to the e-mails.

What he did not reveal was that he and Scanlon had been paying Reed, an avowed foe of gambling, to encourage public support for Cornyn's effort to close *two Indian casinos* [emphasis added] in Texas.

... [And] in the end, Abramoff and Scanlon failed to get the [Tigua] casino reopened.

What was misleading about this article was Schmidt's assertion that Abramoff had intentionally and ruthlessly worked to shut down the Tigua's casino (located in the westernmost part of Texas), so that, motivated by greed, he could then promise to get their casino reopened for a mere $4.2 million. He subsequently—and even more despicably—failed to keep this promise.

The simple fact was that Abramoff had been working to shut down an Indian casino, operating in the *easternmost* part of Texas, which threatened the livelihood of his client—the Louisiana Coushatta—located nearby, across the border in western Louisiana.

Abramoff had no interest in the Tigua, because its casino was located almost 1000 miles away from that of his Louisiana client!

Because gambling was illegal in Texas, people in the eastern part of that state, particularly from Houston, had been flocking to the casino of Abramoff's client in western Louisiana. In fact, there were scores of billboards on Texas I-45 and I-10 that point in the direction of the Louisiana Coushatta casino, resort, and golf course just across the state border. However, the new Indian casino, which had recently opened in the easternmost part of Texas, obviously threatened his client's casino. Both of these Texas tribal casinos—the one operated by the Tigua and the second one, operated by a tribe whose identity and *location* Schmidt did not disclose—had been operating illegally. And John Cornyn, then Texas attorney general, was about to shut both of them down. However, a bill had been introduced in the Texas legislature that would have allowed these two casinos to remain open, something Schmidt also omitted from her story. Abramoff managed to block that bill, because he wanted the *easternmost* Texas casino to be shut down, thus saving his client's business.

The Tigua—located in El Paso in *westernmost* Texas—unfortunately got caught in the collateral crossfire.

Why did Schmidt focus all of her attention on the Tigua and none on the second Texas tribe? Did she even know of the existence, identity, and location of that second tribe?

As a matter of fact, this very tribe had just been mentioned in the *Post*'s previous Abramoff article, written by Thomas B. Edsall, which Schmidt had contributed to.[158] It was the Alabama-Coushatta Tribe of Texas. And was the Alabama-Coushatta casino threatening the Louisiana

Coushatta's casino? The *Post*'s previous article, the one that Schmidt had helped write, had clearly said so:

> **The Louisiana Coushatta Tribe was seeking to prevent development of potentially competitive casinos by the Alabama-Coushatta Tribe of Texas...**

Therefore, Schmidt not only should have known the identity of the second Texas tribe whose casino was shut down, but also should have known it was that very casino that had threatened the livelihood of Abramoff's client, the Louisiana Coushatta. Schmidt certainly knew that the Louisiana Coushatta was Abramoff's client, because she had mentioned it at least *a dozen times* in her previous stories. It is difficult to understand why Schmidt had neglected to mention the Alabama-Coushatta Tribe of Texas in her September 26th story.

If Schmidt had acknowledged the existence, identity, and location of the Alabama-Coushatta, then she would have been forced to concede its relevance. Abramoff wasn't trying to shut down the Tigua. He was simply trying to shut down the Alabama-Coushatta. This revelation would have driven a stake into the heart of her sensational Tigua fairy tale. After all, she had reported in her September 26th story that "*two Indians casinos*" had been shut down.

What's more, Schmidt tried to bolster her story by including several callous-sounding Abramoff e-mails. These e-mails were not yet publicly available. McCain, who had just subpoenaed them, had apparently provided them to her. In her September 26 story, Schmidt also wrote:

> **On Feb. 6, 2002, with the casino's shutdown just two days away, the tribe was desperate. Abramoff made his move. "I'm on the phone with Tigua!" he wrote in a 9:54 a.m. e-mail to Scanlon. "Fire up the jet, baby, we're going to El Paso!!"**
>
> **A week later, a Texas consultant employed by the tribe thanked Abramoff for his visit and said he would push his proposal. Abramoff forwarded the e-mail to Scanlon with the message: "This guy NEEDS us to save his ass!!"**

Days later, on Feb. 19, Scanlon sent Abramoff an *El Paso Times* news story headlined "450 casino employees officially terminated" with the message: "This is on the front page of today's paper while they will be voting on our plan!"

"Is life great or what!!!" responded Abramoff.

Says Abramoff about the e-mails: "I was being jocular. We were privately joking around. Am I the only one in the world who does this?...If I was trying to get the Tigua as a client at any point before February 4, there would have been some mention of this in my many e-mails during the previous months when I was trying to shut down the Alabama-Coushatta."

Abramoff had mentioned the Tigua in earlier e-mails, but only because he knew that shutting down one casino could not be accomplished without shutting down the other. What concerned Abramoff was that the Tigua—who were far more politically savvy and well connected—would apply pressure in subsequent years on the Texas legislature to re-file the bill that would make all tribal casinos legal. If the Tigua succeeded, then the Alabama-Coushatta would have also been able to reopen its casino. Therefore, the reason Abramoff approached the Tigua was to offer them another option, circumventing state control, that would have allowed *only their casino* to reopen. He would try to arrange for the tribe to receive a federal exemption, by quietly inserting a "rider"[159] into a congressional bill, thereby overriding Texas law. The Tigua would be able to reopen its casino, while the Alabama-Coushatta would not.

In this way, Abramoff would have succeeded in protecting the interests of his Louisiana client. "In addition to solving the [Louisiana] Coushatta's problems, we could solve the Tigua's problems, and get another client," says Abramoff. "It was the ultimate gimme five, because it was brilliant."

Schmidt's Sunday story ran on the front page. Two days later, the *Post* ran an editorial praising her reporting and condemning Abramoff in the strongest language possible:

> What the Tigua didn't know, according to a report by the *Post*'s Susan Schmidt, was that just before [Abramoff] hit the tribe up for business, [he was] actively working, on behalf of rival tribes, to shut down the Tigua casino....

> **But the exploitative twist uncovered by Ms. Schmidt—making money by sticking it to the tribe, then making even more by promising to undo the damage—takes the tale to a new level of avarice and duplicity.**

What "rival tribes" was the *Post* referring to? Abramoff's nearest tribal client,[160] the Louisiana Coushatta, as noted, was nearly 1000 miles away.

The following morning, Abramoff was scheduled to appear under subpoena and testify under oath before Sen. John McCain and his committee.

"What Sue Schmidt did [in that story] was beyond contempt. It made me look like the worst villain that ever lived," says Abramoff.

When contacted in mid-June 2008 by phone for an interview, Schmidt, now a reporter for *The Wall Street Journal*, wanted to know what the thrust of the book was and what kinds of questions would she be asked. She was given a sample question: "Was Scott Reed the unnamed lobbyist source for your first story?" She declined to answer the question and immediately ended the call. A series of questions were then e-mailed to Schmidt, but she did not respond to them as well. However, *The Washington Post*'s editor in chief, Len Downie did respond to a series of e-mailed questions about Schmidt's September 26th story: He wrote back: "Your questions involve a level of detail about one particular aspect of the Abramoff coverage that I cannot remember. Our coverage, which continues as the story continues to unfold, has stood up well."

CHAPTER FORTY-FOUR
THE HEARING

The timing and effect of the one-two punch—Schmidt's story on September 26th followed by the *Post*'s scathing editorial on September 28th—was ruinous. Its impact was palpable when McCain and his colleagues publicly grilled the committee's very first witness, Jack Abramoff, the next morning.

McCain had also engineered a timing coup of his own. He had scheduled Abramoff's appearance to coincide with the inauguration of the National Museum of the American Indian in Washington, D.C.

Thousands of Native Americans that had come to town that week would get a twofer. They could celebrate the grand opening of their museum, and they would get a chance to see indignant U. S. Senators rail against a villain to Native Americans. Figuring he might as well sprinkle a bit more fuel on the fire, McCain had just released some of Abramoff's most volatile e-mails in which the lobbyist appeared to have labeled his Indian clients "monkeys," "morons," "idiots," and "troglodytes." It was almost as if Schmidt and McCain had become synchronized swimmers. In fact, Abramoff and his lawyer, Lowell, believed they were indeed colluding.

Both Abramoff and Scanlon[161] had been subpoenaed to testify, but only Abramoff showed up. "Last I had heard," said McCain, "Mr. Scanlon was dodging the U.S. Marshals attempting to serve him." Hearing Room 216 in the Hart Senate Building was packed with reporters, photographs, and Native Americans. The proceedings were being televised. Excerpts would later appear on all the national evening news broadcasts. Of the thirteen senators on the committee, in addition to McCain, seven showed up: Chairman Ben Nighthorse Campbell, vice-chair Daniel Inouye (D-Hawaii), Kent Conrad (D-ND), Maria Cantwell (D-Wash), Brian R. Dorgan (D-ND), Tim Johnson (D-SD), and Lisa Murkowski (R-Alaska). Four were no-shows: Orrin Hatch (R-Utah), Harry Reid (D-Nevada), Gordon Smith (R-OR), and James M. Inhofe (R-OK).

Shortly after 9:30 am, Sen. Campbell—the first Native American elected to the U. S. Senate, who was also responsible for changing the name of the Custer Battlefield Monument in Montana to the Little Bighorn Battlefield National Monument—pounded his gavel and called the hearing to order. He was relishing the massacre of a modern-day Custer, who would be wearing the uniform of a businessman—white shirt, dark suit, and a blue silk tie. Campbell launched into a prepared statement and was soon reading aloud some of Abramoff's e-mails. These had been blown up on cardboard and displayed on an easel for all—including the cameras—to see: "'I have to meet with the monkeys from the Choctaw Tribal Council....' Mind you," Campbell noted, "that these 'monkeys,' as Mr. Abramoff refers to the tribal council of the Mississippi Band of the Choctaw Indians, had enriched him over a five-year period with over $7 million in lobbying fees...." Other e-mails put on display included Abramoff referring to his tribal clients as 'f-ing troglodytes,' which he had defined for Scanlon as 'a lower former of existence.'"

Waiting in the anteroom of the Senate chamber, Abramoff could hear every word. As the word "racist" was being branded on his forehead, he thought he could smell the stink of his own burning flesh.

When Campbell had completed his excoriations, Sen. Inouye—recipient of the Medal of Honor in WWII—read his prepared remarks. After that, it was Sen. McCain's turn. For a while, the ex-POW pontificated and rebuked. Eventually he posed a question: "Why did Mr. Scanlon pay Mr. Abramoff half of his profit? After all, in his interview with the *Post*'s reporter, Mr. Abramoff denied having any *financial interest* in Mr. Scanlon's companies. The answer is surprisingly simple. Mr. Abramoff and Mr. Scanlon were partners. Their partnership apparently began over 3 years ago on June 18, 2001. In an e-mail to Mr. Abramoff, Mr. Scanlon set forth his vision. Mr. Abramoff would develop the client base and Mr. Scanlon would serve them. In Mr. Scanlon's own words: 'Bottomline, if you help me get CCS a client base of $3 million a year, I will get the clients served and the firm acquired at $9 million, we can split up the profits. What do you think?'" McCain paused and then continued: "Lest there be any doubt on this point, one year later, Mr. Abramoff extolled his partner's virtues in an e-mail. After Mr. Scanlon reported on the receipt of $3 million from the Louisiana Coushatta for undisclosed services, Mr. Abramoff replied: 'You are a great partner. What I love about our partnership is that when one of us is down, the other is there. We are going to make dollars for years together.'...What is wrong with this relationship, some may ask? Possibly nothing, had it been disclosed to the tribes, but it never was...."

McCain had just called Abramoff a liar for telling Schmidt that he did not have a "financial interest" in Scanlon's companies. Few in the room would recall that in her first story, Abramoff had denied having an "ownership interest." After March 30th, however, Schmidt had subtly shifted to the phrase "financial interest," even though this had not been Abramoff's response to her original question. It may seem insignificant, but it was the difference between fraud—if Scanlon was not doing the work he'd promised to do and Abramoff was a partner in Scanlon's company—and a referral fee. Ultimately, it became moot, because Abramoff pleaded guilty to whatever the prosecutors stipulated. As for disclosing this arrangement to the tribes, once again McCain was misleading and mistaken. Abramoff was not obliged to tell the tribes.

Soon, it was Sen. Conrad's turn to scold Abramoff, saying that he had been "struck by the [Schmidt] article in *The Washington Post* on Sunday. If you were to set out to write down a scheme that would reveal the basest nature of people," Conrad bristled, "you'd have a hard time coming up with more examples than have been provided by this case. This Jack Abramoff, Michael Scanlon, taking advantage of the political system in the most crass and crude way, all for their own enrichment. You have to ask yourselves, what kind of people are these? What kind of people are these that would cook up such a scheme and then actually carry it out? It's despicable. They deserve the harshest treatment that the legal system can provide."

Conrad had no way of knowing that it was the very article to which he was referring that had been "cooked up."

Still waiting in the anteroom, Abramoff says, "I was in a state of shock. It seemed like for hours I'd listened to this litany of insults they hurled at me. How I was a racist, how I hated my clients, how I stole from them, how I had deceived them."

Finally when the prepared remarks had been exhausted, it was time for the main event. The condemned man would be dragged into the coliseum to be drawn and quartered. Abramoff was instructed to make his entrance. He took a deep breath and walked into the crowded hearing room. "The media was there in full force. It looked like the Iran-Contra hearings. I glanced around the room. There were angry Indians, whipped up by months of bombast from the press. They viewed me as their Hitler. I noticed Larry Rosenthal and Sue Schmidt, looking smug," says Abramoff. "The stone cold, angry stares bore holes into my head as I slowly walked to my seat at the witness table. Some of my former tribal friends had front-row seats. They looked at me with utter disgust and contempt, ready to spit on me."

Abramoff and his lawyer took their seats at the witness table. Campbell asked Abramoff to stand, raise his right hand, and swear to tell the truth. Because of his religious beliefs, he "affirmed" that he would tell the truth.[162] He sat back down. His lawyer then leaned over and passed a pearl of legal wisdom into his ear. "That was my first Michael Corleone photo, with [my lawyer] whispering in my ear. It would grace the newspapers for months," says Abramoff, "until it was replaced with 'The Hat.'"[163]

Abramoff answered the first question—and all subsequent questions—by asserting his Fifth Amendment privilege, on advice of counsel. "As much as I wanted to speak, I had to keep one thing in mind. Don't do anything that could later be construed as a crime," says Abramoff.

If he had answered a single question, Abramoff would have automatically waived his right to remain silent, and then the senators would have kept him there for days, asking hundreds of questions, going through his tax returns line by line, and going through all his e-mails. Abramoff says that the only purpose of a Senate hearing was to trip up the witness and to get him to stumble or contradict himself—just enough for prosecutors to bring perjury charges. "I found it hard to believe that there were actually still people in Washington who thought that availing oneself of the Fifth Amendment was tantamount to an admission of guilt," says Abramoff. "And I still pay the price for not defending myself before that inquisition to this very day."

That exact moment in time became Abramoff's "angle of repose." His life had just come screeching to a halt. Redemption or exoneration of any kind would never be possible. The Schmidt fairy tale and the racist-sounding e-mails had crucified him forever.

Playing to the cameras and the live audience, the senators kept pounding, pummeling, and peppering him with rude and insulting questions. All Abramoff could do was to respectfully repeat his Fifth Amendment mantra: "Senator, on advice of counsel…" He stared back at the eight senators. Exception for McCain, Abramoff had raised funds for every one of them, including the absent committee members, especially Harry Reid.

"Here were all these senators, who, not six months before, had been begging for funds from Abramoff, indulging themselves at his restaurant, kissing up to him and his team," says a source close to the investigation. "Had Chairman Campbell forgotten the breakfast with Abramoff at La Colline—with [Campbell's] former chief of staff, later accused of extortion? That's where Abramoff had dutifully handed him all those $5,000 checks from his clients. Had Campbell forgotten that his staff and Team Abramoff had been thick as thieves on scores of [earlier] issues in front of this very [Senate Indian Affairs] Committee? And what about Senators Dorgan and Conrad? Had they forgotten that Mike Smith, who worked for Abramoff, had provided them with tens of thousands of dollars in campaign contributions? And what about Sen. Inouye?

Had the senior senator from Hawaii forgotten how he'd rammed "his way straight to [Choctaw] Chief Martin, demanding $50,000 for the Democratic Senatorial Committee, reminding the Chief and Abramoff about how much he did for Indians?" Perhaps the ethical thing for these senators would have been to recuse themselves from any involvement in the investigation.

And then there was McCain, who was leading the charge. "Did he really think Abramoff was more corrupt than he, as a line of secretaries provided him with laundered campaign checks, with Charles Keating looking on approvingly? Or all those free flights on Keating's jet until [McCain] 'remembered' to pay for them two years later when the [Keating Five] scandal broke?"[164] wonders a source close to the investigation. "And what about when [McCain] was the chairman [of the Senate Indian Affairs Committee from 1995-1997] and wanted to eviscerate Indian gaming with a slew of legislative attacks, and then he sat back and did nothing when certain House Republicans [in 1996] tried to undo the Indian Child Welfare Act, that Abramoff worked so hard to save, meeting with [McCain] in his office in failed attempts to get him to help out the tribes?"

Standing nearby was Pablo Carrillo, the committee's chief investigative counsel. "Even Pablo used to feast at the trough at Signatures with Michael Williams of Abramoff's staff," says the source close to the investigation, "and never once paid for a meal."

The senators kept taking turns hurling invectives at Abramoff, playing to the cameras. It seemed to go on for days. From time to time, one of them brought up Schmidt's September 26th article. Abramoff says it was that "lie" that probably sickened him the most.

Indeed, nearly two years later when McCain's report was released, he manipulated the evidence to further validate in greater detail the tall tale that Schmidt had spun. But surely, in researching and preparing this report, there must have been a couple of young and idealistic committee staffers who grasped the speciousness of the Tigua allegation against Abramoff. Had they been afraid to challenge the conventional wisdom and defy the apparently explicit wishes of McCain? Surely, there must have been at least one intrepid staffer who cringed at one of the report's most bizarre claims: "Abramoff and Scanlon were representing the... El Paso Tigua, in direct conflict with the interests of [their client] the

Louisiana Coushattas..." Didn't anybody think to check MapQuest? By car, the two casinos were over thirteen hours apart. For those unfamiliar with the sprawl of Texas geography, it took less time to drive from New York City to Atlanta, or from Chicago to Washington, D.C. than to drive from the Tigua in El Paso to the Louisiana Coushatta in Kinder, Louisiana. How could McCain possibly accuse Abramoff of having a conflict of interest in representing two tribes separated by roughly one-third of the distance from sea to shining sea? The treachery and deceit of McCain's report were stunning. And yet, somehow everyone got swept away by the perfect narrative.

Abramoff had bitten his lip and fought to keep his composure to the point of exhaustion. Suddenly and thankfully, he realized the ordeal was about to end. He heard the final words come out of Sen. Conrad's mouth: "I would say to you, Mr. Abramoff, shame on you. Shame on you."

Chairman Campbell informed Abramoff and his lawyer that they were excused. They rose and walked out of the room. "Pablo did provide one nicety," says Abramoff. "He let us leave by a side door, avoiding the throng of media, which wasn't the case [nearly two years later] at the courthouse."

CHAPTER FORTY-FIVE
PURGATORY

Abramoff's appearance at the McCain hearing was televised nationally on C-Span and covered by the media across the country, and in some cases, around the world. And Schmidt's Tigua fairy tale was often repeated or referred to in those stories.

In the weeks and months that followed, things only became worse for Abramoff. Signatures quickly became the restaurant for Capitol Hill staffers and lobbyists to avoid. Even though Abramoff had stopped giving away free meals, business deteriorated and he had to shut down the restaurant.

His new venture in real-estate and film-production stalled, because he was running out of cash. "I tried everything I could think of to earn a living, to support my family and pay my burgeoning legal bills. It was ironic," says Abramoff. "In the past, I was the one who would support not only my family, but scores of other families in need. I was the one sending out bills from my law firm. Now, I was in debt to my attorneys, and my financial future looked bleak."

More stories in *The Washington Post* appeared. Other newspapers wanted their pound of flesh, so they sent out their own investigative reporters to dig up dirt. Other alleged machinations were soon unearthed or expanded upon. These included Abramoff's supposed participation in a $23 million forged wire transfer, Abramoff's possible link to the gangland slaying of Gus Boulis, Abramoff's International Freedom Foundation as a front for apartheid, the Hollywood movie that Abramoff had produced in apartheid-controlled Namibia in violation of UN sanctions, Abramoff's support for a visa for Congo dictator Mobutu Sese Seku, Abramoff's venal exploitation of defenseless women in the Northern Mariana Islands, and so on. Even Abramoff's BMW 745Li, with $50,000 in extras, was used to put him in the worst possible light. At times, he was even front-page fodder in Europe, Israel, South Africa, Russia, China, and Malaysia. Every time he stepped out in public—if he went to a basketball or baseball game, or if he even tried to tee up early one morning at a private golf course—it somehow found its way into the newest story of the day. The unspoken message was that it was unconscionable for Abramoff to be able to continue enjoying his sybaritic lifestyle with his ill-gotten gains.

After a while, to avoid the public eye, he stopped going into Washington, except for his get-togethers with federal prosecutors, with whom he had started meeting in August 2004.

"There may not have been a moment of epiphany, but the cumulative impact was making me wonder where and how the next phase of my life would commence," says Abramoff. That next phrase would commence soon enough with his earning a few pennies an hour as an inmate working in a federal prison. "The prospect of prison time was not real at that point," he says.

Three months after Schmidt's first article, he had also been forced to shut down Eshkol Academy. That November, a judge ordered Abramoff's assets frozen because thirteen former school employees—including nine teachers and the principal—had sued him for $149,000 in unpaid wages. "This [Eshkol lawsuit] was extremely painful and was entirely without merit," says Abramoff. "I was a donor—the only donor, but a donor nevertheless—not the owner of the business, [which was a nonprofit organization,] so the suit has gone nowhere."

Even his personal tailor would take him to court, along with most of his former tribal clients.

As his world continued to disintegrate, he did what little he could to minimize the potential damage. For example, hoping to shed the SunCruz millstone, he reached a settlement in the civil suit with Foothill and Citadel. In June 2005, the SunCruz lenders agreed to dismiss the case against Abramoff in return for his handing over his pension. His old-age safety net was now gone. What was worse was that it proved to be an utterly wasted effort. When he was later sentenced to 70 months in prison, his punishment also included $20 million in restitution to those very lenders.

Meanwhile, federal prosecutors, who had not been in touch with Adam Kidan for over a year, contacted him again. "The thing that had changed was that back at that first meeting, I'd been the big fish. I was the one in the press. I was the one with the Gambino contacts. I was the central figure," says Kidan. "All of a sudden Jack's in the press. Now, they want me again, but I'm not the big fish. I'm the little fish, and everything's changed."

State prosecutors pressed Kidan to testify against the prime suspects in Boulis' murder, who had not yet been indicted. "The chief witness in the case had failed three lie-detector tests. They wanted [the] Boulis [killers] and they wanted Abramoff, so I became someone they thought could help them," says Kidan.

At his own expense, Kidan flew down to Ft. Lauderdale several times for meetings with federal prosecutors. Finally, a deal was struck. "They really scared me. They told me I was facing 30 years in prison. They were going to charge me with a variety of things: bank fraud, wire fraud, conspiracy to commit bank fraud, fraud of financial statements," says Kidan. "So at the last meeting, they finally put a deal on the table. I have to testify against Abramoff, as well as the killers of Boulis. In return, I'll get two and a half years in prison. Well, I'm distraught over serving a single day in prison and I'm worried about testifying against the Mafia."

Kidan vacillated. He read a gloomy book, *Down Time*, about what to expect in federal prison. Finally, against his lawyer's advice, Kidan turned down the deal. The risks were too great. As a former lawyer, he knew that the government was not eager to bring this bank-fraud case to trial. "It would be evident to the jury that the lenders had not been defrauded, since they had colluded in the fraud," says Kidan. "But going to trial would kill me financially."

Still, he says the federal prosecutors remained cordial. He knew they were "being nice" to him, because he was the little fish who could help them catch the big fish. "They told me on Wednesday afternoon that I [would] have to be down in Florida the following morning." He would be indicted, arrested, appear before the judge, and be released on bail. "They let me see the indictment. It was nothing close to what they claimed [they were going to charge me with]. It was just wire fraud and conspiracy to commit wire fraud. They never brought the bank fraud charges, because Foothill [along with Citadel] wasn't a bank," says Kidan. "I was shocked to see that Ben [Waldman] wasn't indicted. I was shocked that no one from the Boulis side was part of it."

Around midnight, Kidan flew from New York and landed in Miami. The next morning he walked into his lawyer's office, ready to surrender at 10 am. "My lawyer tells me there's a problem," says Kidan. "They can't find Jack."

CHAPTER FORTY-SIX
THE SHU

The impact of the negative publicity upon Abramoff's children was enormous. He suggested to them that they change their last name to escape the harassment they were experiencing. They refused out of loyalty to their father.

Nevertheless, Abramoff had tried to maintain a certain routine. Every summer, he had made time to take each of his five children on a weeklong summer trip.

He and one of his twin daughters went to visit family and friends in Los Angeles in August 2005. They had flown out using frequent-flyer miles. They would be staying with his brother in Los Angeles and later with his parents in Rancho Mirage. Abramoff and his daughter went to the movies, dined at some kosher restaurants, and drove around Beverly Hills where Abramoff had grown up. Still trying to find work, he had also arranged a few business meetings.

On Thursday, August 11, 2005, Abramoff took his daughter to meet his childhood friend, Neal Bagg, now a Hollywood agent. "We were in Neal's conference room that overlooked the Hollywood Hills. We'd been joined by a couple of other agents from his firm who wanted to meet me," says Abramoff. "Then my phone rang. I must have turned pale, but I tried to maintain my composure, as I left the room to take the call."

When Abramoff returned, he told them he had something to say. They would hear it on the news soon enough. He was about to be indicted. "My daughter looked at me with confusion. 'Indicted' was not a word she'd studied in her sixth-grade class at the strictly Orthodox Jewish school she attended in Baltimore," says Abramoff. "Had she realized what was about to happen, she might have burst into the tears that were welling up inside of me."

Abramoff says that his lawyers had not been informed about his indictment: "It was the media who told my lawyers. I was ordered to report [to a downtown federal building] at 1 pm."

Acting U.S. attorney Anthony Acosta tried to orchestrate a little side show. He planned to hold a press conference in Miami to take credit for the indictments, while the cameras cut to a handcuffed Abramoff, who would be paraded down the sidewalk next to the courthouse in downtown Los Angeles.

At the Miami press conference later that afternoon, Acosta announced the criminal indictments of Abramoff and Kidan on charges of wire fraud and conspiracy to commit wire fraud. Acosta declared: "Preserving financial security is a top priority of this U.S. Attorney's office." Special agent Timothy Delany added that this was a prime example "of the types of cases that should be prosecuted. Regardless of position, status and association, actions like this will not be tolerated."

This case was hardly a model for touting the "preserving [of] financial security." According to a source close to the U.S. Attorney's office, Acosta was simply trying to further his well-known political ambitions by piggy-backing onto Abramoff's visibility. It was highly doubtful any jury would have found Kidan guilty, never mind Abramoff. But for Acosta this was an extremely low-risk gamble, because the odds were overwhelmingly stacked in his favor. There was only a 5% chance this case would ever go to trial, because affluent and well-educated white-collar defendants—

who had never spent a day in jail, or been charged with a felony or misdemeanor—could so easily be intimidated into pleading guilty.

Abramoff's Miami attorney, Neal Sonnett, told reporters, "We were hopeful we'd be able to convince [Acosta] not to file charges because [Abramoff] was not involved in fraud involving SunCruz." Kidan took a similar tack: "I have cooperated fully with the federal investigation for the past three years because I have nothing to hide. I did nothing wrong and these allegations are totally unfounded."

Although the indictment did not expressly say so, some reporters seemed to grasp that it had been Kidan who had faxed the forged $23 million wire transfer, not Abramoff. When asked at the press conference why Ben Waldman had not been charged as well, Acosta declined to say, stating: "I'm not going to discuss whether someone may or may not be a witness."

Unfortunately for Acosta, his sideshow didn't go as planned. Something unexpected happened. Abramoff didn't show up for the "perp walk." He had failed to surrender at the appointed hour. A phalanx of frustrated cameramen, photographers, and reporters had been waiting in the summer heat for the handcuffed "perp" to emerge from a government vehicle, so he could be extensively photographed and filmed as he walked in handcuffs down the sidewalk for half a block into the federal courthouse. Acosta was hoping to be the lead story on the nightly network news shows. Bush had nominated Acosta as U.S. Attorney for southern Florida, but his confirmation was being held up in the U.S. Senate. Acosta was hoping that this publicity would unclog his nomination.

But where was Abramoff? Had he gone on the lam? The titillating possibility meant that Abramoff might soon be declared the object of a national manhunt. As it turned out, there was a benign explanation. Abramoff says he had been misinformed or misunderstood where he was to go. He had gone to 1100 Wilshire Blvd. The actual address was 11000 Wilshire Blvd. By the time he finally showed up at the correct address, it was 5 pm. The cameras were long gone. Abramoff was quietly handcuffed and taken to the LA Downtown Detention Center, technically a medium-security federal prison. Promptly stripped of all his clothing, including his yarmulke, he was told he'd be spending the night playing ping pong with his fellow inmates. But because his face had graced the prison televisions all day, he was carted off—dressed in a bright orange jumpsuit—to the SHU [special housing unit], also known as "the hole."

Instead of battling the links at St. Andrews as he had in previous Augusts, he struggled through the night in solitary confinement, listening to the shouts and shrieks of his fellow inmates in the cell block.

Early the next morning, he was cuffed, put in leg irons, and marched across the compound to the federal courthouse. In the courtroom, much of the Washington media contingent—who had caught the red-eye out to Los Angeles, and who had helped to make Abramoff a household name—was eagerly waiting.

"Their smirks and glee were not lost on me as I sat in the dock with the other prisoners," says Abramoff. "I tried to stare back at them without showing any emotion." The judge finally called for Abramoff to step forward. Acosta had set the bail at $2.5 million—five times that of Kidan. After Abramoff, his brother, and his father pledged their homes as surety for bail, Abramoff was released shortly before 1 pm. Because it was too late for him to fly home without violating the Sabbath, he spent the night at the airport. Just after dark on Saturday, he took the red-eye back to Washington. He felt badly for his daughter: "What a way to spend a summer vacation."

Three thousand miles away, Kidan had not been subjected to the perp walk. And he had not spent a night in jail. Following his arraignment, he was immediately released on bail. Kidan says that Moscatiello called him right away: "He was very concerned for my welfare. He even told me that he was willing to put up his house as collateral for my bail. I guess that's what people do in his world. But I also think he was afraid if I went down fast, I'd take him down with me."

Several weeks later, Kidan decided to hire new criminal defense attorneys. He interviewed Joseph Conway and Robert LaRusso, two former division heads at the U.S. Attorney's office, who had recently gone into private practice. Kidan was surprised to learn that Conway had been the prosecutor who had charged Moscatiello with heroin smuggling back in the 1980s. Conway told Kidan that the case against Moscatiello had been dropped because of mistaken identity. Kidan says that he even then consulted with Moscatiello about hiring Conway. Moscatiello supposedly told Kidan, "Yeah, Joe was the one who prosecuted me. He was incredible. He's a good lawyer. He's fair. He's a nice guy." Because a high-profile case would be good for business, Kidan says that Conway and LaRusso offered to charge him much less than the other defense attorneys he had considered.

A few days after Kidan's conversation with Moscatiello, there was a stunning development. On September 28th, Moscatiello—along with Anthony "Little Tony" Ferrari and John "Pudgy" Fiorillo—were arrested for the murder of Gus Boulis. *The Miami Herald* quickly pointed out that both "Ferrari and Moscatiello—who had ties to the Gambino crime family in New York—were paid $250,000 for catering and security services by Kidan from the SunCruz coffers." *The Washington Post* would later point out that Kidan had paid $145,000 to Moscatiello, "[even though] there is no evidence that food or drink was [ever] provided."

Moscatiello was taken into custody outside his red-brick home in the Howard Beach section of Queens, New York, where a number of organized-crime figures have resided, including mob bosses John Gotti and Joe Massino. Apparently, Moscatiello was very chatty with the police who arrested him. He joked that he was actually a "wiseguy," because he had an IQ of 152. He also mentioned that he had recently spent $110,000 on his daughter's wedding, but that the marriage had dissolved after 10 days, because her "husband had some Las Vegas stripper on the side."

And in an ironic twist, one of the arresting officers, Det. Richie Fagan, later revealed that years earlier, he had babysat for Chris Paciello, the Miami night club impresario who had confessed in 2001 to the murder of Kidan's mother.

Before Moscatiello was shipped down to Florida, Kidan paid him a visit at Riker's Island, where "Big Tony" was being held without bail. "I just dropped by as a friend to tell him how sorry I was," says Kidan.

But the pressure was mounting on Kidan. On November 21, Michael Scanlon pleaded guilty to one count of conspiracy. He agreed to cooperate with authorities by testifying against Abramoff, Ney, and others. At about the same time, Kidan heard a rumor that Moscatiello was trying to cut his own deal, claiming that Kidan had ordered the hit on Boulis. Kidan was preparing to go to trial and was confident he would not be found guilty. He then got a call from one of his lawyers, who had just been told by the prosecutor, "Oh, by the way, we're also going to indict Kidan for bribing Congressman Bob Ney. The statute of limitations is coming up, so either toll the statute [of limitations] or we'll indict him right away." Kidan says he couldn't afford to defend himself against another indictment. His lawyers, who were feverishly preparing for trial, flew down to Florida to meet with the prosecutors. They also decided to pay a courtesy call on Abramoff's attorney. According to Kidan, not only did Abramoff's attorney not appear to be preparing for trial, he mentioned that he had not been paid in a while, because Abramoff was broke. "My lawyers told me that I'd better hurry up and plead before Jack does," says Kidan. Two days later, the prosecutors had worked out a deal with Kidan. He would plead guilty in the SunCruz case. He would also testify against Abramoff, as well as against the three men who had been charged with Boulis' murder.

What would Kidan get in return? Well, that all depended on the value of his cooperation. The prosecutors were demanding six months in prison and six months of house arrest. Kidan's lawyers were hoping to negotiate the sentence down to probation. But the deal might take as long as two years to finalize, during which time Kidan would be out on bail. "My lawyers told me that after you plead guilty, the judge doesn't sentence you until after you've finished your cooperation," says Kidan. "If the prosecutors are satisfied, the judge signs off on whatever they recommend."

The reason for the two-year delay was that state prosecutors had just filed the paperwork seeking the death penalty against Moscatiello and his two co-defendants.

On December 15, Kidan appeared before Judge Paul C. Huck and agreed to plead guilty to wire fraud and conspiracy to commit wire fraud. "Mr. Kidan has acknowledged today that he, along with co-defendant Jack Abramoff, made false representations to lenders," Kidan's lawyer told reporters after the brief hearing. What was not disclosed was that Kidan had secretly agreed to testify against the mobsters who allegedly murdered Boulis. But the south Florida press could read between the lines. Kidan decided to immediately go into hiding, especially after being told "that Moscatiello had hired a hit man to kill me."

Meanwhile, Abramoff too had decided to bite the bullet. On January 3, 2006, he appeared before Judge Ellen Huvelle in Washington, D.C. and pleaded guilty to conspiracy, fraud, and income tax evasion. The following day, Abramoff appeared before Judge Paul Huck in Miami, Florida, and pleaded guilty to wire fraud and conspiracy to commit wire fraud.

A few days later, Abramoff and Kidan—along with their attorneys and federal prosecutors—were caught off guard. Judge Huck announced that he was not going to wait for the defendants to complete their cooperation. He would go ahead and sentence them at the end of March.

On March 29th, Judge Huck sentenced both Abramoff and Kidan to 70 months in prison, agreeing to stay their sentences for three months so they could continue their cooperation with the investigation.

The prosecutors assumed that Judge Huck would grant any further requests for a stay of sentence until the defendants' cooperation had been completed.

CHAPTER FORTY-SEVEN
THE MCCAIN REPORT

On June 22, 2006, McCain's 373-page Senate Indian Affairs Final Report—*"Gimme Five"—Investigation of Tribal Lobbying Matters, Final Report Before the Committee on Indian Affairs*—was released without fanfare. The members of the Senate committee approved it unanimously. Of course, *The Washington Post* and *The New York Times* covered its release, but the nightly network newscasts did not.

Sen. McCain and his chief investigator, Pablo Carrillo, did not respond to a request for an interview several days after the report was published. McCain's presidential campaign committee also did not respond to a series of e-mailed questions sent in mid-June 2008.

It seemed bizarre that Grover Norquist had not been called to testify. And there were no criminal or civil charges brought against Norquist, Ralph Reed, Gale Norton, or Amy Ridenour for their alleged misuse of their nonprofits—in which they were employed as "pass-throughs" by Abramoff. There seemed to be little doubt that subtle pressure had been applied to McCain to protect the Republican Party from further damage. Of course, McCain's investigation—aided by the media—had already succeeded in eliminating some of the leading right-wing politicians, fundraisers, and political activists who, coincidentally, had long opposed his presidential aspirations

It was deeply troubling that McCain's report, with its sins of omission and its deceitfulness, was repeatedly touted by him as neutral, factual, and fair.

ELDER LEGACY

At every possible opportunity, Schmidt and McCain labored to hammer home the callousness of Abramoff's behavior, either twisting facts to support their allegations, or overlooking or omitting them altogether if they undermined their thesis. One example involved a proposal for a life-insurance program for elderly members of the Tigua tribe, called the Elder Legacy Program, which Abramoff presented to the tribe in mid March of 2003.

Details of the proposal were never explained either by the *Post* or in McCain's report. Abramoff's firm had developed a program called Creative Funding Solutions that raised money for nonprofit charitable concerns. The program enrolled tribal elders, 75 and older, in term life insurance free of charge. The premiums would be financed by Creative Funding Solutions. When the elder passed away, the proceeds would be split. One portion would pay for the financed premiums and the rest would flow into a nonprofit charity established by Abramoff. The nonprofit would, in turn, pay the tribe's lobbying fees to Abramoff's firm. Elders who participated in this program would have no out-of-pocket costs.

It sounded too good to be true, but since the elders did not pay any of the premiums and the program entirely defrayed the cost of the tribe's lobbying fees, why did it matter?

Yet in the right hands, it was fairly easy to distort this into something that sounded despicable. Schmidt was the first to take a stab at it two months after Abramoff's appearance before McCain's committee in a story she wrote in November 18, 2004.

> **Chairman Ben Nighthorse Campbell (R-Colo.) said he was "horrified" to learn how far Abramoff was allegedly willing to go in pursuit of tribal dollars. Documents released yesterday show that when the Tiguas were out of money in 2003, Abramoff came up with a plan to provide term life insurance to tribal elders, who**

> would make their beneficiary a Jewish school Abramoff founded…[Eshkol Academy] would pay Abramoff's lobbying fees at [his] firm…
>
> Campbell expressed dismay that Abramoff allegedly schemed to make money "by putting prices on the lives of tribal elders." The Tiguas rejected the plan.

Without investigating any further, other members of the media would weigh in with mounting disgust. *The Texas Observer* later noted:

> Abramoff planned to purchase term life insurance on Tigua elders and collect the death benefits as they died. It was an imaginative idea by which the deaths of tribal elders would pay for lobbying services for those left behind. It was also more than the Tigua Tribal Council could stomach.

A book later written in 2006 by Peter H. Stone on the Abramoff scandal chimed in:

> One of the most bizarre notions Abramoff suggested involved an insurance scam that the tribe quickly rejected.

Of course, McCain couldn't believe his luck. It just kept getting better and better. He eagerly voiced his outrage over Abramoff's Elder Legacy Program. At a public hearing he held on November 17, 2004, McCain noted, "After brief consideration the Tigua rejected it, because [and then he quoted from a July 30, 2003 email without identifying the date] 'it just wasn't right.'" McCain paused and then continued:

> The story I just shared with you [about the Elder Legacy Program] and which we will learn more about today is tragic. Jack Abramoff and Michael Scanlon preyed upon the tribe and its members when they were most vulnerable. They played upon their hopes and fears. They went to El Paso selling salvation and instead delivered snake oil.

During that same hearing, Sen. Campbell asked Tigua Lt. Gov. Carlos Hisa if the tribe had rejected Abramoff's "offensive" proposal. Hisa testified:

> It was approved initially, but the tribal council got together outside the meeting and we discussed it for 1 or 2 weeks, and then we just decided not to move forward on it anymore.

Sen. Campbell then asked Tigua's director of public relations, Marc Schwartz, who was seated next to Hisa, and asked if his reaction to that [Elder Legacy Program] was "as cynical as mine [when] I had heard it for the first time." Schwartz replied: "It was certainly extremely a morbid subject."

This response did not exactly square with Schwartz' 2003 e-mails that McCain had in his possession and which he never released. These e-mails suggest that the memories of Schwartz and Hisa were either clouded by the passage of time or the need to jump on the bandwagon to please Sen. McCain. In fact, Abramoff's proposal was given serious and extensive consideration—not for a week or two—but for *more than four months*. Below are a series of e-mails from Schwartz to Abramoff which addressed the Elder Legacy Program.

> -----Original Message-----
> From: Mjschwartz@aol.com
> [mailto:Mjschwartz@aol.com]
> Sent: Sunday, March 30, 2003 11:56 PM
> To: Abramoff, Jack (Dir-DC-Gov)
> Subject: IDENTIFIED ELDERS
>
> Jack:
> Any way, Carlos [Hisa] has identified 35 Elders as of today that will meet your criteria (so far). How many do we need to make the thing take off? We still have a way to go, but I wanted to give you some numbers first since we never spoke about them at length.
>
> Marc

At that point, the Tigua had been considering the proposal for the Elder Legacy Program for two weeks. No one appeared to be holding his nose.

> -----Original Message-----
> From: Mjschwartz@aol.com
> [mailto:Mjschwartz@aol.com]
> Sent: Friday, April 04, 2003 10:41 PM
> To: Abramoff, Jack (Dir-DC-Gov)
> Subject: MONDAY MEETING
>
> Jack:...I have received [the Elder Legacy Program's] final package and passed it along to Carlos, who is handling the issue
>
> Marc

According to the Schwartz e-mail, it would appear that Lt. Gov. Hisa had been in charge of implementing the program and was apparently proceeding with it full steam ahead.

> -----Original Message-----
> From: Mjschwartz@aol.com
> [mailto:Mjschwartz@aol.com]
> Sent: Wednesday, April 16, 2003 2:01 PM
> To: Gibson, Duane R. (Shld-DC-Gov/Adm)
> Cc: Abramoff, Jack (Dir-DC-Gov)
> Subject: Re: Tomorrow
>
> As of this morning, they have not scheduled any meeting with Elders. Lt. Governor [Hisa] is handling applications and I haven't spoken with him today.
>
> Marc

Not much to report so far.

> -----Original Message-----
> From: Mjschwartz@aol.com

> [mailto:Mjschwartz@aol.com]
> Sent: Tuesday, May 06, 2003 9:47 AM
> To: Abramoff, Jack (Dir-DC-Gov)
> Subject: Re: Marc, any news on the elders?
>
> Evidentally, from what I am being told, they are talking to them one-on-one (will take way too long). I'll talk with Carlos [Hisa] today and see if we can move it along quicker. Also, I'll include the Governor so he can ratchet it up a notch or two.

Lt. Gov. Hisa was discussing the proposal with the elders, but it seemed to be taking "way too long." Apparently, Schwartz believed enough in the program that he was going to solicit the tribe's governor to help speed things up.

> -----Original Message-----
> From: Mjschwartz@aol.com
> [mailto:Mjschwartz@aol.com]
> Sent: Wednesday, May 28, 2003 10:12 AM
> To: Abramoff, Jack (Dir-DC-Gov)
> Subject: Re: didn't hear back from you. everything go well?
>
> Having a meeting with Council today to discuss Elder program. Need some help from them....Thanks for everything.
>
> Marc

Clearly, tribal officials had been pushing this proposal for a month an a half. There was no indication that anyone was insulted or disgusted.

> -----Original Message-----
> From: Mjschwartz@aol.com
> [mailto:Mjschwartz@aol.com]
> Sent: Tuesday, July 15, 2003 10:25 PM

To: Abramoff, Jack (Dir-DC-Gov)
Subject: Re: WAS IT MY BREATH?

I'll resend the information on Bush and Elders. Have you read about the goings-on in Texas with redistricting?

Marc

It's now mid-July and apparently the Elder Legacy Program was still viable.

-----Original Message-----

From: Mjschwartz@aol.com
[mailto:Mjschwartz@aol.com]
Sent: Wednesday, July 30, 2003 1:03 AM
To: Abramoff, Jack (Dir-DC-Gov)
Subject: MEETING TODAY

Jack:
As I briefly said on the phone…They have been rejected by their Elders on the insurance plan; "just shouldn't be done"…

Marc

Finally, more than four months later, it "just shouldn't be done." Obviously, it was not the tribal officials who had rejected the plan, but the elders themselves. There did not seem to be any ill-will toward Abramoff or any view of the Elder Legacy Program as the least bit inappropriate. In fact, that very evening, Schwartz and several Tigua officials dined at Signatures as guests of the owner. After dinner, Schwartz returned to his hotel and sent his host an effusive e-mail without any hint of how "extremely morbid [a] subject" he found the Elder Legacy Program to be.

-----Original Message-----

From: Mjschwartz@aol.com
[mailto:Mjschwartz@aol.com]

Sent: Wednesday, July 30, 2003 10:18 PM
To: Abramoff, Jack (Dir-DC-Gov)
Subject: THANKS

Jack:
Once again, you have restored their hope....Thanks again for your patience and perseverance...they enjoyed the meal and your positive attitude....Thanks again and I'll talk to you soon. Marc

This was another example of McCain's skullduggery. He had heard the testimony from Schwartz and Hisa in September 2004, which was contradicted by Schwartz's 2003 e-mails, all of which were in McCain's possession. McCain twisted the facts and omitted crucial e-mails to make it appear that Abramoff's proposal was perverted.

When asked about the Elder Legacy Program, Abramoff recalls, "I was approached by a senior partner at GT [Greenberg Traurig], who came to me and said, 'We've developed a program to pitch to elderly Native Americans and Eskimo. In fact, the longer the elders live, the better it would be. The tribe would earn more money. The beneficiary would be the school [Eshkol Academy], and then the school would pay the firm the tribe's lobbying fees. It's complicated but it only works if the beneficiary is a non-profit.' My law firm created it. This was not to suck out the life of their elders...And Schwartz was not only in favor of it, he was enthusiastic about it."

SNIPER SCOPES
Tax law is complex. Non-profit tax law is arcane. But one thing can be said with absolute certainty. The law enforcement of charities like Abramoff's is so lax that many operate openly in violation of their stated charitable purpose and are virtually never prosecuted.

Context is everything. Why was Abramoff garroted into pleading guilty to felonious tax evasion? He poured a vast majority of his own personal income into Capital Athletic Foundation (CAF), the tax-exempt, nonprofit corporation that he founded in 1991. McCain went out of his way to make Abramoff seem as if he had committed some outrageous charitable transgressions. McCain's report included the following:

> CAF was simply another vehicle [that] Abramoff [used to defraud his clients]…and treated [it] as his own personal slush fund, apparently using it to evade taxes, finance lobbying activities such as a golfing trip to Scotland, purchase paramilitary equipment, and for other purposes inconsistent with CAF's tax exempt status and stated mission.

In January 2006, Abramoff pleaded guilty to income-tax evasion for his misuse of CAF:

> to receive income and make expenditures for his own personal benefit…[and] conceal his income from the Internal Revenue Service and others…[and that he] knew these activities constituted a misuse of these tax exempt entities.

All of this was absolutely true. Abramoff was guilty. McCain and the federal prosecutors must have felt proud. They had shut down a fraudulent charity and sent its director to prison. And yet, this may have been unwarranted and even outrageous. In fact, a source close to the federal investigation says that following Abramoff's imprisonment, some prosecutors took the position that Abramoff's tax-evasion conviction should be rescinded, but they were overruled.

Abramoff founded CAF to fund a private school, not unlike a parochial school, except that it would serve Orthodox Jewish male students. Eventually, CAF became the sole source of financial support for Eshkol Academy. CAF's website stated that it was a youth charity that supported "needy and deserving programs." About half of the 75 students who attended Eshkol academy were poor Jewish kids from Miami, Atlanta, Boston, Los Angeles, and San Jose.

How did McCain manage to manipulate this information? First, he repeatedly referred to CAF as Abramoff's "private foundation," as if it were something distinct from other 501(c)3 organizations. In fact, with the exception of universities and hospitals, the IRS treats most 501(c)3s as "private foundations." Second, McCain repeatedly referred to Eshkol Academy as Abramoff's private "Jewish boys' school." The phrasing could be interpreted as having a patina of anti-Semitism. It might have been preferable if McCain had simply called it a private religious school. Thirdly, he focused on how a tiny fraction of CAF's funds were misused. And finally, McCain wanted to mislead the reader into believing that Abramoff had deceived and bamboozled his tribal clients into making huge donations to CAF.

In 2001, the Louisiana Coushatta made a $1 million contribution to CAF. In 2002, the Choctaws donated $1.5 million to Abramoff's charity. But the tribes knew perfectly well they weren't making a donation to a charity. This was how they were paying Michael Scanlon for his grassroots and public relations work. CAF was simply being used as a "pass-through" to pay Scanlon. A "pass-through" was something to which the tribes had paid repeatedly in the past. It had been set up with the tribe's consent to disguise the fact that Ralph Reed had been hired by gamblers to stop gambling, and to conceal the fact the tribe was preventing its nearby brethren from opening a competing casino nearby. Furthermore, McCain—and federal prosecutors—knew that these payments to CAF were simply the, albeit hefty, profits that Scanlon was paying to Abramoff as a referral fee. If Scanlon had paid $1 million to Abramoff and then Abramoff had donated it to CAF, his $1 million donation would have been 100% deductible from his taxable income. Assuming that these referral fees were legitimate, this money was going to a legitimate charity, not into Abramoff's pocket. What's more, in 2002 Abramoff donated to CAF an additional $991,749 of his own personal income. That meant that close to 100% of all CAF's contributions in 2002 came from Abramoff. And how did CAF distribute these funds? Almost all of the money was given to worthy causes: $1,857,704 to Eshkol Academy, $300,000 to a school in Brooklyn for students with disabilities, and an additional $62,000 to other legitimate charities.

Also, what was neither mentioned in CAF's 990 tax forms—nor by McCain—was that Abramoff and his wife provided free room and board in their own home to seven of Eshkol's students and in some cases even paid their dental bills. And the Abramoffs did not pay themselves a single penny—in salary, compensation, or perks—for running CAF.

What then did McCain harp on? He criticized Abramoff for not listing the identity of these large donations—to the two schools—on CAF's website. He also accused Abramoff of "concealing his use of CAF to fund Eshkol, [when for example] Abramoff [had told someone in his firm] that he was personally funding Eshkol Academy." In fact, Abramoff *was* personally funding the whole kit and caboodle.

What did McCain and federal prosecutors choose to focus on? In 2002, Abramoff had donated $97,000—or 4% of CAF's donations that year—to Kollel Ohel Tieferet, an alleged educational institution in Israel. Abramoff was actually helping out Sheldon Greer, an old high-school football teammate, who had changed his name to Shmuel ben Zvi and moved to Israel. He was now living in Beitar Illit, a Jewish city in the Israeli-occupied West Bank of Palestine. "He asked my help in getting for him [and his fellow settlers] night vision glasses, so they could more effectively protect the town he lived in from the Arab terrorist attacks. He told me that the Arabs were firing into their town at night and that they were putting their kids in front of their guns so that the Israelis could not fire back," says Abramoff.

Eventually, he supplied ben Zvi with a couple of sniper scopes, a thermal imager, night-vision binoculars, a jeep, and a ghili suit, which was a camouflage suit that could be purchased from most hunting-supply catalogues. "Anyway, he got the night-vision binoculars and on the first night they used it, he claimed they stopped two terrorists crawling to their village with C4s[165] on their backs," says Abramoff.[166]

What McCain didn't mention was that Abramoff was not the only one bending the tax-exempt rules. Apparently, it's like exceeding the 65 mph speed limit, except that Abramoff was only going 66. His violations were microscopic compared to those of others, who are virtually never prosecuted.

For example, while Abramoff was shipping off a ghili suit to ben Zvi, the Nature Conservancy, one of the premiere environmental groups in America, if not the world, was not exactly leading an exemplary life. Its tax-exempt purpose is to preserve forests, streams, and wildlife sanctuaries. According to *The Washington Post*, while amassing $3 billion in assets, the Nature Conservancy seemed to have violated its expressly stated charitable purpose when it "logged forests, engineered a $64 million deal paving the way for opulent houses on fragile grasslands, and drilled for natural gas—[which it then sold, even though it belonged to someone else]—under the last breeding ground of an endangered bird species."

In 2002, the Nature Conservancy paid its president $420,000. It also loaned him $1.55 million to purchase a home. In 2000, the charity purchased an undeveloped 10-acre parcel of land near the Hamptons for $2.1 million, which it then sold a few weeks later to two of its trustees for $500,000.

Also that year, other well-known charities made sure their presidents were well compensated. The Boy Scouts of America paid its selfless leader $308,000; the American Red Cross, $377.000.

But let's not forget Roger Chapin, the nonprofit guru of all time. According to *The New York Times,* he founded Coalition to Salute America's Heroes and its sister charity, Help Hospitalized Veterans. While prosecutors were putting Abramoff in prison for jaywalking, Chapin, who raised more than $168 million from 2004 to 2006, paid himself and his wife $1.5 million in salary, in addition to $340,000 in meals and other expenses, a $440,000 condominium, and a $17,000 golf club membership.

On July 5th, a staffer for Senate finance Committee chairman, Chuck Grassley (R-IOWA) told a reporter for *The Hill* that McCain's report would be considered part of the committee's three-year probe into tax abuses by nonprofits, such as the Red Cross, American University, and the United Way.

Of course, McCain and federal prosecutors must have known that nonprofit violations were widespread and generally went unpunished. Nevertheless, they treated Abramoff as if he were not only an exception, but an egregious one.

CHAPTER FORTY-EIGHT
TIGUA REDUX

In his report, McCain championed Schmidt's Tigua fairytale with great vigor and passion, even though he clearly had far more evidence in his possession than she, which made his betrayal of the public trust even more egregious.

Gambling is not exactly illegal in Texas. The state has an official lottery, there is horse racing, charity bingos, and "cruises to nowhere" on the Gulf Coast, generating about $7 billion in combined revenue, but there are no Las Vegas-style casinos in Texas. Arguing that it had the legal right to open one, the Tigua[167] tribe of El Paso launched a small illegal casino in 1994, which soon grew into a larger Las Vegas-style operation with annual revenues exceeding $60 million. By 1999, Texas Attorney General John Cornyn decided to take action. He filed a civil lawsuit to shut down the Tigua casino. The tribe fought back in court. As the case slowly wended its way through the legal system, the Tigua shrewdly decided to arrange for "insurance" that would allow it to keep its casino open. On January 9, 2001, Rep. Juan Hinojosa filed a bill in the state legislature, which would have allowed the state's two federally recognized Indian tribes—the Tigua and the Alabama-Coushatta[168]—to operate casinos on their reservations. If the Hinojosa bill became law, it would have made the pending litigation moot.

In March 2001, fearing that the passage of this bill would inspire the Alabama-Coushatta, located outside of Houston, to open its own casino, the Louisiana-Coushatta hired Abramoff—along with Michael Scanlon and Ralph Reed—to prevent this bill from becoming law. At least McCain conceded that:

> The majority of the Louisiana Coushatta casino's customers are from Texas, particularly the Houston area. While the State of Texas was pursuing its case to close the Tigua's…casino …another tribe, the Alabama-Coushatta, was considering opening its own casino in eastern Texas… Abramoff…said that if the Tigua succeeded in its efforts to keep open its casino, the State of Texas would have no choice but to allow the Alabama Coushatta to have a casino.

On April 25, 2001, by a margin of 83 votes, the Texas House of Representatives passed Hinojosa's bill. It then moved over to the Texas Senate, where it was sponsored by state Sen. Eliot Shapleigh of El Paso. Abramoff instructed Reed to quickly mobilize a blistering campaign—whipping up his Christian allies—to defeat the bill. Unfortunately, it wasn't going to succeed. In the state senate, the legislation also enjoyed overwhelming support and would have easily passed. However, in Texas, the Lt. Governor also serves as the president of the state Senate and has the power to refuse to recognize a senator who wishes to bring a bill to the floor for a vote. That was exactly what Lt. Gov. Bill Ratliff did. Abramoff and Reed had somehow persuaded Ratliff that the bill should be blocked. As unbelievable as it might sound, Ratliff subsequently refused to recognize Sen. Shapleigh for the remainder of the legislative session, which ended on May 28. Since the Texas legislature only meets every other year, the bill could not be revived until 2003.

None of this information—readily available—was mentioned either by Schmidt in her news stories or by McCain in his report. Perhaps they omitted it because it clearly demonstrated what an effective lobbyist Abramoff had been. However, McCain did note:

> Abramoff [had] boasted to a colleague: "…Last year we stopped [a bill that would have enabled Indians in Texas to have totally unregulated casinos] after it passed the house using the Lt. Governor (Bill Ratliff) to prevent it from being scheduled in the state senate."

At least McCain confirmed that the bill had been stopped, but without giving Abramoff any credit:

> In fact, former Texas Lt. Governor Ratliff did refuse to schedule the legislation for a floor vote in the previous session…

Meanwhile, the Tigua continued operating its illegal casino, and Attorney General Cornyn continued his court battle to shut it down and also to prevent the Alabama-Coushatta casino from opening its own casino. Due process, however, has a tendency to drag on. Several months later, on November 23, the Alabama-Coushatta opened a small casino near Houston with ambitious plans to expand.

"One day I got a call from [William] Worfel [of the Louisiana Coushatta]. I could hear the sound of slot machines in the background. He said, 'Do you know where I am? I'm standing in the Alabama-Coushatta casino right now.' He sounded perturbed," says Abramoff.

Even McCain conceded that Abramoff realized he was about to lose his most lucrative client if he didn't do something fast. In the following except from his report, at least, McCain seemed to acknowledge that Abramoff's thrust in Texas was to shut down the Alabama-Coushatta—not the Tigua—because the former threatened his client, the Louisiana Coushatta. (The brackets are McCain's.)

> By December 2001, Reed apparently was not achieving satisfactory results. With respect to the Alabama Coushatta's new casino, Abramoff wrote, "We are going to lose this client [Louisiana Coushatta] if we can't get this thing closed...."

It's important to be clear that "this thing" refers to the Alabama-Coushatta casino, not the Tigua casino.

Finally, at the end of 2001, the Tigua had just about exhausted its efforts to delay the inevitable. Cornyn was on the verge of shutting down its casino. For legal reasons, he had to shut down the Tigua casino first, before shutting down the nascent Alabama-Coushatta casino, about which the Louisiana Coushatta, of course, were increasingly anxious. Always quick to toss in a private locker-room e-mail to impute the callousness of Abramoff's soul, McCain had inserted into his report the following communication Abramoff had sent to Michael Scanlon on February 5, 2002:

> "Whining idiot. Close the f'ing thing already!!"

Trying to give the impression that the only thing Abramoff cared about was the closure of the Tigua casino, McCain then wrote:

> [T]he state's legal efforts succeeded, and the Tigua officially closed its casino on February 12, 2002.

But McCain omitted that Cornyn would now focus his attention on closing down the Alabama-Coushatta Tribe of Texas casino, which had clearly been the entire thrust of Abramoff's intense lobbying efforts since March 2001! McCain then suddenly and seamlessly embraced the Schmidt fairy tale. He launched into a long narrative on Abramoff's baseness for persuading the Tigua to hire him to get its casino reopened. McCain cited the following internal memorandum, which a Tigua attorney had written:

> I had a telephone conversation this afternoon with [C.] Bryant Rogers, a lawyer in Santa Fe, who represents a number of Indian Tribes. He advises me that he was asked by Mr. Jack Abramoff, a lobbyist in Washington, D.C. whether the Tiguas were attempting a solution

to the order that may be outside the courts. According to Mr. Rogers, Mr. Abramoff is with a firm that is well connected to the Bush Administration…and has been effective in the past in efforts for other tribes. He is willing to come to El Paso and meet with the Council at no cost to discuss whether he can be of assistance.

This was the first documentary evidence in which Abramoff was ever mentioned that he wanted the Tigua to hire him. This memo, dated February 4, 2002, was written eleven months after the Louisiana Coushatta had first authorized and hired Abramoff to stop Hinojosa's bill in the Texas legislature. And McCain had in his possession all of the March 2001 e-mails, detailing this. This was just one of many examples of why McCain allowed the release of less than 2% or about 8,000 pages of the 750,000 pages of Abramoff documents. McCain had all the evidence. He knew that Abramoff never deliberately set out to shut down the Tigua casino just so he could persuade them to pay him $4.2 million to get it reopened. And yet McCain sat back and allowed Schmidt's Tigua fairy tale to gain currency, even though he knew it to be false. It was axiomatic that if Schmidt's claim had been true, there would have been scores of scheming, sophomoric Abramoff e-mails supporting her claim, whose existence McCain would have loudly proclaimed. The problem was that there weren't any such e-mails. Not one.

And who was C. Bryant Rogers who had telephoned the Tigua on Abramoff's behalf? He was the former husband of the Choctaw's strategic planner, Nell Rogers. In effect, the Choctaw were only too happy to recommend their extraordinary lobbyist to the Tigua. Again, this was something McCain omitted.

"After I killed [Hinojosa's bill], the Tigua and [Alabama-Coushatta] coalition announced they would reload and try to push it through next time around. This was a real threat to the Louisiana Coushatta, considering how close they'd come," says Abramoff. "The problem was my client [the Louisiana Coushatta] were getting spread thin by fighting the Jenas [who were trying to build a nearby casino] and slots at [nearby] race tracks. I had to stop future efforts to pass that Texas bill. If I could remove half of that coalition, it would tilt the odds forever against the Alabama-Coushatta. The Texas threat would be gone and my client could focus on fights within Louisiana. Plus, if it worked, I'd have another huge client. And the Louisiana Coushatta had no problem with the Tigua getting a casino, since they were a world away."

After C. Bryant Rogers's phone call to the Tigua, the tribe's spokesman, Marc Schwartz, was instructed to contact Abramoff. They spoke and agreed that Abramoff and Scanlon would come to El Paso to pitch their solution to the tribe's problem. McCain included another sophomoric Abramoff e-mail, this one written on February 6th:

> **Abramoff: Fire up the jet baby, we're going to El Paso!!**

> **Scanlon: I want all their MONEY!!!**

On February 11th, Ralph Reed, who had been so instrumental in helping to block the Texas legislation, e-mailed Abramoff. Reed alerted him that the Tigua would have to close their casino the following day. McCain, however, deceitfully employed an ellipsis in quoting Reed's email: "**major victory…but note they plan a legislative battle now that they have lost in court.**" The implication was that closing down the Tigua casino was the "**major victory.**"

But McCain had omitted something crucial. What Reed had actually written—along with Abramoff's response—clearly indicated that the Tigua shut down was just a preliminary step towards the goal of shutting down the casino of the Alabama-Coushatta.

> **Reed: Major victory…[and now] on to Livingston [the city where the Alabama-Coushatta were located.]**

> **Abramoff: Ultimately, as you can imagine, the main target is the AC [Alabama Coushatta].**

Those were startling omissions. The probable reason McCain did not include the e-mails was that they would have undermined Schmidt's entire premise. Instead, McCain inserted the following e-mail to drive home once again Abramoff's alleged "disdain" for his tribal clients:

> **I wish those moronic Tiguas were smarter in their political contributions. I'd love us to get our mitts on that moolah!! Oh well, stupid folks get wiped out.**

The following day—which was the day police showed up to close down the Tigua casino—Abramoff and Scanlon flew into El Paso and made a 45-minute presentation before the tribal council. Their plan was to engineer a federal legislative fix. A friendly lawmaker in Washington would slip some innocuous-sounding language into a piece of federal legislation that would allow the Tigua to reopen its casino. Lobbyists and lawmakers did this routinely. The tribe would have to make some strategic political contributions, and Scanlon would have to mount a grassroots campaign to ensure that the language was not stripped from the bill before President Bush signed it into law. Abramoff predicted that all of this could probably be accomplished in about four months. During that time, he would work *pro bono*. Otherwise, he would have to file paperwork in Washington, which might draw unwelcome attention to what he was doing, allowing his or the tribe's enemies to block it.

Once the casino was up and running again, the tribe would pay his firm a monthly retainer of $150,000. Scanlon would submit a proposal to the tribe in a few days, but his total fees would run in the $5 million range. The following day Schwartz e-mailed Abramoff, thanking him for his presentation:

> **Schwartz: Certainly enjoyed your visit and efforts to help our client. I look forward to receiving your proposal and we will do everything possible to make it come to fruition.**
>
> **Abramoff forwarded this email to Scanlon and wrote: "This guy NEEDS us to save his ass!!"**

On February 18, Abramoff sent Schwartz an e-mail with Scanlon's strategy plan, dubbed "Operation Open Doors." Abramoff cautioned that the strategy was not "fool proof...[but] could [not] be classified as high risk either."

> ...Operation Open Doors is a massive undertaking fueled by a nation-wide political operation...The network we are building for you will give you the political clout needed to end...the obstacles you face in your own back yard. Simply put, you need 218 friends

in the U.S. House and 51 Senators on your side very quickly, and we will do that through both love and fear.

On February 19, Scanlon e-mailed Abramoff with an article in *The El Paso Times* that the Tigua had to fire 450 people because its casino had been shut down.

Scanlon: This was on the front page of today's paper while they will be voting on our plan!

Abramoff: Is life great or what!!

"I cannot stress enough how mortified I am to read my jocular and careless juvenile e-mails these many years later" says Abramoff. "The truth is that we had a locker-room atmosphere in our efforts, playing hard and talking hard. Many of my e-mails were joking and some were serious, fueled by the testosterone of the jock lobbyist culture I inhabited. However, any an all that were or can in any way be seen to be hateful, I regret and wish were never typed, let alone sent. It will haunt me to my grave, since they convey impressions which were exactly the opposite of those I held of my clients, whom I loved and was willing and did spill my blood for."

Two weeks later, the Tigua hired Abramoff and agreed to pay Scanlon $4.2 million. Of course, McCain repeated his misleading mantra that Abramoff had never "disclosed...that [he] had any type of financial interests in Scanlon's operation." Furthermore, McCain claimed that the "tribe had no idea that Abramoff, Scanlon, and Reed had just worked to ensure the closure of its casino." This was important to support McCain's and Schmidt's claim that Abramoff had been underhanded, because if the Tigua knew that Abramoff had helped to shut down their casino and still agreed to hire him, it could only mean that its tribal leaders understood that he had worked to shut down the Alabama-Coushatta, and that the closing of the Tigua casino was simply inadvertent, collateral damage.

"It was clear to everyone that one of the reasons that Scanlon and I had credibility with the Tiguas was that we were the very ones responsible for the defeat of the Texas legislation. The Alabama Coushatta's lobbyists spent full time blaming me in particular for their inability to get the AC legalized gaming," says Abramoff," so of course the Tigua knew. It actually became a joke between [the Tigua tribal leadership], Scanlon and me that now the tribe had the devil working for them, instead of against them…but of course, they didn't want the AC to know we were working for them."

Abramoff and his team went right to work. On March 7th, they considered several pieces of pending legislation—an energy bill, a terrorism insurance bill, and an employment insurance bill—into which the "Tigua provision" could be inserted. On March 20th, it seemed the final battle plan was taking shape. Abramoff sent an e-mail to Scanlon, saying that Rep. Bob Ney was on board:

> **Just met with Ney!!! We're f'ing gold!!! He's going to do Tigua. Call me.**

This was how it typically worked. The Tigua's legislative fix would be appended in this case to the 2002 Election Reform Act, euphemistically called the Help America Vote Act. This bill would ban unions and corporations from making "soft" money contributions to political campaigns. Slightly different versions of the bill had passed the U. S. House and Senate. Whenever that occurred, the differences were ironed out in a joint "Conference Committee." The managers of that committee were Ney for the House and Sen. Christopher Dodd (D-CT) for the Senate. Six days later, Abramoff advised Schwartz that it might be a good idea if the Tigua would send checks totaling $32,000 to two Ney political action committees and to his campaign committee. This the tribe promptly did. Abramoff also wanted the tribe to make $300,000 in other contributions to Washington lawmakers on both sides of the aisle. The tribe promptly did this as well.

Two years later, Ney would deny any knowledge of the tribe's existence. In a private interview with McCain's Senate Indian Affairs Committee in the fall of 2004, the Ohio congressman would claim that Abramoff had told him that Sen. Dodd wanted to insert a provision into the bill to benefit a gaming tribe in the state of Connecticut. Furthermore, Ney claimed there was never any mention of a tribe in Texas and that he was not even familiar with the Tigua.

Apparently, Ney's interview with McCain was leaked to *The Washington Post*, because six days later Susan Schmidt reported that Ney had met with Tigua tribal officials in August 2002, and praised Abramoff and said he would support inserting the Tigua provision into the election bill. Interestingly, the meeting, which lasted almost two hours, took place just a few days after Ney had returned from the Scotland golf junket for which Abramoff, Volz, Safavian, Heaton, and Ney would later be indicted. The tribe's Lt. Gov. Carlos Hisa remembered that Ney "had a terrible sunburn. He was red like a lobster from that Scotland trip." And on June 27, 2006, the Tigua released a photograph, showing a smiling Ney meeting with Hisa and another tribal member in a House hearing room on August 14, 2002.

Back in May 2002, Abramoff was busy engineering the Tigua legislative fix. He had taken care of the House side of the Conference Committee by enlisting Ney's support. Abramoff had given him the following language to insert into the Help America Vote Act:

> **Public Law 100-89 is amended by striking section 107 (101 Stat. 668, 672.)**

It was intentionally arcane. Those thirteen words and numbers would magically remove the anti-gambling provisions of the federal law that recognized the Tigua as an official Indian tribe (under the Restoration Act) and would instantly place the tribe under a different federal law (Indian Gaming Regulatory Act), which would have allowed the Tigua to eventually reopen their Las Vegas-style casino.

The Tigua would later complain to McCain that they'd been defrauded, especially by Scanlon. But at the time, the tribe's e-mails suggest that it was excited about its lobbyist. Over the years, Abramoff and legions of other lobbyists had routinely inserted riders and earmarks into congressional bills. In fact, it used to be a regular event and was how business got done in the nation's capital.

"The language was the essence of stealth and it would pass through without any fight, which is what I wanted," says Abramoff. "No one who was not intimately involved with the Tiguas would have any clue what this was and [the Tigua] knew how important it was to not alert [the Alabama-Coushatta] that they were getting screwed, who also had lobbyists in DC...It was not out of the goodness of my heart that my firm would work *pro bono* and I told them this. It was because every time I landed a client, *The Washington Post*, *The Hill*, or *Roll Call* would write about it. I could not make a move which was not noted in the press. In those days, though, the coverage was positive. The Tigua would start paying [my firm] once the provision became law and [their casino] was [back] open for business."

But Abramoff had badly blundered. He had placed Scanlon in charge of handling the Senate side. His job was to enlist Dodd's support. Soon, Scanlon would tell the Tigua:

> We began to target Senator Dodd using a system of repeated contact from influential members of his political family. At the cornerstone of the project was the vice chairperson of the DNC and a member of [Dodd's] finance committee, Lottie Shackelford.

Apparently, Scanlon did make about $50,000 in political contributions to achieve this goal, but there was subsequently a spate of explanations, denials, excuses, and contradictions from the parties involved. Thanks to reassurances from Scanlon, Abramoff was confident that Dodd was on board and the Tigua fix was assured. For example, on May 13, 2002, Scanlon wrote to Schwartz, with a copy to Abramoff, updating him about the situation:

> All of the major players on the election reform package have given their support.

By mid-July, the staffs of the conference committee, who had been meeting regularly to iron out the differences between the House and Senate versions, were close to resolving all remaining issues. Finally, Ney approached Dodd about the Tigua provision and discovered there was a "fly in the ointment." On July 25th, a dumbfounded Abramoff sent Scanlon the following e-mail:

> I just spoke to Ney who met today with Dodd on the bill and raised our provision. Dodd looked at him like a "deer in headlights" and said he has never made such a commitment and that, with the problems of new casinos in Connecticut, it is a problem!!! Mike, please call me immediately to tell me how we wired this, or were supposed to wire it. Ney feels we left him out to dry. Please call me!!!

Two years later, McCain would ask Michael Scanlon, who appeared under subpoena before the Senate Indian Affairs Committee but refused to answer questions, about this very matter:

> **You were responsible for lining up political supporters to assist the Tigua Tribe in reopening its casino. You told Mr. Abramoff and the tribal council you had the Senate's support. You told them, "All the major players on the election reform package have given their support on our issue." In fact… numerous witnesses have told the committee that nothing you told Mr. Abramoff and the tribe about Senate support was accurate. When Mr. Abramoff found out that you did not have the Senate's support you had bragged about…He later demanded that you "get our money back from the person who was supposed to take care of arranging Senate support."**
> **When did you come up with this scheme to not only con the tribe but con your partner?**

Abramoff had believed Scanlon's version that there had simply been an apparent mix-up in communication. Abramoff didn't share the bad news with the Tigua. Instead, he told them there was a snafu, which would cause a delay in the final vote on the bill. And when Congress went into its August recess, it gave Abramoff some breathing room to somehow persuade Dodd to change his mind. The Election Reform bill would now come up for a vote sometime in the fall.

When Ney returned from the Scotland golf junket and met with the Tigua representatives on August 14th, Schwartz remembered that Ney's chief of staff, William Heaton, gave Abramoff a warm bear hug, and Lt. Gov. Hisa recalled that Ney informed him that "he and Senator Dodd were committed to getting the language in the bill and that he did not foresee any problem with the Tigua-related provision." This was obviously less than truthful.

In early October, the Election Reform bill passed without the Tigua rider. According to Schwartz, Abramoff told him that "Congressman Ney had reported Senator Dodd had gone back on his word and stripped the

THE PERFECT VILLAIN

measure from the committee report." During a conference call between Ney and Tigua officials a few days later, Schwartz said that Ney expressed "disbelief that Senator Dodd had gone back on his word"... and said "that [Ney] would continue to work on the issue and believed that the tribe was entitled to their gaming operation." Ney would find a way to insert the Tigua provision into another measure in 2003.

Abramoff says he was determined to keep trying and the tribe continued to believe in its lobbyist with great enthusiasm, which was made clear in the following e-mail from Marc Schwartz to Abramoff:

-----Original Message-----

From: Mjschwartz@aol.com
[mailto:Mjschwartz@aol.com]

Sent: Wednesday, January 08, 2003 11:08 PM
To: abramoffj@gtlaw.com
Subject: OUTSTANDING!

What can I say...you are an impressive guy! Art [Senclair, the new chief] is still raving about your drive, dedication and compassion. Thanks for keeping us alive...Thanks for everything!!! Marc

And Abramoff maintains that he never stopped trying to solve the Tigua problem until he was forced to resign from Greenberg Traurig a year later

* * * * * * * * * * * * * *

In addition to its dishonesty, the McCain report was also incompetent. McCain had accused Abramoff of charging outrageous fees and receiving "kickbacks"—none of which was illegal. McCain had also accused Abramoff of defrauding his tribal clients, a claim overwhelmingly contradicted by the evidence in McCain's possession. And yet when he had the opportunity to accuse Abramoff of an apparently egregious conflict of interest, McCain blew it. He had the evidence in the palm of his hand, because he had all the e-mails, but he didn't realize what he had.

In the spring of 2002, shortly after the Tigua had hired Abramoff and Scanlon to get their casino reopened, the tribe was concerned about what would happen when it became known that they had obtained an exclusive legislative fix to reopen its casino. Would the Alabama-Coushatta go ballistic? Would they scream bloody murder? What if the Alabama-Coushatta's outrage caused Congress to rescind the Tigua legislative fix? Should Abramoff consider including the Alabama-Coushatta in that legislative fix as well?

Abramoff did agree to include the Alabama-Coushatta and apparently wanted additional compensation for doing so. Was Abramoff now working against his Louisiana Coushatta client?

In an April 18, 2002 e-mail, Abramoff asked an associate in his firm to redraft the language of the rider so that the Alabama-Coushatta would enjoy the exemption as well:

> **I might have worked the deal with the Alabama-Coushattas. Don't tell anyone for now.**

Abramoff asked the same associate—in a June 27, 2002 e-mail—to write up a consulting agreement with the Alabama-Coushatta:

> **Draft an airtight agreement between XYZ corporation (to be named later) and the Alabama-Coushatta Tribe of Texas.**

According to a lawsuit later filed by the Alabama-Coushatta tribe against Abramoff and others, Abramoff wanted 10% of the Tribe's gaming revenue in perpetuity, in exchange for getting its casino reopened. Interestingly, the lawsuit failed to provide any Abramoff e-mail to support this claim.

The following day, on June 28, 2002, Abramoff e-mailed the consulting agreement to Schwartz, who was dealing directly with the Alabama-Coushatta.

On another matter, Abramoff had also e-mailed Schwartz to ask if the Tigua would help fund Ney's golf trip to Scotland with a $50,000 donation. There was no mention of his asking for a donation from the Alabama-Coushatta. Abramoff brought up the subject again in an e-mail to Schwartz on July 8, 2002. Abramoff asked if the Tigua were going to make a donation to the upcoming Scotland golf trip, and if the Alabama-Coushatta had reviewed his consulting contract. Again, there was no mention of his asking the Alabama-Coushatta to contribute to the golf trip.

According to the Alabama-Coushatta lawsuit (filed in July 2006), Schwartz claimed that on that very same day, he telephoned Abramoff informing him that the Alabama-Coushatta had refused to sign the consulting agreement, and that the Tigua would not be subsidizing Ney's "educational" and "fact-finding" trip to Scotland. Schwartz claimed that Abramoff then asked if the Alabama-Coushatta might be willing to help sponsor the golf trip. However, there were no e-mails corroborating Schwartz' claim that Abramoff had asked for a contribution from the Alabama-Coushatta.

Two days later Schwartz did write a memo to the tribe's Lt. Gov. Carlos Hisa about the golf trip, and again Schwartz never mentioned any request by Abramoff for a donation from the Alabama-Coushatta. In fact, Schwartz stated the following:

> **Neither the Tiguas nor the Alabama-Coushattas has been solicited to underwrite this educational trip abroad, but I would strongly recommend that both Tribes consider [it]...There is an educational foundation that will actually be sending the delegation abroad and if you and the Alabama-Coushatta Tribe were to divide the [$100,000] cost, it would send a very strong message to the very powerful member of the Congressional leadership team.**

The Tigua then contacted and successfully persuaded the Alabama-Coushatta to donate to the golf trip. The Tigua implied that they too were helping to fund the trip. On July 18th, Schwartz sent an e-mail to Kevin Battise, the Alabama-Coushatta's chairman:

> **Thanks to you and your Council for agreeing to assist in the effort. Your $50,000 check should be made payable to the Capital Athletic Foundation.**[169]

On July 24th, Abramoff deposited the $50,000 check from the Alabama-Coushatta into the foundation's account at the Sun Trust Bank. The tribe was under the impression that the Tigua would be funding the other half of the golf trip, but the Tigua never did.

On the same day he made that deposit, Abramoff received an e-mail from Ralph Reed informing him that the court had finally given Attorney General Cornyn the final order to shut down the Alabama-Coushatta casino.

According to the 2006 lawsuit, Abramoff then forwarded this e-mail to Scanlon, asking him to tell the Louisiana Coushatta that he and Scanlon needed more money to keep the Alabama-Coushatta from reopening their casino.

According to Abramoff, a very different series of events had unfolded.

"Our consistent goal was to prevent the AC [Alabama-Coushatta] from operating a casino, which would have hurt our client's casino in [Louisiana]. That meant stopping a class-3 casino," says Abramoff. A class-3 casino is a full-scale Las Vegas-style casino. A class-2 casino is a bingo parlor. According to Abramoff, the Louisiana Coushatta didn't care if the Alabama-Coushatta operated a class-2 casino. It was only their operation of a class-3 casino that would threaten the Louisiana Coushatta's livelihood.

"At first, we were going to stop them from anything, and in fact, we worked to shut down their illegally opened class-3 casino, as you know," says Abramoff.

He did not want any attention drawn to his efforts on Capitol Hill, because Sen. Phil Gramm (R-TX), "who was an implacable foe of the Tigua—one of their chiefs had said something racist about Gramm's Asian wife, Wendy, I believe—would put a hold on the bill. Therefore, the effort [to get the legislative fix for the Tigua] required stealth, which is why we did not register, for better or worse."[170]

Abramoff says the Tigua wanted to somehow include the Alabama-Coushatta in the federal legislative fix, and he agreed to consider it only if this was acceptable to his Louisiana client: "I went to Worfel, since at every step along the way I consulted him for approval. Schwartz continually was more into peacemaking with the AC, but he always put the Tigua first. And [the Tigua] were not at all unhappy to smash the AC to bits if that's what it took for them to get their casino back. Anyway, Worfel agreed that if we got them [the Alabama-Coushatta] into [the rider], they would be eligible [only] for a class-2 casino, which would not be a threat to [the Louisiana Coushatta's] class-3 casino. But—and this is the key—he wanted either to have a share of their revenue for [his tribe] or that they should put up money into a political contributions pot and [help] pay for all the political efforts going forward. That was the genesis of the agreement to the XYZ corporation for 10%, which I drafted and sent to Schwartz to send to them."[171]

Abramoff says that the 10% was entirely for the Louisiana Coushatta. None of that money would have been going into his pocket.

As for the Alabama-Coushatta's $50,000 contribution to the Capital Athletic Foundation for the 2002 golf junket to Scotland, Abramoff says, "I guess my approach was that the money which we got from the AC... was really money that we were supposed to get from the Tigua and that they got it from the AC. In my mind this did not create a fiduciary relationship with the AC, since I never asked them to put in the money and since the money was to 'cover' the obligation of the Tigua."

Abramoff shakes his head and shrugs. He knows this is complex and difficult to understand.

After reflecting for a moment, he adds, "I don't think I was skullduggerous, other than the normal of the business. I had two clients with a set of subtle, consistent interests, and I wanted to maximize the financial opportunity for all of us and still win. That is what I did everywhere."

CHAPTER FORTY-NINE
JUDGE HUCK

It was tense in the Miami courtroom of federal district Judge Paul C. Huck in the early afternoon of September 28, 2006. His official court reporter, Patricia Sanders, waited for the judge's clerk to finish adjusting the speaker phones. Finally, all of the far-flung participants in the teleconference hearing announced their presence. Edward Nucci, acting head of the Public Integrity Division of the Department of Justice and his assistant Kendall Day, along with Abramoff's attorney's Abbe Lowell and Pamela Marple were calling in from Washington, D.C.; Kidan's attorney Joseph Conway was in Mineola, New York; assistant U. S. Attorneys Lawrence LaVecchio and Paul Schwartz were in Ft. Lauderdale; and Kidan's local attorney Jonathan Rosenthal and Abramoff's attorney local Neal Sonnett were in Miami.

Six months before Judge Huck had sentenced Abramoff and Kidan to 70 months in prison, but had stayed their sentences for 90 days to allow them to continue cooperating with prosecutors. It was assumed that Huck would behave like most judges and grant all future requests for extension. At the end of June, Huck did renew the prosecutors' request, staying the defendants' sentences for another 90 days. But three months later, Huck decided to send them to prison.

During the September 28th telephone conference call, Huck told Nucci, the acting head of Public Integrity for the Department of Justice:

> There comes a time when people must pay the piper. I think that time has come.

Nucci could not believe what he was hearing. Huck was going to destroy or seriously impede the investigation by unnecessarily putting Abramoff in prison long before his cooperation was completed. Nucci, who until just a few weeks earlier had served as a federal prosecutor in south Florida and had appeared before Huck many times, pleaded with him by phone to grant the 90-day extension:

> What we need to get from Mr. Abramoff is going to be impossible to get if he is incarcerated… At this point I would ask your honor to take my word as an officer of the court how hard we have been working, how much time was spent with Mr. Abramoff and how much needs to be done.

Apparently Judge Huck, a former bankruptcy lawyer, who may not have had a clue as to how tortuous political corruption cases could be, did not accept Nucci's word. Huck seemed more concerned about his conception of public perception than about putting the kibosh on perhaps the most far-reaching Washington corruption scandal in the nation's history.

> This is a relatively high profile case, [which] has received a great deal of media attention. And I am concerned about the public's confidence in the judicial process. Back in March sentencing occurred. It is now the end of

> September, almost October, and [Abramoff] is still out [of prison]…
>
> There is no reason what you are saying you want to accomplish in the next ninety days could not have been accomplished in the past nine months…All we're talking about now is historical facts and data. Now it's a matter of putting those things in the proper form and reviewing them. If you have a case, then indict it or seek a plea agreement, whatever you need to do… I don't want to tie the government's hands but until there is some pressure, until there's a deadline, nothing gets accomplished…
>
> It's not my responsibility to get this work done, it's your responsibility.

Huck then ordered Abramoff to report to prison on November 15th.[172] The following day the House Government Reform Committee released a report documenting 485 contacts Abramoff and his team had had with the White House, including nearly 100 with Karl Rove.

CHAPTER FIFTY
TIME MACHINE

The day of reckoning had been fast approaching, and now it was November 14, 2006. In a few hours, Abramoff would report to prison. There were many last-minute things to attend to. "It feels like I'm going to my funeral," Abramoff says, as I drove him to the barbershop, "except it's worse, because I'm not actually dying."

He got a buzz cut, so he could postpone a prison haircut as long as possible. We then had lunch at a sushi restaurant. He seemed to savor every morsel. This would be his last taste of raw fish for several years. As always, we split the bill. After lunch, we took his black BMW 745Li with tinted windows to be washed and detailed, because later that afternoon he would be selling the car. He needed the money. "I used to be a millionaire," he says. "Now, I'm a thousandaire."

The media had touted his BMW as an example of Abramoff's greedy and sybaritic lifestyle, because he used to have a driver and had the vehicle equipped with nearly $50,000 in extras, including a radar detector etched into the rearview mirror.[173]

For a man heading off to a long prison term, Abramoff seemed remarkably composed. He sounded philosophical, apparently drawing on his deep faith, which presumably was saving him from utter collapse. He did not seem despondent. He spoke articulately and even joked about his impending confinement. He received a steady stream of phone calls from saddened friends. Incredibly, it was he who seemed to be doing the comforting.

What had Abramoff been like before his disgrace and humiliation? Had his tone and spirit been markedly different? How had his personality changed? Was he as respectful and deferential back then? Did he listen as attentively, patiently, and sympathetically as he does now? The Abramoff I know never cut off or interrupted the person he was talking to. On occasion, because his telephone number was listed, he received nasty calls. Instead of hanging up, he simply listened as the caller vented. Occasionally, he might quietly respond monosyllabically. Was Abramoff so thoroughly beaten down that taking abuse from total strangers was now a part of his penance?

Obviously, it would be impossible to know what he used to be like. And then suddenly, a glimpse of the past magically appeared on my computer screen.

A blogger from the DailyKos, who had never forgiven Abramoff for lobbying for the Northern Mariana Islands, had been obsessively following his career since 1999. The blogger, a superb researcher, had a treasure trove of materials on the lobbyist, including an "archived" speech Abramoff gave to the College Republican National Convention in late June 2001. The blogger happened to send it to me as an e-mail attachment in the waning hours of Abramoff's freedom.

Abramoff had just wandered off with his children, so I sat alone in his study, which was walled with books, mostly in Hebrew. Next to his three computers, a prescription bottle of Ambien sat on his desk. He had been taking the drug for the past two years to help him sleep. I began watching the blogger's video. It opened with Ralph Reed in mid-speech at the podium. He was giving a superbly smooth and intelligent extemporaneous speech, occasionally punctuated with a diabolical laugh.[174]

Near the end of Reed's speech, Abramoff suddenly appeared. He was bearded, wearing rimless glasses, and packing a few extra pounds. Invited up to the podium, Abramoff was introduced as "probably the best chairman the College Republicans have ever had."

The convention was being held in a large conference room in the Capitol Hilton Hotel, filled with mostly well-dressed college students. All of the usual suspects were slated to address the conservative youngsters: House Majority Whip Tom DeLay, former College Republican chairman and current presidential advisor Karl Rove, retired Col. Oliver North, and Grover Norquist.

Abramoff adjusted the microphone and began. Like Reed, he was articulate and spoke extemporaneously. But Abramoff seemed more likeable, engaging, warm, and humble. And while Reed had been slick and strictly business, Abramoff was funny, irreverent, and gestured with enthusiasm, almost joyfully. Viewing the footage of his upbeat manner, knowing that he was a doomed man, I found mesmerizing and poignant.

Abramoff told the audience how much he loathed the "political-correctness movement" and referred to himself as a "Reagan baby." He recounted a story about a trip he took to Germany when he was College Republican chairman 20 years before. Youth members of the Socialist Democrats, the leftist government in power at the time, were sitting around a room, saying how evil and moronic Ronald Reagan was.

His eyes twinkling, Abramoff told his listeners, "In an intemperate moment, I said, 'Look, he's our president; we love him; he's our hero. And frankly, we don't appreciate that and we don't pick on you guys.'" Then switching to a perfect German accent, Abramoff continued, "'And vat do you mean *pick* on uz?'" Abramoff paused, smiling, "'Well, you know you're not faring much better than the last Socialist Party that ran Germany,' which, of course, was [Hitler's] National Socialist Party." The audience laughed. "Well, that got me kicked out of the building and sent to the airport." The audience erupted into applause.

Abramoff also spoke about his tenure in 1980 as head of the Massachusetts College Republicans when he attended Brandeis, and how he and Norquist had drummed up support for Ronald Reagan.

"Massachusetts wasn't a target state…[The Republican National Committee] never thought they'd win Massachusetts, so we literally got nothing [from them]. We had no bumper stickers…[and we] had like seven Reagan buttons…We didn't have e-mail…there were no fax machines back then. This was ancient times. There wasn't even Federal Express…There was a guy on a horse who carried the mail around and that was it."

There was audience laughter.

"Grover and I used to have a saying that to take the Soviets out you needed two atomic weapons: one to go to Moscow; the other to take out Harvard Square…"

There was more laughter from the audience. I put the video on pause and stared out the window. It seemed amazing that Abramoff and I had never discussed my politics, which are quite different from his. He did know that I live in the People's Republic of Cambridge, Massachusetts, which should have told him something. He didn't know that for the past 20 years I've actually lived at ground zero—in the heart of Harvard Square.

I clicked the play button and watched the rest of the video. For the past twenty-four minutes, the original Jack Abramoff had appeared before me. He didn't seem so different from the man who had just walked back into the room, sat down behind his desk, and was now checking his e-mail, perhaps for the last time in a while. For someone about to surrender himself into the clutches of the federal prison system as a convicted felon, he seemed at peace, or at least resigned.

He apologized for leaving me alone for so long and asked me what I had been doing. I closed my computer and shook my head: "Nothing much."

It was now 10 pm. In about six hours, he would depart on a two-and-a-half hour journey to a federal prison near the Maryland-West Virginia border.

I asked him if he had any final thoughts.

"It is what it is," he says sadly.

EPILOGUE
IT ISN'T WHAT IT IS

Dubbed the "Abramoff prosecutor," Noel L. Hillman, chief of the Public Integrity Division of the Justice Department, suddenly stepped down on January 26, 2006. His resignation was announced just three weeks after Abramoff had pleaded guilty and agreed to cooperate in an ever-widening probe, whose targets were clearly Republican lawmakers and government officials. Abramoff was in an excellent position to provide incriminating information, because of his close links to so many of the GOP elite and their staff.

Hillman had been described in the media as hands-on, aggressive and relentless prosecutor. He was known for being independent-minded and highly respected. He was someone who would not bend to political pressure from his superiors.

President Bush had nominated Hillman for a federal judgeship. Bush, who claimed that this nomination had been in the works for nearly a year, was effectively getting rid of Hillman by kicking him upstairs. The timing of this announcement seemed highly suspicious. Sen. Charles Schumer (D-NY) worried that Bush "might have something to risk" and might "choose a particular type of person" to replace Hillman who was less aggressive and less committed to uncovering the truth.

The Abramoff scandal was perhaps the most serious corruption probe since Watergate. There had even been calls for Bush to name a special prosecutor, which he had ignored.

Hillman's temporary replacement was Andrew Lourie, a seasoned south Florida prosecutor. This would be his second stint as the Acting Section Chief of the Public Integrity Division. Few doubted he would last long. They were wrong.

Lourie would now report directly to the Chief of the Justice Department's Criminal Division, Alice Fisher, a Bush political appointee. Her appointment had been controversial, due to her lack of any prior experience as a federal prosecutor.

A veteran former Washington D.C. federal prosecutor, Nancy Luque, who was not involved in the Abramoff probe but was familiar with it, points out, "[The] Public Integrity [Division] was allowed to drift [in the Abramoff investigation.]" Indeed, Bush left Hillman's post vacant, never appointing his permanent replacement. Lourie continued as "acting" chief for more than two years until he finally resigned in February 2008. Alice Fisher quit three months after that.

The effect of Judge Huck's decision to prematurely imprison Abramoff was to severely limit the probe, all but silencing its star witness. The five-hour round-trip journey that the prosecutors would now have to endure between Washington and Abramoff's new residence in Cumberland, Maryland, proved to be an inefficient use of time. During Abramoff's first year of incarceration, prosecutors visited him infrequently. This was in stark contrast to their five-day-a-week meetings with him, often for ten hours at a stretch, for the many months before he went to prison. Back then, Abramoff would even be given "homework"—reams of his e-mails on computer discs—to study and explain the following day. Once in prison, he reportedly could not prepare for these visits, because prisoners were not allowed to have personal computers.

Therefore, thanks to Huck's decision, the Bush Administration could breathe a sign of relief. Many GOP lawmakers and government officials—who had been so cozy with Abramoff—were keeping a watchful eye on the clock, hoping that the five-year statute of limitations would run out on any crimes that they might have committed.

Another problem handicapping the investigation was that there was frequent turnover among the prosecutors and investigators at the Department of Justice. New arrivals would need time to get up to speed on the investigation, which would also slow down the probe.

Nancy Luque points out that in reality there was not even a need for the Abramoff prosecutors to make the five-hour round-trip journey. "If I had been in charge [and had a grand-jury nearby], I would have simply issued a 'writ,' ordering a federal marshal to deliver Abramoff to my office in Washington, D.C.," she says. "I could have put him in the DC jail each night, or stuck him in a motel with a marshal sitting outside his room for months or years until I had run out of questions to ask him."

Except for Rep. Bob Ney, who had been caught pocketing over $50,000 from an Arab arms merchant, no other congressmen or high government officials had been indicted. On April 22, 2008, Robert Coughlin, a minor Justice Department official, pleaded guilty to a conflict-of-interest felony, for having accepted a few free meals and sports tickets from Team Abramoff's Kevin Ring. On June 2, 2008 John Albaugh, the former chief of staff for former congressman Ernest Istook (R-OK), pleaded guilty to one count of bribery. He'd accepted tickets to Abramoff's private boxes for sports events and concerts, and enjoyed some free meals at Abramoff's restaurant.

"In the business, these guilty pleas of minor officials are called 'road kill,'" says Luque, now a nationally respected private attorney who defended Jonathan Pollard and Brent Wilkes, among other high-profile cases. "There have been no high-value indictments" in the Abramoff case.

A source close to the investigation says, "[The Department of] Justice wants [Tom] DeLay and [Karl] Rove, but so far they're refusing to plead [guilty]."

Abramoff had not yet been sentenced in Washington D. C. There, U. S. District Court Judge Ellen Huvelle had been following the usual practice of waiting for Abramoff to complete his cooperation, so that she could then consent to the prosecutors' recommendation for a reduction of sentence.

Finally, on June 9, 2008 prosecutors appeared before Judge Huvelle to request that she schedule Abramoff's sentencing for September 4, 2008—at which time they would recommend a reduction of sentence— for the three felony counts to which he had pleaded guilty back in January 2006: bribery, honest-services fraud, and tax evasion.

Normally, prosecutors requested a sentence reduction—called a Rule 35—when the defendant's cooperation had been substantially completed.

Therefore, it could be inferred that—as far as the prosecutors were concerned—Abramoff's cooperation was drawing to a close.

According to federal sentencing guidelines, Abramoff was probably facing a total of 9 ½ years in prison for the three felony counts. It was expected that the prosecutors would recommend a 50% reduction in his sentence, bringing it to 4 years and 9 months. (In addition, it was expected that prosecutors in south Florida would ask Judge Huck for a 50% reduction in Abramoff's 70-month sentence for wire fraud, bringing that to just under 3 years. Since both sentences would run concurrently, Abramoff would serve time only for the longer sentence, and would be credited for the 22 months already served.)

Based on Abramoff's time served, along with a probable one-year reduction for completing a drug rehab program (due to his previous dependency on Ambien) and a seven-month reduction for good behavior, Abramoff would be released from prison in April or May 2009, to a six-month stay in a half-way house. (After six weeks, however, he would probably be transferred to home confinement and required to wear an ankle bracelet.)

In the final analysis, Abramoff's decision to plead guilty and cooperate with prosecutors saved him from a possible life sentence in a maximum-security prison with violent offenders. Instead, he would most likely return to his wife and five children after having served less than three years in a minimum-security prison camp.

* * * * * * * * * * * * * * *

It is clear that Abramoff never bribed anyone. He never had to. He was the best at what he did. He simply played the game—along with the other 35,000 registered lobbyists—in order to gain access to lawmakers and public officials so that his clients' concerns could be heard. His right to petition Congress was guaranteed by the First Amendment.

It seems that Abramoff's tax-evasion charge was simply tacked on to placate prosecutors in the Department of Justice's Tax-Fraud Division. Abramoff donated so much of his money to charitable organizations—all of it deductible from his taxable income—that this charge seemed grossly unfair and unjust. In fact, Abramoff is reportedly owed a sizeable refund from the IRS.

As for the wire fraud charges that landed him in prison prematurely, it is highly unlikely that any jury would have found Abramoff guilty.

He was, however, guilty of one charge: honest-services fraud. It is probably safe to say that every adult in America is guilty of this crime to some extent. What is honest-services fraud? It is defined as a scheme or artifice to deprive another of the "intangible right of honest services." Unfortunately, it is difficult to define "honest-services" without using it in the definition. Nancy Luque says, "I'm an expert in honest services fraud and I have no idea what it means...It's one of those laws that prosecutors use to indict anybody they want."

Many defense attorneys agree with Luque. They say it is a catchall statute that is an ill-defined way for prosecutors to convert almost any kind of behavior into a felony.[175]

Finally, this particular mythic narrative seems to be missing something. Where are the heroes in this story?

Abramoff, the protagonist, is certainly not a hero. Abramoff says that if he had it to do over again, he would never have become a lobbyist, given that lobbyists often inhabit a murky world involving dubious moral conduct. But if influence-peddling is not the most heroic of pursuits, neither is Abramoff the perfect villain as portrayed by the media and McCain. In fact, to the hundreds of recipients of his extraordinary generosity, and to all of his friends and family who stood by him throughout his ordeal, he was a hero.

Neither Susan Schmidt, in particular, nor the media, in general, behaved heroically. Their reporting was disappointing at best, and misleading and less than honorable at worst.

Certainly, Sen. John McCain cannot in this instance be touted as a hero. His manipulation of the evidence in his Senate Indian Affairs Report was dishonest and appalling. If he truly were a man of courage and integrity, he would publicly apologize to Abramoff.

Finally, the Justice Department cannot be viewed as heroic. Federal prosecutors have become the Torquemada, the Grand Inquisitor of the American justice system, unwittingly corrupted by their unlimited power. They suborn perjury by terrifying white-collar defendants into pleading guilty to crimes they may not have committed. Instead, prosecutors seem driven by the pursuit of high conviction rates. They seem to have lost sight of their oath of office—to seek justice.

In the end, no matter how "incontrovertible" the evidence, there will always be other sides to any human story. And there will always be Jack Abramoffs, fallible, larger than life, ambitious, generous, shrewd, foolish.

The perfect villain only exists in stories like *Othello*.

ACKNOWLEDGEMENTS

I would like to thank the following people for their support and assistance in editing and/or researching this book: Carolyn Rieder, Deanne Peterson, Marc Chafetz, Richard Meibers, Al Divver, Jay Weaver, Harry Levy, Leslie Carr, Alex Gibney, Dan Aaron, Jeremiah Healy, James Barretto, Sybille Barrasso, Tom Buckmaster, Fran Barkan, David Brody, and Mark Harty.

FOOTNOTES
PROLOGUE

1. After Ney completed a drug rehabilitation program for alcoholism, his sentence was reduced by one year. He was released in February 2008, having served less than 12 months in prison of his 30 month sentence.

2. Police and prosecutors often pressure suspects to plead guilty. For example, in November 2007, *The New York Times* reported that over a quarter of all convicted rapists and murderers later cleared by DNA evidence had confessed to the crimes for which they were later exonerated.

3. In addition to a 70-month prison sentence, Abramoff must pay millions of dollars in restitution to the tribes he allegedly defrauded.

CHAPTER ONE
FATHER OF ABRAMOFF

4. This was about the same hourly wage Abramoff would later earn in prison.

CHAPTER TWO
EPIPHANY

5. For his restaurant reviews, Gold won the 2007 Pulitzer Prize in criticism.

CHAPTER THREE
THEN THERE WAS ADAM

6. The bettor made a wager on the last digit of the combined gross revenue of all racetracks in New York City. That number would be published the next day in many newspapers. The payoff was about 600 to 1.

CHAPTER FIVE
GETTING ACQUAINTED

7. In 1980, Reagan won 489 electoral votes to incumbent President Jimmy Carter's 89.

8. According to Abramoff, it was the only time a member of the 1980 GOP ticket set foot in Massachusetts.

9. Abramoff persuaded his only opponent, Amy Ridenour, to withdraw from the race. She would go on to found and direct a political nonprofit, the National

Center for Public Policy Research, which would later become entangled in the scandal.

10. This position had once been held by Karl Rove, President George W. Bush's chief political strategist, who would also become embroiled in the Abramoff scandal. The manager of Rove's College Republican campaign was the infamous political trickster, Lee Atwater, nicknamed "Darth Vader." Before Atwater died of a brain tumor in 1991, he apologized for his behavior.

CHAPTER EIGHT
A LESSON

11. Crystal described the purpose of his first meeting with Abramoff as "a grand alliance of conservative students…an alliance that would represent the swing to the right amongst the youth in America and Western Europe."

12. Knowing a veto would be overridden, President Reagan signed the bill in to law.

13. Claims that this invasion was to divert attention from a terrorist attack two days earlier in Lebanon that had killed 239 U.S. Marines was viewed by Abramoff as outrageous.

14. The criminal convictions of John Poindexter and Oliver North were overturned on technicalities. Later, President George W. H. Bush pardoned all Iran-Contra conspirators, including former Defense Secretary Caspar Weinberger, former national security advisor Robert McFarlane, former assistant secretary of state Elliot Abrams; and three former CIA employees. Oliver North, who later ran for Senate from Virginia and lost, became a best-selling author, speech giver, and Fox-News correspondent. And Ronald Reagan, who left office with popularity ratings higher than any departing president since Franklin Roosevelt, was honored by having Washington's National Airport named after him.

CHAPTER TEN
FUNDING FREEDOM

15. Mbeki, who died in 2001, was the father of Thabo Mbeki, South Africa's president from 1999 to 2009.

16. The official presidential announcement omitted the full name of the company: Atlantic City Boardwalk Associates (no ampersand).

CHAPTER ELEVEN
SCORPION

17. Robert Blake, the actor who was acquitted in 2005 of murdering his wife, put it succinctly: "Innocent, until proven broke."

18. South West African Political Organization, now a political party, then a liberation movement.

CHAPTER THIRTEEN
TRANSITION

19. What may have clinched Bush's decision to meet with Dr. Mahathir was Malaysia's immediate support for the war on terrorism after the September 11, 2001, attacks on the United States.

20. Usually for male Orthodox students, a yeshiva is a school for the study of the Torah and the Talmud.

21. The conservative newspaper is owned by the controversial Rev. Sun Myung Moon, founder of the Unification Church. Many conservatives subscribe to The Washington Times, because they loath *The Washington Post*, Abramoff, however, did have a subscription to the Post during most of the scandal.

22. This was a Doers, not a Dewers Scotch, profile.

23. "K-Street" is a commonly used metonym for the think tanks, lobbying firms, law firms that flock to this particular street in Washington, D.C.

24. In 2007, the firm merged with Kirkpatrick & Lockhart Nicholson Graham and became K&L Gates.

25. A TV news talk show distributed by the Christian Broadcasting Network, co-hosted by Pat Robertson.

26. Norquist, whose reputation was later sullied by the Abramoff scandal, was one of the few friends—along with Dana Rohrabacher and Morton Blackwell—who remained loyal to him.

27. In 1992, Norquist invited conservatives to his office for meetings to discuss policy and strategy. These Wednesday meetings soon became an important Washington institution. Years later, even President Bush and Vice President Cheney sent their own aides to these informal get-togethers.

28. Waller is currently on the faculty of the Institute of World Politics in Washington, D.C.

CHAPTER FOURTEEN
DISTANT SPECKS

29. It is officially known as the Commonwealth of Northern Mariana Islands or CNMI.

30. About 14 percent of the native population was receiving food stamps, yet most could afford to hire a Filipino maid. It became so embarrassing that a law was passed forbidding it, which did little to stop the practice.

31. Most of the Northern Marianas population resides on the three largest islands: Tinian, Saipan, and Rota.

32. The Enola Gay, a B-29 Superfortress bomber, dropped the first wartime atomic bomb on the Japanese city of Hiroshima on August 6, 1945.

33. Without admitting wrongdoing, Tan paid $9 million to the workers—the largest fine ever paid to the Labor Department at that time—and promised to spend $1.3 million for renovations in his factories.

34. Allen Stayman was the official over which the media would later vilify Abramoff. He would be accused of forcing Stayman out of his job in July, 2001, with the help of Ralph Reed and Karl Rove. However, Stayman was a Clinton holdover, who would have lost his job anyway.

35. The Office of Insular Affairs oversees federal administration of all United States possessions: American Samoa, Guam, Northern Mariana Islands, U.S. Virgin Islands, Marshall Islands, the Federated States of Micronesia, and Palau.

36. Union of Needletrades, Industrial and Textile Employees.

37. "[Waller] used to work for me when I was chairman of the College Republicans. He was an extremely rightwing college kid, a bit nuts actually, who saw the world and everyone in it in white and black terms. He did some good work for me…but ultimately either left or was fired, and then started this lifelong attack on me…I basically ignored him. He did, however, have his allies…and his contacts in the press. When convenient, he is made to look like a credible source for the media, but for the most part he is a fringe player," says Abramoff.

38. From 1965 to 1979, Meeds—the consummate tree hugger and leaf peeper—served as a liberal Democrat congressman from the state of Washington. Known for his work on conservation and education, he was instrumental in creating the Alpine Lakes Wilderness Area and the North Cascades National Park. Meeds died in 2005.

CHAPTER FIFTEEN
CAME, SAW, GOLFED

39. In an April 3, 2002, *The New York Times* claimed that Abramoff had arranged for 150 congressmen and staff to visit the Marianas, a claim that was not supported by the Preston Gates' billing records.

40. It is said this mass suicide was the final straw in persuading President Harry Truman to drop atomic bombs on Hiroshima and Nagasaki. He feared relentless resistance to an allied invasion of the Japanese homeland would cost a million allied lives.

41. Later, in a secretly (and probably illegally) taped interview, Tan would boast that DeLay had reassured him not to worry. "I make the schedule of the Congress, and I'm not going to put it on the schedule," Tan said, allegedly quoting DeLay. "Forget it, Willie. No chance." Perhaps coincidentally, Tan subsequently made a $650,000 donation to DeLay's favorite charity—the U.S. Family Network, whose stated purpose was the restoration of America's

"moral fitness." The charity was run by Ed Buckham, DeLay's former chief of staff.

CHAPTER SIXTEEN
CROSSING THE LINE?

42. The award-winning filmmaker claimed that several congressmen, who visited the Northern Marianas at Abramoff's behest, frequented Fitial's bars and received sexual favors.

43. "DeLay helps foster kids, because this is where the criminal class comes from," Abramoff told me. "I really admired him and learned a lot from him."

44. A term for a Congressional bill, often a minor one, to which many amendments are attached usually to benefit of constituents or special interests.

45. At the time, there was a one-year ban on former staff having any contact with the lawmakers for which they had worked. The ban has been extended to two years.

46. As of August 2008, Rudy's and Scanlon's final sentences continued to be deferred pending completion of their cooperation.

47. On April 10, 2008, Congress finally passed legislation, extending U.S. immigration laws to and establishing a guest-worker program for the Mariana Islands. Rep. George Miller praised the new law: "We sought these changes so that we could put a stop to the well-documented and widespread abuse of poor men and women in the garment and tourism industry in the CNMI." Ben Fitial, CNMI governor, was disappointed. "I believe this new federal immigration policy would have a very severe adverse impact on our economy and community," he said. His spokesman added, "Our apparel manufacturing industry is almost dead, with only a handful of factories remaining. We expect all factories to shut down within a year or less. We cannot compete with China, India, Vietnam and other low-wage countries without federal protections." Several weeks later, Bush signed the bill into law.

CHAPTER SEVENTEEN
CHOCTAW

48. Abramoff says that one of the biggest threats to an Indian casino's revenues was the effort to allow slot machines at racetracks. That became clear when visiting the casinos of Abramoff's former tribal clients. The casinos were essentially huge smoke-filled slot-machine warehouses with only a handful of blackjack, poker, and roulette tables.

49. In fact during a five-year period from 1997 to 2002, DeLay traveled on eighteen all-expenses-paid junkets. Five involved Abramoff: The Choctaw, Moscow, the Northern Mariana Islands, Scotland, and Korea.

50. Despite the fact that a federally recognized tribe is a "sovereign nation" within the United States, an individual state that bans gambling statewide

can ban Indian casinos as well. But if a state allows any gambling whatsoever, including a lottery, it must allow Indian gambling too. However, a state cannot tax Indian gambling revenues, unless Congress allows it to. But a state may circumvent that prohibition by requesting an "in lieu of tax," a euphemism for a tax.

51. In *Heist*, Peter Stone claimed it only saved the Choctaws about $180,000 a year.
52. A month after Siegelman took office, U.S. Attorney Leura Canary, a Bush appointee and the wife of the campaign manager of Siegelman's gubernatorial opponent, began a federal investigation of the governor that six years later resulted in a conviction on corruption charges. Siegelman was sentenced to seven years in prison, mostly for honest-services fraud. In 2007, *The New York Times* opined that "There is reason to believe [Siegelman's] prosecution may have been a political hit." There was some evidence the hit may have been encouraged by Abramoff's friend, Karl Rove.
53. Many Alabama grade-school students were being taught in trailers, called "portable" classrooms.

CHAPTER EIGHTEEN
SNAKE EYES

54. Betting at racetracks was not considered gambling and therefore not unconstitutional. There were vociferous debates over the constitutionality of video poker and video blackjack at racetracks. Everyone seemed to agree that a state-run lottery was unconstitutional.
55. Honorary titles for campaign contributors in George W. Bush's presidential bids included a "pioneer," who raised $100,000 and a "ranger," who raised $200,000. Many of these elite donors ended up with ambassadorships and political appointments.
56. Actually, Lt. Gov. Andrew Applegate (1868-70) and Lt. Gov. Alexander McKinstry (1872-74) were both elected as Republicans.
57. William Worfel, chief of the Coushatta, a future Abramoff client, also employed Reed.

CHAPTER NINETEEN
DISCRETION

58. Abramoff would become the lobbyist for the Coushatta in March 2001.
59. "Chief Martin met with [the Poarch Creek] Chief and asked them to put their casino in the southern part of Alabama, so it would not draw from the Choctaw market, but he refused. So [Martin] took the necessary steps to make sure his casino was not destroyed," says Abramoff.

THE PERFECT VILLAIN

60. Coincidentally, The Republican Governors' Association failed to disclose this massive contribution "due to a clerical error" until May 2004, 16 months after Riley's election.

61. Before working for DeLay, Scanlon had served on Rep. Riley's staff.

62. As of August 2008, Riley remained the Alabama governor, thanks in large part to Abramoff's and Scanlon's original efforts. As a result, the Choctaw casino continues to thrive.

63. Like the Jena Band Indians whose casino Abramoff later stopped on behalf of the Mississippi Coushatta, Abramoff was also instrumental in killing the proposed Poarch Creek Indian casino which would have diminished revenues at the Choctaw casino.

64, Siegelman does make an interesting point. Neither Reed nor Norquist were called to testify before McCain's committee.

65. Even the Northern Mariana Islands got into the act. In January 2006, its governor wrote a letter to the two firms Abramoff had worked for demanding that his $11 million in lobbying fees should be returned.

CHAPTER TWENTY
THE GAME

66. Another paladin of the politically incorrect, Burns told a local Montana newspaper that an elderly Montana rancher had once asked him, "Conrad, how can you live back there [in Washington, D.C.] with all those niggers?" Burns replied that it was "a hell of a challenge." Later, Burns referred to Arabs as "ragheads." In 2008, the Justice Department made an announcement: Sen. Burns was no longer under investigation in the Abramoff scandal. There was speculation that this surprising decision had been made not by the career prosecutors, but by their politically appointed superiors.

67. In 2004, the maximum allowable amount was $2,000.

68. According to the Internal Revenue Tax Code, a 501(c)4 is a tax-exempt, non-profit organization that can engage in lobbying and political campaigning. Contributions to the organization, however, are not deductible.

69. A 527 Group is a type of tax-exempt organization created primarily to influence the nomination, election, appointment or defeat of candidates for public office, and is not regulated by the Federal Election Commission. A Political Action Committee, commonly called a PAC is also a group which raises and spends money to elect or defeat a candidate.

CHAPTER TWENTY-TWO
INTRIGUE

70. NaftaSib is "a major shareholder in Gazprom—the state-controlled Russian oil and gas giant…[and its] largest clients [are] the ministries of defense and internal affairs."[Washington Post: 6 April 2005] The conglomerate also owns a significant interest in a Russian bank[AKM News: 1 August 2003], refineries, and construction projects.[Russian Oil and Gas Report: 23 August 2004].

71. Over several years, the US Family Network also received generous contributions from two other Abramoff clients—$250,000 from the Choctaws and $500,000 from Mariana Island textile manufacturers. According to a Post story in March 2006, Abramoff reportedly boasted that he had invested $1 million in Buckham and that his clients would reap the benefits as a result. Sources say, "Abramoff did this because Buckham was very important to him, as was DeLay…But there was never any specific quid pro quo. Buckham, however, did tell Abramoff frequently that DeLay was either grateful or interested in Abramoff giving more money to USFN," according to a confidential source.

72. These included Washington Times Editorial Page editor Todd Lindberg, North Carolina journalist Bart Adams, Insight Magazine's James Lucier, Sr., and National Interest's Assistant Managing Editor Erica Tuttle.

73. In 1999, Curt Weldon (R-PA)— whom the FBI would later investigate in connection with the Abramoff lobbying scandal—praised Koulakovsky in the *Congressional Record* for opening the school.

74. Greeslin later told the Post that at first the Russians wanted to make the contribution in cash to be picked up at an airport near Washington, D.C. According to Abramoff, this claim is absurd: "Greeslin was just reveling in his 15 minutes of fame."

75. The former IRS official, Marcus Owen, also told the Post that "such a donor would not be entitled to claim the tax deduction allowed for U.S. citizens." However, Owen was mistaken. "The donation not getting the foreigners a tax deduction is idiotic," says Abramoff. "No American can deduct money to a 501(c)4 either." According to IRS records, The US Family Network was indeed a 501(c)4.

76. Technically, Russia delayed paying its obligations for 90 days, forcing lenders to restructure the loans.

77. The Committee recommended only $3.4 billion.

78. Russia bounced back from the August 1998 financial crash, in large part, because world oil prices rose sharply 1999–2000.

CHAPTER TWENTY-THREE
JEWISH OIL

79. By coincidence, that was very same day that Gus Boulis was gunned down in a mob-style slaying in southern Florida by associates of Adam Kidan. A prominent and colorful Miami businessman, Boulis had recently sold SunCruz, a fleet of floating casino boats, to Abramoff and Kidan. In fact, Abramoff had approached Koulakovsky to help finance the SunCruz acquisition. Initially, he expressed interest but then bowed out. Eventually, with Boulis' permission, a $23 million forged wire transfer was used to secure the purchase, which was what, years later, landed Abramoff and Kidan in federal prison.

80. The Heletz oil field has proven reserves of 18 million barrels, of which only about 20% is recoverable. Saudi Arabia, with the world's largest proven reserves, pumps out 12 million barrels a day.

CHAPTER TWENTY-FOUR
RECONNECTION

81. Warren Bell, Brooklyn's bialy (similar to a bagel) king, was briefly a partner.

82. Kidan also squired around town many attractive women, including Naomi Seligman, a staffer for Rep. Sam Farr (R-CA). Seligman would later became deputy director for Citizens for Responsible Ethics in Washington (CREW), a nonprofit watchdog group that eventually sued the Secret Service for the release of the complete records of Abramoff's visits to the White House.

83. According to Continetti, "Kidan told people that he had founded Dial-a-Mattress. He had not. Kidan told people that he had been a 'principal' in and 'general counsel' to the St. Maarten Hotel Beach Club and Casino. No such establishment exists. Kidan told people that he was a 'former partner' at the law firm 'Duncan, Fish, Bergen & Kidan.' I have found no evidence that there was ever such a firm." First, there is no evidence that Kidan actually claimed he founded Dial-A-Mattress, only that he founded its initial franchise. However, local newspapers would often abridge this, referring to him as the founder, which did not make Kidan a liar. Second, in Kidan's August 17, 2005 indictment prosecutors accused him of falsely claiming to have previously worked in the casino industry. However, there was documentary proof that the St. Maarten Hotel Beach Club and Casino did exist. It is now defunct. Finally, as for Kidan's law firm, all Continetti had to do was conduct a cursory search in the New York State Supreme Courthouse in Mineola, Long Island, and the U.S. Appellate Court Second Judicial Department in Brooklyn, where the documents in Shemtov's lawsuit against Kidan were filed, in which Kidan's law firm—Duncan, Fish, Bergen & Kidan—was listed as the co-defendant.

CHAPTER TWENTY-FIVE
DEAL OF THE CENTURY

84. This was taken from Waldman's letter to Judge Huck, allegedly mailed just prior to Abramoff's sentencing March 28, 2006. However, this letter, which Waldman made available to the author, was not included with Abramoff's 277 letters of support released by the court. Why Waldman's letter was not included remained a mystery. Kidan wondered if it had never been mailed.

85. Florida jurisdiction ends three nautical miles off the Atlantic coast and nine miles off the gulf coast.

86. Although Boulis was not an American citizen at the time he purchased his first boat, he subsequently became one. As far as federal prosecutors were concerned, this didn't matter.

87. If prospective buyers knew he was being forced to sell by a certain date, it would drive down the price.

CHAPTER TWENTY-SIX
BANKERS

88. Without admitting that he had misled Abramoff, Kidan did concede that he promised Abramoff that he would be reimbursed his costs at the closing. Later, when the bankers refused, Kidan promised Abramoff that the company would repay him.

89. Arthur Andersen would later be forced out of business by the Enron scandal in 2002.

CHAPTER TWENTY-SEVEN
WIRED

90. Indeed, this would later be used by federal prosecutors to coerce Kidan into pleading guilty. "After I'd been indicted for wire fraud on August 18, 2005, I pleaded not guilty. But a couple weeks later when they told me they were also going to indict me for bribing a congressman, I gave up the fight. I just couldn't afford it," says Kidan. "I decided to plead guilty and start cooperating."

91. For lenders, the purpose of this cash "equity" contribution was similar to the requirement of a down payment on the purchase of a home. It ensured that Kidan and Abramoff had a significant personal stake in the company that they were about to purchase.

92. In a long series on Washington lobbyist, Gerald Cassidy, that began on March 4, 2007, *The Washington Post* reported that in 1999 "…Cassidy sold the firm… in a stock transaction that netted [him]…just over $15 million."

93. "Liens, attachment, and executions, as well as two bankruptcies" was redundant, because liens, attachments, and executions were automatically triggered by a bankruptcy.

94. Total closing costs came to $5,094, 500, of which the lenders and their lawyers received $3,394.500.

95. At that point, only Boulis knew that his retention of any ownership interest in SunCruz was illegal. It violated his agreement with federal prosecutors.

96. Kidan and Abramoff would each own 40% of SunCruz; Waldman and Boulis would each own 10%. If Boulis' second mortgage was not retired by the deadline, Kidan's and Abramoff's share would drop to 35% each and Boulis' would increase to 20%.

CHAPTER TWENTY-EIGHT
OFFSETS

97. On March 5, 2005, the sports complex became the Verizon Center.

98. Abramoff helped direct others contributions into several Republican PACs for which Ney was given credit. This enhanced his standing among fellow Republicans. A few months later, with Tom Delay's assistance, Ney was rewarded with the Chairmanship of the Committee on House Administration on January 20, 2001, which made him the 11th most powerful man in Congress.

99. "Tony, who has m.s. [multiple sclerosis], has a wife and three kids and is very devoted to his family. He's heavy set, maybe 5'10", 220lbs. He's a really nice guy, great sense of humor, not a tough guy at all. Well, he can be if you push him. I think he was turned on by the mafia when he was younger, but later had regrets about it. Tony was never a "made" man. I don't think he wanted to be…[In 2004] he had a big wedding for his daughter, which I went to. Cost him a bundle. And then two weeks later, Tony finds out that his new son-in-law was having an affair, so she moved out and had the marriage annulled."

CHAPTER TWENTY-NINE
HONEST HANDS

100. It was unclear how Waldman could have confirmed "the facts independently."

101. Broward County would play a decisive role in the 2000 election, in which George W. Bush was elected president. Bush won the state of Florida by a margin of 537 votes.

102. The term became famous because many voters, particularly in Broward County, had left partially punched holes—chads—in their paper punch-card ballots. Some chads were still attached, but dimpled. A controversy

grew over which, if any, of these ballots should be counted in the 2000 presidential election.

103. Shemtov filed a complaint with the state's Attorney's Grievance Committee against his stepson Kidan in 1994, claiming that Kidan had mishandled $100,000 Shemtov had given him to be held in escrow. Kidan claimed the money was to be invested in a joint business venture. And a review of court documents did indicate that Kidan's position had some merit. According to Kidan, Shemtov became enraged when he learned that Kidan and his sisters had hired a private investigator to determine if their stepfather was involved in their mother's murder, when they learned that he secretly owned "Sensations," a string of adult video stores. "I returned every penny," says Kidan. "[Shemtov] fabricated the complaint and then apologized." Shemtov could not be reached for comment to confirm this apology. However, if true, it is doubtful that Shemtov would have openly admitted this alleged "fabrication," because such an confession would have left him open to prosecution for fraud. But he did write a letter on October 13, 1995 to the Attorney's Grievance Committee and to the District Attorney stating, "[We] have now resolved our differences amicably. I hereby withdraw my earlier correspondence and…request that your office cease its investigation, if any." The District Attorney halted its inquiry, but the Grievance Committee's automatic policy was to complete its investigation, which dragged on for over five years. "I'd already moved to Florida to run SunCruz," says Kidan. "I saw no point in paying a lawyer to fight these charges. It was just easier to resign and forget about the whole thing. Never in a million years did I think the press would someday use it against me." He was officially disbarred on November 13, 2000. Hence, claims that he had misled Abramoff and the lenders by failing to reveal that he had been disbarred were not true. He simply did not inform them of the pending complaint.

CHAPTER THIRTY
GANGLAND SLAYING

104. Actually, Abramoff did retain 3% of the company.

CHAPTER THIRTY-ONE
SMEAR CAMPAIGN

105. Eight years later, the venom had not subsided. In early 2008, former House Majority leader DeLay—badly damaged by the Abramoff scandal and no longer a member of Congress, never mind House Majority leader—would resurface to denounce McCain, then the presumptive Republican nominee for president. DeLay told Fox News, "McCain has done more to hurt the Republican Party than any elected official I know of" and that the McCain-Feingold campaign finance laws had "completely neutered the Republican Party."

106. McCain was uncomfortable talking about this incident, because he desperately needed conservative Republican support for his 2008 presidential bid. For example, in March 2008, McCain's famous temper erupted when a New York Times reporter asked him repeatedly about controversial discussions he had in 2004 with Kerry about accepting the vice presidency.

107. In many cases, the language in the flyers and e-mails was obscene.

108. It wasn't until 2007, when Bridget turned 16, that she googled herself and learned for the first time about the smear campaign. McCain later said he would not have run for president in 2008, without the consent of his wife and daughter.

109. Released during the height of the Cold War in 1962, The Manchurian Candidate was a popular film that played on the public's fears about Communism. Directed by John Frankenheimer and starring Frank Sinatra, the story revolved around a brainwashed American POW in the Korean War, whom the Communists groomed to return home as a political assassin.

110. This last paragraph sounded like pure propaganda. Even though American involvement in Vietnam was condemned around the world and at home, this would not have been consistent with how McCain viewed the situation.

111. McCain was shot down on October 26, 1967. The Tet Offensive did not begin until January 30, 1968. McCain and his fellow POWs, however, learned of it the day after it began. Faith of My Fathers: Page 218.

112. Mark Salter, McCain's chief of staff, would later observe after the scandal broke: "Grover couldn't be any closer to Abramoff if they moved to Massachusetts and got married." John Weaver, McCain's political adviser, added: "I think [Norquist is] just lonely with [disgraced lobbyist] Jack Abramoff gone to prison. I think he's probably just sad and lonely and delusional." In mid 2008, Norquist surprised many by announcing his support for McCain for president. Some say it was out of gratitude, because McCain did not require Norquist to testify before the Senate Indian Affairs Committee during the Abramoff probe.

CHAPTER THIRTY-TWO
MUSIC, GOLF, LUCK

113. Several months later, the law was changed requiring the disclosure of—but not banning—these kinds of political donations.

114. Abramoff leased a skybox at the MCI Center for eight years. The value of the skybox that evening was approximately $3,500.

115. According to the Center for Public Integrity study, however, Rep. Tom DeLay was the king of the junketeers. He and his staffers accepted about a half-million dollars in free trips from the year 2000 to June 2005.

116. Preston Gates reimbursed Abramoff, but Ridenour's organization never reimbursed Preston Gates.

117. However, according to *The Washington Post*, on three occasions in 2004, the House Ethics Committee would admonish DeLay, who by then was the House Majority Leader, "for infringing rules governing lawmakers' activities and their contacts with registered lobbyists."

118. The Old Course at St. Andrews, Scotland is the oldest golf course in the world. The game, however, was apparently invented in the Netherlands.

119. James Dobson, who had unwittingly helped Abramoff defeat the Alabama state lottery on behalf of the Choctaw Indians, had written an op-ed piece in *The New York Times* praising the bill.

120. The bill would have also permitted online gambling for jai lai, a sport played professionally only in the state of Florida.

121. This second "lie" referred to the biggest scandal of Clinton's presidency, which would lead to his impeachment, but not conviction. Clinton asserted that his involvement with Monica Lewinsky, a White House intern, did not constitute sex, because there had been no intercourse, only fellatio. A surprising number of Americans actually agreed with Clinton's definition.

122. Forty-four Republicans, including DeLay, and 114 Democrats voted against the bill. One hundred and sixty five Republicans and seventy-nine Democrats voted in favor of it.

123. Safavian would later become implicated in the Abramoff scandal. On October 27, 2006, he was sentenced to 18 months in prison for making false statements and obstruction of justice. Abramoff was distraught over this verdict. He says he would prefer to add five years to his sentence rather than have Safavian go to prison.

CHAPTER THIRTY-THREE
THE STARS LINE UP

124. According to a 1900 census, only three full-blooded Chitimacha tribal members remained.

125. The Secret Service claimed that it did not have to disclose all of Abramoff's White House visits because some of them may have fallen under the rubric of "sensitive security visits." For a complete chronology of efforts to force the release of those records, see http://www.citizensforethics.org/node/30542

126. Rove resigned from the White House a year later on August 31, 2007, about a year and a half before the end of Bush's second term. He became a consultant and a Fox TV News analyst. He is reportedly under investigation by the Justice Department for his involvement in the Abramoff scandal.

127. One of the most intriguing references to Rove came in a March 18, 2002 e-mail that Abramoff sent to Ben Zvi, an old high-school friend, who had moved to Israel. Despite Bush's claim to have exhausted all diplomatic options, Rove apparently told Abramoff that the president had actually made up to go to war with Iraq more than a year before the start of hostilities on March 20, 2003: "I was sitting yesterday with Karl Rove, Bush's top advisor, at the NCAA basketball game, discussing Israel…It seems that the President was very sad to have to come out negatively regarding Israel, but that they needed to mollify the Arabs for the upcoming war on Iraq."

128. Although the Zachares effort did not succeed, Abramoff did put in a good word for Patrick Pizzella, his friend and lobbying colleague at Preston Gates, whom Bush nominated as assistant Secretary of Labor on the very same day of Abramoff's White House visit. See http://www.whitehouse.gov/news/releases/2001/03/20010306-7.html

CHAPTER THIRTY-FOUR
ADJUSTMENTS

129. The Senate had an equal number of Republicans and Democrats. Tie votes would be broken by Vice President Dick Cheney. However, the Republicans lost control of the Senate on May 24, 2001, when Vermont Sen. James Jeffords left the Republican Party, became an independent, and agreed to caucus with the Democrats.

130. The controversial Channel One beamed a 12-minute news program—which included advertisements—into the classrooms of thousands of private and public middle-and high-school students in exchange for the free loan of electronic equipment, including televisions and VCRs.

131. Fitial lost the race, but defeated Babauta in the next election and became governor in 2006. Although he took political heat for saying it, Fitial said he still considered Abramoff a "good friend."

CHAPTER THIRTY-FIVE
COUSHATTA COMPACT

132. Terry Martin was no relation to Philip Martin, the chief of the Mississippi Choctaws, also Abramoff's tribal client.

133. Often, charitable tax-exempt entities, such as universities, pay municipalities an "in lieu of tax" to compensate them for a portion of the property tax revenue they would have otherwise collected.

CHAPTER THIRTY-SIX
JENAS

134. Their full name was the Jena Band of Choctaws. To avoid confusion with the Mississippi Choctaw, the tribe will simply be referred to as the Jenas.

135. In July 2007, Vitter, who had been recently elected to the U. S. Senate from Louisiana, was identified as a client of a prostitution ring in Washington, D.C.

136. In Part Two of the report "Analysis by Entity," the Jena Band was finally mentioned, but only in the context of how Abramoff concealed and funneled into various organizations the referral fees or "kickbacks" that Scanlon had paid him.

137. Reid became Senate Majority leader after the 2006 mid-term elections.

138. In 2007, Griles pleaded guilty to obstruction of justice. Prosecutors had recommended a five-month sentence. However, because the judge did not find Griles sufficiently contrite, she doubled it.

139. Gov. Foster was barred from running for reelection, because by state law, the governor cannot serve more than two consecutive terms.

CHAPTER THIRTY-SEVEN
BIN LADEN

140. Williams was one of the three of seven adults on Abramoff's 2002 golf junket to Scotland, who did not end up getting indicted.

141. According to a footnote in the McCain report, "[Khaled} Saffuri appears to have been a lobbyist at an Abramoff owned or controlled entity called the Lexington Group. At one time, Saffuri was reportedly the Assistant Executive Director of the American Muslim Council ("AMC"), where he apparently served as a lobbyist. The AMC was apparently founded in 1990 by Abdurahman Mohamed Alamoudi, an open supporter of Palestinian terror organization Hamas. A few years ago, Alamoudi was implicated in a plot to assassinate the Saudi Crown Prince Abdullah."

CHAPTER THIRTY-EIGHT
SAGCHIPS

142. The Gun Lake Indians are officially known as the Pokagon band of Potawatomi Indians.

143. For gamblers and conventioneers who wish to spend the night, the 514-room Soaring Eagle hotel is available.

144. The second election was Ben Fitial's defeat in the race for governor in the Mariana Islands.

145. About a year later, the tribal council voted to raise the monthly retainer to $180,000.

146. According to the tribe's Legislative Affairs Department, from 2002 to 2004, Abramoff obtained $19,682,311 for the Saginaw Chippewa.

CHAPTER FORTY
QUADRUPLE BOGEY

147. On February 26, 2007, Heaton pleaded guilty to one count of conspiracy to commit fraud. In return for his cooperation, he was sentenced to 24 months of probation.

148. Ney was still a congressman. After pleading guilty, he promptly checked himself into an alcohol rehabilitation facility, but he had not yet resigned. Even after officially pleading guilty before Judge Ellen Huvelle in Washington District Court on October 13, he still refused to resign. Ney finally handed in his resignation on November 3rd, four days before the elections.

149. Ney would technically have to spend the next six months in a half-way house. But after a few weeks, most are released to home confinement.

CHAPTER FORTY-ONE
CALM BEFORE THE FIRESTORM

150. Istook's chief of staff, John C. Albaugh, plead guilty to one count of conspiracy to commit honest-services wire fraud on June 2, 2008.

151. The author of this book was the freelance writer that Kidan had hired.

152. The reason prosecutors had cancelled his wire continued to puzzle Kidan. He would have to wait until *The Miami Herald* broke the story in April 2006. Everyone involved was stunned. Moscatiello—now sitting in a Miami jail awaiting trial for Boulis' murder—had been an FBI informant for the past fifteen years.

153. In May 2004, she received some notoriety by cutting off a live interview on NBC's "Meet the Press" with then-Secretary of State Colin Powell.

154. Ring, who refused to testify before McCain's committee in 2005, was a former aide to Rep. John Doolittle (R-CA) and teamed up with Abramoff as a lobbyist in 2001. He was cited as "Lobbyist C" when Rep. Ernest Istook's former chief of staff, John Albaugh pleaded guilty to honest-fraud wire conspiracy on June 2, 2008.

155. In his report, McCain included this excerpt from the interview with a slanted editorial comment: "Schmidt finally cut to the chase: 'Do you have an ownership stake in [any of Scanlon's firms]'? Even a pregnant pause here might be looked on with some suspicion So, Abramoff had no choice [emphasis added]: 'No. No, I don't ....'"

156. In *Heist*, author Peter H. Stone called Abramoff a liar for denying in the Schmidt interview that he had a "financial stake," in any of Scanlon's businesses, but the question she asked him was if he had an "ownership interest," which was not the same. In fact, it could be argued that a referral fee is not a financial stake.

CHAPTER FORTY-TWO
OPENING SALVO

157. This speech also appeared in the opening paragraph of McCain's 373-page report, issued more than two years later on June 22, 2006.

CHAPTER FORTY-THREE
THE SECOND CASINO

158. Her name appeared at the end of the story as a "tag line," which meant that she had contributed to the story.

159. It was not an earmark, which involves money.

160. The Sandia tribe of New Mexico would not hire Abramoff until March 2002.

CHAPTER FORTY-FOUR
THE HEARING

161. Scanlon had not been properly subpoenaed. McCain's committee had faxed the cover page of the summons to Scanlon's lawyer without attaching the actual summons. Scanlon did not believe it was his obligation to appear if he had not been properly summoned.

162. Jewish law forbids Jews to swear an oath to God, because that would mean taking the Lord's name in vain, prohibited by the Ten Commandments.

163. This refers to the supposed "fedora" Abramoff wore leaving the courthouse after pleading guilty on January 3, 2006, in Miami, Florida, which he claimed was a fold-up plastic rain hat.

164. This was in reference to the 1989 Keating Five Scandal. One of the five senators was McCain.

CHAPTER FORTY-SEVEN
THE MCCAIN REPORT

165. C-4 is plastic explosive and is 1.34 times as explosive as TNT.

166. There were some other expenditure violations with Capital Athletic Foundation: a $10,000 loean to Mark Zachares, a $50,000 loan repayment to Ralph Nuremberger, and of course the $150,000 for the 2002 golf trip to Scotland.

CHAPTER FORTY-EIGHT
TIGUA REDUX

167. The Tigua's official name is the Ysleta Del Sur Pueblo

168. There is a third federally recognized tribe in Texas, the Kickapoo, but for reasons too complex to explain, it operates under a different set of federal regulations.

169. When questioned by Sen. Conrad during the Indian Affairs Committee hearing on November 4, 2004, Marc Schwartz and Carlos Hisa testified that the Tigua did not make any contribution to the 2002 Scotland golf trip. Later, Sen. Conrad asked Hisa again. Hisa said, "I think in total the golfing trip was going to be $100,000, my understanding is that the Mississippi Choctaw paid $50,000 and the Alabama Coushatta paid another $50,000."

170. According to the Alabama-Coushatta 2006 lawsuit, Abramoff's firm knew about this non-disclosure. See page 43.

171. Abramoff says that if the Alabama-Coushatta had been included in the legislative fix, they would have obtained a class-2 casino license. In order for them to obtain a class-3 license, the tribe would have had to obtained a compact with the governor of Texas, which Abramoff says he was confident he could have stopped, since the Alabama-Coushatta were close to DeLay's congressional district.

CHAPTER FORTY-NINE
JUDGE HUCK

172. Kidan was ordered to report to prison on October 23rd. On June 25, 2008, Judge Huck accepted the government's recommendation that Kidan's 70-month sentence be reduced by 50 percent. Therefore, Kidan will probably be released to a half-way house in September 2008.

CHAPTER FIFTY
TIME MACHINE

173. The radar unit was "designed to perform over hills, around corners and across distances of several miles [and was]...augmented by a pair of 'laser diffusers' in front and back to avoid detection further." The car also featured a 15.2 inch wide-screen flip-down monitor with cordless headphone transmitters and a wireless keyboard. According to *The New York Times*, "For $7,390, he added a hands-free cell phone system, with a special antenna amplifier to boost the signal...[and] paid $6,495 for [handmade] seat-back tables."

174. "The media loved Ralph, but a lot of people didn't really like him," Abramoff says. "I happened to like him a lot, even though he was one of the most arrogant people alive. When he'd hit a great tee shot, Ralph would say, 'Isn't that a beautiful shot!' Usually when a golfer hits a great shot, he admires it in silence and waits for others to express their admiration—but not Ralph."

EPILOGUE
IT ISN'T WHAT IT IS

175. For further explanation on honest-services fraud, see http://library.findlaw.com/2002/jul/8/132494.html

CHAPTER NOTES

PROLOGUE

p. xii: I would think I was Satan. [The experience has been] "Kafkaesque: *The New York Times Magazine*, by Michael Crowley, May 1, 2005.

CHAPTER ONE
FATHER OF ABRAMOFF

p. 3–4: securing …[a] franchise for their area.: *The Washington Post*, April 26, 1963, page C19.

p. 4: But I can't say that I didn't ever meet him." *The Buffalo News*, by William Douglas, January 27, 2006, page A5.

p. 4: that [Abramoff] attended, then a few staff-level meetings on top of that.": The White House, Press Briefing by Scott McClellan, January 17, 2006.

p. 4: "pure political purposes" and "they're not relevant to the investigation: KnightRidder/Tribune News Service, Bush Says He Doesn't Abramoff, Remember Photos Being Taken, January 27, 2006.

p. 5: "president of Diners Franchise Systems, a new subsidiary of Diners' Club.": *The New York Times*, March 16, 1969, page F9.

p. 6: The murder has never been solved.: *The Toronto Star* (Ontario, Canada), Montreal Mob Boss had Volpe killed, Informant says, December 18, 1986.

p. 7: take steps to determine if the landfill had been properly closed.": United States, Appellant v. Charles Price [and others including] Bernard Abramoff, Lee Garrell, Frank Abramoff, United States Court of Appeals Third Circuit, 688F.2d 204, U. S. v. Price, (C.A.3 [NJ] 1982).

CHAPTER TWO
EPIPHANY

p. 8: "one of Jack's proudest accomplishments: Abramoff's Memorandum in Aid of Sentencing, page 15. Available on PACER.

p. 9: that [the message of secular Judaism] was gibberish: *Jewish Journal of Greater Los Angeles*, by David Klinghoffer, February 5, 1006.

p. 9: in order to preserve the faith in our family," said Abramoff.:, *The New York Times Magazine* by Michael Crowley, May 1, 2005.

p. 10: newspapers and magazines around the country—didn't dig deep enough: *The Los Angeles Times*, by Faye Fiore and Martha Groves, January 4, 2006, page 1.

p. 12: Rowen recalled, who enjoyed attending the high-school football games: *Rolling Stone*, Meet Mr. Republican: The Secret History of the Most Corrupt Man in Washington, by Matt Taibi, March 24, 2006.

p. 12: his first Rocky film, to help him raise funds: Abramoff's Memorandum In Aid of Sentencing, page 15.

p. 13: used to call Abramoff "Abraham Jackoff" behind his back: *Slate.com*, Jack Abramoff's School Days: The Making of a Sleazeball, by Timothy Noah, April 27, 2005, http://www.Slate.com/toolbar.aspz?action=print&id+2117520

p. 13: Who wouldn't feel satisfied that he was getting his comeuppance: Interview on National Public Radio, This American Life with Ira Glass, aired June 23, 2006.

CHAPTER THREE
THEN THERE WAS ADAM

p. 15: liar, claiming the St. Maarten's Casino and Beach Club didn't exist.): *The Weekly Standard*, Money, Mobsters, Murder: The sordid tale of a GOP lobbyist's casino deal gone bad, by Matthew Continetti, November 28, 2005.

CHAPTER FOUR
REAGAN TAKES NOTICE

p. 16: not in a suit," said a conservative activist and an old friend: *The New York Times Magazine*, A Lobbyist in Full, by Michael Crowley, May 1, 2005, page 32.

p. 17: that he was a guy who would be in the trenches with me.": *Jewish Journal of Greater Los Angeles*, In Defense of Jack Abramoff, by David Klinghoffer, February 4, 2006.

p. 18: Jack, if you carry Massachusetts for Reagan, we'll win in a national landslide: *The American Spectator*, Some thoughts on Jack Abramoff, by Morton Blackwell, March 23, 2006.

p. 18: services [with me] at an early hour of the morning for a year: Abramoff's Memorandum In Aid of Sentencing, page 19.

p. 19: never even knew who specifically had helped them out," wrote Klein: Abramoff's Memorandum In Aid of Sentencing, attached letters (no pagination).

CHAPTER SIX
PURGE THE BUSHYITES

p. 25: Abramoff told a reporter for *The Atlantic City Press*.: *The Atlantic City Press*, by Frank J. Prendergast, December 21, 1981.

p. 26: but we wanted the College Republicans to remain conservative: *Gang of Five*, by Nina J. Easton, page 141.

p. 26: student newspapers and radio stations, student governments, and academia: *Ibid*, page 143.

p. 26: Wade into them. Spill their blood. Shoot them in the belly!: *Ibid*.

p. 26: "The goal is to win, not to incite: *Ibid*, page 146.

p. 27: power broker like Abramoff remained so naïve about money: Abramoff's Memorandum In Aid of Sentencing, attached letters (no pagination).

p. 28: It was damn the torpedoes, full speed ahead: *The Boston Globe*, by Nina J. Easton, February 6, 2006.

p. 28: leading anti-Reagan and anti-free market forces on campus: *The New York Times*, College Republicans Open a Drive Against

Student Activist Groups, by Joseph B. Treaster, March 13, 1983, page 28.

p. 28: Abramoff's efforts did have the support of the Republican National Committee: *Ibid.*

p. 29: obligatory funds, that's something we generally support: *Ibid.*

p. 29: he has his USA [Foundation] hat on, he's nonpartisan: *The Washington Post*, Two 'Nonpolitical' Foundations Push Grenada Rallies, by Howard Kurtz and Charles R. Babcock, October 4, 1984, page 1.

p. 30: we must become financially self-sufficient: This letter is housed in the College Republicans collection of the National Archives in Washington, D.C.

p. 30: David Barron, former head of the Young Republicans: *Mother Jones*, by Barry Yeoman, The Fall of a True Believer, September 1, 2005.

p. 31: between freedom and tyranny by the Berlin Wall for too long: *The Boston Globe*, by Nina J. Easton, February 6, 2006, page 152.

p. 31: It was probably a blessing: *Mother Jones*, by Barry Yeoman, The Fall of a True Believer, September 1, 2005.

CHAPTER SEVEN
SMALL-WORLD DEPARTMENT

p. 33: I [knew] who [had] experience in feeding large groups of people: *The Weekly Standard,* by Matthew Continetti, Money, Mobsters, Murder, November 28, 2005.

CHAPTER NINE
JAMBOREE

p. 38: Abramoff had been assigned responsibility for organizing briefings by Contra speakers: NSC Intelligence Document: Exhibit OLN-217 [declassified].

p. 38: Abramoff was in touch with North almost daily: *The Washington Post*, McFarlane Aide Facilitates Policy; Marine Officer Nurtures Connections With Contras, Conservatives, by Joanne Omang, August 11, 1985, page 1.

p. 38: Abramoff was in touch with North almost daily: *The Washington Post*, McFarlane Aide Facilitates Policy; Marine Officer Nurtures Connections with Contras, Conservatives, by Joanne Omang, August 11, 1985, page 1.

p. 38: "It was Ollie this and Ollie that: *The Washington Post*, Reagan Doctrine's Passionate Advocate; North, Rallying the Right, Forged a Political Base for Contra Aid, by Sidney Blumenthal, December 17, 1986, page 1.

p. 40: hand-deliver the invitation to the leader of the Contras: *Ibid*.

p. 40: Angola, and then driven a two-hour bumpy ride to Jamba: *Gang of Five*, by Nina J. Easton, page 166.

p.41: has a full-time director at the KGB for disinformation: *Mother Jones*, The Fall of a True Believer, by Barry Yeoman, September/October 2005.

p. 41: one of the few authentic heroes of our time: *The New York Times*, The World; Exit Savimbi, and the Cold War in Africa, by Howard French, March 3, 2002, Week in Review Desk, page 5.

p. 41: articulate charismatic homicidal maniac I've ever met: http://www.salon.com/ent/feature/ 2005/08/17/abramoff/print/ html. By James Verini.

p. 43: was one big party…[Abramoff] had gone hog wild: *The Washington Post*, Staff Shakeup Hits Conservative Group; 7 Fired at Lehrman's Citizens for America by Sidney Blumenthal, July 27, 1985, page 10.

p. 44: "We didn't get any money from the Ayatollah: United Press International, by Judi Hasson, December 16, 1986.

CHAPTER TEN
FUNDING FREEDOM

p. 45: "has emerged as an influential and occasionally controversial character: *The New York Times*, Nicaraguan Rebel Tells of Killings as Device for Forced Recruitment, by Joel Brinkley, September 12, 1985, page 10.

p. 45: opened other offices in Johannesburg, London, Hamburg, Brussels, and Rome: *Covert Action Information Bulletin*, by David Ivon [pseudonym], winter of 1989, number 31, page 62.

p. 48: hardly believe cooperated with us politically when it came to the Soviets: *Newsday*, Front for Apartheid, by Dele Olojede and Timothy M. Phelps, July 16, 1995, page 1.

p. 48: "was a former South African Defense Force project: *Ibid.*

p. 48: including the murder of Ruth First: *Ibid.*

p. 48: we steered them. That was the point: *Ibid.*

p. 49: As chairman [of the IFF], he understood where the money was coming from: *Harpers*, The Making of a Lobbyist, by Ken Silverstein, April 17, 2006. Also in The Texas Observer, Stranger than Paradise, http://www.texasobserver.org/showArticle.asp?ArticleID=1743.

p. 49: The staff thought it was the hard work of fundraising: *Harpers*, The Making of a Lobbyist, by Ken Silverstein, April 17, 2006.

p. 49: I would have put a stop to it: *Newsday*, Front for Apartheid, by Dele Olojede and Timothy M. Phelps, July 16, 1995, page 1.

p. 49: good in intelligence, but in political warfare: *Ibid.*

p. 50: chaired by his good friend, Rep. Dan Burton: : *Covert Action Information Bulletin*, by David Ivon [pseudonym], winter of 1989, number 31, page 64.

p. 51: being a mouthpiece for Soviet and Cuban terrorism: *Ibid.*

p. 51: sporting a badge with the beguiling motto: "Hang Nelson Mandela: *Ibid.*

p. 52: Mandela failed to receive the honorary "key to the city: *Newsday*, Front for Apartheid, by Dele Olojede and Timothy M. Phelps, July 16, 1995, page 1.

p. 53: sometimes more frequently, sometimes less: *The Washington Post*, Reagan's Doctrine's Passionate Advocate; North; Rallying the Right, Forged a Political Base for Contra Aid, by Sidney Blumenthal, December 17, 1986, page 1.

p. 54: included battle footage of his guerrillas in action: *The New York Times*, Washington Talk: Briefing; That North Video, May 10, 2006.

CHAPTER ELEVEN
SCORPION

p. 59: Frank Rich described it as "seriously God-awful: *The Washington Post*, by Peters Carlson, November 27, 2005, Page N1

p. 59: reflective moments belong to Mr. Lundgren's sweaty chest: *The New York Times*, by Stephen Holden, April 21, 1989, Page C17

p. 59: called it "a numbskull live-action comic book: *The Washington Post*, by Peters Carlson, November 27, 2005, Page N1.

p. 59: character development, which is unheard of in such epics: *The San Diego Union-Tribune*, by Bill Hagen, April 27, 1989, Page D12.

p. 59: Red Scorpion opened in 1,268 movie theaters across America: *The Texas Observer*, Stranger in Paradise; How Tom DeLay's Deregulatory Ideology Stretched to the Island of Saipan, By Lou Dubose and Jan Reid, September 10, 2004 [excerpted from *The Hammer*, by Lou Dubose and Jan Reid].

p. 59: "Why would you want to make a documentary: *The Weekly Standard*, My Dinner with Jack, by Mark Hemingway, April 3, 2006.

p. 60: "steroid-enhanced, genetically engineered" Soviet boxer in Rocky IV: *New American*, Seeing Russia the Abramoff Way, by William Norman Grigg, http://www.thenewamerican.com/artman/publish/article_3117.shtml.

p. 60: of him [shaking hands] with [President] Ronald Reagan: *The New Republic*, Mr. Abramoff Goes to Hollywood, by Franklin Foer, January 24, 2006.

p. 61: for exploitation and of course trying to make money: http://www.salon.com/ent/feature/ 2005/08/17/abramoff/print/ html. By James Verini.

p. 63: "Sometimes the deductions totaled twice or three times the investments: *The New Republic*, Mr. Abramoff Goes to Hollywood, by Franklin Foer, January 24, 2006.

p. 63: Beverly Hills Jewish kids—were doing this: http://www.salon.com/ent/feature/ 2005/08/17/ abramoff/print/ html. By James Verini.

p. 64: "I strongly advised him against filming [in Namibia]: *The New Republic*, Mr. Abramoff Goes to Hollywood, by Franklin Foer, January 24, 2006.

p. 65; Namibia "to patch up [her] relationship with Dolph: *The New York Times*, by James Brooke, South Africa Helps U.S. film Makers in Namibia with Troops and Trucks, January 9, 1988, page 11.

p. 65: intimidated by their temperamental leading man: *The Weekly Standard*, My Dinner with Jack, by Mark Hemingway, April 3, 2006.

p. 66: Samil troop transports and Casspir and Buffel armored personnel carriers: *Ibid*.

p. 66; The filmmakers are paying for this assistance: *Ibid*.

p. 66 Arthur Ashe, the black American tennis star: *Ibid*.

p. 66: involved even before [Abramoff] decided to shoot in Namibia: *Ibid*.

CHAPTER TWELVE
HOME INVASION

p. 68: and hurled the murder weapon into the icy water below.: Much of the material in this chapter comes from interviews with Adam Kidan, confidential sources, and *Mob over Miami*, by Michele McPhee, 2002.

CHAPTER THIRTEEN
TRANSITION

p. 72: my answer now if you like. My offer is this: nothing: *The Washington Post*, The Fast Rise and Steep Fall of Jack Abramoff: How a Well-Connect Lobbyist Became the Center of a Far-Reaching Corruption Scandal, by Susan Schmidt and James V. Grimaldi, December 29, 2005, page 1.

p. 73: He wouldn't see it again for another 10 years: *Mother Jones*, by Barry Yeoman, The Fall of a True Believer, September 1, 2005.

p. 74: but in Malaysia they could not do so: *The New York Times*, Malaysian Premier Sees Jews Behind Nation's Money Crisis, by Seth Mydans, October 16, 1997, page 8.

p. 74: They get others to fight and die for them: *The Forward*, by E. J. Kessler, April 22, 2005

p. 74: If it works there will be a lot more. Reed: Sure: *Heist*, by Peter H. Stone, page 143.

p. 74: and then met again in Washington on May 14, 2002.: *National Journal*, July 7, 2006.

p. 75: unheard of in the Orthodox world," said Abramoff.: *Washington Business Forward*, November/December 2002.

p. 76: policy without a revolution in fundraising: PBS Documentary, *Moyers on America*, Capitol Crimes, aired October 6, 2006.

p. 76: punish your enemies and reward your friends," said DeLay: *The Washington Post*, Speaker and His Directors Make the Cash Flow Right by David Maraniss and Michael Weisskopf, November 27, 1995, page 1.

p. 76: "the ditch digger who makes it all happen: *The Texas Observer*, DeLay, Incorporated, by Robert Dreyfuss, February 4, 2000.

p. 77: with tax liens for not paying payroll and income taxes: *The Washington Post Magazine*, Absolute Truth; Tom DeLay is certain that Christian family values will solve America's problems. But he's uncertain how to face his own family, by Peter Perl, May 13, 2001, page W12.

p. 77: Environmental Protection Agency, because it banned a certain pesticide he favored: *The Texas Observer*, The DeLay Chronicles: A Nice Guy in Austin, by Julie Hollar, February 4, 2000.

p. 77: that he "was no longer committing adultery: *The New Yorker*, Party Unfaithful, by Jeffrey Goldberg, June 4, 2007.

p. 78: Committee Chairman Chris Cox and their staffs,": PR Newswire, December 30, 1994, Preston Gates Ellis & Rouvelas Meeds Announces Well Known Republican Party And Conservative Movement Leader Joins Firm: Jack Abramoff Hired as Government Affairs Counselor

p. 78: victory'—powerful words that you don't usually hear in D.C.: *Mother Jones*, The Fall of a True Believer, by Barry Yeoman, September 1, 2005.

p. 79: the religious right's war to reunite church and state: *The Seattle Weekly*, May 11, 2005

THE PERFECT VILLAIN

p. 79: one of his favorite programs was *The 700 Club*.: http://www.cbn.com/cbnnews/news/ 040225_passion.aspx

p. 80: both Tom DeLay and Jack Abramoff were present: *The Seattle Weekly*, January 18, 2006

p. 80: our side," said Buckham, "he has access to DeLay: *National Journal*, Jack Abramoff: A Lobbyist With a Line to Capitol Hill, by W. John Moore, July 29, 1995.

p. 80: ATR meetings, but became disenchanted with Norquist: *Heist*, by Peter H. Stone, page 40.

p. 80: PACs and through giving to our coalition groups: *Ibid*

p. 81: [Washington, D.C.] becomes a different town: Jack Abramoff: *National Journal*, A Lobbyist With a Line to Capitol Hill, by John Moore, July 29, 1995.

p. 80: he's accused of doing that's illegal, immoral, or fattening: *The Weekly Standard*, December 20, 2004.

p. 81: "[Abramoff] was able to deliver DeLay very fast: *Heist*, by Peter H. Stone, page 40.

p. 81: followed is no less remarkable. He made it happen: Confidential interview.

CHAPTER FOURTEEN
DISTANT SPECKS

p. 83: would have earned, for example, in Guangdong, China: *The Weekend Standard*, The Island that Lost its Shirt, by Zach Coleman, December 18-19, 2004.

p. 83: low-paid second-class foreigners do the drudge work: *The Dallas Observer*, Our Man in Saipan; Dick Armey thinks he's found a free-market paradise in the Marianas Islands, a U.S. territory where the workers never complain, the factories never quit, and wages are so low, even welfare mothers can hire a Filipino maid, by Thomas Korosec, February 19, 1998.

p. 84: strip the Northern Mariana's wage and immigration exemptions.: *ABC 20/20*: Airdate: 24 May 1999

p. 85: by unanimous consent; another had 234 sponsors in the House!: *The Los Angeles Times*, A Question of Influence; Two

Former Aides to DeLay Paved Way for Lobbyist's Deal; Their Work on Saipan Helped Get a Contract for a Lawyer Now the Target of a Corruption Probe., by Walter F. Roche Jr. and Chuck Neubauer, May 6, 2005, page 1.

p. 85: textile manufacturer and the islands largest employer: *The Washington Post*, Former DeLay Aide Enriched By Nonprofit; Bulk of Group's Funds Tied to Abramoff, by R. Jeffrey Smith, March 26, 2006, page 1.

p. 85: ventilation, filthy toilets, and overcrowded conditions: *The Weekend Standard*, Sweating it out in Saipan, by Zach Coleman, August 13-14, 2005

p. 86: and labor departments are essentially organized crime: http://www.time.com/time/ magazine/article.0,9171,987745,00.html

p. 87: because their employer said they were still trainees: CNN.com, Report: Indian supplier used forced child labor, October 28, 2007: http://www.cnn.com/2007/BUSINESS/10/28/britain.gap. ap/index.html

p. 87: "perfect Petri dish of capitalism…my Galapagos Island: *The Washington Post*, A 'Petri Dish' in the Pacific; Conservative Network Aligned With DeLay Makes Marianas a Profitable Cause, by Juliet Eilperin, July 26, 2000, page 1.

p. 88: wonderful experiment in free market and low taxes at work: PBS Documentary, *Moyers on America*, Capitol Crimes, aired October 6, 2006.

p. 88: 1995, "but he is a very innovative and very productive guy: *National Journal*, Jack Abramoff: A Lobbyist with a Line to Capitol Hill, by W. John Moore, July 29, 1995.

p. 88: Rep. George Miller's proposals to "gut their economy: Http://www.foxnews.com/story/ 0,2933,158968,00.html.

p. 88: accounting for one-quarter of the firm's lobbying revenues: *The Seattle Times*, Seattle firm aids 'sweatshops,' critics say — Preston Gates Fighting Labor Protections For Pacific Territory, by Danny Westneat, March 24, 1998, page 1.

p. 88: said let's make a move on their economy: *The New York Times*, Congressional Fact-Finding in Saipan: They Came. They Saw. They Golfed., by Lizette Alvarez, January 20, 1998, page 14.

CHAPTER FIFTEEN
CAME, SAW, GOLFED

p. 89: freedom," said a furious Rep. George Miller: *The New York Times*, At $500 an Hour, Lobbyist's Influence Rises With G.O.P., by David E. Rosenbaum, April 3, 2002, page 1.

p. 89: have convinced Congress to support the system he describes: Ibid.

p. 90: Tom DeLay would go even further, denouncing [opponents] as "evil.": *Contemporary Women's Issues*, Trapped-Human Trafficking for Forced Labor in the Commonwealth of the Northern Mariana Islands (a U.S. Territory) [Part 4 of 5], no by-line, 1999, pages 21–27.

p. 90: be viewed as a "lavishly funded public relations [stunt]: *The Dallas Observer*, Our Man in Saipan; Dick Armey thinks he's found a free-market paradise in the Marianas Islands, a U.S. territory where the workers never complain, the factories never quit, and wages are so low, even welfare mothers can hire a Filipino maid, by Thomas Korosec, February 19, 1998.

p. 90: Interior, as well as visits to various apparel manufacturers: Preston Gates billing records, House Committee on Oversight and Government Reform: http://oversight.house.gov/.

p. 90: something the print and TV media neglected to mention: *The New York Times*, Columnist Resigns His Post, Admitting Lobbyist Paid Him, by Anne E. Kornblut and Philip Shenon, December 17, 2005.

p. 91: pundits trade their ability to shape public perception for cash: *BusinessWeek*, Op-Eds for Sale: A columnist from a libertarian think tank admits accepting payments to promote an indicted lobbyist's clients. Will more examples follow?, by Eamon Javers, December 16, 2005: http://www.businessweek.com/bwdaily/dnflash/dec2005/nf20051216_1037_db016.htm

p. 91: the Marianas. They were a "stunning economic success: *The Seattle Times*, Seattle firm aids 'sweatshops,' critics say — Preston Gates Fighting Labor Protections For Pacific Territory, by Danny Westneat, March 24, 1998, page 1.

p. 91: Bandow did, she said, "isn't a lapse in judgment, it's soul-selling: *Editor & Publisher*, December 2005.

p. 91: think tanks who have similar arrangements: *BusinessWeek*, Op-Eds for Sale: A columnist from a libertarian think tank admits accepting payments to promote an indicted lobbyist's clients. Will more examples follow?, by Eamon Javers, December 16, 2005: http://www. businessweek.com/bwdaily/dnflash/dec2005/nf20051216_1037_db016.htm

p. 91: favorable to Abramoff's clients in *The Washington Times*: Hardball, with Chris Mathews and David Shuster, October 13, 2006. Transcript 101301cb.461.

p. 92: DeLay and 104 conversations with Ed Buckham, DeLay's chief of staff: *The Washington Post*, Former DeLay Aide Enriched by Nonprofit, by R. Jeffrey Smith: March 26, 2006, page 1.

p. 93: "I didn't see anyone sweating," DeLay reportedly joked: *The Dallas Observer*, Our Man in Saipan; Dick Armey thinks he's found a free-market paradise in the Marianas Islands, a U.S. territory where the workers never complain, the factories never quit, and wages are so low, even welfare mothers can hire a Filipino maid, by Thomas Korosec, February 19, 1998.

p. 93: bias, mistruth, and sensationalism in order to win a TV ratings war: http://www.talking pointsmemo.com/docs/doolittle-dear-colleague/

p. 94: the forces of big labor and the radical left: *The Dallas Observer*, Our Man in Saipan; Dick Armey thinks he's found a free-market paradise in the Marianas Islands, a U.S. territory where the workers never complain, the factories never quit, and wages are so low, even welfare mothers can hire a Filipino maid, by Thomas Korosec, February 19, 1998.

p. 94: When one of my closest and dearest friends: *Ibid*.

p. 94: corral-encrusted lagoon on the exclusive Managaha Island: *Ibid*.

p. 94: cockfight, according to one of the participants: *The Washington Post*, Former DeLay Aide Enriched By Nonprofit; Bulk of Group's Funds Tied to Abramoff, by R. Jeffrey Smith, March 26, 2006, page 1.

CHAPTER SIXTEEN
CROSSING THE LINE?

p. 95: paid Abramoff a whopping $1.8 millions in fees: *National Journal*, From the K Street Corridor, by Peter H. Stone, March 31, 2001, [page 962].

p. 95: was signed: "YOUR 'ADOPTED' BROTHER BEN: *The Washington Post*, Former DeLay Aide Enriched By Nonprofit; Bulk of Group's Funds Tied to Abramoff, by R. Jeffrey Smith, March 26, 2006, page 1.

p. 96: Although Scanlon, who was still paying off his student loans: *The Washington Post*, A Jackpot From Indian Gaming Tribes; Lobbying, PR Firms Paid $45 Million Over 3 Years, by Susan Schmidt, February 22, 2004, page 1.

p. 96: buttonholed Mendiola; Scanlon waylaid Norman S. Palacios: *The Los Angeles Times*, A Question of Influence; Two Former Aides to DeLay Paved Way for Lobbyist's Deal; Their work on Saipan helped get a contract for a lawyer now the target of a corruption probe, by Walter F. Roche, Jr. and Chuck Neubauer, May 6, 2005, page 1.

p. 97: lobbying business and that had been sought by Abramoff: Michael Scanlon Plea Agreement, Attachment A: Factual Basis for the Plea, November 21, 2005, see PACER.

p. 97: I give you something, you give me something," he insisted: *The Los Angeles Times*, A Question of Influence; Two Former Aides to DeLay Paved Way for Lobbyist's Deal; Their work on Saipan helped get a contract for a lawyer now the target of a corruption probe, by Walter F. Roche, Jr. and Chuck Neubauer, May 6, 2005, page 1.

p. 97: if possible, say National Center for Public Policy Research: *The Washington Post*, Nonprofit Groups Funneled Money for Abramoff, by Susan Schmidt and James V. Grimaldi, June 25, 2006, page 1.

p. 98: criminal activity — trading congressional appropriations for votes: *The Seattle Weekly*, Meet the Lapin Brothers, by Rick Anderson, May 11, 2005.

p. 99: Microsoft paid its 13 lobbying firms for the same period: *The Wall Street Journal*, Mississippi's Choctaw Find an Unlikely Ally in a GOP Stalwart, by Jim Vandehei, July 3, 2000, page 1.

p. 99: "top-paying single client of any lobbying" firm in the entire country: *National Journal*, Helping the Choctaw for $ 3 Million a Year, by Shawn Zeller, May 27, 2000.

CHAPTER SEVENTEEN
CHOCTAW

p. 99: we get our money's worth, or we wouldn't be doing it: *The Wall Street Journal*, Mississippi's Choctaw Find an Unlikely Ally in a GOP Stalwart, by Jim Vandehei, July 3, 2000, page 1.

p. 100: Indian casinos to be taxed in the same manner as Las Vegas gambling facilities: *The Washington Post*, Abramoff Allies Keeping Distance; Lobbyist Under Scrutiny for Dealings With Indian Tribes, by Thomas B. Edsall, November 8, 2004, page 23.

p. 100: essential governmental services to the some-10,000 tribal members: Hearing Before the Committee on Indian Affairs United States Senate, June 22, 2005, Testimony of Nell Rogers, planner, Mississippi Band of Choctaw Indians.

p. 100: occupy an Indian reservation, but a "free-enterprise zone: *The Washingtonian*, Local Lawyers and Lobbyists Have Big Stakes in Gambling, by Kim Eisler, November, 1998.

p. 101: campaign to say [about the Choctaws] 'these are good guys: *The Washington Post*, November 18, 2004, page 23.

p. 101: Choctaw's "lucrative perks," in order to pocket "hefty: *The Wall Street Journal*, Mississippi's Choctaw Find an Unlikely Ally in a GOP Stalwart, by Jim Vandehei, July 3, 2000, page 1.

p. 103: golf course designer Tom Fazio and PGA great Jerry Pate: http://www.dancingrabbitgolf. Com/.

p. 103: charitable event." That trip set the tribe back $6,935: *The Weekly Standard*, The Friends of Tom DeLay: What was the staff of the former majority leader up to anyway?, by Matthew Continetti, April 17, 2006.

p. 103: spirit…[who] offer a model for other tribes: *BusinessWeek*, Op-Eds for Sale: A columnist from a libertarian think tank admits accepting payments to promote an indicted lobbyist's clients. Will more examples follow?, by Eamon Javers, December 16, 2005: http

p. 103: but they surely knew tax reform," said Abramoff: *The Wall Street Journal*, Mississippi's Choctaw Find an Unlikely Ally in a GOP Stalwart, by Jim Vandehei, July 3, 2000, page 1.

p. 104: and conservatives should never be in favor of new taxes: *The New York Times*, At $500 an Hour, Lobbyist's Influence Rises With G.O.P., by David E. Rosenbaum, April 3, 2002, page 1.

p. 104: the tribe's ability to take its gambling operations online: *National Journal*, Helping the Choctaw for $ 3 Million a Year, by Shawn Zeller, May 27, 2000.

p. 104: in Congress, called this exemption "unprecedented: *The Wall Street Journal*, Mississippi's Choctaw Find an Unlikely Ally in a GOP Stalwart, by Jim Vandehei, July 3, 2000, page 1.

p. 107: of deliberately building trust and then betraying it: "Gimme Five"—Investigation of Tribal Lobbying Matters, Final Report before the Committee on Indian Affairs, June 22, 2006, page 22.

CHAPTER EIGHTEEN
SNAKE EYES

p. 108: important piece of education legislation in this state's history: http://www.stateline.org/ live/ViewPage.action?siteNodeId=136&languageId=1&contentId=13643

p. 109: please be sure to join me for the Redskins' quest for imperfection.": "Gimme Five"—Investigation of Tribal Lobbying Matters, Final Report before the Committee on Indian Affairs, June 22, 2006, Exhibit: Pre 2001.

p. 112: were not aware of every specific client or interest: *The Washington Post*, Reed Confirms Fees From Indian Casino Lobbyists, by Thomas Edsall, tagline by Susan Schmidt, August 30, 2004, page 3.

p. 112: hindsight that this is a piece of business I should have declined.": The Associated Press, Washington Tax-Cut Advocate Aided Abramoff, by Peter Yost, June 23, 2006, and "Gimme

Five"—Investigation of Tribal Lobbying Matters, Final Report before the Committee on Indian Affairs, June 22, 2006,

p. 112: By October, the referendum was defeated by a margin of 54-46: http://archive.salon.com/news/feature/1999/10/27/gambling/index.html

p. 112: a degree of sense, but it also means…[Abramoff] can justify huge fees.": *National Journal*, Lobbying: Helping the Choctaw for $3 Million a Year, by Shawn Zeller, May 27, 2000.

p. 112: tribal clients: "squelching supposedly ubiquitous threats": "Gimme Five"—Investigation of Tribal Lobbying Matters, Final Report before the Committee on Indian Affairs, June 22, 2006, page 11.

p. 112: that threats to the Tribe's gaming interests were everywhere: *Ibid*, page 54.

p. 112: threats—both real and imagined—that the Tribe faced: *Ibid*, page 55.

p. 113: falsely, about threats to their sovereignty or gaming interests: *Ibid*, page 211-212

CHAPTER NINETEEN
DISCRETION

p. 115: to sending payments through conduits at Abramoff's direction.": "Gimme Five"—Investigation of Tribal Lobbying Matters, Final Report before the Committee on Indian Affairs, June 22, 2006, pages 33-34.

p. 116: she understood that this was "the cost of operating under the radar.": "Gimme Five"—Investigation of Tribal Lobbying Matters, Final Report before the Committee on Indian Affairs, June 22, 2006, page 32.

p. 116: inform the borrower, who may have fared better with another lender.: *The Boston Globe*: October 2, 2007, Mortgage Brokers' Sleight of Hand, by Elizabeth Warren, Harvard Law professor, Op-Ed page.

p. 117: implants that the surgeon uses without ever informing their patients: *The Boston Globe*: November 7, 2007, Business Section

p. 117: It was unethical and ultimately it may have been illegal.": Senate Indian Affairs Committee Hearing, September 29, 2004, Sen. McCain's prepared statement.

p. 117: **Preston Gates, which were likely expensed to the Tribes:** "Gimme Five"—Investigation of Tribal Lobbying Matters, Final Report before the Committee on Indian Affairs, June 22, 2006,, footnote 105, Part II, Chapter II, page 272.

p. 118: scheme to not only con the tribe but con your partner: Senate Indian Affairs Committee, Public Hearing, November 17, 2004.

p. 118: contributions from Scanlon's company, Capitol Campaign Strategies: *The Washington Post*, May 18, 2004, page 17

p. 118: to accept any contributions from gambling interests: *Ibid*.

p. 118: controversial election and by a margin of only 3,120: http://www.sos.state.al.us/election /2002/index.aspx

p. 119: out of Alabama so it wouldn't hurt [the tribe's casino].": "Gimme Five"—Investigation of Tribal Lobbying Matters, Final Report before the Committee on Indian Affairs, June 22, 2006, page 48, see footnote 59.

p. 119: used as conduits by Rove and Abramoff…to destroy me.": http://rawstory.com/news/ 2008/ iegelman_Exposing_Rove_worth_every_day_0430.html

p. 119: $250,000 payment to the Governors' Association showed up: "Gimme Five"—Investigation of Tribal Lobbying Matters, Final Report before the Committee on Indian Affairs, June 22, 2006, page 231.

p. 120: $250,000 payments on October 14 and 22, 2002—were omitted: "Gimme Five"—Investigation of Tribal Lobbying Matters, Final Report before the Committee on Indian Affairs, June 22, 2006, page 217.

p. 120: Riley's gubernatorial campaign in the summer of 2004: *The Washington Post*, May 18, 2004, page A 17

p. 120: single largest that the Republican Governors' Association received in 2002: *Texas Observer*, November 19, 2004, K Street Croupiers, by Louis Dubose: http://www.Texasobserver. org/article.php?aid=1800

p. 120: ability to settle that civil matter with those parties.": Senate Indian Affairs Committee Public Hearing, June 22, 2005, page 27.

p. 122: hard to believe, coming from a lobbyist, but it's true.": *National Journal*, May 5, 2000.

p. 122:"rise to concerns that Abramoff had defrauded the Tribe…": "Gimme Five"—Investigation of Tribal Lobbying Matters, Final Report before the Committee on Indian Affairs, June 22, 2006, page 137.

CHAPTER TWENTY
THE GAME

p. 123: anti-NACS [National Association of Convenience Stores] work: "Gimme Five"—Investigation of Tribal Lobbying Matters, Final Report before the Committee on Indian Affairs, June 22, 2006, page 36.

p. 125: Choctaws donated $100,000 to the Republican State Elections Committee: *National Journal*, May 27, 2000.

p. 125: unreported donations to a network of conservative groups: *The Wall Street Journal*, July 3, 2000.

p. 125: Abramoff's clout was so effective and pervasive on Capital Hill: http://www.capitaleye. org/abramoff.asp.

p. 126: we wanted from Sen. Conrad Burns' committee we got: *Vanity Fair*, Washington's Invisible Man, by David Margolick, April 6, 2006.

CHAPTER TWENTY-ONE
MOBUTU

p. 128: to do was dig up my letter to the editor to *The Seattle Times*: *The Seattle Times*, Letters to the Editor, April 27, 1995, page B5.

CHAPTER TWENTY-TWO
INTRIGUE

p. 129: to sell a critical foreign-aid vote to the Russian mob.: *The New American*, Seeing Russia the Abramoff Way, by William Norman Grigg, February 6, 2006.

p. 129: Justice Department…issued subpoenas in early 2006: *National Journal*, "Investigators Issue New Subpoena in Abramoff Case" by Peter H. Stone: February 13, 2006.

p. 129: ministry, or office holder or agent of the Russian Government.: *The Boston Globe*, Abramoff's Ties to Russians Probed, by Michael Kranish, February 23, 2006.

p. 129: the whole dynamic of the Middle East.": United Press International: "Abramoff Tried to Get Israeli Oil Rights": 1 March 2006

p. 130: and were protected by bodyguards with machine guns.: *The Washington Post*, The DeLay-Abramoff Money Trail by R. Jeffrey Smith: December 31, 2005, page 1.

p. 131: Soviet-era internal security and intelligence agencies: http://www.exile.ru/articles/detial.php?ARTICLE_ID=7718&IBLOCK_ID=35

p. 131: school for Russian military intelligence agents.: *Russia Reform Monitor*, No. 302, 25 August 1997: American Foreign Policy Council

p. 131: progressive market reforms and bilateral trade.: *Ibid*.

p. 131: Abramoff received $260,000 in fees from Chelsea: *The Washington Post*, A 3rd DeLay Trip Under Scrutiny; 1997 Russia Visit Reportedly Backed by Business Interests, by R. Jeffrey Smith and James V. Grimaldi, April 6, 2005, page 1.

p. 131: a semi-independent tax-haven off the coast of France.: *Ibid*

p. 132: US Family Network, a "pro family" and "moral fitness: *The Washington Post*, Former DeLay Aide Enriched by Nonprofit, by R. Jeffrey Smith: March 26, 2006, page 1.

p. 132: Buckham had set up a few months earlier: *Ibid*.

p. 132: to provide money to evangelical Christian charities.: *The Boston Globe*, Abramoff's Ties to Russians Probed, by Michael Kranish, February 23, 2006, page 1.

p. 132: to restoring our government to citizen control.": *National Journal*: "Abramoff's Network" by Peter H. Stone, March 11, 2006.

p. 132: to himself and other volunteer board members.: *The Boston Globe*, Abramoff's Ties to Russians Probed, by Michael Kranish, February 23, 2006, page 1.

p. 132: were several conservative scholars and journalists: *The New Republic*, Abramoff's Shadow Lobby, by Franklin Foer, May 16, 2005.

p. 133: Abramoff served as a board member: *The Boston Globe*, Abramoff's Ties to Russians Probed, by Michael Kranish, February 23, 2006, page 1.

p. 133: as "THE CENTER for conservative communications,": *The Wall Street Journal*: "Conservative Center Stands By DeLay—As Majority Leader Fends Off Ethics Questions, Washington Think Tank Remains an Ally," by David Rogers: May 23, 2005.

p. 133: Houston to businessmen interested in expanding trade: *National Journal*: "Abramoff's Network" by Peter H. Stone, March 11, 2006.

p. 134: to jail and [Koulakovsky] would go to jail.": *The Washington Post*, The DeLay-Abramoff Money Trail by R. Jeffrey Smith: December 31, 2005, page 1.

p. 134: staff's portion of the trip came to $57,238.: *The Washington Post*, A 3rd DeLay Trip Under Scrutiny; 1997 Russia Visit Reportedly Backed by Business Interests, by R. Jeffrey Smith and James V. Grimaldi, April 6, 2005, page 1.

p. 134: the Russian stock market tumbled 50%.: *The New York Times*: Rescuing Russia: A Special Report: The Bailout of the Kremlin: How the U.S. Pressed the I.M.F., by Michael R. Gordon and David E. Sanger: July 17, 1998, page 1.

p. 134: export, had bottomed out under $15.: http://www.wtrg.com/pices.htm

p. 135: an additional $18 billion for funding the IMF: http://www.rferl.org/reports/ corruptionwatch/2002/06/25-270602.asp

p. 135: boost tax collection and cut government spending: *The Washington Post*, Russia, IMF Reach Bailout Agreement, by Daniel Williams, July 14, 1998, page 1.

p. 135: forwarded again by James & Sarch.: *The Washington Post*, The DeLay-Abramoff Money Trail by R. Jeffrey Smith: December 31, 2005, page 1.

p. 135: amount of money to come from a foreign source.": *Ibid*.

p. 135: promptly vanished the day it arrived.: *The Washington Post:*, IMF Ready to Resume Russia Aid, $4.5 Billion Loan Tied to Aid, by Paul Blustein, April 29, 1999, page E1.

p. 135: treasury bills and devalued the ruble.: *The New York Times*, "Russia Acts to Save Sinking Finances," by Celestine Bohlen: August 18, 1998, page 1.

p. 135: That's just outrageous," DeLay said.: *The Washington Post*, The DeLay-Abramoff Money Trail by R. Jeffrey Smith: December 31, 2005, page 1.

p. 135: new funds to replenish the IMF account.": *Ibid.*

p. 136: the IMF is now bailing out the bankrupt.": *The New York Times*, House Panel Blocks New Funds for I.M.F., by Katharine Q. Seelye, September 11, 1998, page 12.

p. 136: did vote "to replenish the IMF account,": *The Washington Post*, The DeLay-Abramoff Money Trail by R. Jeffrey Smith: December 31, 2005, page 1.

p. 136: of the $18 billion Clinton had requested.: *The New York Times*, House Votes Small Fraction of Money Sought for I.M.F., by Katharine Q. Seeyle, September, 18, 1998, page 12.

p. 137: other issues "pertaining to defense and security.": *The Boston Globe*, Abramoff's Ties to Russians Probed, by Michael Kranish, February 23, 2006, page 1.

p. 137: I said, 'I think this will never happen.'": *Ibid.*

p. 137: no assets, no activity, and listed no shareholders.: *Ibid.*

p. 137: 2004, Abramoff's firm forced him to resign.: *The Washington Post*, Lobbyist Quits as Firm Probes Work With Tribes, by Susan Schmidt: March 4, 2004, page 1.

p. 137: resignation, Voor Huisen was quietly dissolved.: *Vrij Nederlander*, Abramoff: The Dutch Connection, by Freke Vuijst, January 14, 2006.

CHAPTER TWENTY-THREE
JEWISH OIL

p. 129: change the whole dynamic of the Middle East: *The Boston Globe*,. Abramoff Pushed Plan to Drill for Oil in Israel: Established Firm With Two Russians, by Michael Kranish, March 1, 2006, page 1.

p. 138: and we are running short of time: "Gimme Five"— Investigation of Tribal Lobbying Matters, Final Report before the Committee on Indian Affairs, June 22, 2006.

p. 138: unable to obtain the required permits: *The Boston Globe*,. Abramoff Pushed Plan to Drill for Oil in Israel: Established Firm With Two Russians, by Michael Kranish, March 1, 2006, page 1.

p. 139: of oil a day—an inconsequential amount: http://www.haaretz.com/hasen/pages/ ShArt.jhtml?itemNo=434666&contrassID=1&subContrassID= 1&sbSubContrassID=0&listSrc=Y

CHAPTER TWENTY-FOUR
RECONNECTION

p. 142: for the arrest of his mother's murderers: *The Weekly Standard*, by Matthew Continetti, November 28, 2005

p. 142: a decision we didn't have to sleep on: PR Newswire: February 15, 1994.

p. 142: got national coverage on that," he said: *Ibid*

p. 142: Greater Washington Urban League: *The Washington Post*, Appointments, June 1, 1998, pF20.

p. 142: Commerce Political Action Committee: *Washington Business Journal*, October 9, 1998; page 1

p. 142: and Greater D.C. Cares: *The Washington Post*, August 16, 1999; page D17.

p. 142: "We do this on a regular basis: *The Virginia Pilot (Norfolk)*, July 20, 1995, by Scott McCaskey, page 5.

p. 142: illustrating his purported mendacity: *The Weekly Standard*, Money, Mobster, and Murder: The Sordid Tale of a GOP Lobbyist's Casino Deal Gone Bad; by Matthew Continetti; November 28, 2005.

p. 143: The next day I got a check: *The Washington Times*, February 17, 1995 by John McCaslin; page A5

p. 143: last 'S,' that's for solicitations: *Ibid.*

p. 143: to prevent a takeover by the parent firm: *The Washington Post*, April 26, 1996; page F3

p. 143: said Kidan of the bankruptcy filing: *The Washington Post*, August 25, 1997, page 10.

p. 143: Robert Isler, Barragan's assistant general counsel: *Washington Business Journal*, July 2, 1999, page 3.

p. 144: Dial-A-Mattress for an "eight-figure payoff: Abramoff deposition

p. 144: paid Kidan $800,000 in cash for the franchise: A confidential source.

p. 144: Kidan was driving a 1995 Dodge: Kidan's bankruptcy filed in U. S. federal court in Baltimore, MD, available online from Public Access to Court Electronic Records (PACER).

CHAPTER TWENTY-FIVE
DEAL OF THE CENTURY

p. 145: stake,' recalled a former colleague of Abramoff's: *Heist*, by Peter H. Stone, page 66

p. 146: Boulis told the firm he did not care: *The Washington Post*, Untangling a Lobbyist's Stake in a Casino Fleet; With Millions of Dollars Unaccounted for, Another Federal Investigation Targets Abramoff, by Susan Schmidt and James V. Grimaldi, May 1, 2005, page 1.

p. 149: We hire lawyers if we have to: *The St. Petersburg Times (Florida)*, February 8, 2001, by Thomas C. Tobin

p. 149: fleet and pay a $2 million fine: *The Miami Herald*, February 2, 2001, Judge Urged to Air Casino-Boat Mogul's Secret Deal, by Erika Bolstead, page B3.

CHAPTER TWENTY-SIX
BANKERS

p. 151: so I would suffer for the rest of my life.": *The Broward-Palm Beach NewTimes,* November 10, 2005, The Bad Bet, by Trevor Aaronson

CHAPTER TWENTY-SEVEN
WIRED

p. 154: to place a statement in the Congressional Record: *Heist,* by Peter H. Stone, page 69

p. 155: that we can protect consumers across the country: http://frwb-gate4.access.gpo.gov/cgi-bin/waisgate.cgi?WAISdocID=796962488896+0+0+0&WAISaction=retrieve

p. 155: flown…over the U.S. Capitol, courtesy of DeLay: *The Washington Post,* Untangling a Lobbyist's Stake in a Casino Fleet; With Millions of Dollars Unaccounted for, Another Federal Investigation Targets Abramoff, by Susan Schmidt and James V. Grimaldi, May 1, 2005, page 1.

p. 156: shareholders agreement. Regards, Adam: e-mail never publicly released, in author's possession.

p. 157: Gus. Will we be OK with this?: e-mail never publicly released, in author's possession.

p. 158: is carefully planned out. Regards, Adam.: e-mail never publicly released, in author's possession.

p. 159: deferred to Kidan on all things financial.": Waldman's letter to Judge Huck.

p. 159: said. "He's a very honest man.": http://frwbgate4.access.gpo.gov/cgi-bin/waisgate.cgi?WAISdocID=796962488896+0+0+0&WAISaction=retrieve

p. 159: partner in the law firm of Preston Gates…": Criminal indictment, United States District Court Southern District of Florida, United States of America v. Adam R. Kidan and Jack A. Abramoff, Case # 05-60204 CR-HUCK, August 17, 2005, page 8.

p. 162: "The credit has to stand on its own.": *The Washington Post,* Untangling a Lobbyist's Stake in a Casino Fleet; With Millions of

Dollars Unaccounted for, Another Federal Investigation Targets Abramoff, by Susan Schmidt and James V. Grimaldi, May 1, 2005, page 1.

p. 165: the substituted notes from the lenders.": *Ibid*

p. 165: who are we hiding these items from & why?": *Ibid*

p. 165: going on and are a party to it," he said: *Ibid*

p. 166: requested that Ms. Glait attend the closing: Citadel Equity Fund Ltd. v. Wells Fargo Foothill, The United States District Court for the Southern District of New York, file # 04CV08648, November 1, 2004, pages 15-16.

CHAPTER TWENTY-EIGHT
OFFSETS

p. 167: they paid the interest on the loans.": *The Village Voice*, October 24, 2006, In the Beginning, There was Adam: The Man Who Helped Bring Abramoff Down Goes to Prison for his own Misdeeds, by Sean Gardiner.

p. 167: riches and his exit from hourly fees.": *Heist*, by Peter H. Stone, page 66

p. 168: initially just six years ago with a single boat.": *Business Wire*, September 27, 2000

p. 168: violated every environmental rule.": *The St. Petersburg Times (Florida)*, September 28, 2000

p. 168: in charitable contributions annually.": *The Miami Herald*, SunCruz Changes Owners Bigger Gambling Ships Planned, by Cynthia Corzo, September 27, 2000, page 1.

p. 168: He was not a good corporate citizen.": *Ibid*.

p. 170: by the government to sell…SunCruz.":*Heist*, by Peter H. Stone, page 65.

p. 171: enterprise to an upstanding establishment.: http://frwebgate4.access.gpo.gov/cgi-bin/ waisgate.cgi?WAISdocID=7969501601+0+0+0&WAISaction=retrieve

p. 172: Boulis grew up in a culture of violence.": *The Miami Herald*, Businessman Was Worried that Boulis Might Kill Him, by Erika Bolstad, February 8, 2001, page 21.

p. 172: troubles or alleged Gambino affiliations.": *The Washington Post*, Untangling a Lobbyist's Stake in a Casino Fleet; With Millions of Dollars Unaccounted for, Another Federal Investigation Targets Abramoff, by Susan Schmidt and James V. Grimaldi, May 1, 2005, page 1.

p. 172: charges against Moscatiello were dropped: *Ibid*.

p. 173: because it was top secret: *The Miami Herald,* Wiseguy Defendant Doubled as FBI Snitch: The Star Defendant in the Murder of Konstantinos "Gus" Boulis had Secretly Been Playing Both Sides of the Law, by Wanda DeMarzo and Jay Weaver, April 1, 2006, page 1.

CHAPTER TWENTY-NINE
HONEST HANDS

p. 174: I immediately told Jack," said Waldman: Waldman's unpublished letter to Judge Huck in author's possession.

p. 174: the company to honest hands.": *Ibid*

p. 174: "Abramoff was flabbergasted by this news.": *The Washington Post*, Untangling a Lobbyist's Stake in a Casino Fleet, by Susan Schmidt and James Grimaldi, May 1, 2005, page 1.

p. 174: Kidan "beaten and/or killed.": *The Miami Herald*, February 2, 2001, page 1B.

p. 175: Embarrassed, Kidan threatened to sue: *The Washington Post*, Untangling a Lobbyist's Stake in a Casino Fleet, by Susan Schmidt and James Grimaldi, May 1, 2005, page 1.

p. 175: from Kidan and any SunCruz operation.": *The Miami Herald*, Businessman Was Worried that Boulis Might Kill Him, by Erika Bolstad, February 8, 2001, page 21.

p. 176: implicitly supporting Kidan's version: *The Washington Post*, Untangling a Lobbyist's Stake in a Casino Fleet, by Susan Schmidt and James Grimaldi, May 1, 2005, page 1.

p. 176: Department of State Division of Licensing: *The Boston Herald*, "Sea of Trouble; Gloucester Gambling Boat Navigates Mob Ties," by Jonathan Wells, Jack Meyers, and Maggie Mulvihill, November 13, 2002, page 1.

p. 176: but the situation is at a critical point: *The Washington Post*, Untangling a Lobbyist's Stake in a Casino Fleet, by Susan Schmidt and James Grimaldi, May 1, 2005, page 1.

CHAPTER THIRTY
GANGLAND SLAYING

p. 179: saddened by the death of Gus Boulis.": *The Miami Herald*, Businessman Was Worried that Boulis Might Kill Him, by Erika Bolstad, February 8, 2001, page 21.

p. 179: "He didn't seem to have too many friends.": *The St. Petersburg Times (Florida)*, February 8, 2001

p. 180: across from one of his "Miami Subs: *The Miami Herald*, Florida Development Mogul Gunned Down in Fort Lauderdale, by Wanda J. DeMarzo and William Yardley, February 7, 2001, page 1. Also, Associated Press, Miami Businessmen Killed in Ambush, by Adrian Sainz, February 7, 2001.

p. 181: was laid to rest in a platinum casket..: The description of Boulis' murder comes from news reports, confidential interviews, and interviews with Adam Kidan.

p. 181: point-blank range. He killed my mother: *Mob Over Miami*, by Michele McPhee, 2002, page 288.

p. 184: not something I would repeat.": *The Washington Post*, Untangling a Lobbyist's Stake in a Casino, by Susan Schmidt and James Grimaldi, May 1, 2005, page 1.

p. 184: ha ha, you shouldn't be in the business.": *The Miami Herald*, by Fred Grim, December 25, 2005.

p. 186: one of Florida's most "notorious": *The Miami Herald*, February 7, 2001, page 1B

p. 187: "'It's called Three Miles Out.'": *Forbes* magazine, Going for Broke, by Michael Freedman, September 17, 2001

p. 187: through his business dealings.": document in author's possession.

CHAPTER THIRTY-ONE
SMEAR CAMPAIGN

p. 190: You don't know until election night: *Norfolk Virginia-Pilot*, Robertson Political Arm to Help GOP in Other States, September, 9, 1991. Also, carried by United Press International, same date.

p. 190: contemplated switching to the Democratic Party: *The New York Times*, Two Divergent McCain Moments, Rarely Mentioned, by Elisabeth Bumiller, March 24, 2008, page 16.

p. 191: as if he is morally superior to them: *The Week*, February 1, 2008, page 2.

p. 192: fathered an illegitimate black child?: *The New York Times*, Confronting Ghost of 2000 in South Carolina, by Jennifer Steinhauer, October 19, 2007, page 1.

p. 192: openly gay people for his administration: *The New York Times*, by Frank Rich, Everybody Into the Mudfight, February 26, 2000, page 15.

p. 193: prisoner of war in North Vietnam: *The New York Times*, Two Divergent McCain Moments, Rarely Mentioned, by Elisabeth Bumiller, March 24, 2008, page 16.

p. 194: information" he gave to the enemy in return: *U.S. News & World Report*, How POW's Fought Back, by John S. McCain III, May 14, 1973, page 46.

p. 194: cities that had already been bombed: *Faith of My Fathers*, by John McCain with Mark Salter, 1999, page 191-194.

p. 194: black crimes, and other generalities: *U.S. News & World Report*, How POW's Fought Back, by John S. McCain III, May 14, 1973, page 46.

p. 195: an operation that I did not deserve: *Faith of My Fathers*, by John McCain with Mark Salter, 1999, page 244.

p. 195: is always worse than the crime.: *Why Courage Matters*, by John McCain with Mark Salter, 2004, page 71.

p. 195: having lost the courage it demanded: *Ibid*, pages 107-8.

p. 195: I felt when I didn't measure up: *Ibid*, pages 168-9.

THE PERFECT VILLAIN 405

p. 196: alone, so much in its isolation: http://www.vietnamveteransagainstjohnmccain.com/ declassified_nhan_dan_interview_11_09_1967.pdf

p. 197: This isn't Paris, but it's alright: http://www.vietnamveteransagainstjohnmccain.com/ declassified_chalais_interview_12_29_1967.pdf

p. 197: much of my health and strength: http://www.vietnamveteransagainstjohnmccain.com/ declassified__Laird_interview_June%202_%201969.pdf

p. 203: at a cocktail party [emphasis ended: http://www.vietnam-veteransagainstjohnmccain. com/declassified_fernando_interview_1_24_1970.pdf

p. 204: let me tell you what it is—deceit: http://www.dailymail.co.uk/femail/article-1024927/The-wife-John-McCain-callously-left-behind.html#comments.

p. 204: imprisonment by the North Vietnamese communists: http://www.Salon.com/opinion/ conason/2006/03/03/mccain_candidacy/ind:ex.html

p. 204: advocating the policies of "Big Labor: *The Boston Globe*, Attack Ad says McCain's 'Soft Money' legislation hurts GOP, by Jill Zuckman, December 24, 1999

p. 204: just politics, John. It doesn't mean anything: *The Boston Globe*, Book Review: Divided We Stand: How Al Gore Beat George Bush and Lost the Presidency, by Roger Simon, October 9, 2001, page C5

p. 205: for his rival "through gritted teeth: *The New Yorker*, McCain's Party, by Connie Bruck, May 30, 2005.

p. 205: smiles and pledges to work together: *USA Today*, GOP's Future on the Table at Bush-McCain Meeting, page 8A

p. 206: not pretend the Indians are stupid: *Vanity Fair*, Washington's Invisible Man, by David Margolick, April 2006.

p. 207: protect and obtain more gaming opportunities: *New American Media*, American Indian Media: Tribes' Greed Led Them Into Abramoff Scandal, by Peter Micek, January 11, 2006.

p. 207: until he appeared before the committee: *Ibid*.

CHAPTER THIRTY-TWO
MUSIC, GOLF, LUCK

p. 208: Carreras, Placido Domingo, and Luciano Pavarotti.: The Associated Press, April 20, 2005, http://www.msnbc.msn.com/id/7577057/.

p. 210: according to the Center for Public Integrity.: *The Center for Public Integrity Report*, published June 5, 2006. http://www.publicintegrity.org/powertrips/report.aspx?aid=799

p. 210: DeLay departed on the trip," according to *The Washington Post*.: *The Washington Post*, Gambling Interests Funded DeLay Trip, March 12, 2005, page 1.

p. 210: the donations from Choctaw and eLottery.: *Ibid*.

p. 211: frolic and detour to the links at St. Andrews.: "Gimme Five"— Investigation of Tribal Lobbying Matters, Final Report before the Committee on Indian Affairs, June 22, 2006.

p. 211: as long as they were promptly reimbursed.: *The Washington Post*, April 24, 2005, DeLay Airfare was Charged to Lobbyist's Credit Card, page 1.

p. 211: some [of] the things we had done.": *The Washington Post*, Gambling Interests Funded DeLay Trip, March 12, 2005, page 1.

p. 212: paying her $115,000 over a three-year period.: *The Galveston News (Galveston County)*, January 10, 2006, http://www.galvnews.com/story.lasso?ewcd=c029f447454b3364.

p. 212: to hire Rudy's wife as a consultant.": *Los Angeles Times*, February 11, 2006, page 1.

p. 213: provided him with things of value.": Department of Justice press release, March 31, 2005. http://www.usdoj.gov/opa/pr/2006/march/06_crm_197.html

p. 213: cocktail parties I have to go to?": *The New York Times*, A Developer, His Deals and His Ties to McCain, April 22, 2008, page 1; and The Trouble With not Being Earnest, April 25, 2008, page 26.

p. 213: whose executives were major campaign donors: *The New York Times*, by Ariel Alexovich, May 16, 2008. http://thecaucus.blogs.nytimes.com/2008/05/16/the-early-word-conflict-issue-for-McCain/

p. 213: corporations that had business before his committee.: http://cgi.cnn.com/TRANSCRIPTS/ 0002/07/ip.00.html.

p. 214: the business of eLottery, Abramoff's client.: *The Washington Post*, Gambling Interests Funded DeLay Trip, March 12, 2005, page 1.

p. 214: "We wouldn't have been able to operate.": *Ibid.*

p. 216: conservatives back on this or we are doomed.": *The Washington Post*, October 16, 2005, How A Lobbyist Stacked the Deck; Abramoff Used DeLay Aide, Attacks on Allies to Defeat Anti-Gambling Bill, by Susan Schmidt and James V. Grimaldi, page 1.

p. 216: "I told him I strongly opposed the bill.": *The Congressional Quarterly*, July 13/14, 2000.

p. 216: "based on sound public policy and principle.": *The Washington Post*, October 16, 2005, How A Lobbyist Stacked the Deck; Abramoff Used DeLay Aide, Attacks on Allies to Defeat Anti-Gambling Bill, by Susan Schmidt and James V. Grimaldi, page 1.

p. 217: have to deal with all those amendments.": *Ibid.*

p. 217: "eroded just enough votes" to defeat the bill: *Ibid.*

p. 218: I'm shocked out of my socks," said Sheldon.: *Ibid.*

CHAPTER THIRTY-THREE
THE STARS LINE UP

p. 222: they're ready to 'hang on the wall.': "Gimme Five"—Investigation of Tribal Lobbying Matters, Final Report before the Committee on Indian Affairs, June 22, 2006. Exhibit 31

p. 222: read aloud at one of McCain's hearings.: *The Washington Post*, One Committee's Three Hours of Inquiry, In Surreal Time, June 23, 2005, p. 1.

p. 222: "[f]rom my side it was tongue-in-cheek.": *The Washington Post*, The Republicans' Rabbi in Arms, page C1.

p. 222: wallpaper his office with awards.": *The Seattle Weekly*, A Rabbi's Regrets, January 18, 2006.

p. 222: on the Greenberg Traurig official website,: The website, http://GTLAW.com/bios/govadmin/abramoff.html, has been deleted. The author is in possession of a hard copy of Abramoff's profile.

p. 223: 82 contacts with Rove's office.: *The New York Times*, Report Finds 82 Contacts Between Abramoff and Rove, September 29, 2006

p. 224: would describe him as a casual acquaintance.": Associated Press, White House: Rove Considered Abramoff 'A Casual Acquaintance', February 14, 2006.

p. 224: even encouraged me, to repeat a lie.": *The Los Angeles Times*, May 26, 2008, page 1.

p. 225: a notorious Republican dirty trickster.: *Too Close to Call*, by Jeffrey Toobin, Random House, 2001.

p. 226: the eighth largest law firm in the world,: Alabama-Coushatta Tribe of Texas v. Jack Abramoff, Michael Scanlon, Jon van Horne, Neil Volz, and Ralph Reed, United States District Court Western District of Texas Austin Division, July 12, 2006. Page 7.

p. 226: immediately replied, [Be] happy to.": "Gimme Five"— Investigation of Tribal Lobbying Matters, Final Report before the Committee on Indian Affairs, June 22, 2006.

p. 226: White House to meet with Rove to discuss it.: *The Washington Post*, Log Shows 2 Abramoff visits to White House, May 10, 2006.

p. 226: have shown much interest in Zachares.": House Government Reform Committee Report: Jack Abramoff's Contacts with White House Officials (updated June 11, 2008), page 24: e-mail exchange between Doug Hoelscher, Ken Mehlman, Matt Schlapp, and Paul Dyck (November 9, 2001.)

p. 227: worth of tickets to sporting events and concerts.: *The Hill*, April 24, 2007: http://thehill.com/ leading-the-news/feeney-fbi-probe-of-his-ties-to-abramoff-is-unthreatening-2007-04-24.html

p. 227: specifications: "no smokers or fats please.": .": *The Weekly Standard*, Roger Stone: Political Animal, November 5, 2007: http://www.weeklystandard.com/Utilities/printer_preview.asp?idArticle14278&R= 1163A318CF

p. 228: from the wealthy Indian gaming tribes.: *The Village Voice*, by Wayne Barrett, The Man Who Stopped Miami Recount Makes Gaming Millions: A Dirty Trickster's Bush Bonanza, April 19, 2005

p. 228: Reed later denied saying this.: *The Washingtonian*, by Kim Eisler, June 2006.

CHAPTER THIRTY-FOUR
ADJUSTMENTS

p. 229: end up dead, disgraced, or in jail.": *The Washington Post*, Untangling a Lobbyist's Stake in a Casino, by Susan Schmidt and James Grimaldi, May 1, 2005, page 1.

p. 230: heavy into the relationship side.: *The Washington Post*, December 14, 2000.

p. 230: "vaulted" into the upper tier.": The House Government Reform Committee Report on Jack Abramoff's White House Lobbying, September, 29, 2006, page 14.

p. 230: the reputation we want to have.": *The Hill*, April 4, 2001.

p. 231: four Wizards tickets worth $1,300.: The House Government Reform Committee Report on Jack Abramoff's White House Lobbying, September, 29, 2006

p. 232: [Abramoff] influence-peddling scandal.: *The Washington Post*, October 7, 2006, page 1.

CHAPTER THIRTY-FIVE
COUSHATTA COMPACT

p. 232: "I call Jack and I get results: *The New York Times*, At $500 an Hour, Lobbyist's Interests Rise with GOP, by David E. Rosenbaum, April 2, 2002.

p. 232: took every opportunity [to rob] us: "Gimme Five"— Investigation of Tribal Lobbying Matters, Final Report before the Committee on Indian Affairs, June 22, 2006.

p. 233: revenue came from its casino profits: Senate Indian Affairs Committee interview of William Worfel on September 13-15, 2005.

p. 233: expecting a "very vigorous fight: Senate Indian Affairs Committee interview of Kathryn Van Hoof, former outside counsel, Coushatta Tribe of Louisiana, in Lecompte, Louisiana (September 21, 2005).

p. 234: a sophisticated business-oriented tribe: Statement by William Worfel to Senate Indian Affairs Committee, November 2, 2004.

p. 236: mistreated, been misled," said Worfel.: *Time* Magazine, January 8, 2006, Cover Story.

p. 236: give them real "stroke" in Washington.: *Ibid*.

p. 238: about his renewing the Coushatta's compact.: *The Washington Post*, Casino Bid Prompted High-Stakes Lobbyist; Probe Scrutinizes Efforts Against Tribe, by Susan Schmidt, March 13, 2005, page 1.

p. 238: Norton—along with Steven Griles, her deputy.: *Ibid*.

p. 240: issues for gaming tribes on the horizon: *The Washington Post*, A Jackpot From Indian Gaming Tribes: Lobbying, PR Firms Paid $45 Million Over 3 Years, by Susan Schmidt, February 22, 2004, page 1.

p. 239: Ashcroft and his guys will also be there: *Heist*, by Peter Stone, page 96.

p. 240: lying to" McCain Senate committee.: *The Hill*, Norton Aide Cops a Plea, June 7, 2007

p. 241: four years probation was considered relatively mild.: *The Washington Post*, Republican With Links to Abramoff Sentenced; Judge Insists She Serve Time, Rejects Request for Harsher Sentence for Colleague at Environmental Group, By Susan Schmidt, December 15, 2007, page 7.

CHAPTER THIRTY-SIX
JENAS

p. 240: considered sovereign nations, they are state-tax exempt: National Journal, Helping the Choctaw for $ 3 Million a Year, by Shawn Zeller, May 27, 2000.

p. 241: being approved by the Texas Legislature.": "Gimme Five"— Investigation of Tribal Lobbying Matters, Final Report before the Committee on Indian Affairs, June 22, 2006.

p. 242: whom the Jenas had hired to build their casino.: *The Village Voice*, by Wayne Barrett, The Man Who Stopped Miami Recount

Makes Gaming Millions: A Dirty Trickster's Bush Bonanza, April 19, 2005

p. 242: not Abramoff, who got it quashed.: *The Texas Observer*, November 19, 2004, K Street Croupiers, by Louis Dubose: http://www.texasobserver.org/article.php?aid=1800

p. 242: Coushattas, was extensive and successful.": *The Washington Post*, Casino Bid Prompted High-Stakes Lobbyist; Probe Scrutinizes Efforts Against Tribe, by Susan Schmidt, March 13, 2005, page 1.

p. 242: over 220 million people worldwide.: http://www.focusonfamily.com/press/focusvoices/ A000000025.cfm

p. 243: play it in the [White House] and Interior.": *The Washington Post*, Casino Bid Prompted High-Stakes Lobbyist; Probe Scrutinizes Efforts Against Tribe, by Susan Schmidt, March 13, 2005, page 1.

p. 243: Interior official later told *The Washington Post*.: Ibid.

p. 243: Michael Rossetti, Norton's legal councilor.: *Heist*, by Peter Stone, page 97-8.

p. 243: [Norton] and the President slamming [her].": *The Village Voice*, by Wayne Barrett, The Man Who Stopped Miami Recount Makes Gaming Millions: A Dirty Trickster's Bush Bonanza, April 19, 2005

p. 243: the Jena Band's bid for a casino.: *The Washington Post*, Casino Bid Prompted High-Stakes Lobbyist; Probe Scrutinizes Efforts Against Tribe, by Susan Schmidt, March 13, 2005, page 1.

p. 244: Reed told Abramoff in an e-mail. "Gimme Five"—Investigation of Tribal Lobbying Matters, Final Report before the Committee on Indian Affairs, June 22, 2006, page 98.

p. 244: in political donations from Abramoff's clients: "Gimme Five"—Investigation of Tribal Lobbying Matters, Final Report before the Committee on Indian Affairs, June 22, 2006.

p. 244: his decision to deny an Indian casino license.: *The Village Voice*, by Wayne Barrett, The Man Who Stopped Miami Recount Makes Gaming Millions: A Dirty Trickster's Bush Bonanza, April 19, 2005

p. 244: [including] a $100,000 check to CREA.": *The Washington Post*, Casino Bid Prompted High-Stakes Lobbyist; Probe Scrutinizes Efforts Against Tribe, by Susan Schmidt, March 13, 2005, page 1.

p. 244: "influenced by any outside kind of pressure,": *Ibid.*

p. 244: income tax on a sovereign Indian nation.: *The Village Voice*, by Wayne Barrett, The Man Who Stopped Miami Recount Makes Gaming Millions: A Dirty Trickster's Bush Bonanza, April 19, 2005

p. 245: Las Vegas-based Pinnacle Development, Inc.: http://www.secinfo.com/dV5Ff.36V5

p. 246: a Jena lobbyist, no doubt with a tinge of envy.: *Heist*, by Peter H. Stone, page 99.

p. 247: no option except to give it to…Michael Rossetti.": "Gimme Five"—Investigation of Tribal Lobbying Matters, Final Report before the Committee on Indian Affairs, June 22, 2006. Part II.

p. 248: her opposition to the expansion of gambling.: *The Village Voice*, by Wayne Barrett, The Man Who Stopped Miami Recount Makes Gaming Millions: A Dirty Trickster's Bush Bonanza, April 19, 2005

CHAPTER THIRTY-SEVEN
BIN LADEN

p. 248: Isaacson, of the American Jewish Congress.: *The Forward*, by E.J. Kessler, April 22, 2005.

p. 249: was used heavily by Osama bin Laden.: *Heist*, by Peter H. Stone, page 117.

p. 249: because he served on the House Financial Services.: *Ibid.*

CHAPTER THIRTY-EIGHT
SAGCHIPS

p. 250: guidelines and there was no unemployment.: http://www.itcm.org/thehistorytribal6.htlm.

p. 251 one of Abramoff's keenest competitors.": "Gimme Five"—Investigation of Tribal Lobbying Matters, Final Report before the Committee on Indian Affairs, June 22, 2006, page 63.

p. 251: "Rosenthal has been badmouthing us nonstop.": *Ibid*, page 64.

p. 251: appropriations are zeroed out, they'll be back.": *Ibid*

p. 252: Saginaw's market, between 10 and 17 percent.": Bernie Sprague Interview with Senate Indian Affairs Committee, September 14, 2004.

p. 252: assisting his uncle's tribe to obtain a casino.: Speech given by Sprague during Saginaw Chippewa "State of the Tribe" Community Meeting, January 29, 2006.

p. 252: casino was poised to open in 2009.: *The Kalamazoo Gazette (Michigan)*, February 10, 2008.

p. 253: scandal-plagued politics of this tribe in the past.": "Gimme Five"—Investigation of Tribal Lobbying Matters, Final Report before the Committee on Indian Affairs, June 22, 2006, page 68.

p. 253: like a chance to work for the tribe.": *Ibid.*

p. 254: and was unemployed for six months.: *Heist*, by Peter H. Stone, page 108.

p. 254: in tribal elections was "unheard of.": Senate Indian Affairs Committee hearings on September 29, 2004, prepared statement by Bernie Sprague. Also, see page 73–74 of the Report.

p. 254: tribal funds to conduct campaign activity…": "Gimme Five"—Investigation of Tribal Lobbying Matters, Final Report before the Committee on Indian Affairs, June 22, 2006, page 91.

p. 254: knew Scanlon and that he was a professional.: "Gimme Five"—Investigation of Tribal Lobbying Matters, Final Report before the Committee on Indian Affairs, June 22, 2006, page 75

p. 254: denied the charge and then backed down.: *Heist*, by Peter H. Stone, page 107-8.

p. 255: [Abramoff's restaurant] and their cafeteria.": *Vanity Fair*, by David Margolick, April 2006.

p. 255: operational costs of running the school.: *Heist*, by Peter H. Stone, page 110.

p. 257: around "keeping our people in power.": "Gimme Five"—Investigation of Tribal Lobbying Matters, Final Report before the Committee on Indian Affairs, June 22, 2006, page 79.

CHAPTER THIRTY-NINE
MORE TRIBES

p. 260: spiritual sustenance for hundreds of years.: http://www.sandiapueblo.nsn.us/mountain/ what_changes.html#why_important.

p. 260: his firm's $125,000 monthly retainer.: "Gimme Five"—Investigation of Tribal Lobbying Matters, Final Report before the Committee on Indian Affairs, June 22, 2006, page 186-7.

p. 261: when COush [Coushatta] comes to town!: *Ibid*, page 175.

p. 261: the tribe renewed its contract with Abramoff.: *Ibid*, page 192

p. 264: learn about their secret partnership.": *Ibid*, page 128.

CHAPTER FORTY
QUADRUPLE BOGEY

p. 264: and make contributions so this is easier.": "Gimme Five"—Investigation of Tribal Lobbying Matters, Final Report before the Committee on Indian Affairs, June 22, 2006, page 165.

p. 265: Scotland golf trip for him and some staff.": *The New York Times*, The Muddying of the Greens, by Anne E. Kornblut, January 22, 2006, page 1.

p. 266: is asking, please do. I already have.: "Gimme Five"—Investigation of Tribal Lobbying Matters, Final Report before the Committee on Indian Affairs, June 22, 2006, page 280.

p. 266: the charity [CAF] from their clients.": Factual Basis for Plea Agreement, U.S. v. Tony Rudy, D.C. District Court, March 31, 2006.: Factual Basis for Plea Agreement, U.S. v. Jack A. Abramoff, D.C. District Court, January 3, 2006.

p. 266: members of his staff, and others.": *The New York Times*, Ex-White House Aide Charged in Corruption Case, by Philip Shenon and Anne E. Kornblut, September 20, 2005, page 1.

p. 266: of GSA [Government Services Administration].": Department of Justice Press Release, October 6, 2006: http://www.usdoj.gov/opa/pr/October/06_crm_733.html.

p. 266: Committee about this trip to Scotland.: *The New York Times*, The Muddying of the Greens, by Anne E. Kornblut, January 22, 2005, page 1.

THE PERFECT VILLAIN

p. 267: and had borrowed his son's clubs.: *The Columbus Dispatch*, by Jack Torry and Jonathan Riskind, February 27, 2007, page 3, and September 16, 2006, page 1.

p. 268: $34,000 of the cash in his possession.: The Factual Basis for Bob Ney's Plea Agreement, September, 15, 2006. See PACER.

p. 268: mischaracterized the purpose of the trip.": *The New York Times*, Former Top Aide to DeLay Pleads Guilty, by Philip Shenon, November 22, 2005, page 21.

p. 269: in exchange for a series of official acts,: Department of Justice press release, January 3, 2006: www. doj%20official%20news%20on%20abr%20plea.html

p. 269: announced that he was running for reelection.: Associated Press, Embattled Rep. Ney to Seek Reelection, by David Hammer, January 25, 2006.

p. 270: no longer put them through this ordeal.": *The Washington Post*, Embattled Rep. Ney Won't Seek Reelection; Abramoff Ties Let GOP to Urge his Withdrawal, by Jonathan Weisman, August 8, 2006, page 1

p. 270: to the GOP campaign committee was improper.": *The Miami Herald*, Lobby scandal topples U.S. rep: Rep. Bob Ney pleaded guilty to corruption charges in a case with South Florida roots that grew into a wide-ranging Washington scandal, by Jay Weaver, September 16, 2006.

CHAPTER FORTY-ONE
CALM BEFORE THE FIRESTORM

p. 272: rock star. His hourly fee was $750.: *The Forward*, by Ori Nir, page 2.

p. 274: perhaps for those who preferred discretion.: *The New York Times*, For Lobbyist, a Seat of Power Came With a Plate, by Glenn Justice, July 6, 2005

p. 274: way it's sort of a sweetheart deal.: *The New York Times*, Steak and Chips, and a Side of Politics, by Marian Burros, August 30, 2000

p. 275: a portion of a 1997 appropriations bill.: *The Washingtonian*, Show Me the Money, by Kim Eisler, January 1998, page 78.

p. 276: were free meals for the owner and his guests.: *The New York Times*, For Lobbyist, a Seat of Power Came With a Plate, by Glenn Justice, July 6, 2005

p. 277: Super Bowl party at Stacks…his [delicatessen: *Heist*, by Peter H. Stone, page 119

p. 278: associate of the New York Gambino crime family.: *The Boston Herald*, "Sea of Trouble; Gloucester Gambling Boat Navigates Mob Ties," by Jonathan Wells, Jack Meyers, and Maggie Mulvihill, November 13, 2002, page 1.

p. 280: took a 90% pay cut to join the lobbying field: *The Hill*, March 26, 2003, page 20.

p. 281: who had contacted her in the fall of 2003.: *The Washington Post*, The Fast Rise and Steep Fall of Jack Abramoff: How a Well-Connect Lobbyist Became the Center of a Far-Reaching Corruption Scandal, by Susan Schmidt and James Grimaldi, December 29, 2005, page 1. Also, see: *The Washington Post*, Getting the Story on Jack Abramoff, by Deborah Howell, January 15, 2006, page B6, [which refers to a single lobbyist "called to tip Schmidt."]

p. 282: a seafood restaurant, whom he later married.: *The Wall Street Journal*, End of the Affair, by Brody Mullins, March 31, 2006

p. 283: would later call Abramoff's response a lie.: "Gimme Five"— Investigation of Tribal Lobbying Matters, Final Report before the Committee on Indian Affairs, June 22, 2006, page 5.

p. 285: Can't wait to see you on the 23rd.": *Ibid*, page 17.

p. 285: if Abramoff should file a lawsuit for slander.: *Ibid*

p. 285: "We just keep coming back to SunCruz: *The Miami Herald*, One Year Later, Boulis Slaying Still a Mystery, by Monica Rhor and Caroline Keough, February 6, 2002.

CHAPTER FORTY-TWO
OPENING SALVO

p. 290: gain something off your casino revenues,": Hearing Before The Committee on Indian Affairs, United States Senate, Oversight Hearing Regarding Tribal Lobbying Matters, November 2, 2005.

p. 290: "Hey, boy, here's your next project: *Heist,* by Peter H. Stone, 2006, page 153-4.

p. 290: who was very helpful on this issue.": Senate Indian Affairs Committee exhibits, released on June 22, 2006. Sen. McCain's letter to Chief Audrey Falcon, Saginaw Chippewa Tribe, March 4, 2004.

p. 292: "still living on [a] subsistence level: *Roll Call,* by Paul Kane, McCain to Probe Lobbying Contracts, February 26, 2004.

p. 292: Sen…Campbell, chairman of the…Committee.: *Ibid.*

p. 292: running for reelection for health reasons.: *The New York Times,* G.O.P Senator Campbell of Colorado Will Retire, by Michael Janovsky, March 4, 2004.

p. 293: as an attack on tribal sovereignty: *Heist,* by Peter H. Stone, 2006, page 155

p. 293: "that is wrong and they should stop it: *Roll Call,* by Paul Kane, McCain to Probe Lobbying Contracts, February 26, 2004.

p. 293: that have been raised by recent news reports: *The Hill,* March 4, 2005.

p. 293: I hope I am reading it wrong: *Heist,* by Peter H. Stone, 2006, page 155

p. 294: Abramoff reportedly broke into tears.: *Ibid,* page 156.

p. 294: related conduct which are unacceptable to the firm: *The Washington Post,* by Susan Schmidt, Lobbyist Quits As Firm Probes Work With Tribes, March 4, 2004, page 1.

p. 295: let's discuss when we are together.: "Gimme Five"— Investigation of Tribal Lobbying Matters, Final Report before the Committee on Indian Affairs, June 22, 2006.

p. 296: significantly in excess of [his] costs.": Scanlon's Plea Agreement: November 11, 2005: See PACER.

p. 297: we hired him [on March 23] on a consulting basis.": *Washingtonpost.com,* June 20, 2007, by Robert G. Kaiser, Chapter 24: Gerald Cassidy Slips on the Jack Abramoff Banana Peel. http://blog.washingtonpost.com/citizen-k-street/

p. 297: "Get rid of him today.": *Ibid.*

p. 297: Abramoff and Cassidy & Associates had parted company.: *The Washington Post*, by Judy Sarasohn, page A15.

p. 297: which Abramoff previously represented.: *The Washingtonian*, by Kim Eisler, Abramoff's Fall—A Windfall for [Scott] Reed and Stone?, June 2004, page 21.

CHAPTER FORTY-THREE
THE SECOND CASINO

p. 300: billboards on Texas I-45 and I-10 [to] Louisiana Coushatta casino,: *The Texas Observer*, by Louis Dubose, August 26, 2005. http://www.texasobserver.org/article.php?aid=2016.

p. 300: **by the Alabama-Coushatta Tribe of Texas…**: *The Washington Post*, Reed Confirms Fees From Indian Casino Lobbyists, by Thomas B. Edsall, August 30, 2004. At the end of the story: "Staff Writer Susan Schmidt contributed to this article from Washington."

p. 302: **tale to a new level of avarice and duplicity**.: *The Washington Post*, Editorial: Tribal Trickery, September 28, 2004, page A26.

CHAPTER FORTY-FOUR
THE HEARING

p. 305: it been disclosed to the tribes, but it never was….": Hearing Before The Committee on Indian Affairs, United States Senate, Oversight Hearing Regarding Tribal Lobbying Matters, September 29, 2004.

p. 305: Schmidt had subtly shifted to the phrase "financial interest: *The Washington Post*, by Susan Schmidt, Probe Finds $10 million in Payments to Lobbyist; Indian Tribes Unaware of Fees, March 30, 2004, page 1.

p. 308: representing the…Tigua, in direct conflict with…the Louisiana Coushattas…": "Gimme Five"—Investigation of Tribal Lobbying Matters, Final Report before the Committee on Indian Affairs, June 22, 2006.

CHAPTER FORTY-FIVE
PURGATORY

p. 310: had sued him for $149,000 in unpaid wages.: *The Washington Post:* Ex-Lobbyist Assets Frozen, by Susan Schmidt, page A13.

p. 311: Even his personal tailor would take him to court,: *The Washington Post,* Abramoff's Tailor-Made (Law) Suit, by Amy Argetsinger and Roxanne Roberts, September 24, 2007, page C3.

p. 311: the SunCruz lenders agreed to dismiss the case against Abramoff: US District Court Southern District of Florida Miami Division, case # 04-20690-CIV, filed June 8, 2005.

CHAPTER FORTY-SIX
THE SHU

p. 312: association, actions like this will not be tolerated: *Daily Business Review,* by Jessica M. Walker, August 12, 2005.

p. 312: wrong and these allegations are totally unfounded: The Associated Press, by Curt Anderson, August 11, 2005.

p. 313: to discuss whether someone may or may not be a witness: *The Washington Post,* by James Grimaldi, August 12, 2005, page 1.

p. 314: Acosta was hoping that this publicity would unclog his nomination: *The Miami Herald,* Alito Protégé Sworn in as U.S. Attorney in Miami: R. Alexander Acosta was officially Sworn in as the U.S. Attorney in Miami by His Former Boss, Supreme Court Justice Samuel Alito, by Jay Weaver.

p. 316: $250,000 for catering and security services by Kidan from the SunCruz coffers: *The Miami Herald,* by Wanda J. DeMarzo and Jay Weaver, 4 Years Later, 3 Jailed in Boulis Murder Case, page 1.

p. 316: no evidence that food or drink was [ever] provided: *The Washington Post,* by Susan Schmidt and James V. Grimaldi,3 Charged in Killing of Fla. Businessman; Boulis Slain After 2000 Abramoff Deal, September 28, 2005, page 3.

p. 316: a "wiseguy," because he had an IQ of 152.: *The Miami Herald,* by Dan Christensen, September 28, 2005.

p. 316: "husband had some Las Vegas stripper on the side: *The Miami Herald*, by Wanda J. DeMarzo and Evan S. Ben, September 29, 2005.

p. 316: babysat…Chris Paciello… night club impresario…confessed…to the murder of Kidan's mother.: *The Miami Herald*, by Wanda J. DeMarzo and Jay Weaver, Kidan's Tale 'Stranger Than Fiction,' October 2, 2005, page 1.

p. 317: made false representations to lenders: *The Miami Herald*, by Jay Weaver and Wanda J. DeMarzo, December 16, 2005, page 1.

CHAPTER FORTY-SEVEN
THE MCCAIN REPORT

p. 320: The Tiguas rejected the plan.: *The Washington Post*, by Susan Schmidt, November 18, 2004, page 1.

p. 320: more than the Tigua Tribal Council could stomach: *The Texas Observer*, by Louis Dubose, August 26, 2005. http://www.texasobserver.org/article.php?aid=2016.

p. 320: involved an insurance scam that the tribe quickly rejected.: *Heist*, by Peter H. Stone, page 73.

p. 321: From: Mjschwartz@aol.com: McCain did not publicly release these Schwartz e-mails; obtained by the author.

p. 326: IRS treats most 501(c)3s as "private foundations: www.irs.gov/charities/article/ 0d+96114.htlm

p. 328: last breeding ground of an endangered bird species: *The Washington Post*, by David B. Ottoway and Joe Stevens, May 4, 2003, page 1.

p. 328: It also loaned him $1.55 million to purchase a home.: *Ibid*.

p. 329: a few weeks later to two of its trustees for $500,000.: *The Washington Post*, by David B. Ottoway and Joe Stevens, May 6, 2003, page 1.

p. 329: a $440,000 condominium, and a $17,000 golf club membership: *The New York Times*, Editorial, February 8, 2006.

CHAPTER FORTY-EIGHT
TIGUA REDUX

p. 334: **"major victory...but note they plan a legislative battle now that they have lost in court."**: "Gimme Five"—Investigation of Tribal Lobbying Matters, Final Report before the Committee on Indian Affairs, June 22, 2006, page 152.

p. 334: **"major victory...[now] on to Livingston"** the city in which the Alabama-Coushatta were located. Abramoff's responded: **"Ultimately, as you can imagine, the main target is the AC [Alabama Coushatta]."**: Alabama-Coushatta Tribe of Texas v. Jack Abramoff, Michael Scanlon, Jon van Horne, Neil Volz, and Ralph Reed, United States District Court Western District of Texas Austin Division, July 12, 2006. http://alabama-coushatta.com/Portals/0/Filing_1752084_1.pdf, page 32.

p. 337: make $300,000 in contributions to Washington lawmakers on both sides of the aisle.: *The Washington Post*, by Susan Schmidt, November 18, 2004, page 1.

p. 338: inserting the Tigua provision into the election bill: *Ibid.*

p. 338: another tribal member in a House hearing room on August 14, 2002: Photo Shows Ney at Meeting He Can't Remember: Picture Connects Congressman to Tribe That was an Abramoff Client, by Joel Seidman, June 27, 2006, http://www.msnbc.msn.com/id/13582611/

p. 338: **Public Law 100-89 is amended by striking section 107(101 Stat. 668, 672.)**: never publicly released by McCain, obtained by author.

p. 341: he did not foresee any problem with the Tigua-related provision.": "Gimme Five"—Investigation of Tribal Lobbying Matters, Final Report before the Committee on Indian Affairs, June 22, 2006, page 176.

p. 342: **deal with the Alabama-Coushattas. Don't tell anyone for now.**: Alabama-Coushatta Tribe of Texas v. Jack Abramoff, Michael Scanlon, Jon van Horne, Neil Volz, and Ralph Reed, United States District Court Western District of Texas Austin Division, July 12, 2006. http://alabama-coushatta.com/Portals/0/Filing_1752084_1.pdf, page 36.

p. 342: **between XYZ corporation (to be named later) and the Alabama-Coushatta Tribe of Texas.:** *Ibid*, page 37..

p. 343: Schwartz claimed that Abramoff then asked if Alabama-Coushatta might be willing to help sponsor it.: *Ibid*, page 39–40.

p. 343: very strong message to the very powerful member of the Congressional leadership team.: "Gimme Five"—Investigation of Tribal Lobbying Matters, Final Report before the Committee on Indian Affairs, June 22, 2006, page 174.

p. 344: **Your $50,000 check should be made payable to the Capital Athletic Foundation**: "Gimme Five"—Investigation of Tribal Lobbying Matters, Final Report before the Committee on Indian Affairs, June 22, 2006, page 167.

p. 344: the impression that the Tigua would be funding the other half of the golf, but the Tigua never did: When questioned by Sen. Conrad during the Indian Affairs Committee hearing on November 4, 2004, Marc Schwartz and Carlos Hisa testified that the Tigua did not make any contribution to the 2002 Scotland golf trip. Later, Sen. Conrad asked Hisa again. Hisa said, "I think in total the golfing trip was going to be $100,000, my understanding is that the Mississippi Choctaw paid $50,000 and the Alabama Coushatta paid another $50,000." See Senate Indian Affairs Committee Hearings: November 4, 2004.

CHAPTER FORTY-NINE
JUDGE HUCK

p. 346: **pay the piper. I think that time has come.** (and all other excerpts): United States District Court Southern District of Florida, case no. 05-60204-cr-pch, the United States of America, plaintiff vs. Jack Abramoff, Adam R. Kidan defendants, telephonic hearing held 9-28-06, before the honorable Paul C. Huck, reported by: Patricia Sanders, RPR, official court reporter. (Not available in PACER, author obtained transcript directly from Ms. Sanders.)

p. 346: putting the kibosh on perhaps the most far-reaching Washington corruption scandal in the nation's history: Associated

Press, Judge May Have Stymied Abramoff Probe, by Matt Apuzzo, September 29, 2006.

EPILOGUE
IT ISN'T WHAT IT IS

p. 351: Noel L. Hillman, chief of the Public Integrity Division of the Justice Department, suddenly stepped down on January 26, 2006.: *The New York Times*, by Philip Shenon and Elisabeth Bumiller, Prosecutor, Picked by Bush for US Judgeship, Will Step Down from Lobbyist Case, January 27, 2006, page 21.

p. 351: as hands-on, aggressive and relentless prosecutor: *Time* Magazine, Off Abramoff's Case, by Brian Bennett, January 29, 2006, http://www.time.com/time/magazine/article/0,9171,1154211,00.html

p. 351: calls for Bush to name a special prosecutor,: States News Service, 36 Senators Urge Gonzales to Appoint Special Prosecutor to Lead Abramoff Scandal Case, February 2, 2006.

p. 352: temporary replacement was Andrew Lourie, a seasoned south Florida prosecutor.: *Roll Call*, DOJ: Abramoff Probe Will Stay on Track, by Paul Kane, January 30, 2006.

p. 352: Alice Fisher, a Bush political appointee. Her appointment had been controversial, due to her lack of any prior experience as a federal prosecutor.: *Statement of Senator Patrick J. Leahy: Hearing for Nominees to be Assistant Attorney General for the Criminal Division, Assistant Attorney General for the Office of Legal Policy, and Assistant Attorney General for the Office of Justice Programs* - May 12, 2005. http://www.senate.gov/comm/judiciary/general/member_statement.cfm?id=1500&wit_id=2629

p. 352: Lourie continued as "acting" chief for more than two years until he finally resigned in February 2008.: http://legaltimes.typepad.com/blt/2008/02/2-doj-senior-ai.html

p. 352: Alice Fisher quit three months after that.: *The Washington Post*, Justice Official Who Oversees Cases on Corruption, Fraud is Quitting, by Carrie Johnson, May 1, 2008, page 17.

p. 353: on June 9, 2008 prosecutors [asked] Huvelle to…schedule Abramoff's sentencing for September: *Roll Call*, June 9, 2008.

INDEX

A

Abdullah, Saudi Crown Prince, 372n141
Abramoff, Alex, 73, 268
Abramoff, Bernard, 1–2, 5–7
Abramoff, Daniel, 73
Abramoff, Frank, 1–8, 21, 45, 84, 99
Abramoff, Jack: accusations against, viii; birth of, 3; childhood in California, 8–14; in college, 14, 16–21, 73; family background, 1–8; good works of, x–xi, 8, 18–19, 75, 273; indictment of, 312–18; prison sentence of, vii, 349; reporting to prison, xv; wife of, 23–24, 53
Abramoff, Jane, 2–3, 10–11
Abramoff, Levi, 73
Abramoff, Linda, 3
Abramoff, Livia, 73
Abramoff, Robert, 3, 59–61
Abramoff, Sarah, 73
Abrams, Elliot, 358n14
Acosta, Anthony, 313–15
Adams, Bart, 364n72
Aderholt, Robert, 218
African National Congress (ANC), 47, 50–51
Agassi, Andre, 3
Agua Caliente band, 2, 119, 262–64, 285
Alabama-Coushatta Indians, Abramoff battle against and, 114, 241; Cornyn and, 332; donations from, 342–45; Edsall article on, 300; Hinojosa bill and, 330–31, 335; lawsuit filed by, 343, 375n170; Schwartz and, 344, 346; shutting down casino, 233, 300–02, 333–34, 336, 338, 340
Alamoudi, Abdurahman Mohamed, 372n141
Albaugh, John, 353, 373n150, 373n154
Alexander, Pamela, 23–24, 53
All Things Considered radio show, 21

Allende, Salvador, 36, 49
al-Zayat, Fouad, 268
Amato, Andy, 14–15, 53
American International Center, 75, 116, 284
American Jewish Congress, 248
American Muslim Council, 372n141
American Red Cross, 329
American University, 329
Americans for a Republican Majority (ARMPAC), 132, 208
Americans for Tax Reform (ATR), 19, 80, 102–3, 114, 216, 284
America's Most Wanted TV show, 182, 185
Ames, Mark, 130
Angola, 38–44, 276
Angola Peace Monitor, 45
Anti-Defamation League, 79
apartheid, 35, 46–47, 50–51, 66
Applegate, Andrew, 362n56
Arafat, Yasser, 52
Archer, Bill, 100, 102
Argenziano, Carmen, 63
Armey, Dick, 76, 78, 92, 219
Arnold Palmer Enterprises, 4–5
Arthur Andersen, 152, 368n89
Artisis and Athletes Against Apartheid, 66
Ashe, Arthur, 66
Asia-Pacific Economic Cooperation (APEC), 74
Asner, Ed, 193
Atlantic City Press, 25
Atta, Mohammed, 174
Atwater, Lee, 358n10
Aviv, Jonathan, 12

B

Babauta, Juan, 232, 371n131
Babbitt, Bruce, 244
Bagg, Neal, 313
Baggett, Fred, 230, 246

Baker, Howard, 32
Baker, James, 225
Baldwin, Steve, 28
Bandow, Doug, 91, 103
Barbieri, Paula, 65
Barbour, Haley, 274–75
Barragan, Napoleon, 67, 142–44, 399n143
Barral, Fernando, 197–204
Barrales, Ruben, 232
Barron, David, 30
Batista, Fulgencio, 34
Bell, Alexander Graham, 221
Bell, Jeffrey, 36
Bell, Warren, 365n81
Bello, Al, 68
ben Zvi Schmuel (Sheldon Greer), 328, 371n127
Biegun, Steve, 131
bin Laden, Osama, 248–49
Black Panthers, 17, 23
Blackwell, Morton, 17, 359n26
Blake, Robert, 358n17
Blanco, Kathleen, 248
Blank, Jonathan, 78, 81, 111, 230
Bloomingdale, Alfred, 5, 29
Blumenthal, Sidney, 43
Blunt, Roy, 245
Bocelli, Andrea, 231
Boesky, Ivan, 36
Boeta, P. W., 42
Boggs, Patton, 245–46
Boggs, Thomas H., Jr., 274
Bogolubov, Andre, 38
Boland Amendment, 36
Boland II Amendment, 37
Boles Knop & Co., 162
Bonanno crime family, 68
Bond, Richard, 30
Borg, Bjorn, 3
Borgnine, Ernest, 12
Boston Globe, 132, 135
Boston Herald, 277–78

Bostoner Rebbe, 20
Boulanger, Todd, 224, 265–66, 282, 285, 291
Boulis, Christos, 147
Boulis, Efronsini, 147
Boulis, Gus: background, 146–48; citizenship of, 366n86; creating SunCruz, 148–49; filing lawsuit, 177, 182–83, 280–81; Kidan and, 168, 173–78; multiple entities of, 162; murder of, 33, 141, 178–87, 254, 278, 310, 316; Ney on, 154, 269; seller financing for SunCruz, 153–66, 367n95; selling SunCruz, 150–53, 170–73; Shipping Act and, 149, 169; Waldman and, 173–76
Boulis, Panagiotis, 147
Bowie, Datuk Paddy, 73–74
Boy Scouts of America, 329
Braden, Mark, 28
Bradley, Bill, 36
Brandeis University, 13–14, 16–21, 73
Branigan, William, 84
Breaux, John, 244–45
Brokaw, Tom, 22, 42
Brooks Brothers Riot, 224–25
Brown, Nicole, 65
Brown, Robert, 16
Buckham, Ed: Choctaw Indians and, 103; election of 2000 and, 224; Fitial and, 95, 232; introducing Abramoff and DeLay, 79–80, 92; under investigation, 136; NaftaSib and, 212; Northern Marianas and, 97; resignation of, 96; St. Andrews golf junket, 211; trip to Moscow, 132–33; U.S. Family Network and, 132, 135, 361n41
Buckley, William F., 25
Budget Reconciliation Act (1995), 102
Buffalino crime family, 15, 32
Burchfield, Roger, 211

Bureau of Indian Affairs (BIA), 105, 225–28, 242, 250
Burns, Conrad, 24, 125–26, 255, 363n66
Burton, Dan, 46, 50
Bush, George H. W., 15, 20, 26, 32
Bush, George W.: Abramoff and, 12, 78; Abramoff family and, 4–5; Babauta and, 232; campaign contributors titles, 362n55; Coushattas and, 237–38; election of 2000, 225, 367n101; Hillman and, 351; inauguration of, 177; Kidan and, 15; Mahathir and, 74, 361n19; McCain smear campaign and, xiii, 189–90, 192, 204–05; Reed and, 109
Bush, Jeb, 149
Butterworth, Robert, 148–49, 154, 168, 179

C

Caan, James, 12
Cadwalader Wickersham and Taft, 131
Calero, Adolfo, 40, 54
Campbell, Ben Nighthorse, 292, 304–07, 319–21
Canary, Leura, 362n52
Cantor, Eric, 245
Cantwell, Maria, 304
Capital Athletic Foundation (CAF): Abramoff's personal financing of, 327–30; expenditure violations, 374n166; Indian tribes contributions to, 116, 284, 345–46; name change to, 75; Signatures restaurant and, 275; St. Andrews golf junket and, 264–66; Zachares and, 226
Capital Campaign Strategies, 116, 118
Carbo, Art, 285
Card, Andrew, 243
Carelo, Adolfo, 40–41
Carreras, José, 208
Carrillo, Pablo, 291–92, 308–09, 318
Carter, Jimmy, 19–20, 357n7

casinos: Agua Caliente band, 262–64; in Atlantic City, 5–6; Chitimacha Indians, 220–21; Choctaw Indians, 98–108; Coushatta Indians, 233–40; Indian tax exemption and, 240–48; in international waters, 148; Jena Band Indians, 233, 241–49; organized crime and, 6; riverboat, 235; Saginaw Chippewa Indians, 249–59; in St. Maarten, 15, 32; Tigua Indians, 319–26, 331–46; wars over turf, 114. *See also* SunCruz Casinos
Cassidy, Gerald, 296–97, 366n92
Cassidy and Associates, 294, 297
Castro, Fidel, 49, 52
Cato Institute, 91
Cauhilla Indians, 2, 119, 262–64
Cavallo, Michael, 33
Center for Public Integrity, 369n115
Center for Responsive Politics, 125–26
Century Strategies, 109
Chafetz, Gary S., 373n151
Chalais, Francois, 196
Chang Kai-shek, 34
Channel One, 371n130
Chapin, Roger, 330
Charles, Ray, 32
Chelsea Commercial Enterprises Ltd., 131, 133, 136
Cheney, Dick, 227, 359n27, 371n129
Chernomyrdin, Viktor, 130–33
Chitimacha Indians (Louisiana), 212, 220–21, 234–35, 370n124
Choctaw Indians: Abramoff's derogatory remarks, 56, 304; Chitimacha Indians and, 220; fees paid to Abramoff by, xiii; gambling in Alabama and, 105, 107–13; Levin and, 21; lobbying efforts for, 98–108; strict confidentiality and, 113–22
The Choctaw Revolution (Ferrera), 103
Christian Coalition, 27, 109–10, 215, 237, 284

CIA (Central Intelligence Agency), 36, 39
Citadel Equity Fund (Cayman Islands), 160, 162–63, 165, 177, 181, 280–81, 311
Citizens for America, 35–36, 38, 44
Citizens for Responsible Ethics in Washington (CREW), 365n82
Cleaver, Eldridge, 23
Clifton, Laura, 276
Clinton, Bill, 76, 85, 134–35, 142–43, 192, 216, 370n120
Clinton, Hillary, 191
Clooney, George, 13
Coalition to Salute America's Heroes, 329
Cochran, Thad, 104, 244
Cohen, Andrew J., x
Cohen, David, 226
Cohen, Herman, 48
Cohn, Roy, 29–30
Colby, William, 46
Cold War, 39, 369n109
College Democrats, 22
College Republicans, 19, 21–22, 24–25, 27–31, 35
Commerce Department, U.S., 90
The Committee Against Gambling Expansion, 243–44
Commonwealth of the Northern Mariana Islands. *See* Northern Mariana Islands
Communism, 34–39, 41, 369n109
Comprehensive Anti-Apartheid Act (1986), 46, 62
Congress, U.S.: Boland Amendment, 36; Boland II Amendment, 37; Budget Reconciliation Act, 102; Comprehensive Anti-Apartheid Act, 46, 62; elections of 1994, 76; Foreign Agents Registration Act, 75; Internet gambling and, 212, 214–20; SunCruz Casinos and, 154–55

Conrad, Kent, 304, 306–7, 309, 375n169
Conservative Caucus, 35
Conservative Digest, 38
Continetti, Matthew, 144, 365n83
Conway, Joseph, 173, 315–16, 345
Coors, Joseph, 25, 36
Copley News Service, 91
Cornyn, John, 299–300, 331, 344
Cosby, Bill, 12
Cotton, Joseph, 4
Coughlin, Robert, 353
Coulter, Anne, 191
Council of Republicans for Environmental Advocacy (CREA), 238–39, 244, 284
Coushatta Indians (Louisiana): casinos and, 233–42; donations to CAF, 327; donations to CREA, 244; Hinojosa bill and, 331, 334–35; Reed and, 237, 242, 328, 362n57; Scanlon and, 114, 119, 288, 328; Schmidt on, 288; Texas casino and, 329, 330, 342, 345
Cox, Chris, 78
Crane, Arlene, 274
Crane, Phil, 19, 46, 53, 274
Creative Management Agency (CMA), 5
Crystal, Russel: IFF and, 44–46; links to South African military intelligence, 35, 40, 48, 50; on Mbeki, 51; National Student Federation and, 35, 39, 358n11; *Red Scorpion* and, 62; Williamson and, 42
Cuba, 36
Cuomo, Mario, 36

D

Daschle, Tom, 190
Davenport, Christina, 169
Davis, Angela, 16
Day, Kendall, 345
de Klerk, F. W., 47
Delany, Timothy, 313
DeLay, Christine, 133, 211–12, 224, 293

DeLay, Tom: Abramoff and, 43, 77, 79–80, 128, 293; ARMPAC and, 208; Choctaws and, 105; Coushattas and, 236; early careers, 77; election of 2000 and, 224; Fitial and, 95; Internet gambling and, 214, 216–18; investigation of, vii, 355; Jena Band Indians and, 245; junkets by, 74, 103, 209–14, 265, 363n49, 371n115; Kidan and, 177; Lapin and, 79; lobbyists and, 78; as Majority Leader, 273; as Majority Whip, 76, 80; McCain and, 189, 206, 257–58, 370n105; NaftaSib and, 212; Ney and, 154; Norquist and, 80, 92–93; Northern Mariana Islands and, 86–87, 92–94, 97; PACs and, 369n98; Russian oil/gas conglomerate and, 129–37; Sandia Indians and, 260; Scanlon and, 177, 291; at Signatures restaurant, 275–76; speeches by, 219, 350; SunCruz Casinos and, 155; Tan and, 362n41; Walker and, 161
Democratic Party, 76, 100, 190–91
Diamond, Donald K., 213
DiMaria, Lenny, 15, 33
Dimopoulos, Art, 145–46, 149–50, 169–70
Diners' Club, 5
Divac, Jane. *See* Abramoff, Jane
Dobson, James, 218, 242–43, 370n119
Dodd, Christopher, 337–41
Dolan, Terry, 25
Dole, Bob, 32, 50, 227, 297
Domenech, Doug, 243
Domingo, Plácido, 208
Doolittle, John, vii, 93, 246, 373n154
Dorgan, Brian R., 304, 307
Dorgan, Byron L., vii, 246
Dornan, Robert, 46
Dowd, Maureen, 192
Downie, Len, 303

Druckman, Yehezkiel, 138
DuPont, Pete, 22

E

Edsall, Thomas B., 300
Eisenhower, Dwight, 21
El Paso Times, 302, 336
Elder Legacy Program, 319–26
Election Reform Act, 337, 339, 340
eLottery, 212, 214–20
The Emperor's Gold (film), 73
Enola Gay, 361n32
Enron Corporation, 109, 366n89
Erickson, Paul, 53
Eshkol Academy, 75, 79, 272–73, 310–11, 320, 325–28
Ethiopia, 36
Ethnics Liberation Organization of Laos, 40
Evert, Chris, 3
eXile magazine, 130

F

Factor, David, 10–11
Factor, Max, 10
Fagan, Richie, 316
Faith and Family Reliance, 216
Faith of My Fathers (McCain), 194–95
Fallout radio show, 22, 24
Falwell, Jerry, 189
Farr, Sam, 365n82
Fazio, Tom, 103
FBI (Federal Bureau of Investigation): Heaton and, 270; investigating ties to Abramoff, vii, 290–91, 366n73; Kahgegab and, 256; Kidan and, 278–79; Martin and, 221; Moscatiello and, 375n152
Federici, Italia, 238–39, 243, 245–46, 284
Feinstein, Diane, 215, 217
Fennel, Randy, 84
Ferrara, Peter, 91, 103
Ferrari, Anthony, 172, 176, 182, 185, 316

Fiddler on the Roof play, 9, 72
filmmaking, 55–67, 73
Fiorillo, John "Pudgy," 316
First, Ruth, 48
First Gate Resources, 138
Fischetti, Ronald, 173
Fisher, Alice, 354
Fitial, Benigno, 95–98, 232, 361n42, 361n47, 371n131, 372n144
501(c)4 organizations, 126, 365n68
527 Group, 126, 363n69
Florida Sun-Sentinel, 177
Focus on the Family, 215, 242–43
Foothill Capital, 159–63, 165–66, 177, 181, 186, 280–81, 311
Forbes magazine, 187
Ford, Gerald, 32, 274
Foreign Agents Registration Act, 75
Forges, George, 11
Foster, Allen, 282
Foster, Gary and Greg, 60
Foster, Mike, 234–35, 237–38, 241–42, 244, 372n139
Fox News Sunday news show, 135
Frankenheimer, John, 369n109
Freedom Bulletin (publication), 45, 51
Freeman, Judy, 14
Friedman, Rob, 63–64, 66

G

Gambino crime family, 33, 172, 183–84, 278, 316
gaming. *See* legalized gambling
Garell, Lee, 6
garment industry in Northern Mariana Islands, 83–88, 93, 310
Gates, Bill, 78, 256
General Council for Islamic Banks, 249
George Washington University, 21–24
Georgetown University, 21, 35
Gianovetti, Tom, 91
Gibson, Duane, 224, 323
Gibson, Mel, 79

Gimme Five (secret kickback scheme), 105–06
Gingrich, Newt, 22, 26, 76, 78, 80
Glait, Phyllis, 165–66
Glogower, Rod, 17
The Godfather (film), 72
Goland, Michael, x, 53
Gold, Jonathan, 13, 357n5
Goldman, Ron, 65
Goldwater, Barry, 22, 32
golf: first golf lessons, 3; miniature golf, 3–4; Moscow junket, 134; Northern Mariana Islands, 93, 95; Pebble Beach junket, 155, 213; St. Andrews junket, 74, 123, 209–14, 220, 264–72, 338, 340, 342
Goodlatte, Robert W., 214–19
Gore, Al, 131, 224
Gorton, Slade, 104
Gotti, Gene, 172
Gotti, John, 33, 172, 316
Gould, Elliot, 12
Government Services Administration, 266
Grace, J. Peter, 36
Gramm, Phil, 4, 344
Gramm, Wendy, 346
Grassley, Ernest "Chuck," vii, 329
Greenberg Traurig: Abramoff joining, 226, 230; Bush and, 224; Foreign Agents Registration Act and, 75; Griles and, 246–47; Kidan and, 181; Miller and, 282; resignation from, 294; subpoenaed e-mails, 157, 293; tribal clients and, 112, 121, 233, 277
Greener, William I., 26, 28–29
Greer, Sheldon (*See* ben Zvi Schmuel)
Greeslin, Chris, 132, 135–36, 364n74
Grenada (island), 29, 36
Griles, J. Stephen, vii, 238–39, 245–47, 275, 372n138
Guam, 84
Guilanti, Mara, 179

Gun Lake tribe, 252, 372n142
Gurino, Johnny, 180

H
Hackman, Gene, 8
Harpers Magazine, 49
Harris, Katherine, 225
Hastert, Dennis, vii, 245–46, 273, 275–76
Hastings, Doc, 88
Hatch, Orrin, 304
Hayes, Robin, 218
Hayworth, J. D., vii
Heaton, William, 267–70, 339, 342, 373n147
Helms, Jesse, 46, 131, 193
Help America Vote Act, 337–39
Help Hospitalized Veterans, 329
Henderson, Wallace, 245
Hendrix, Jimmy, 16
Henson, Lisa, 62
Her, Pa Kao, 40–41
Hercenberg, Jerrold, 18
Heritage Foundation, 25, 29, 35
The Hill, 279, 330, 340
Hillman, Noel L., 351–52
Hinojosa, Juan, 330, 33
Hirsch, David, 12
Hirschmann, Susan, 103, 133, 212
Hisa, Carlos, 321–23, 325, 338, 340, 343, 375n169, 422 (p. 345)
Hoffa, Jimmy, 15
Hoile, David, 51
Holden, Stephen, 59
Holzman, Mark, 36
Honest-Services Fraud, 98, 206, 296, 353, 355, 362n52, 376n175
Hoover, Herbert, 221
House Appropriations Committee, 96, 136
House Ethics Committee, 372n117
House Financial Services, 249
House Government Reform Committee, xiv, 5, 122, 231–32, 347
House Republican Study Committee, 50
House Ways and Means Committee, 44
Hren, Margaret, 147, 151
Huck, Paul C., ix, xiv, 317–18, 345–47, 352, 354, 366n84, 375n172
Hume, Jack, 35–36
Hunt, Nelson Bunker, 25, 36
Hussein, Saddam, 34
Huvelle, Ellen, ix, 317, 353, 373n148
Hyman, Paul G., 184

I
Ietan Consulting, 251
Indian Affairs Committee (Senate), viii, 257, 289, 291–92, 303–9. *See also* McCain report
Indian Child Welfare Act, 308
Indian Gaming Regulatory Act, 338
Indian tribes: Abramoff's derogatory remarks about, xiii, 56, 304; Democratic Party and, 100; tax exemption and, 240–48, 361n50. *See also* casinos; *specific tribes*
Influence (publication), 127
Inhofe, James M., 304
Inouye, Daniel, 126, 297, 304–5, 307–8
Institute for Policy Innovation, 91
Interior Department, U.S., 85–86, 90, 226–27, 239, 360n35
International Freedom Foundation (IFF), 44–52, 54, 310
International Management Group (IMG), 3
International Monetary Fund, 135–36
Internet gambling, 212, 214–20
Iran-Contra Affair, 37–38, 40, 44–45, 53–54, 358n14
Isaacson, Jason, 248
Islamic Unity of Afghanistan, 40
Isler, Robert, 143

Israel: anti-communisim summit, 39; Jamba Jamboree, 39; oil and, 35, 137–39, 230, 365n80
Istook, Ernest, vii, 104, 276, 355, 373n154

J

Jackson, Delores, 252, 258
Jackson, Jesse, 31
Jaffe, Martin, 165
Jamba Jamboree (Angola), 38–44, 276
James & Sarch law firm, 132, 135
Jeffries and Company, 170
Jena Band Indians, 233, 241–49, 363n63, 371n134, 372n136
Jennings, Peter, 22
Johannesburg Star, 51
Johnson, Tim, 304
Johnston, J. Bennett, 234
Jones, Grace, 60, 64–65
Judaism: Brandeis University and, 16–17; on burials, 69; marking end of Sabbath, 99; Pam Alexander and, 24, 53; religious epiphany about, 9–10; on swearing oaths, 374n162; worry about growing divide in, 75
Jungle Jamboree (Angola), 38–44, 276
Justice Department, vii, xiv, 4, 129, 173, 209, 214, 259, 274, 345–46, 351–55, 363n66, 372n126

K

Kabila, Laurent, 127
Kahgegab, Maynard, Jr., 251–54, 256, 258, 288, 290, 293
Kamel, Salh Abdullah, 249
Kaplan, Julius "Jay," 131, 222
Keating, Charles, 308, 374n164
Keep Our Majority (KOMPAC), 246
Kemp, Jack, 4, 22, 26, 53
Kennedy, Edward, 50, 190
Kerry, John, 190, 204, 369n106
Keyes, Alan, 50, 52

Khadafy, Moammar, 52
Kickapoo tribe, 374n168
Kidan, Adam: Abramoff and, 7, 22, 53; background, 14–16, 367n83; Barragan and, 142–44; Boulis and, 168, 173–78; Chafetz and, 373n151; in college, 21–24; DeLay and, 80–81, 177; disbarment of, 174, 368n103; divesting SunCruz ownership, 185; early legal career, 32–33, 67; federal prosecutors and, 311–14, 366n90; gangland slaying of Boulis and, 178–87; indictment of, 315–17; Israel and, 230; Moscatiello and, 33, 172, 177, 182–85, 315; Ney on, 171, 269; organized crime and, 171–73, 175; prison sentence for, 69–70, 377n172; on Ralston, 231; on *Red Scorpion*, 59; on Reed, 27; Shemtov and, 67–68, 368n103; Sun Coast Casinos and, 278; USA Foundation, 32. *See also* SunCruz Casinos
Kidan, April, 14
Kidan, Arlyn, 14, 68–69
Kidan, Steven, 14
Kildee, Dale, 104
Kilgore, Donald, 116, 120–21
Kirkpatrick, Jeanne, 41
Kissinger, Henry, 9, 46, 221
Klein, Jeffrey, 18
Kleinberger, Avi, 60, 64
Kollel Ohel Tieferet, 328
Koulakovsky, Alexander, 130–34, 137–39, 152, 178, 212, 364n73, 365n79
Kristol, Bill, 24
The K-Street Gang (Continetti), 144
K-Street Project, 76, 359n22

L

LA Weekly, 13
Laird, Melvin, 15, 197
Laissez-faire (publication), 46

Langley, Bertney, 234, 241, 244
Laos, 40
Lapin, Daniel, 43, 79, 212, 219, 221–22
Lapin, David, 43, 79
LaRusso, Robert P., 173, 315–16
LaTourette, Larry, 78
LaVecchio, Lawrence, 278–79, 345
Laver, Rod, 3
Lebanon, 37
Lee, Moonyee, 63
Legal Times, 127
legalized gambling: in Alabama, 105, 107–13, 118–19; in Atlantic City, 5; eLottery, 212, 214–20; in international waters, 148; racetracks and, 364n54; Reed and, 110–13. *See also* casinos
Lehrman, Lew, 35–36, 41–42
Leon, Peter, 63–64
Lesotho (Africa), 63
Levin, Marc, 21, 99–100, 121
Lewinsky, Monica, 142, 370n120
Lewis, Joe, 4
Lexington Group, 372n141
Liberty Consulting Services, 123
Liddy, G. Gordon, 22
Limbaugh, Rush, 191
Lindberg, Todd, 364n72
Lloyd's of London, 61, 162
Lobbying Disclosure Act, 136, 249
lobbyists: for foreign governments, 75; influence of, 56–57; perception of access and, 223–24; typical perks to clients, 208–9
Log Cabin Republicans, 192
Los Angeles Times, 10, 59
Lott, Trent, 244
Lourie, Andrew, 352
Lovelin, Chief, 235, 244
Lowell, Abbe, 294, 345
Lucier, James, Sr., 193, 364n72
Lumumba, Patrice, 48
Lundgren, Dolph, 58–61, 64–65

Luque, Nancy, 352–3, 355
Lytle-Kyser, Velma, 252

M

MacFarlane, Robert "Bud," 37
Madden, Kevin, 136
Madonna, 144
Magazine Publishers of America, 212
Mahathir Mohamed, 74–75, 359n19
Malaysia, 73–74
Manchurian Candidate (film), 369n109
Mandela, Nelson, 47, 49–52
Mandelker, Philip, 138
Manley, Michael, 48
Mao Zedung, 34
Marianas. *See* Northern Mariana Islands
Marple, Pamela, xv, 345
Martin, Aurene, 227, 258
Martin, Philip, 56, 99–103, 107, 114–16, 126, 220, 308, 362n59, 371n132
Martin, Terry, 212, 220–21, 234–35, 241, 281, 371n132
Marx, Groucho, 4
Mashpee Indians (Massachusetts), 221
Massino, Joe, 316
Mbeki, Govan, 51, 358n15
Mbeki, Thabo, 358n15
McCain, Bridget, 192, 205, 369n108
McCain, Carol, 202
McCain, Cindy, 192, 205
McCain, John: DeLay and, 189, 206, 257–58, 368n105; Kerry and, 369n106; launching investigation, viii, 292; relationship with Abramoff, xiii; Senate hearing and, 303–9; smear campaign against, xiii, 189–208, 371n108; view of Indian tribes, 101
McCain report: on Abramoff's charities, 75; on Abramoff's tribal clients, 112–16, 236–38, 241, 244–45, 250–51, 255–57; on finder's fees, 117–18; omissions in, 123; overview,

318–30; on Scanlon, 119–20; on
  Tigua Indians, 331–46
McCaleb, Neal, 227–28, 244
McClellan, Scott, 4, 224
McConnell, Mitch, 215, 217
McCormack, Mark, 3–4
McEnroe, John, 3
McFarlane, Robert, 358n14
McGovern, George, 20
McGuinn, Edwin, 214
McKinstry, Alexander, 363n56
McPherson, Vic, 49
Meeds, Lloyd, 88, 100, 360n38
Mehlman, Ken, vii
Mendiola, Alejo, 96
Miami Herald, 168, 285, 316, 373n152
Milan Film Market, 61
Miller, Emily, 281–82
Miller, George, 84, 87–89, 98, 361n47
Minnery, Thomas, 243
Mississippi Choctaw Indians. *See* Choctaw Indians
Mobutu Sese Seku, viii, 82, 127–28, 310
Moon, Sun Myung, 359n21
Moon Over Miami security firm, 176
Moore, Roger, 60
Moral Majority, 25, 215
Morrow, Colleen, 45, 54
Moscatiello, Anthony: Cavallo and, 33; daughter's wedding, 367n99; DiMaria and, 33; FBI and, 375n152; Ferrari and, 176; Kidan and, 33, 172, 177, 182–85, 315; LaRusso and, 173; murder of Boulis and, 33, 179, 279, 316; Sun Coast Casino and, 278
movie production, 55–67, 73
Murdoch, Rupert, 277–78
Murdock, Jason, 267
Murkowski, Lisa, 304

N

Nader, Ralph, 28
NaftaSib, 129–37, 212, 364n70
Namibia, viii, 39, 64–67, 310
National Center for Public Policy Research, 97, 114, 133, 210, 223, 268, 357n9
National Conservative Political Action Committee (NCPAC), 25
National Geographic Society, 221
National Indian Gaming Commission, 104, 228
National Institute of Torah, 75
National Journal, 99
National Museum of the American Indian, 303
National Public Radio, 20–21, 80
National Society of Newspaper Columnists, 91
National Student Federation (South Africa), 35, 39
National Union for Total Independence of Angola (UNITA), 39, 41–42
Nationscorp, 132
Native American Caucus, 104
Native American Times, 207
Native American tribes: Abramoff's derogatory remarks, xiii, 56, 304; Democratic Party and, 100; tax exemption and, 240–48, 361n50. *See also* casinos; *specific tribes*
Nature Conservancy, 328
Nevskaya, Marina V., 130–31, 134, 137–38
"New Right," 24
New York Times: on Abramoff overcharging clients, 99; on Bernard Abramoff, 6; on Chapin, 330; on Coushatta Indians, 233; on Frank Abramoff, 5; on IMF, 136; on McCain report, 318; on Northern Marianas, 85; on Oliver North, 45; on *Red Scorpion,* 65–66

Newsday, 48–49, 51

Ney, Robert: conspiracy charges and, vii; DeLay and, 154; fundraising event as skybox, 181; Heaton and, 269–70; indictment against, 355, 357n1; investigation against, xiv; Islamic banking officials and, 249; Kidan and, 316; PACs and, 367n98; plea agreement of, 270–72; resignation of, 373n148; at Signatures restaurant, 276; St. Andrews golf junket, 265, 267–69, 339, 342, 344; statement on Boulis, 154, 269; statement on Kidan, 171, 269; SunCruz and, 126, 270; Tigua Indians and, 338–39

Nicaragua, 36–38, 40, 42, 54

Nicaraguan Democratic Force, 40

Nicholson, Dwayne, 176

Nicklaus, Jack, 3

Nixon, Richard, 16, 19–20, 274

Noah, Timothy, 13

Norquist, Grover: Abramoff and, 19–20, 53, 91, 286; ATR and, 80; Choctaws and, 102–3; College Republicans and, 31; Coushattas and, 238; firing of, 42; Jena Band Indians and, 244; "Jews for Reagan," 20–21; loyalty of, 361n26; McCain and, 189, 205–6; resolutions of, 26; Salter on, 371n112; Schmidt and, 284; Senate hearings and, 318; speech by, 219, 350; Waller and, 88

Norris, Chuck, 62

North, Oliver, 37–38, 40, 44–45, 53–54, 294, 350, 358n14

Northern Mariana Islands: Abramoff's lobbying efforts for, viii–ix, 79, 82–90, 94–98; exploring feasibility of casinos in, 7; Fitial and, 232; junkets to, 90–94; sex trade in, 84–85, 89; textile industry in, 83–88, 93, 310; Zachares and, 226

Norton, Gale, vii, 238–39, 242–44, 247, 318

Nucci, Ed, xiv, 345–46

Nuremberger, Ralph, 374n166

O

Occupational Safety and Health Administration (OSHA), 85–86

O'Connor, Sandra Day, 221

oil/gas industry: Israel and, 35, 137–39, 230, 367n80; Russia and, 129–37

Olsen, Arne, 60–61

O'Neill, Tip, 32

organized crime: Amato and, 14–15, 53; Bonanno crime family, 68; Boulis assassination and, 141; Buffalino crime family, 15, 32; casinos and, 6; Gambino crime family, 33, 172, 183–84, 278, 316; gangland slaying of Boulis and, 178–87; Gotti and, 33, 172; Kidan and, 171–73, 175; Shemtov and, 67–68

Otto, David, 253, 257

Owen, Marcus, 364n75

P

Pace-Capstone, 262

Paciello, Chris, 144, 316

PACs (Political Action Committees), 126, 142, 363n69, 367n98

Palacios, Norman S., 96

Palmer, Amy, 4

Palmer, Arnold, 3, 5

Palmer, Becky, 4

Palmer, Winnie, 4

Pandin, Jeff: on Abramoff, 25, 29, 82; at Abramoff's wedding, 53; on apartheid, 51; IFF and, 45–46, 49, 54; on Jamba Jamboree, 40, 42–43

Parker, Jay, 52

Pate, Jerry, 103

Patencio, Candace, 262–64, 285

Patton, George S., 26

Pavarotti, Luciano, 208
Peace and Freedom Party, 23
Percy, Charles H., 27
Perry, Jill, 282, 285
Peters, Patricia, 252, 257
Petras, Chris, 253, 288
Philips, Kevin, 24
Phillips, Howard, 25
Pickens, T. Boone, 36
Pickle, J. J., 44
Pinnacle Development, Inc., 245, 248
Pinochet, Augusto, 34
Pizzella, Patrick, 371n128
Platt, Ronald, 137–39, 230
Poarch Creek Indians, 108, 113–14, 116, 362n59, 363n63
Poindexter, John, 37, 358n14
Pokagon band, 372n142
Pollack, Sidney, 62
Pollard, Jonathan, 353
Poncho, Chief, 237–38
Potawatomi Indians, 372n142
Potomac Outdoor Advertising, 145
Powell, Colin, 52, 373n153
Preston Gates Ellis & Rouvelas Meeds: Abramoff and, 81, 122; background, 78; Choctaw Indians and, 99, 103, 121; disenchantment with, 229–30; eLottery and, 215; Northern Mariana Islands and, 88, 90; as pass-through, 111, 116; subpoenaed e-mails, 157, 293; SunCruz Casinos and, 146, 154
Price's Pit, 6–7
Project Relief, 76, 359n22
Pucci, Angelo, 6
Pueblo Sandia Indians, 259–61, 374n160
push polling, 192–93

R

Ragucci, Frederic, 164
Ralston, Susan: Northern Marianas and, 97; Rove and, xiv, 109, 225, 230–31; as Special Assistant to the President, 231; on Stayman, 232; SunCruz and, 174
Rather, Dan, 42
Ratliff, Bill, 330–31
Reader's Digest, 85
Reagan, Maureen, 20
Reagan, Nancy, 23
Reagan, Ronald: Abramoff and, 4, 17–18, 22–23, 25; Bush and, 20; Citizens for America and, 35; College Republicans and, 32; on Communism, 36–37; Comprehensive Anti-Apartheid Act, 46, 62; election of 1980, 357n7; on evil empire, 47; Iran-Contra Affair and, 53, 358n14; Jungle Jamboree and, 42; Kidan and, 15; Lundgren and, 60; "personnel make policy" slogan, 226; "plausible deniability," 37; purging Bushyites, 25–26; Savimbi and, 41; South Africa and, 38–39, 48; taking naps, 23, 30; U.S. Holocaust Memorial Council, 52
realpolitik, 34
Red Scorpion (film), 58–62, 72–73
Redford, Robert, 62
Reed, Mike, 182
Reed, Ralph: Abramoff and, 23, 27, 53, 80, 108–9; APEC and, 74; background, 109; Choctaws and, 110–16; College Republicans and, 31; Coushattas and, 237, 242, 328, 364n56; Georgia lieutenant governor campaign, vii–viii, 27; Hinojosa and, 332; Internet gambling and, 216, 218; McCain and, 189–91, 205–6, 208, 259; media and, 377n174; Ralston and, 231; Rove and, 243;

Schmidt and, 284; Schmidt on, 299; Senate hearings and, 318; Smith and, 228; speech by, 338-50; St. Andrews golf junket, 264, 267; Stayman and, 363n64; Tigua Indians and, 330, 332, 334, 336, 344; Zachares and, 226
Reed, Scott W., 225, 227–28, 242, 258–59, 281, 292, 297, 303
Regula, Ralph, 281
Reid, Harry, 246, 304, 307, 372n137
Republican National Committee (RNC), 25–26
Republican Party, 76, 100, 190–91, 225
Republikein (publication), 65
Restoration Act, 339
Rich, Frank, 58–59
Ridenour, Amy Moritz, 97, 114, 133, 210–11, 222–23, 318, 357n9
Riley, Bob, 118–20, 363n60
Ring, Kevin, 282, 285, 291, 353, 373n154
Rishe, Melvin, 53
Robertson, Pat, 109, 145, 189, 359n25
Robinson, Randall, 51, 66
Robinson, Sugar Ray, 4, 12
Rockefeller, Nelson, 221
Rodman, Dennis, 144
Roe v. Wade, 24
Rogan, James E., 218
Rogers, C. Bryant, 114, 332–3
Rogers, Kenny, 8
Rogers, Nell, 99–100, 106–07, 110–11, 114–16, 120–21, 333
Rohrbacher, Dana, 40, 159, 246, 276, 359n26
Rolt, John, 48
Rosen, Marvin, 282
Rosen, Michael, 275
Rosenbaum, Richard, 294
Rosenthal, Jonathan, 345
Rosenthal, Larry, 251, 253–54, 256–58, 306
Rossetti, Michael, 243, 246–47
Rouvelas, Manuel, 229–30

Rove, Karl: APEC and, 74; Atwater and, 358n10; Babauta and, 232; election of 2000, 225; House Government Affairs Committee report on, xiv; investigation of, vii, 355; lobbyist access and, 223–24, 348; McCain and, 191, 193, 205, 208, 259; Ralston and, xiv, 109, 225, 230–31; Reed and, 243; resignation of, 372n126; Siegelman and, 119, 362n52; at Signatures restaurant, 275; speech by, 350; Stayman and, 362n34; Zachares and, 226
Rowen, Milton, 10–12
Rudy, Lisa, 79, 97, 212, 219
Rudy, Tony: Choctaw Indians and, 103, 123; deferred sentencing, 361n46; election of 2000 and, 224; Greenberg Traurig and, 230; Internet gambling and, 217–18; Ney and, 269; Northern Marianas and, 97; Rohrbacher and, 159; St. Andrews golf junket and, 155, 212, 265–66; SunCruz and, 213
Ruebelmann, Louis, 27
Ruff, Eric, 243
Rule 35, 353
Russia, 26, 30, 39, 47, 129–37, 366n76
Russo, Anthony, 278
Russo, Rose Marie, 278

S

Safavian, David, 219, 266–67, 275, 338, 370n123
Saffuri, Khaled, 249, 372n141
Sagan, Carl, 221
Saginaw Chippewa Indians, 126, 249–59, 265–66, 288, 291, 372n146
Saipan Tribune newspaper, 93, 98
Salon, 205
Salter, Mark, 207, 369n112
Sampley, Ted, 204
Sampras, Pete, 3

San Diego-Union Tribune, 59
Sanders, David, 50
Sanders, Patricia, 345
Sandia Indians, 259–61, 374n160
Sansonetti, Tom, 227
Saudi Arabia, 37, 365n80
Savimbi, Jonas, 39–41, 59
Scaife, Richard Mellon, 25
Scanlon, Michael: Agua Caliente band, 263–64; American International Center and, 75; Choctaws and, 115–18, 236; conspiracy charges, 316; Coushattas and, 114, 119, 235, 237, 288, 328; deferred sentencing, 363n46; DeLay and, 177, 291; derogatory remarks about Indians, 56; Fitial and, 232; gangland slaying of Boulis and, 178; Gimme Five kickbacks, 105–6; Greenberg Traurig and, 230; Miller and, 282; Ney and, 269; Northern Marianas and, 96–97; referral fees from, 277, 295–96, 305; Riley and, 363n61; Saginaw Chippewas and, 250–51, 255–58, 288; Sandia Indians and, 260–61; Schmidt on, 282–84, 289–90, 299; Schwartz and, 340; Senate hearing and, 304–6, 308; Sprague and, 254; subpoenaed, 374n161; SunCruz Casinos and, 154, 171; Tigua Indians and, 320, 331, 333, 336–41, 343; Worfel and, 293
Schiavo, Terri, 79
Schmidt, Susan: on Abramoff defrauding clients, 117; on CAF, 75; calling Abramoff, 281; December 2005 article, 289; e-mails from, xv; on Eshkol Academy, 75; February 2004 article, xiii, 286, 288; at Greenberg Traurig, 282–85; March 2004 article, 294; McCain and, 292; November 2004 article, 319–20; omissions by, 51, 290–91, 332; Reed and, 228, 281; Scanlon and, 294–95; at Senate hearings, 306; September 2004 article, 298–303, 308; Sprague and, 250, 281; on Tigua Indians, 334, 339
Schoon, Marius, 48
Schulte Roth & Zabel, 161
Schumer, Charles, 351
Schwartz, Marc: Abramoff's presentation to Tiguas, 335–37; Alabama-Coushattas and, 344–46; Campbell and, 321; donations to Ney PACs, 338; Elder Legacy Program and, 321, 324–25; Hisa and, 322–23, 325; Ney and, 342; Scanlon and, 340; Senate hearings and, 375n169; Tigua Indians and, 291, 321, 324–25
Schwartz, Paul, 278–79, 347
Schwarzenegger, Arnold, 4, 275
Sciandra, Eddie, 15, 32–33
Scotland golf trip, 74, 123, 209–14, 220, 264–72, 338, 340-3, 345
Seattle Times, 229
SecureCar Worldwide, 186–87
Seligman, Naomi, 365n82
Sellars, Duncan, 45, 49, 54
Senate Ethics Committee, 294
Senate Finance Committee, 213
Senate Foreign Relations Committee, 131, 193
Senate Indian Affairs Committee, viii, 257, 289, 291–92, 303–9. *See also* McCain report
700 Club, The, 79
sex trade, 84–85, 89
Shackelford, Lottie, 339
Shapleigh, Eliot, 330
Sheldon, Louis P., 216, 218–19
Shemtov, Judy, 67–68, 316
Shemtov, Sami, 67–68, 141, 368n103
Shipping Act (1916), 149, 169
Shultz, George, 50
Sibbison, Heather, 246
Sidransky, David, 19

Siegelman, Don, 107–08, 118–19, 362n52, 363n64
Signatures restaurant, 123, 223–24, 227, 232, 249, 273–74, 309
Silva, Virginia, 262
Simon, Paul, 27
Simpson, O. J., 65
Sinatra, Frank, 369n109
Sincere, Rick, 49
Slate.com, 13
smear campaigns, xiii, 189–208, 369n108
Smith, Gordon, 304
Smith, Kevin, 58
Smith, Mike, 307
Smith, Wayne, 228, 297
Smith, William French, 22
Sonnett, Neal, 314, 347
Soussan, Andre, 127
South Africa, Republic of: apartheid and, 46–47, 51; Crystal and, 35, 39–40, 42, 44–46, 48, 50–51, 62, 360n11; Jamba Jamboree and, 38–39; opposition to sanctions against, 52; *Red Scorpion* and, 62
South African National Student Federation, 39
Soviet Perspective (publication), 46
Soviet Union, 26, 30, 39, 47, 129–37, 364n76
Speiser, Mark, 182
Sprague, Bernie, 250, 252, 254–55, 257–58, 281, 288, 290, 292
Sprague, D. K. "Richard," 252
Sprague, Gary, 258
Springsteen, Bruce, 231
Spur magazine, 51
St. Andrews golf junket, 74, 123, 209–14, 220, 264–72, 339, 342, 344
St. Maarten, 15, 32, 365n83
Stacks and Archives delicatessen, 273
Stalling, Stephen, 175
Standring, Suzette, 91

Stanley, H. K., 242
Stansbury, Bill, 11–12
Starr, Kenneth, 142
Stayman, Allen, 86, 232, 360n34
Steinberg, Martin, 186
Steinburg, Don, 41
Stockholm Syndrome, xii
Stone, Nydia, 227
Stone, Peter H., 283, 320, 362n51, 373n156
Stone, Roger, Jr., 225, 227, 242, 245, 248, 258–59, 297
Streep, Meryl, 62
Sub-Sahara Monitor (publication), 46
Sugar Ray Robinson Youth Foundation, 12
Sullivan, Brendan, 54, 294
Sun Coast Casinos, 187, 278
SunCruz Casinos: appraisal of value, 182–83; attempts to keep afloat, 173–78; background, 141, 145–50; civil suit and, 311; new owners taking charge, 166–73; Ney and, 126, 270; purchasing, 7, 34–35, 150–53, 369n96; Rudy and, 213; Schmidt and, 284; seller financing for, 153–66
Sunkin, Neil, 18
Sun-Sentinel, 285
Swaziland, 62

T

Tambo, Oliver, 50
Tan, William, 85, 93–97, 360n33, 360n41
Target America, 26
Target Marketing, 5
Tauzin, Billy, 217, 219, 245
tax-exempt organizations, 28–29, 240–48, 371n133
Tenorio, Froilan, 84, 92
Tenorio, Pedro, 94, 98
Texas Observer, 320
textile industry in Northern Mariana Islands, 83–88, 93, 310

Thatcher, Margaret, 211
Thomas, Danny, 8
Thurmond, Strom, 192
Tigua Indians, 264, 291, 299–302, 308, 318–26, 328–46, 374n167
Time magazine, vii, 42, 86, 109, 235
Toward Tradition, 79, 212, 218, 221
Town Talk newspaper, xiii
toxic clean-up sites, 6–7
Traditional Values Coalition, 216
TransAfrica, 51, 66
Truman, Harry, 362n40
Trump, Donald, 7
Truth and Reconciliation Commission, 47–48
Tuttle, Erica, 364n72
20/20 news show, 86, 93

U
UBIT (unrelated business income tax), 100, 102–4, 283
UNITA (National Union for Total Independence of Angola), 39, 41–42
UNITE (Union of Needletrades, Industrial and Textile Employees), 86, 360n36
United Way, 329
U.S. Family Network, 132, 135, 360n41, 364n71
U.S. Holocaust Memorial Council, 52
U.S. News & World Report, 193–94
USA Foundation, 29, 32
Usery, Tracy, 193

V
van Horne, Jon, 282–83
Vanity Fair, 206
Vasell, Shawn, 224
Vietnam War, 9, 16–17, 36, 193–204, 369n110
Viguerie, Richard A., 24
Vinovich, Paul D., 267

Vitter, David, 243–44, 247–48, 276, 372n135
Volpe, Paul, 6
Volz, Neil, 154, 249, 267, 269, 277, 291, 338
Voor Huisen (firm), 136–37

W
Wagner, Joan, 155, 165
Waldman, Ben: Boulis and, 173–76; charges against, 314; divesting SunCruz ownership, 184; Huck and, 366n84; Kidan on, 314; Potomac Outdoor Advertising and, 145; Sun-Cruz Casino purchase, 141, 151–52, 154–55, 158, 162–66, 172, 185
Walker, Greg C., 161–62, 164
Wall Street Journal, 99, 303
Waller, J. Michael, 80, 88, 359n28, 360n37
Wardak, Ghulam, 40–41
Washington Post: on Abramoff and DeLay, 79, 135–36; on Abramoff and North, 38, 53; on Abramoff and tribal clients, viii, 99, 101, 106, 228, 239, 286, 310, 318; on Abramoff quoting movie lines, 72; Frank Abramoff and, 3–5; on Internet gambling, 214, 217, 219; McCain and, 206–7; on Nature Conservancy, 330
Washington Times, 75, 91, 359n21
The Washingtonian, 297
Watts, J. C., 218
Weaver, John, 369n112
Weekly Standard, 144, 191
Weinberger, Caspar, 56, 358n14
Weldon, Curt, 364n73
Western Pacific Economic Council, 95
Weyrich, Paul, 25
Wheeler, Jack, 39
Why Courage Matters (McCain), 195
Wilkes, Brent, 353

Williams, H. DeWayne, 186
Williams, Mike, 249, 308, 372n140
Williamson, Craig, 42, 47–48, 63
Wilson, Woodrow, 221
Windom, Steve, 109
Woods, Tiger, 3, 155
Wooldridge, Sue Ellen, 247
Worfel, William: as Coushatta representative, 233–34, 290, 330, 344; Jena Band Indians and, 244; Martin and, 234, 241; Reed and, 364n56; Scanlon and, 235, 288; on Schmidt, 293

Y

Yeltsin, Boris, 130, 134
Yeshiva University, 16
Young, Don, 226
Young, Robert, 8
Young Americans for Freedom, 25

Z

Zachares, Mark, 226–27, 371n128, 374n166
al-Zayat, Fouad, 268
Zionism, 10
Zito, Joseph, 61–62